ADVANCE PRAISE FOR *OWÓKNAGE*

"Né makóce né Nakóda téhą ųbi no Wóyabi né ta'ówowįcaknagabi cá okná én Togáda giyá nená knuzábįkta no Wóyabi ne eháhtiya cá Nína pinámaya! / These are the stories of the Nakóda people, they have retained them for generations. The future Nakóda people will retain them. This book provides a truthful Nakóda perspective." —MICHAEL TURCOTTE, Fort Peck Húdešana Nakóda (Red Bottom Nakóda)

"A beautiful expression of the history, migration, and pre- and post-reserve era of the Nakoda tribe. A must read!" —CHIEF IRA MCARTHUR, Pheasant Rump Nakota First Nation

"A brilliant resource that tells the history of the Nakoda Oyate from precontact to the present day." —INFORED/BRAD BELLEGARDE, Nakoda/Cree Hip-Hop Artist and Journalist

"A monumental collaboration between academics and community Knowledge Keepers that traces the 700-year odyssey of the Nakoda Nation from their ancestral lands in the Woodlands across the Northern Great Plains, to their homes in the Borderlands and in the Cypress Hills, to their forced exile from their chosen home in Cypress to the reserve imposed on them, and their strategies to surviving the reserve. This encyclopedic—even epic—story traces Nakoda history from the deep past to contemporary concerns with climate change, environmental degradations, and pipeline developments. Its balance of the regional and the local sheds light on the broad sweep of western and trans-border history, as well as the detailed pattern of local reserve use by a nation that has, until now, gone largely under-recognized and misunderstood."
—JAMES DASCHUK, author of *Clearing the Plains*

OWÓKNAGE

THE STORY OF CARRY THE KETTLE NAKODA FIRST NATION

Čegá K'iŋna Nakóda Oyáde

WITH JIM TANNER, DAVID R. MILLER, TRACEY TANNER, AND PEGGY MARTIN MCGUIRE

Copyright © 2022 by Carry The Kettle Nakoda First Nation.

All rights reserved. No part of this work covered by the copyrights hereon may be reproduced or used in any form or by any means—graphic, electronic, or mechanical—without the prior written permission of the publisher. Any request for photocopying, recording, taping or placement in information storage and retrieval systems of any sort shall be directed in writing to Access Copyright.

ON THE COVER: Fort Walsh, 1878: Grizzly Bear, Mosquito, Lean Man, The Man Who Took the Coat, Is Not a Young Man, One Who Chops Wood, Little Mountain, and Long Lodge. Caption: Assiniboine Council Near Fort Walsh, Saskatchewan. Credit: Glenbow Archives, NA-936-34.
Originally published in 2017 as a Traditional Land Use Study by Nicomacian Press

COVER AND TEXT DESIGN: Duncan Noel Campbell
COPY EDITOR: Dallas Harrison
PROOFREADER: Kirsten Craven
INDEXER: Patricia Furdek

MAPS: Weldon Hiebert. All maps based on original maps by Terri Quintal, except Figure 4, which is adapted from a map by Walde, Meyer, and Unfreed from "The Late Period on the Canadian and Adjacent Plains"; and Figure 8, which is adapted from a map by Cassie Theurer in F.P. Prucha, *Atlas of American Indian Affairs*. All maps made with Natural Earth, except Figures 13 and 17 which contain map data licenced under the Open Government Licence – Canada and whose background imagery is courtesy NASA/JPL-Caltech.

Library and Archives Canada Cataloguing in Publication

TITLE: Owóknage : the story of Carry the Kettle First Nation / Cegá K'iŋna Nakoda Oyáte ; with Jim Tanner, David R. Miller, Tracey Tanner, and Peggy Martin Mcguire.

OTHER TITLES: Story of Carry the Kettle First Nation

NAMES: Tanner, James N., author. | Miller, David Reed, 1949- author. | Tanner, Tracey, author. | Martin-McGuire, Peggy, author. | Carry the Kettle (First Nation), author.

DESCRIPTION: Adaptation of: Carry the Kettle Nakota First Nation : historical and current traditional land use study. | Includes bibliographical references and index.

IDENTIFIERS: Canadiana (print) 20220193754 | Canadiana (ebook) 20220203334 | ISBN 9780889778146 (softcover) | ISBN 9780889778153 (hardcover) | ISBN 9780889778160 (PDF) | ISBN 9780889778177 (EPUB)

SUBJECTS: LCSH: Carry the Kettle (First Nation) | LCSH: Carry the Kettle (First Nation)—History. | CSH: First Nations—Land tenure—Saskatchewan. | LCSH: Land use—Saskatchewan—History. | CSH: First Nations—Saskatchewan—History.

CLASSIFICATION: LCC E99.A84 T36 2022 | DDC 333.2—dc23

University of Regina Press

University of Regina, Regina, Saskatchewan, Canada, S4S 0A2
TEL: (306) 585-4758 FAX: (306) 585-4699
WEB: www.uofrpress.ca

10 9 8 7 6 5 4 3 2 1

We acknowledge the support of the Canada Council for the Arts for our publishing program. We acknowledge the financial support of the Government of Canada. / Nous reconnaissons l'appui financier du gouvernement du Canada. This publication was made possible with support from Creative Saskatchewan's Book Publishing Production Grant Program.

CONTENTS

List of Figures **ix**

Publisher's Note **xi**

Letter from Carry The Kettle First Nation
Chief Elsie Jack **xiii**

Letter from Carry The Kettle First Nation
Councillor Kurt Adams **xv**

Assiniboine Tribe of Indians Elder and Traditional
Land User Interviewees, September 1929 **xx**

Cypress Hills Group Interviewees, November 5, 2015 **xx**

Carry The Kettle First Nation Elder and
Current User Interviewees, July 2015 **xvii**

Preface and Acknowledgements **xxi**

Introduction **1**

PART I:
Ne Wanágaša Owóknaga / *The History of the Nakoda People*

CHAPTER 1: Nakódabi Žehaŋ Maká Wiyutá /
Early Land Use of the Nakoda People **7**

CHAPTER 2: Wašíčubi Togáda Nakóda Wiyágabi /
Assiniboine at Contact **23**

CHAPTER 3: Nakódabi 1799–1855 Čagúsam Makóče Missouri ičiyab /
Upper Missouri Country and the Assiniboine, 1799–1855 **45**

CHAPTER 4: Wiyóȟpeyadagiya Knaškíŋyaŋbi /
The Wild West **63**

CHAPTER 5: Oyáde Wowábiyutaŋibi hiŋkda Makóče Wokšúbi /
Treaty 4 and Reserve Farming **87**

CHAPTER 6: Wazi Ȟe Makóče Žedáhaŋ Nakódabi Baȟeyam iyéya hiŋkda ne Canadian's Išta Mneǧá Hiyúbi Ičíyabi /
The Assiniboine Removal from Cypress Hills and the "Canadian" Trail of Tears, 1883 **117**

CHAPTER 7: Nakóda Makóče En Piyábi Dagu Wičóni nagu T'abi Owóknága / Life and Death on the New Reserve **137**

CHAPTER 8: Makóče ne Wičákibi / Loss of Lands **155**

PART 2:
Nakón Wičóȟa Iyamé I nagu Wošbebi / *Spirituality and Traditional Hunting and Gathering*

CHAPTER 9: Nakón Wičóȟaŋga, wičói'ábi, wakaŋ makáwida, Owapiya / Spirituality, Language, Sacred Sites, and Burial Grounds **173**

CHAPTER 10: Wanúyabi Wokšubi / Harvesting Big Game **199**

CHAPTER 11: Iyátaga nagu Hokúwa, Zik'daŋna, Wanúyabi Čusína Wokšubi / Harvesting Smaller Game and Birds, Fishing, and Trapping **225**

CHAPTER 12: Pežúda Wošpíbi, Wibázoka, Wokšubi / Gathering Medicines, Herbs, Berries, and Wild Vegetables **239**

CHAPTER 13: Wičóȟaŋga Ičúŋbi: Wašiču Owáŋga Tibi, Maká En Wokšúbi nagu Woyúda / Farms, Gardens, Traditional Diet, and Other Traditional Activities **255**

CHAPTER 14: Nakón Wósuye, Makóče at'a Iŋhákta nagu Iknúšta / Indigenous Rights and Environmental Concerns **273**

Conclusion **291**

Notes **299**

Bibliography **323**

Index **329**

LIST OF FIGURES

FIGURE 1: Traditional and Current Lands of Carry The Kettle Nakoda First Nation **2**

FIGURE 2: Current Traditional Land Use of Carry The Kettle Nakoda First Nation **3**

FIGURE 3: Geographical Range of the Besant Phase **14**

FIGURE 4: Locations of Precontact Phases and Traditions **15**

FIGURE 5: Western Fur Trade, c. 1700–20 **30**

FIGURE 6: Assiniboine Early Annual Rounds **38**

FIGURE 7: Annual Hunting Cycle of Assiniboine, c. 1821 **42**

FIGURE 8: Lands Reserved by the Mandan, Hidatsa, and Arikara under the 1851 Fort Laramie Treaty **65**

FIGURE 9: Trails Used by First Nations People for Migration and Trades **86**

FIGURE 10: Original Indian Head Reserve Map **131**

FIGURE 11: Surrendered Lands and Band Amalgamation **141**

FIGURE 12: 1905 Surrendered Land **166**

FIGURE 13: Original Cypress Hills Reserve and Current Reserve Details **169**

FIGURE 14: Carry The Kettle Heritage Sites (Sacred Sites and Burial Grounds) **192**

FIGURE 15: Big Game Hunting Areas **216**

FIGURE 16: Traditional Land Use Areas and Crown
Lands (National/Provincial Parks) **221**

FIGURE 17: Waterfowl, Fish, and Trap/Snare Harvest Areas **234**

FIGURE 18: Medicines, Plants, and Berry Harvest Areas **240**

FIGURE 19: Surrendered Lands and Pipelines **286**

Publisher's Note

This publication is the result of a collaboration between Čeǧá K'iŋna Nakóda Oyáde / Carry The Kettle Nakoda First Nation and the University of Regina Press, with assistance from Twin Rivers Consulting, led by James Tanner. It stems from a previously published land use study, *Carry the Kettle Nakota First Nation: Historical and Current Traditional Land Use Study*. This book uses first-hand accounts and interviews, as well as much intensive research into the archives, to help record the true story of the Čeǧá K'iŋna Nakóda Oyáde.

University of Regina Press would like to acknowledge and express gratitude to the Elders of Carry The Kettle Nakoda First Nation, and to Chief Elsie Jack, for asking us to be a part of telling their stories. University of Regina Press would also like to acknowledge and express gratitude to Dr. David Miller, former professor of Indigenous Studies at the First Nations University of Canada, for his tireless efforts and commitments to the press and to Nakoda Peoples and history. He has spent his life devoted to his research, and this book would not have happened without him. Also, a special thank-you to University of Regina Press editorial intern Jellyn Ayudan, who helped compile many of the original sources and citations.

Finally, we want to respectfully acknowledge the recent discovery of residential school student bodies throughout the country, including those children lost from the Čeǧá K'iŋna Nakóda Oyáde. University of Regina Press remains committed to purp*oseful action* and will continue to respond to the Calls of Action set forward by the Truth and Reconciliation Commission.

LETTER FROM CARRY THE KETTLE FIRST NATION CHIEF ELSIE JACK

In moving toward healing of our lands, our community, and the generations before and after us, this land use study gives us a new beginning and an opportunity to move forward in partnership to a healthy, sustainable, and brighter future. —ELSIE JACK

Dear Reader,

I have had the privilege and honour of working with our Nakoda Elders for the past twenty-five years, and I am pleased to present this book on traditional land use compiled from historical research, land claims, Elder and land user interviews, and traditional practices of our people.

Carry The Kettle has a unique and rich history, including precontact traditional land use, the effects of European settlement, our signing of Treaty 4, the Cypress Hills Massacre, and the forced removal of our people from our sacred Cypress Hills homelands. Our people have survived the many acts of genocide inflicted on our nation through government policies initiated by John A. Macdonald and believe that these atrocities need to be recognized, addressed, and atoned.

I would like to thank our Elders for their contributions to and wealth of knowledge attained for this book. Some have passed on to the spirit world since this project began but remain in our hearts and memories. It would be remiss of me not to share my gratitude for the vital roles and contributions of former Chiefs, Councils, and other community members who greatly supported this project from its conception and pioneered the way to its completion.

We strongly believe that the education of our children is a fundamental and sacred responsibility, both a right and a duty of our First Nation. With this in mind, we will provide this book to our educators to teach our youth the rich culture and history of their First Nation. The book will also be imperative for consultations and negotiations with governments and industry regarding our traditional and current land uses in order to assert our Indigenous Rights and defend our lands and people.

Carry The Kettle is resolute and determined to honour this reality by respecting our rights as a nation and as a people that demand clear actions to advance our position and achieve a better future for the generations to come. Our hope is that our First Nation members and families, Elders, educators, leaders, governments, libraries, industry, private sector, and others will find this study beneficial in learning about the strength and pride of Carry The Kettle First Nation.

Sincerely,
Chief Elsie Jack,
Carry The Kettle First Nation
2017

LETTER FROM CARRY THE KETTLE FIRST NATION COUNCILLOR KURT ADAMS

RE: Compilation of Book on Carry The Kettle Land Use Study
TO: All Carry The Kettle Band Members

I would like to take this opportunity to thank all the members who contributed to the research and compilation of the Land Use Plan for Carry The Kettle Nakoda Nation that has since been used for the creation of this book. A very special thank-you to all the Elders for their recollections, oral teachings, and wisdom. I also want to thank all the hunters for their recollections, time, and patience.

This book identifies and depicts all the lands that our ancestors utilized for living, thriving, and surviving through the generations. It will greatly help the Nakoda First Nation's continued leadership in the ongoing negotiations with pipeline companies and other similar aspects of industry. Additionally, the book will help substantially with current and future land claims.

Furthermore, it will be used as a guide for our educators to teach the generations coming after us about the vibrant history of our nation.

Finally, I would like to thank all past leaders for having the vision and fortitude to bring this book to fruition.

Respectfully,
Councillor Kurt Adams
Carry The Kettle First Nation
2017

ASSINIBOINE TRIBE OF INDIANS ELDER AND TRADITIONAL LAND USER INTERVIEWEES, SEPTEMBER 1929

The following members of the Assiniboine Tribe of Indians were interviewed in September 1929 at Wolf Point, Montana, for the case *The Assiniboine Indian Tribe, Plaintiff v. The United States, Defendant*, Court of Claims of the United States, No. J-31, 1929.

Bear Cub	Last	Red Feather
Blue Cloud	Looking	Sam King
Blue Horn	Many Coos	Speaks Thunder
Crazy Bull	Martin Mitchell	Talks Differently
First Eagle	Mrs. Medicine Bear/ Iron Cradle	The Man
Gabriel Beauchman		Thomas Duck
	Nick Alvares	
Iron Horn		Warren Carl/ Brings Back
	Night	

CYPRESS HILLS GROUP INTERVIEWEES, NOVEMBER 5, 2015

O'WATCH, FREDA. Video interviews MVI0002–MVI0018.

PRETTYSHIELD, GLADYS. Video interviews MVI0002–MVI0018.

PRETTYSHIELD, VICTORIA. Video interviews MVI0002–MVI0018.

SAULTEAUX, DARWIN. Video interviews MVI0002–MVI0018.

SPENCER, LYLE. Video interviews MVI0002–MVI0018.

CARRY THE KETTLE FIRST NATION ELDER AND CURRENT USER INTERVIEWEES, JULY 2015

ADAMS, ART.
Interview 15, videotapes 0274 and 0275.

ASHDOHONK, FELIX.
Interview 13, videotapes 0271 and 0272.

ASHDOHONK, TONY.
Interview 10, videotapes 0265 and 0266.

EASHAPPIE, NANCY.
Interview 2, videotapes 0241, 0242, and 0243.

EASHAPPIE, SARAH.
Interview 8, videotape 0261.

HASSLER, LEROY.
Interview 7, videotapes 0258, 0259, and 0260.

HASSLER, MYRTLE.
Interview 7, videotapes 0258, 0259, and 0260.

HAYWAHE, CLINT.
Interview 21, videotapes 0286, 0287, and 0288.

HOTOMANI, STACEY.
Interview 12, videotapes 0268 and 0269.

JACK, DARRELL. Interview 2, videotape 0285.

O'WATCH, JAMES LEON. Interview 6, videotapes 0254, 0255, 0256, and 0257.

PRETTYSHIELD, GLADYS. Interview 3, videotapes 0245 and 0246.

PRETTYSHIELD, JOYCE. Interview 3, videotapes 0245 and 0246.

PRETTYSHIELD, KEITH. Interview 18, videotapes 0281 and 0282.

PRETTYSHIELD, TERRI. Interview 2, videotapes 0241, 0242, and 0243.

PRETTYSHIELD, VICTORIA. Interview 3, videotapes 0245 and 0246.

PRETTYSHIELD, WANDA. Interview 16, videotapes 0276, 0277, and 0278.

RUNS, DELMAR. Interview 1, videotapes 0236, 0237, 0238, 0239, and 0240.

RYDER, JOYCE (RENA).
Interview 12, videotapes
0268 and 0269.

RYDER, KURT.
Interview 19, videotapes
0283 and 0284.

RYDER, VINCENT.
Interview 5, videotapes 0250, 0251, 0252, and 0253.

SAULTEAUX, BERNICE. Interview 22, videotape 0289.

SAULTEAUX, DERRICK. Interview 14, videotape 0273.

SAULTEAUX, ROSWELL (ROSS). Interview 9, videotapes 0262, 0263, and 0264.

SPENCER, EDNA. Interview 11, videotape 0267.

SPENCER, LYLE. Interview 17, videotapes 0279 and 0280.

SPENCER, ORVAL. Interview 11, videotape 0267.

THOMSON, CLAYTON.
Interview 23, video-
tape 0290.

THOMSON, DELBERT.
Interview 23, video-
tape 0290.

THOMSON, DUNCAN.
Interview 9, videotapes
0262, 0263, and 0264.

WALKER, LEROY.
Interview 18, videotapes
0281 and 0282.

WHITECAP, DARLENE.
Interview 4, videotapes
0247, 0248, and 0249.

WHITECAP, GARRY.
Interview 4, videotapes
0247, 0248, and 0249.

Preface and Acknowledgements

The purpose of the traditional land use study that forms much of this book was to collect, record, and protect information about historical and current traditional land use activities, as well as the cultural traditions of Carry The Kettle First Nation (CTK). In addition, one of the goals was to present a fuller, updated description of the history of the First Nation, particularly the precontact occupation of Saskatchewan followed by trade-induced migrations. The book presents the devastation caused by the loss of the bison herds, the effects of the creation of the international border, and the appalling treatment of the Nakoda People by the American and Canadian governments.

Two major data collection methodologies were used. The historical and anthropological data were obtained primarily through the research of Dr. David R. Miller, who has spent a major portion of his professional career researching and accumulating information on the history and prehistory of the Assiniboine People. This publication would not have been possible without his participation. The second source of data was the interviews with Elders, who spoke about their history, their historical and current patterns of land use, as well as their cultural practices and language.

We expect that the maps and data presented here will enhance the processes of consultation required for governments and industry and for the First Nation to protect its constitutional, Treaty, and Indigenous Rights. The book can also be utilized to strengthen and enhance further knowledge about the Nakoda (Assiniboine) culture within Carry The Kettle by passing on some oral traditions to youth and all community members.

We have incorporated detailed traditional land use data collected from thirty-three Elders and current land users, interviews from a large group meeting held in Cypress Hills with the Mosquito First Nation, as well as interview data from 1929 obtained from the Assiniboine Tribe of Indians in Wolf Point, Montana. The historical and archaeological research obtained through Dr. Miller involved a thorough review of all available information in various archives, rare historical documents and libraries, as well as up-to-date discussions with other Nakoda scholars.

In addition to the preliminary research, this project hired Dr. Peggy Martin McGuire to research historical sources from the time of Treaty 4 to the band's forced migration to Indian Head. This material is presented in Chapters 5 and 6.

This project was managed by Dr. James Tanner of Twin Rivers Consulting and facilitated by Chief Elsie Jack, Valerie Ryder, Kristal Jack, and Senator James O'Watch. Dr. Miller provided a series of historical and anthropological materials, as well as drafts of early chapters. Dr. Tanner conducted interviews, collected data, and assisted in writing and editing the book. Tracey Tanner reviewed the research and interviews with Carry The Kettle members, as well as the historical interviews with the Assiniboine in Montana, and prepared and edited the portions of the book pertaining to the spirituality, culture, and historical and current land use practices of Carry The Kettle People and their ancestors. Dr. McGuire prepared a report on the period immediately after Treaty 4, portions of which are included in Chapters 5 and 6. Terri Quintal designed the original maps based on the information provided by the interviews and other historical and anthropological data, and those informed the maps that appear in this book, created by Weldon Hiebert. Thank you to Iris O'Watch for providing the Nakoda names and spelling for the book's title and chapter headings.

ACKNOWLEDGEMENTS FROM CHIEF ELSIE JACK

First, I would like to acknowledge my grandmother, Kate Jack (wife of Joseph Jack, son of Chief The Man Who Took the Coat), who instilled in me the oral history of our people; and my niece, Kaye Thompson, who had a rich history of our nation.

There was a group of Elders who persevered with our historical land claims. Without this perseverance and the oral history of our nation, our nation would not be successful. We are forever indebted to them for their work that occurred from the 1960s through to the 1990s. They are: Katherine (Kaye) Thompson; Andrew C. Ryder; Chief William Burrell (Willy) Gray, Jr.; Dr. Jessie Saulteaux (Mrs. David Saulteaux); Dennis (Young Man) Walker, Jr.; Paul (Moon Face) Leader; and, the only surviving member, Delmar (Runs with Another) Runns.

I would also like to thank my colleagues, Valerie Rider and Kristalee Jack-Crowbuffalo. Without them, this book would not have been completed.

Owóknage (oh-*woh*-kna-geh):
a telling of stories, news, stories
of deeds, honourable stories

—*translation by* IRIS O'WATCH,
Nakoda language specialist

Introduction

Carry The Kettle First Nation is a large band of Nakoda (Assiniboine) People (2,826 registered members) with a residential reserve located southeast of the town of Indian Head, Saskatchewan, in Canada. There are currently 940 registered members of CTK living on reserve and 1,886 members living off reserve. Over the past few years, as a result of the successful Treaty Land Entitlement (TLE) claim, the First Nation has been able to recover small portions of its lands throughout Saskatchewan. These lands are located within the nation's traditional hunting and gathering territories.

Both anthropological and historical evidence show that the Nakoda People originally occupied what is now mid- and southern Manitoba, northern Minnesota, and lands stretching into both Ontario and Saskatchewan, and approximately 700 years ago they appear to have moved farther onto the prairies of Saskatchewan and the northern United States. It appears that the Nakoda originally occupied the parkland, the boreal forest, and the adjacent prairie to sustain their livelihood during different times of the year. Manitoba has acknowledged this original occupation by retaining the name of the Assiniboine River and other important Assiniboine namesakes. However, the Nakoda People moved westward starting around 750 BP likely to utilize the huge bison herds as a primary source of livelihood. The following chapters also describe further movements and reactions to the arrival of the fur trade and European settlement. The archaeological evidence showing

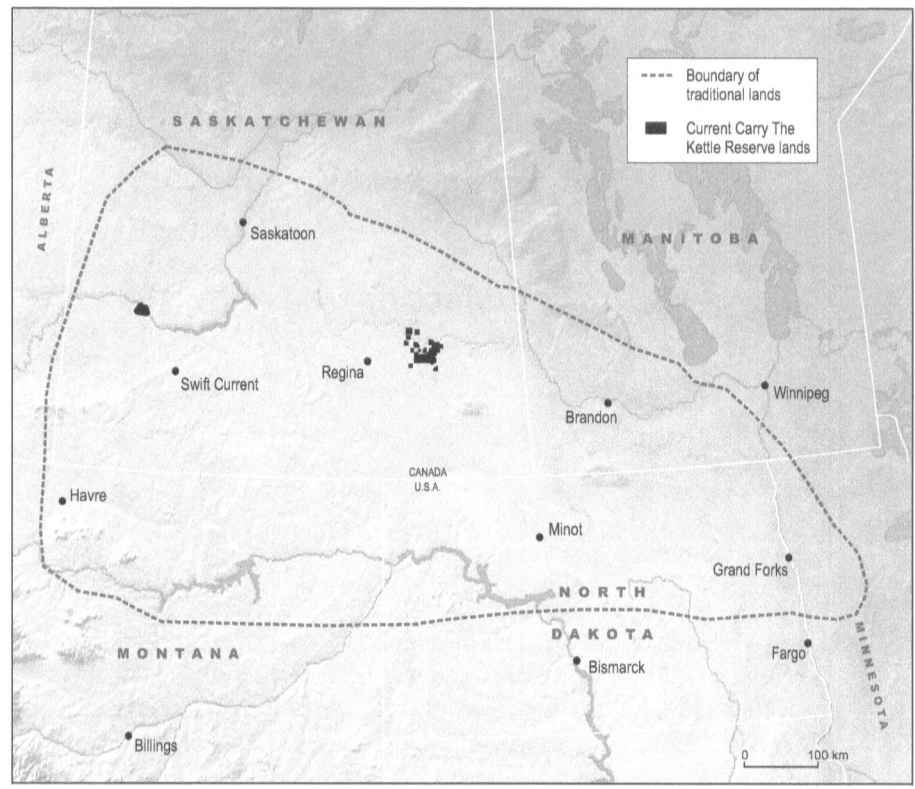

FIGURE I: Traditional and Current Lands of Carry The Kettle Nakoda First Nation

the earlier Nakoda People's occupation of the plains contradicts many of the observations of explorers and fur traders and the conclusions of many settler-based historians and scholars. The error in understanding is characterized by Dale Russell as "displaced observations," simply meaning that it was not the Indigenous people who were moving but the explorers and traders themselves.[1]

Instead, the destruction of the bison, the devastating effects of disease, the imposition of borders and reserves, and other government regulations have been responsible for the significant changes in the lives of the Nakoda People. This book contains descriptions of the historical events and the adaptations of the Nakoda, specifically the ancestors of Carry The Kettle First Nation. The effects of disease on the Assiniboine People were extreme, partially because of their friendly commercial relationships with the white traders who brought with them the diseases. After particularly devastating losses from smallpox,

INTRODUCTION

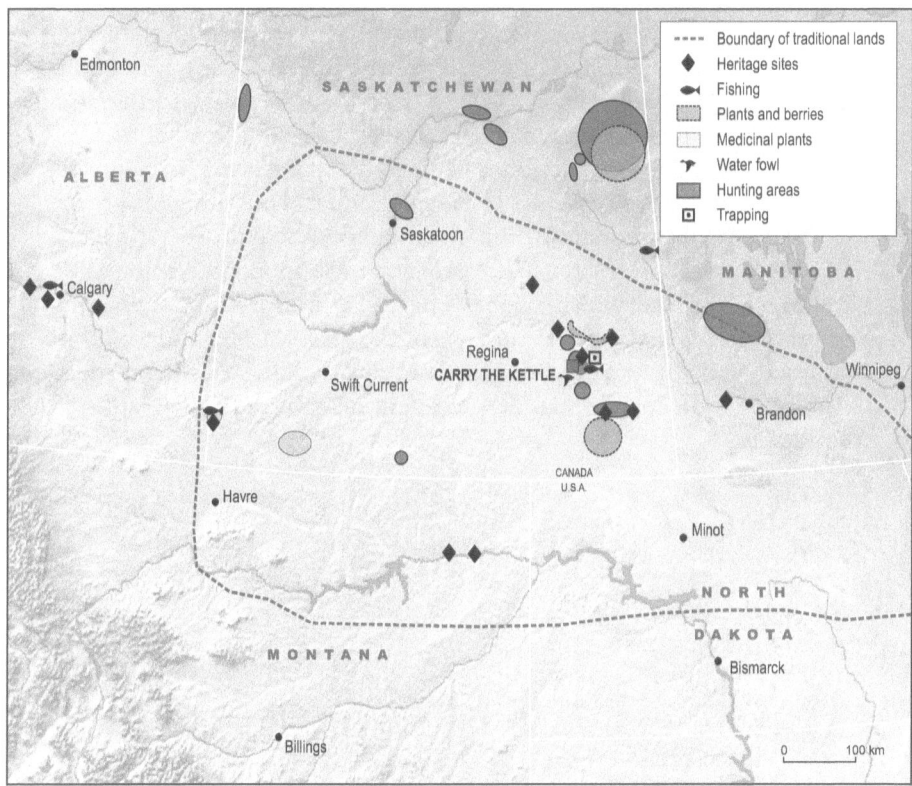

FIGURE 2: Current Traditional Land Use of Carry The Kettle Nakoda First Nation

some Assiniboine People merged with others, often with similar language and culture, such as the Gros Ventre. Also, they appear to have developed adaptations to a plains livelihood, and during their long-term friendship with the Cree Nation they have joined with several mixed Nakoda-Cree bands, such as the Young Dogs.

Carry The Kettle ancestors have endured many hardships during their exposure to settler society. Most of the victims of the Cypress Hills Massacre were ancestors of Carry The Kettle First Nation. The nation endured a forced relocation from its preferred lands in the Cypress Hills to the bald prairie of Indian Head in 1882 and 1883. This is referred to within the CTK community as the "Canadian" Trail of Tears. We also discuss in this book the early reserve life and livelihood on the prairie, where Treaty Lands were taken from the First Nation and agricultural efforts were stymied. The struggles and challenges that the First Nation has survived are truly amazing.

Currently, Carry The Kettle First Nation is resolving some of the claims that have developed as a result of the inappropriate treatment that the people have received over the years. This has allowed them to obtain additional lands, but they have at least two additional outstanding land claims. The First Nation is dedicated to preserving its language and culture despite the assaults of the past, and it is pursuing programs to promote its traditional livelihood, language, and culture. CTK First Nation is pursuing infrastructural projects to support its membership both on and off reserve. This book is part of the efforts to understand and promote the history and land use of the First Nation, and we hope that it will assist in the consultation that must take place with respect to industrial and commercial development on the traditional lands of CTK People.

PART I
Ne Wanágaša Owóknaga
The History of the Nakoda People

CHAPTER I:

Nakódabi Žehaŋ Maká Wiyutá

Early Land Use of the Nakoda People

To determine the lands used historically by Carry The Kettle First Nation, we have endeavoured to reconstruct their prehistory based on the archaeological record. Before written records and non-Indigenous observations, there is evidence of human occupation in this area, and an analysis of this residual material can yield a great part of the story of the activity and behaviour of the people.

Research on the Nakoda language has also provided important insights into the divisions of the Siouan Peoples. The "dialect continuum" of Sioux, Assiniboine, and Stoney Peoples represents this portion of the Siouan language family. The Assiniboine People appear to have separated from the Sioux dating approximately to 600 BP.[1] The Assiniboine and Stoney languages appear to be at the end of a long continuum of language development in that they are not simply divisions of the Dakota/Lakota language[2] but likely had formed their own separate dialects many years before.[3] However, the description of the precise divergence of the Assiniboine language remains an approximation, and this reconstruction contributes context to other lines of research.

The creation story as recited by Fort Belknap Elders clearly identifies the area around Lake Winnipeg as a centre of early Assiniboine use. There appear to be many stories and oral histories describing the origin of the alliance between Assiniboine and Cree Peoples. The stories often propose that the Nakoda and other Siouan tribes separated as a result of a conflict over a woman. Another story suggests that the Nakoda allied themselves with the Cree because they gave them a large source of protection. The time when the nations became allies is difficult to determine but might have been long before contact.

THE CREATION LEGEND

According to Assiniboine legend, Lake Winnipeg was the great water where Ik-Tomi went down to create the world. To the Assiniboine, Lake Winnipeg represents the centre of the world. They believe that they were created there.

The Creation legend describes Ik-Tomi, who is not to be confused with the Great Spirit, God-Wakan-Tanka. Ik-Tomi made the waters and the lands. He made heaven, as well as the night and the day. He made everything that we now see. After he made all the universe, he made men and women. Seven men and seven women he made from the earth. But, after he made these people, he did not want them to multiply and increase on this land that he made. Because he thought that the land that they were on was not the right place for them, he wanted to find another place. He looked around and hunted but found nothing else. Then he found some large oyster shells; these he floated on the water in the manner of a canoe. He sat in the first one and had the seven people sit in the others. They all paddled for many days in the great water, but fearing that they would die because of thirst and hunger, he called all the fowl of the water that had been following them. "Brothers and Sisters," Ik-Tomi said to the fowl, "I am going to select seven from among you. Those that I select must dive down to the bottom of this water and bring me some mud. And you must not come back unless you bring me the mud."

All the seven fowl that Ik-Tomi selected went down. For seven days and nights, the people waited and watched for their return. Finally on the seventh night, the birds who had gone down began to float to the surface of the water. Ik-Tomi examined the tiny claws or webs of each of the birds but found no mud.

"We have made a mistake," he said, "and so we must try again. This time I am going to select the muskrat, the mink, the beaver, and the fisher. Now each of you dive down and don't come back unless you can bring back some mud."

Down they went. At the end of the fourth day, they began to float back to the surface of the water, just as the fowl had done before. The muskrat came first, next the mink, then the beaver, and lastly the fisher.

CHAPTER 1

All of them, like the birds before them, were dead. But Ik-Tomi looked over their little paws, and to his amazement and joy he found tiny specks of mud clinging to them. Carefully, he took the mud from each of the animals, and from this mud he made the land that we are now on for his people. Ik-Tomi knew, however, that his people could not survive on the land alone, so he then made some large lakes, and there at the edge of the lake he put his people....

According to Assiniboine legend, Lake Winnipeg was the great water where Ik-Tomi was sent down to create the world.... The Assiniboine who remained around Lake Winnipeg grew into countless numbers, migrating in every direction seeking new territory, food, and game. The band of people grew to many thousands and inhabited the land of the countless small wooded lakes and streams of the Lake Winnipeg area. And because of the peculiar monster that was seen in Lake Winnipeg, it was named Holy Lake (Minee-Wakan), and the name was applied to its inhabitants as Holy Lake villagers.[4]

ARCHAEOLOGICAL EVIDENCE

Archaeology systematically investigates prehistoric sites by excavation and uses the spatial and stratigraphic locations of discovered artifacts to estimate when and how sites were occupied. Using information accumulated from various studies, anthropologists have implied that early hunter-gatherer societies focused on seasonal subsistence activities.

Generations of archaeologists have interpreted what they have found about the emergence of groups from the woodlands/parklands of northeastern North America onto the plains. The primary evidence supporting this idea is the similarity of artifacts between the regions. The precise motivations for these movements are the subject of speculation. What is evident is that these migrations did occur. There are many eras in which and regions where various cultures were active, but our focus in this book is on the precursors of the Assiniboine. We will discuss interactions and other factors associated with other cultural groups as they entered into regional spheres of influence that had impacts on the Assiniboine.

A series of transformations was occurring, which "began as early as 6000 BP with a long trend involving intensive foraging, semi-sedentism and population growth" in the Eastern Woodlands that then spread to the Northern Plains. "A widespread increase in population density and

Archaeological Research Excavations at the Gull Lake Bison Drive
Courtesy of the Royal Saskatchewan Museum.

commitment to sedentary life . . . [were] sustained first by intensive foraging and later by horticultural production." This became evident during the subsequent Woodland period, presumably because of the intensification of this socio-cultural pattern. Changes in modes of subsistence (ways of life) would inevitably bring innovations in "forms of political integration that involved multi-family co-residence, territorial circumscription, and the emergence of status inequality." With the growth of population in the Eastern Woodlands of the contemporary United States and southeastern Canada, the competition for strategic and ecological resources increased. These changes arose in the transitions from Woodland and Mississippian Traditions in the eastern midwest, and "some populations were pressed to move westward in a search of new lands in [the] face of population pressure, and declining resource productivity (especially in situations of semi-sedentary horticultural or intensive foraging)," which gave rise to the "sustained expression of the Plains Woodland (and later Plains Village) Traditions."[5]

The Plains Woodland Tradition[6] (2000–1000 BP)[7] provides a broad cultural context (basis for understanding influences) for later historical developments, one being general influences on what became pre-Assiniboine groups.[8] Groups moved from the woodlands to the prairies and established fortified villages in various locations along rivers and lakes in the eastern segments of the prairies. Still remaining close to the parklands, which were rich in animal and plant resources, they also moved to exploit the bison on the prairies. During this period, the spread of bow-and-arrow technology across plains culture was an important technological innovation. Village horticulture was another innovation that advanced the new adaptation to the region.[9]

Consequently, more pottery fragments appeared than on the northwestern plains. The cultivation of maize was critical as an alternative food staple; however, was all of it the product of the local groups, or was it traded from sources outside the region? This remains a subject of debate. Moreover, the presence of maize and other cultivars was important to the annual cycle of these groups. Obviously, evidence of earthenware cooking containers indicates specific patterns and means of consumption. These groups constructed earthen burial mounds, and evidence of grave goods suggests ceremonial and funerary rites in which the acquisition and exchange of "exotic raw materials or finished goods" were necessary for these people to fulfill their religious obligations.[10] Moreover,

> these "Woodland cultural influences" occurred gradually with the emergence of ... some generalized foragers in the forested valleys of the eastern Plains, and eventually, the spread of horticultural production and settled village life. These cultural traits do not have uniform expression, but rather, exhibit considerable variability throughout time and across space.... Note that some archaeologically defined cultures originally deriving from woodland habitats chose to become mobile bison-hunting specialists. Indeed, some even engaged in large-scale communal bison hunting.[11]

This was consistent with a pattern over 2,000 years of the Northern Plains being connected by "an exchange of ideas, technology and people."[12] The early plains woodland societies had an "extra-regional cultural influence" as they adapted to the scattered wooded areas in valleys of the eastern plains and later expanded into similar ecotones throughout the Northern Plains. These populations brought new ideas, primarily horticulture, to the plains. Besides improved earthenware cooking vessels, they introduced burial mound ceremonies and associated funerary practices.[13]

Bison was the major resource drawing new groups onto the Northern Plains, and modes of predation were diverse. The "communal mass killing of bison" came to the fore during the late precontact period with the Besant and Sonota archaeological complexes. This form of resource exploitation "reflects a sophisticated understanding of bison behaviour and how to manipulate them using the landscape." Consequently, this method of procurement "required a large and coordinated labour force to affect [sic] such communal mass killing, and implies multi-family effort."[14]

The extent and type of tribal organization, based on organizational prototypes, suggest imported and increased influences from the Eastern Woodlands.[15] This often meant that smaller-scale bison hunting by individuals or small families occurred as late as the latter part of the nineteenth century.[16] These adaptations formed part of the larger pattern of cultural and demographic influences derived ultimately from the Eastern Woodlands.[17] This importation became the foundation for "new innovations involving the development of horticultural village life throughout much of the Eastern Plains after c. 1000 BP. While most strongly expressed in the Central Plains and the Middle Missouri regions, such communities appear in the northeastern Plains (eastern Dakotas, western Minnesota, and southern Manitoba), and exert widespread influence throughout much of the rest of the northern Plains."[18] Simply put, this was a formative period that underpinned a series of archaeological cultures that became the proto-historical era (the period of time just prior to direct contact with Euro-Canadians) for the region.

EARLY TRADITIONS IN THE REGION

Besant (200 BC–AD 500) presumably begat Avonlea (AD 500–800), with Besant artifacts often below Avonlea artifacts stratigraphically, but other studies show co-occurring materials from both traditions. This era saw the rise of groups that appear to have migrated into the Northern Plains from the east and southeast and brought with them Knife River Flint from the Middle Missouri River region to be used in Besant culture. Avonlea culture appears archaeologically to have had some interaction with Laurel mound builders to the east and demonstrates evidence of various trade influences, based on specific materials found in the various sites. Clearly, there were stylistic similarities with Minnesota ceramics. Avonlea Peoples were consummate bison hunters, but there was also evidence of spring use of fish weirs and processing to prepare for the season of hunting bison. They were also persistent users of plains side-notched projectile points.

In the late precontact period, c. 500 BP, it is possible finally to assign historical ethnic identities to archaeological assemblages—but

CHAPTER I

Plaines Hunting Camp, Summer
Artist, M. François Girard; courtesy of the Canadian Museum of History, I-A-44, S95-23507.

not without some questions about the veracity of the designations. For example, Walde asserts that the Mortlach culture represents Proto-Assiniboine; however, Nicholson and others argue that the Mortlach was possibly of Hidatsa origin (coming from the Middle Missouri).[19] The Mortlach response to disease is one of Nicholson's arguments, but there remain problems with evidence. For example, why is there not a mirror reflection of Middle Missouri materials also identified to be Hidatsa in the archaeological evidence of the Mortlach for which there was not a definitive connection?[20]

By the late proto-historical era (c. 1150-650 BP), archaeological assemblages called Blackduck, Early Old Women's, and Psinomani emerged as cultural manifestations in the north-central and northeastern plains. For example, a plains variant of Blackduck, with origins in northern Minnesota forests and adjacent Ontario and Manitoba, was evident: "These people used the bow-and-arrow, making small triangular and side-notched arrow points, and produced good quality pottery. The latter were globular vessels with textile-impressed exteriors and whose necks and rims were elaborately decorated with core-wrapped tool impressions. In the Boundary Waters region of northern Minnesota and adjacent Ontario, it is clear that these people relied on a productive

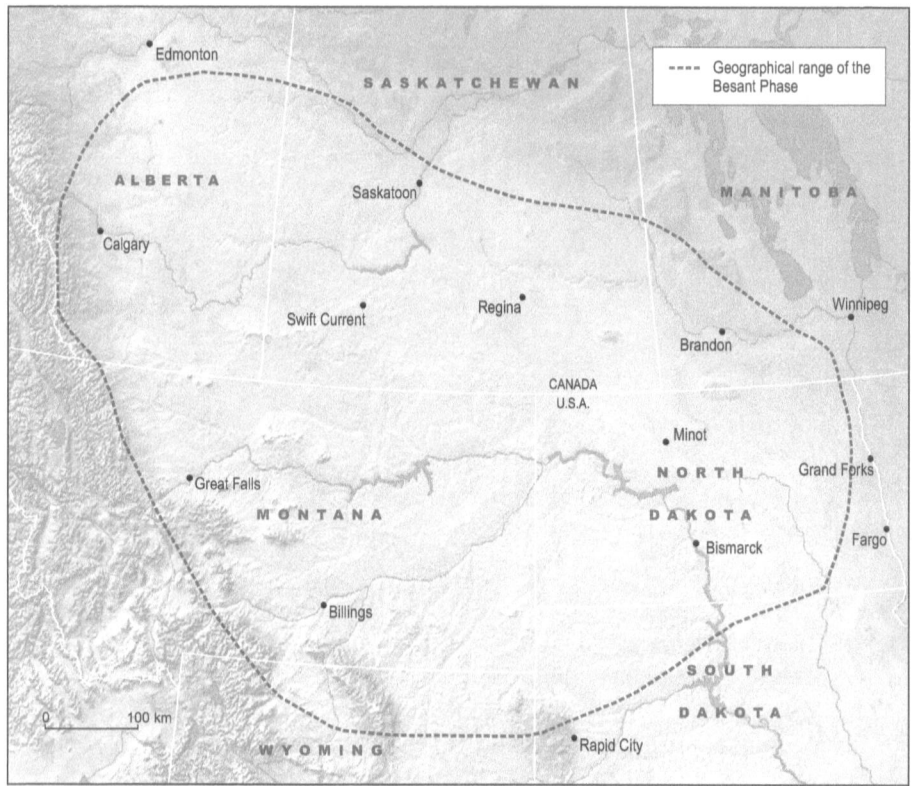

FIGURE 3: Geographical Range of the Besant Phase

subsistence economy based on harvesting wild rice, operating fish weirs and hunting game, especially moose."[21]

The most western plains Blackduck site was the Stott site outside present-day Brandon, Manitoba. Meyer and Hamilton noted that "the Blackduck occupation at this site seems to have occurred in two main periods, around 1150-1050 BP and [again] around 850-750 BP."[22] The reasons for the interruption in continuity remain unexplained. These later people would interact with Mortlach Peoples.

The search for post-Avonlea assemblages in southern Alberta revealed a cluster of sites that eventually was labelled Old Women's archaeological culture. The Old Women's Phase, initially characterized by Reeves as "nebulously defined concepts," is a conceptual frame in which to define post-Besant prehistoric materials recovered in southern Alberta. Initially, earlier Old Women's Peoples occupied the regions where Mortlach Peoples eventually lived. "Old Women's phase tied into a larger model of in situ evolutionary development on the prehistoric

CHAPTER I

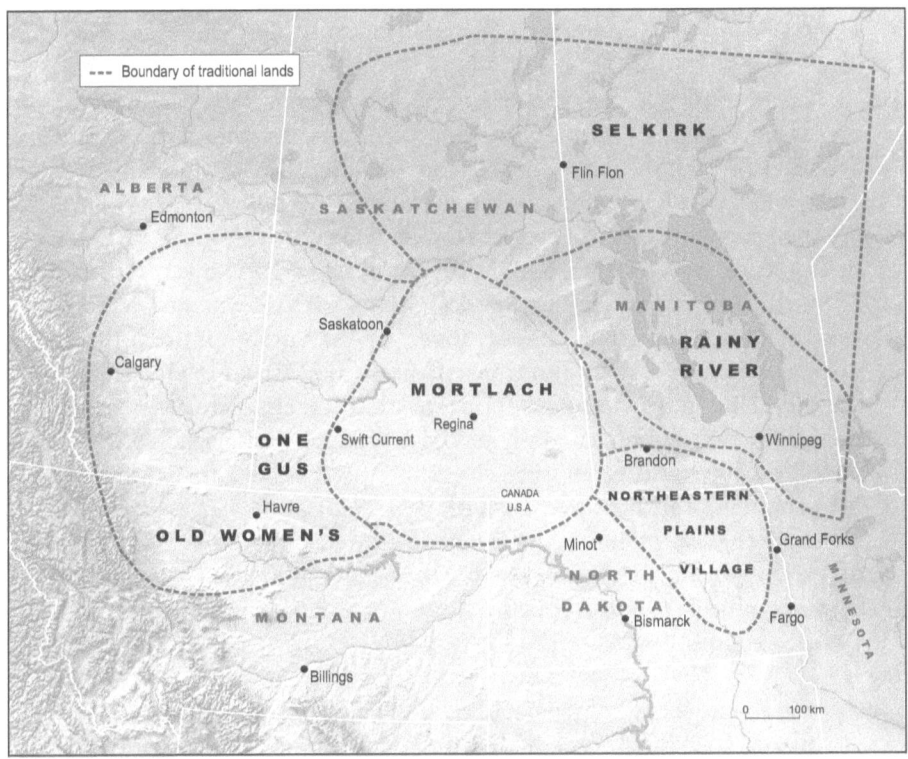

FIGURE 4: Locations of Precontact Phases and Traditions[24]

plains."[23] In other words, these changes made by late Old Women's Peoples developed in their present-day approximate locations, all west of the Mortlach sites.

Again, for the Old Women's Phase, it is possible, judging from the number of winter kill sites, that "these peoples occupied special environments during the winter. These were the valley complexes or the anomalous areas with wooded copses, such as areas of stabilized sand dunes or hilly uplands."[25] In contrast, "it is thought that the warmer seasons were spent on the open grasslands with the bison. At this time of the year the tipi camps were placed in exposed uplands where it was necessary to anchor the dwellings with stones placed around the bases of the tent covers. This produced the large tipi ring sites which are very common on the grasslands."[26] However, few artifacts were found in these sites. Representative sites, such as DhNi-50 located in the Big Muddy Valley in south-central Saskatchewan, have artifacts with Old Women's Phase materials that characterized their shorter occupation before moving westward into Alberta.[27] Old Women's occupation of the areas that eventually became occupied by Mortlach was short lived, soon to be farther west.

The end of the precontact period included a series of developments significant for our discussion. The "northeastern complexities" included a series of cultural expressions—notably Mortlach, Cluny (One Gun), and Late Old Women's—all occurring c. 650–200 BP. "Around 650 BP the spatial extent of the Old Women's phase was reduced when a new cultural group (Mortlach) moved onto the Saskatchewan plains."[28] From this era until contact, the Old Women's Phase was restricted to west of the South Saskatchewan River, in the Saskatoon area to the Rockies. The use of dogs and traps of various kinds was evident in late Old Women's sites, what Blackfoot oral tradition characterized as "the dog days" before horses. Many of these were characterized as winter and spring kill and processing sites, sheltered valleys for winter, yet bison hunting continued year-round.[29]

Another development significant to this discussion was the entry of Psinomani culture onto the northeastern prairies. Tracing what appears to be the source of its cultural innovations, Walde, Meyer, and Unfreed suggest that

> the complexity of sociocultural events on the Manitoba plains following Blackduck is only beginning to be appreciated. About 950 BP the Psinomani culture abruptly replaced Blackduck in central Minnesota.... The pottery of this culture is termed "Sandy Lake Ware" and is characterized by vessels with only slight neck constrictions and no shoulders.... In southern and central portions of the range, Sandy Lake is shell tempered, but is almost always grit tempered on the northern end of its distribution.... By about 1250 AD, the Psinomani culture had expanded as far north as the Boundary Waters region of Minnesota and by 1500 AD was present in northwestern Ontario and southeastern Manitoba.... In the past, Sandy Lake vessels in south central and southeastern Manitoba have often been misidentified as other wares and, therefore, "a broader distribution of Sandy Lake Ware to the west might be expected" (Meyer and Hamilton, 1994: 125; and Walde et al., 1995: 38–39).[30]

These developments, though somewhat sequential, were also to some degree interactive with and influential on one another in ways that are not easily intuited.[31] A series of sites predominantly in eastern

North Dakota have been characterized as the Northeastern Plains Village Complex.[32] In another series of sites in southwestern Manitoba, influences of the complex are demonstrated and provide evidence of some Middle Missouri–style vessels. However, characteristic to these sites is an extensive presence of Sandy Lake Ware–style ceramics, which also means that there were definite influences of Oneota and Plains Village ceramics. In these particular sites, there is no evidence of earth lodges, palisades, or horticulture.[33] They are connected to the rise of the Psinomani Phase and eventually the Mortlach Phase, considered to be Proto-Assiniboine.

The Mortlach Phase, based on ceramic evidence found in central and southern Saskatchewan, is represented in a style of decoration of and associated finishes on ceramic vessels. The initial identification was of some controversy because of the diversity of its vessel forms and decorations, presumably interpreted as influences from neighbouring groups:

> In particular, northern Mortlach sites contain evidence of *Selkirk* [thought to be Proto-Cree] contacts, southern Mortlach reflect Middle Missouri village contacts (LeBeau ware), and eastern Mortlach contains vessels with single cord impressions, a decorative technique characteristic of assemblages of northeastern North Dakota and adjacent southern Manitoba. In addition, western Mortlach components such as the Sykes... site have a few Old Women's phase vessels in them. Therefore, once "foreign" vessels and foreign decorative techniques are accounted for, it is apparent that Mortlach assemblages are characterized by relatively thin and compact earthenware pottery formed and decorated in a wide variety of manners.[34]

Tools for producing the diverse styles are also evident in the various sites. The larger Mortlach pottery assemblages are "almost invariably associated with equally large collections of plains side-notched projectile points... possibly fashioned from Knife River Flint (KRF) and Fused Shale are present in some of these collections—particularly those on the grasslands."[35]

Various artifacts found in the Mortlach inventory—slot knives with bone handles similar to the Middle Missouri, end scrapers, pot sherd gaming disks also similar to the Middle Missouri, bone objects (including ice gliders), among others—demonstrate the niche among cultural influences. All of this led Walde, Meyer, and Unfreed to declare that

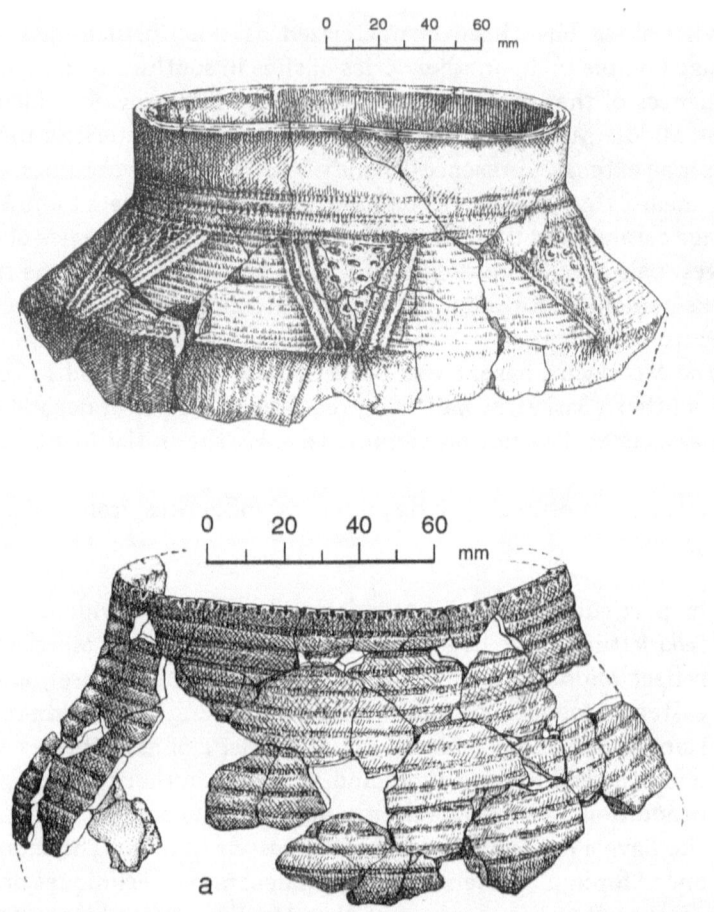

Mortlach Phase Materials (upper, vessel from the Lake Midden site; lower, vessel from the Mollberg site)
Drawings by Phyllis Lodoen; courtesy of the Saskatchewan Archaeological Society.

the spatial boundaries of the Mortlach phase seem reasonably well-defined. The Selkirk Composite along the southern edge of the boreal forest in Saskatchewan forms the northern boundary while single cord-impressed pottery aggregate(s) are present to the east and south in southwestern Manitoba and northeastern North Dakota. At the earliest known appearance of the Mortlach phase, Blackduck and Sandy Lake Wares were also present in southwestern Manitoba. Middle Missouri village cultures delimit the southern borderlands. The eastern boundaries of the Mortlach phase in eastern Saskatchewan remain undefined due to a lack of archaeological investigation in that area. On the west the Mortlach phase is bounded largely by the Old Women's phase in west central Saskatchewan with occasional intrusions of Cluny Complex components in southwestern Saskatchewan.[36]

Early dating of the Mortlach Phase has yielded dates as early as 750 BP. The discovery of European trade goods in select sites suggests direct contact post-450 BP.[37] "The culture content, distribution, and temporal parameters of Mortlach are now sufficiently well understood to warrant designation of Mortlach as a phase. While the diversity of Mortlach pottery continues to be an interesting phenomenon, when 'foreign' vessels and decorative techniques are accounted for in Mortlach assemblages, the ceramic inventory is seen to be quite distinct."[38]

Women were usually the makers of ceramics and reflected the general styles of their mothers and grandmothers. Captives taken in warfare were often adopted into their new social situations. Different exchange networks, including trade, influenced the particular configuration of "foreign" vessels in the Mortlach assemblages (i.e., syncretic Selkirk/Mortlach cultural residues in the parklands), but it is important to note that this has not been found to date south of the parklands: "Mortlach assemblages south of the parklands regularly contain small numbers of single cord-impressed vessels similar to those found east and southeast of the Mortlach region as well as very small numbers of sherds of LeBeau Ware from the Middle Missouri villages to the south."[39]

"Visible social contacts" demonstrate a pattern of orientations to the south and east. The patterns of distribution of Knife River Flint, the preferred lithic material (malleable rock) for manufacturing projectile points and scrapers/knives, as opposed to fused shale points, are reflective of south of the parklands and the parklands proper. Trade relationships with the Middle Missouri are evident from at least 450 BP to the appearance of trade goods in the Mortlach Phase assemblages.[40] Trade for corn must also have begun. Walde, Meyer, and Unfreed argue that Mortlach is Proto-Assiniboine.

Mortlach subsistence-settlement patterns focus primarily on the utilization of bison by following herds in Saskatchewan and Montana. Some bands wintered on the northern edge of the grasslands. The utilization of valley complexes was associated with the Qu'Appelle Valley and Last Mountain Lake, not far from bison herds. Spring fisheries were also evident, as at the Lebret site, providing a food source until bison could be located and exploited. By summer, the Proto-Assiniboine followed the bison south onto the open grasslands. Also, there is evidence of travelling south to trade at the Missouri River villages. The pattern of wintering in coulees/valleys was evident possibly as far south as the Missouri River.[41] There is equally strong evidence that Northern Plains groups maintained "loosely defined territories" and that there was an awareness of claims and frontiers between and among groups.[42]

The ethnicity associated with Psinomani assemblages is patterned by the distribution of Sandy Lake Ware, which has a concentration in the northeastern plains and adjoining woodlands during the late precontact and indirect contact periods. These have been asserted to be Siouan Dakota (or Sioux proper) Peoples, and these areas were occupied at historical contact by the Santee (Mdewakanton, Wahpeton, Wapakute, and Sisseton), Teton (western L dialect speakers), and Yankton and Yanktonai (the middle division Dakota bands), all considered the Dakota Peoples.[43] "It has been further suggested that the grit-tempered, fabric impressed Sandy Lake Ware found at the northern periphery of its distribution was produced by the most northerly branch of these Siouans: the Assiniboines.... Ethnic continuity as well as continuity in aspects of material culture and external exchange relationships between Mortlach and Sandy Lake may be suggested."[44]

Based on the evidence of interactions in ceramic features of Selkirk and Rainy Lake (thought to be Proto-Algonquian-Cree and Ojibwa), such as "fabric-impressed exteriors and grit temper" (as well as punctuation in the surface designs of vessels),[45] there is an indication of "interaction between northern Sandy Lake Peoples (Assiniboine) and Selkirk/Rainy River groups (northern Algonquians such as the Cree). It seems reasonable to suggest that the historically known 'alliances' of some Cree and Assiniboine groups may have been present by at least late Sandy Lake times."[46] Based on his re-examination of transborder regional archaeological collections, Walde asserts that the "people represented by the Mortlach assemblages were ancestors of Assiniboine groups."[47]

The arrival of groups with a cultural history in the eastern woodlands onto the tall-grass prairie and the short-grass plains characterized the period 1500–500 BP, and the Mortlach Peoples, thought to be Proto-Assiniboine, are the subject of this discussion. The resources of these new lands allowed various groups to live abundantly from bison and other game and fish and a range of flora. The extensive ethnogeographic terrain was utilized effectively for the fulfillment of a variety of needs. The early immigrants into this region brought with them knowledge of horticulture and sedentary technologies such as elaborate pottery designs, and it appears that these early cultures interacted through trading and in other ways. Assiniboine emerge in this region as a cultural and social group distinguished by specific choices and circumscribing factors.

CHAPTER 2

Wašíčubi Togáda Nakóda Wiyágabi

Assiniboine at Contact

It was not until fifty years after contact that any understanding of the Nakoda lands emerged. The early European explorers obtained limited information from their brief encounters with the Nakoda fur traders. We discuss in this chapter the records of missionaries and traders from 1640 to 1690, along with later observations by explorers Kelsey and La Vérendrye that provide an estimate of the lands occupied during those earlier times. A westward movement of the Assiniboine is assumed since the traders encountered Assiniboine and Cree farther west. First the early location of the Assiniboine was approximated, and then traders observed Assiniboine and Cree apparently moving westward, possibly because of the fur trade but also because of disease and wildlife depletion. However, this timing of the westward movement of the Assiniboine is contradicted by the Mortlach dating depicted in Chapter 1. Nevertheless, a review of the early encounters with the Assiniboine is valuable.

The first mention of the Assiniboine (Nakoda) in the Euro-Canadian literature was by Jesuit Father Marest in 1640. Marest speculated about the relationship among the Algonquian, Assiniboine, and Sioux. The Assiniboine, called middlemen in the fur trade, were reported at Lake Nipigon north of Lake Superior in *The Jesuit Relations* of 1658.[1] Arthur Ray presents Marest's assessment:

Perhaps for a time prior to 1670 the Assiniboine had lived at peace with other Siouan [sic] bands to the south and yet had differed enough from them, either in terms of culture or geographic location, to be recognized as a separate tribe by their Algonquian neighbours. Or, more likely, the Assiniboine may have developed trade contacts with other Algonquian groups and consequently lived in relative peace with them. As hostilities intensified between Algonquian and Sioux groups after 1670, when the English fur trade began to push into the interior, the Assiniboine then may very well have allied themselves to the Cree, as the Indians suggested, because of the growing military superiority that the latter group gained as a consequence of their more reliable supply of goods (English rather than French). Such a theory may explain why the Indians attributed the outbreak of the Assiniboine-Sioux hostilities to the English intrusion in the Bay, even though the tribe appeared as an identifiable group before the English were established.[2]

This quotation demonstrates the speculation about the Nakoda People during those early days. Further information about the Assiniboine was provided in *The Jesuit Relations* of 1658: "Thirty-five leagues or thereabouts from Lake Alimibeg [Lake Nipigon] is called the Nation of the Assinipoualak or Warriors of the Rock."[3] Ray provides further context for this reference:

Considering that the league was a rough time-distance measurement (the amount of territory canoeists could travel in an hour, approximately three miles), it follows from this account that the Assiniboine lived some one or two days' travel, or a hundred miles to the west of Lake Nipigon. This would put the eastern limit of their territory somewhere in the vicinity of the Pigeon and Kamanistiquia Rivers on the northwest shore of Lake Superior and Sturgeon Lake in northern Ontario. The Assiniboine travelled to Lake Nipigon via the Rainy River, Pigeon River, Lake Superior, and Nipigon River.[4]

In 1660, Father François du Creux drafted a map based on the geographic knowledge of his day that reported locations of Indian nations, including those north of Lake Superior and regions farther west. Father Gabriel Druillettes wrote in 1657–58 that three rivers were identified that appeared to be canoe routes from west to east, information that he learned from the traders Radisson and Grosseilliers.[5] More certainty about the geography of the northwest shore of Lake Superior and information on the movements of groups such as the Assiniboine were not obtained until Father Allouez visited the northwest shore of the great lake in 1667. Based on the De Creux map and *The Jesuit Relations* of 1657–58, the location of the Assiniboine appeared to be some three days or 100 miles west of Lake Nipigon, suggesting along the Pigeon River. By implication, the Assiniboine appear to have been regular visitors to the northwestern shore of Lake Superior and to Lake Nipigon.[6]

The Assiniboine operating in this area had their first direct contact with the French in 1678 when they were encountered by Daniel Greysolon, Sieur du Luth, who attempted to secure a peace between the Assiniboine and the Sioux to the south. In 1684, some six years later, he built a post on Lake Nipigon to trade with the Assiniboine and their Cree counterparts to divert their trade from the English posts already established on Hudson Bay.[7]

In 1685, since the Assiniboine were one of the key links to other Algonquians who were part of the Ottawa-Indian-French trading system, the need for peace to ensure trade between the Assiniboine and the Sioux proper was again emphasized.[8] An earlier memoir, dated November 13, 1681, and written to the minister by M. Duchesnau, pointed out that the Ottawa obtained most of their furs from the Cree, Assiniboine, and Sioux.[9] Du Luth reported to Denonville in a memoir in 1687 that trade was successful at Lake Nipigon and that exchanges were made with some 1,500 Indians.[10] Consequently, Du Luth's strategy of locating a post at Lake Nipigon was to serve one of the major canoe routes that the Assiniboine and Cree traders utilized to travel down to the bay. The post was also a key sphere of interaction between the Assiniboine and various eastern Algonquian groups.[11] This constituted the eastern margins of the Assiniboine interactions.

In 1688, Jacques de Noyon, while travelling from Kaministikwa to Lake of the Woods, met Assiniboine and Cree in the vicinity of Rainy Lake. There was no sense that the Assiniboine resided in the area; rather, they simply used the waterways for trade expeditions. De Noyon noted that Rainy Lake was called Lac des Cristineau and that Lake of the Woods was called Lac des Assiniboils.[12] Some Assiniboine were observed and identified in the area of Rainy Lake as late as 1696, and Beauharnois and Intendant Giles Hocquart indicated that, even though Lake of the Woods was still locally called Lac of the Assiniboins, the Assiniboine were not likely the only tribe in the vicinity of this body of water.[13]

Henry Kelsey Sees the Buffalo
Artist, Charles William Jefferys, c. 1690–92; courtesy of Library and Archives Canada, C-024390.

As detailed, the first fifty years of contact with the Assiniboine show a lack of information on their broader locations and land uses. However, the little information obtained does not contradict the oral histories of the Nakoda People, whose early folklore indicates that they originally occupied lands around Lake Winnipeg. Given the archaeological data, it is probable that the Assiniboine migrated to the lands as defined by Walde, Meyer, and Unfreed in the previous chapter and then after contact moved both back east to trade at Hudson Bay and farther west and south, sharing lands with the bands with whom they traded.

In 1690–91, Hudson's Bay Company (HBC) employee Henry Kelsey made a tour of the northern prairies and adjacent parklands from York

CHAPTER 2

La Vérendrye at Lake of the Woods
Artist, Arthur H. Hinder, c. 1900–33; courtesy of Library and Archives Canada, ID 289594.

Factory to the Touchwood Hills of Saskatchewan. He lived and travelled with the Assiniboine, observed their territories, and demarcated what he thought was Assiniboine territory farther west. Kelsey observed the Assiniboine occupying lands along the Carrot River and south to the Touchwood Hills. He also suggested that there were two divisions of the Assiniboine, Northern and Southern, with various subgroups stemming from both. It is a bit difficult to identify exactly the names that he used for what would now be the modern Cree, Assiniboine, and Hidatsa Peoples, but he did mention the Stone Indians, who were clearly Assiniboine; the Eagle Brich [Birch] Indians; the Eagle Creek or Hills Assiniboine; the Mountain Poets Assiniboine, located near the Touchwood Hills; and the Naywatame Poets, possibly Hidatsa, along the Assiniboine River. These territories therefore were occupied by the Assiniboine and their neighbours, matching the oral tradition of the Assiniboine People and the archaeological information discussed in Chapter 1.

The Assiniboine territories appear to have been vast, and the number of Assiniboine People was likely proportionate to the territories occupied. Another explorer-fur trader, Radisson, estimated that over 400 Assiniboine had travelled to York Factory in 1684.[14] The residential patterns of these Assiniboine and associated Cree appeared to be west of Lake Winnipeg.

It is difficult to set limits or divisions between Cree and Assiniboine lands. Kelsey suggested that the Cree were located primarily in the forest region between the lower Nelson River and the lower Saskatchewan River, north of the Assiniboine River.[15] However, Jacques de Noyon encountered some Cree much farther south, southwest of Rainy Lake. Nevertheless, "Kelsey travelled south through Cree territory passing beyond 'Dering's Point' which is generally thought to have been located on the lower Saskatchewan River in the vicinity of The Pas, Manitoba. He indicated that he was entering the territory of the Assiniboine."[16] It appears to be reasonable to postulate that the Cree territory was farther north than that of the Assiniboine. However, during the early fur trade travel patterns, Indigenous Peoples were responding to trade opportunities, making it difficult to determine previous territorial limits or travel patterns.

Once La Vérendrye reached Lake of the Woods/Lake of the Assiniboine in 1733, he reported that there were few Assiniboine there, but the Cree whom he encountered said that the Assiniboine were "near." La Vérendrye travelled overland from Lake of the Woods to his outpost, Fort Maurepas, initially located on the lower Red River, and once there he met with a group of Cree and Assiniboine and asked them where he should locate additional fur trading posts. An Assiniboine headman proposed that, if a post were built at the forks of the Red River (the confluence of the Red and Assiniboine Rivers), he would bring his group to support such a place of trade.[17]

Joseph La France depicted the locations of various Assiniboine groups on his map titled "New Map of Part of North America, 1739-1742."[18] La France located and labelled one band of Assiniboine as

CHAPTER 2

"Eagle Eyed Indians to the east of Lake Winnipeg and thought to be in the vicinity of the Poplar River." Several other sources confirm that the Eagle Eyed Indians were Assiniboine.[19] A reference from a York Factory (HBC) account book indicated that gifts were given in 1717 to a headman from this vicinity, implying that this Assiniboine group resided there prior to 1742.[20] La France's map also locates the Assiniboines of the Meadows and the Assiniboines of the Woods west of Lake Winnipeg.

Cree and Assiniboine were joined occasionally by Ojibwa in retaliatory forays in the Sioux country. These raiding parties effectively kept the Sioux from expanding north, ensuring that the Assiniboine maintained their established use of southwestern Manitoba while providing an Assiniboine presence in southeastern Manitoba. Farther east, the Cree and Ojibwa were able to thwart the Sioux in the Rainy Lake area.[21]

Buffalo jumps and pounds were very efficient and did not require guns. Therefore, firearms were generally more useful for raiding than for harvesting. Also, guns at this time were of poor quality and needed constant repair; the functioning period of any firearm rarely lasted three years. "As many as 400 firearms were distributed each year for a population of 3,400 or one for every seven persons."[22] "Being well-armed, the Assiniboine and Cree had a decided military advantage over their neighbours; the Dakota Sioux to the south; the Gros Ventres and Blackfoot to the southwest; and the Chipewyan to the north who lacked this direct and steady source of supply."[23] However, the Cree and Assiniboine were overly dependent on firearms, making them vulnerable when numbers of working firearms and supplies of ammunition fluctuated. These supplies could not be consistently restored until the regularity of English supply ships was restored. Governor James Knight reported in 1716 that

> the wars has almost ruin'd this Country it being so thin peopled as the best. there has been all those Indians as they Call em Sinnepoets Destroyed so that of about 60 Canos as us'd to Come Yearly there is not Above 6 familys left wch they told me this Reason for it that they had lost the Use of their Bows and Arrows by having Guns so long Amongst them and when they were disappointed of Powdr Shott wch was Often by the Ships not coming here Enemies found They had no guns to Defend themselves with made war Upon them & Destry'd above 100 Tents Men, Women and Children .[24]

During the French control of Hudson Bay between 1694 and 1714, three maps were drawn representing the interior, providing

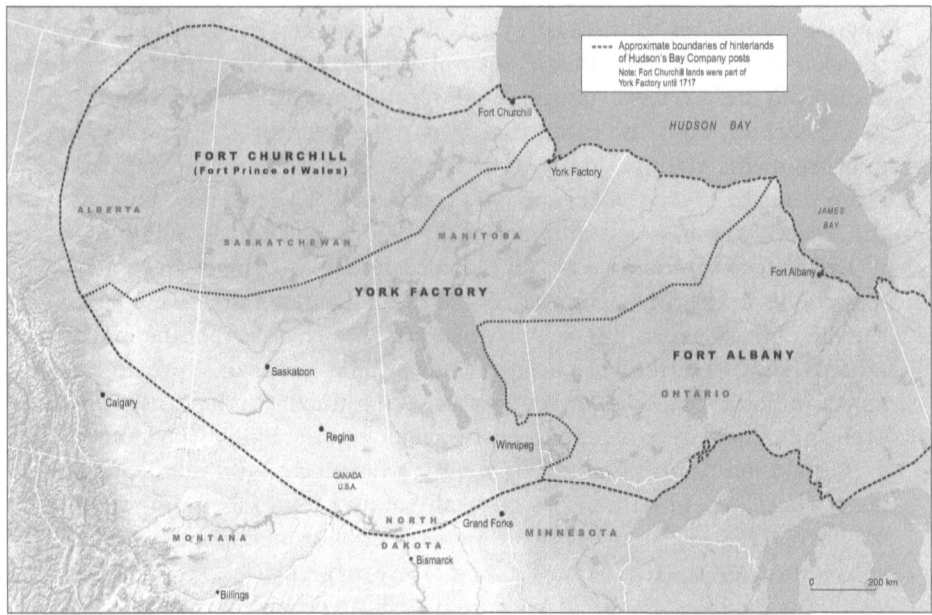

FIGURE 5: Western Fur Trade, c. 1700-20

information about the northern boundaries of Cree and Assiniboine territorial influence. The Woodland portions of these groups were represented as holding "the land between the lower Saskatchewan and upper Nelson rivers and the middle Churchill River between Southern Indian Lake and Reindeer Lake."[25] This era came to an end, and the English regained control of the bay at the conclusion of King William's War, when trade was restored with the Assiniboine and Cree Peoples. This new westerly expansion meant that trapping and trading were occurring between the Churchill and Saskatchewan Rivers. Ray asserts that the York Factory journals between 1714 and 1720 reported "that the territory of the Woodland Assiniboine and Cree reached as far as the head of the Churchill River."[26]

Some Assiniboine still occupied the Touchwood Hills seasonally and otherwise lived beyond that area. This evidence is again consistent with the oral history of the First Nation, included in its legends and Elder interviews. However, the effects of the trade were felt. By the 1700s, trade had begun to alter the nature of traditional land use and extended it through travel for trade for many First Nations.[27]

The sizes of these Indigenous groups might contribute some knowledge about the minimum size of territory required to sustain a population. Ray postulated that by 1685 (based partly on Wissler's reconstructed demographics) population estimates for the Northern Plains "averaged three to six times the total number of adult males."[28] With the entrance of the horse in the region, diseases such as smallpox spread more quickly and were less likely to be contained as with previous practices.[29] There is no clear picture of the impact of the smallpox epidemic of the 1730s on the Cree and Assiniboine populations. Although some smallpox was reported to have reached Red River, this epidemic did not get to the Mandan villages.

Ray surmises based on his reading of the York Factory Journals that after 1720 the Assiniboine were expanding in a "west-northwesterly direction, through the parkland corridor."[30] In 1755, Anthony Henday made a trip from York Factory to eastern Alberta and reported meeting many groups of Assiniboine exploiting the parkland ecotone. His most westward visit was to a location at Sounding Creek, Alberta, "at a longitude of approximately 111 degrees west."[31] It was unclear to Henday if the Woodland Assiniboine whom he encountered in the parklands had been forced westward or come peacefully. He observed these Assiniboine "camping and travelling with the Gros Ventre [Atsina] and Blackfoot on numerous occasions, and the area seemed to be quite tranquil."[32] The most western Assiniboine were those who became the Stoney in the foothills of the Rockies. Meanwhile, the Cree territory had expanded to the parkland and woodland regions between Reindeer Lake and Lake Athabasca. Although their northern expansion had ebbed by 1720, their westward expansion continued well into the mid-century, extending into northwestern Saskatchewan and Alberta.[33]

Ray suggests that this westward expansion was completed by 1720, fostered by the middlemen role played by select Assiniboine and Cree with interethnic trading captains taking the supply of furs to Hudson Bay for exchange.[34] According to Assiniboine Traditional Knowledge, the Assiniboine had used the Cypress Hills since before memory, well before Ray suggests their livelihood cycles shifted southwest. It appears that he recorded movements related to the fur trade that do not account for the homeland established by the Nakoda well before contact as indicated by the archaeological research. This re-emphasizes the need to consider all the available information to understand the probable lands of the Nakoda (Carry The Kettle) People.

Walde, Meyer, and Unfreed state that "it is clear from Russell's discussion that the earliest written (fur trade) records indicate that the northern and eastern boundaries of [the] Mortlach area were occupied by Assiniboine groups." And "the earliest written records . . . place Assiniboine groups on the northern, eastern, and southern boundaries of the study area and are either silent or ambiguous as to the ethnicity of the inhabitants of the study area at the earliest recorded times."[35] It appears to be clear that the Mortlach culture was in fact Proto-Assiniboine. This conclusion implies that earlier research suffered from "displaced observations" as proposed by Dale Russell.[36] It implies that the traders encountered Assiniboine within the Assiniboine heartland and that it was the traders who were moving westward, not the Assiniboine, who were already at home.

This information suggests that the Assiniboine occupied south-central Saskatchewan and farther south as early as 1300 and perhaps included the One Gun area close to the Cypress Hills as reflected in their oral legends. The Cree, however, were likely more recent occupants of the southern area, with the important exception of the mixed Cree-Assiniboine bands. The fur trade likely encouraged the Assiniboine to return to the Hudson Bay area to take advantage of the trade in association with their allies, the Cree. The Cree were also eventually drawn farther southwest with the Assiniboine, their long-term allies.

ASSINIBOINE LAND USE HABITATS AND CYCLES

Ray identifies three distinct types of habitat that characterized the territories occupied by the Assiniboine and Western Cree during the seventeenth and eighteenth centuries: the forest, the parklands, and the grasslands. It is likely that the inhabitation and land use within these habitats were affected by seasonal and disease-related changes. Seasonal changes influenced the availability of food supplies that led to predictable outcomes. Ray observed that,

> significantly, the cyclic variations of the forest, parkland, and grassland habitats did not parallel each other, but rather, tended to be complementary. For example, the summer season, particularly the late spring–early summer and later summer–early autumn, were times of relative food abundance in the woodlands when the fishing was good and waterfowl was plentiful. Food supplies were spatially concentrated around lakes and along rivers at that time. In the winter months, the situation was quite different. By mid-October most of the waterfowl abandoned the area and the fisheries fell off as temperatures plummeted and fish sought out deeper waters. December, January, and February were often grim months for the Indians,

and the threat of starvation was always present. Large game animals could be taken, but they were widely scattered, since many sections of the boreal forests could not support sizeable game populations. These lean conditions did not improve until the arrival of spring.[37]

The parkland region supports a food cycle that has some characteristics of the forest cycle, but there are differences. During the winter season, always long and often with episodes of severe food shortage, the parklands and valleys were sought for shelter and the diverse game usually available. Although food was available in all three zones, regional variations in weather conditions, especially in microclimates, made the parklands preferable:

> During the summer months fish and waterfowl were plentiful, although the former were taken primarily in the spring when the sturgeon were running in the rivers. The fall fishing season was of limited importance compared to that of the forest region. Even though large game was present in the area all summer, the most important animal, the bison, migrated toward the open grassland during the summer and was not abundant. With the onset of winter the situation changed and increasingly harsh weather conditions led the animals to seek shelter. The bison moved into the parklands in greater numbers, grazing in small prairies during mild spells and taking refuge in wooded sections during periods of severe weather. Consequently, food was plentiful in the winter season when it was becoming scarce in the adjacent forest. Indeed, contrary to what one would expect, mild winters in the parklands produced hardships, since the bison remained on the open grasslands and game was scarce.[38]

The third habitat, the grasslands, exhibited characteristics that closely parallel the forest cycle:

> Summer was a time of plenty as the bison massed in large herds during the rutting season. In the winter, the circumstances changed considerably. Under average or severe weather conditions bison scattered in search of shelter. Other game responded in a similar fashion since they could not survive on the open grasslands in the face of the chilling winter winds. At these times it would have been difficult for any Indians to

remain in that environment, and there is little evidence that many did.[39]

Regional economic adaptations meant that local environments were extensively exploited when a resource represented an opportunity. Bison and fish represented seasonal opportunities. Ray discusses this pattern: "It is likely that in the late prehistoric period the Assiniboine and Cree travelled in migratory bands the size of which depended upon the season and local resources. Furthermore, it seems reasonable to assume that through these movements many bands exploited two or three major environmental zones on a seasonal basis."[40]

There were reports of some Assiniboine groups harvesting wild rice, but the Assiniboine were directly observed more in the parklands and grasslands. La Vérendrye's direct observations in the 1730s were the first of the Assiniboine in this region. Attitudes toward the three zones were recorded. The forests/woodlands were feared in winter as a place of starvation.[41] Higher concentrations of people presented particular challenges in provisioning themselves with sufficient game. In spring and early summer, many bands gathered on shores of lakes known to have fish as a resource. By middle and late summer, bison were hunted in the grasslands after they had fattened on grass and become slower. Summer hunts could extend to the Missouri River and were combined with a trade expedition to the Mandan trade centre. La Vérendrye reported in 1737 that he had "inquired of the Assiniboine where they meant to spend the summer; and they said that on returning from war they would go to the country of the Kouathéattes [Mandan] to buy Indian corn and beans.... They promised to bring all these things [items that La Vérendrye had requested] at the fall of the leaves to Fort Maurepas."[42]

Consequently, the more southern Assiniboine at this time would hunt and travel in the direction of the Missouri, often along either side of the Souris or White Earth River, and eventually head farther south to the Mandan villages for trade. Although a direct route would have taken much less time, the objects were to be self-sufficient on the route and to accumulate some surplus to be available for trade with the Mandan. Most important was to live on the land and the numbers of bison on these prairies.

Ray's proposal that the Assiniboine travelled in seasonal cycles is reasonable and supported by the testimony of Elders. However, these cycles involved harvesting the resources when they were available, including harvesting bison during the winter months in northern regions. Walde describes harvests of larger numbers of bison in the

CHAPTER 2

"MIH-TUTTA-HANG-KUSCH"—a Mandan Village
Artist, Karl Bodmer, 1833; courtesy of the Library of Congress, Control Number LC-DIG-pga-04448.

winter and spring to accumulate surplus tradable provisions in advance of their trips south to trade with the more southern horticultural peoples, and this pattern was likely occurring well before contact.[43] Walde opens a precontact trading and cultural window reflected in the Elders' stories but not frequently found in the limited understandings of traders' written reports.

One was an observation by Henry Kelsey of the meeting place at Dering's Point near The Pas, where he observed Woodland Assiniboine gathering in July before their annual departure to live the next few months in the parklands. The vicinity of The Pas was important for harvesting fish, likely done before the Assiniboine moved onto the prairies with the bison. It was also a place to leave family members as trading expeditions headed northeast or to prepare for the bison hunts southwest. Note that Arthur discusses bison wintering regularly around the Touchwood Hills.[44] That would fit with the observations of Kelsey, though he might not have understood the precontact time when bison were more plentiful. He also observed that the Assiniboine travelled along the forest edge until late August, gradually moving into the parkland in late July to take bison using pounds. La Vérendrye gave the first description of a pound during his trip with the Assiniboine to the Mandan in 1737.[45] Further details of how the pound system worked are provided in Chapter 10 via an interview from 1929 with Blue Horn of the Assiniboine Tribe of Indians.

In the 1750s, HBC explorers Joseph Smith and Joseph Waggoner made three trips to assess the state of trade in southwestern Manitoba and into Saskatchewan in areas east and southeast of where Kelsey had travelled seventy years earlier. They described in considerable detail the seasonal activities of the Indigenous people with whom they travelled. Smith and Waggoner identified how the Cree groups travelled between places based on the richness of resources, stayed longer when the resources were plentiful, and moved on when the resources became diminished. In 1763–64, in mid-winter out on the grasslands at the edge of the parklands, Smith described how some of the Assiniboine group were hunting bison while others were located where it was conducive to build canoes. The pattern of leaving families in the spring and early summer at fishing locations enabled the men to make their canoe trip to the factories at Hudson Bay.[46]

In 1767, another HBC man, William Pink, left York Factory and journeyed to the Saskatchewan River up to the area around present-day Prince Albert. He also travelled with "Indians" and observed various subgroups separating from the larger group to pursue their own winter hunts in specific areas. As the larger aggregation fissioned seasonally into smaller groups, Pink travelled to the southwest parklands to make snowshoes and sleds. The Indigenous people with whom he was travelling were joined by one of the last subgroups that had departed earlier, approximately twenty families. Jointly, they strung snowshoes for the last two weeks of December and then spent January in the parklands. By February, the groups were moving to the river and the canoe-building grounds. While they were making this gradual relocation, some groups of men were sent to where meat and hides had been cached in the fall. Another group was sent off to the Birch Hills to harvest birch bark. Over the next two months, they stayed by the river to build their canoes but also fished, hunted waterfowl, and trapped fur animals in the vicinity. The new canoes were ready for departure on May 14, and a portion of the group departed for Hudson Bay. Pink's account of the way of life of the "trading bands of central Saskatchewan" was very similar to the pattern previously observed by Smith and Waggoner.[47]

CHAPTER 2

Other observers—Matthew Cocking, Samuel Hearne, Alexander Henry, as well as Assiniboine Elders—all commented that various Indigenous groups, including the Assiniboine, wintered not in the boreal forest but in the parkland, returning only to fishing sites in the spring to early summer.[48]

Both French and English accounts for the period 1690–1765 report cycles of exploitation characteristic of tribal groups living in central and southern Manitoba and Saskatchewan. Ray explains this parkland cycle:

> One of these [cycles] was based in the forests and parklands and was most common among the Cree and certain bands of Assiniboines who maintained direct contact with Hudson's Bay Company posts. This cycle was one in which tribal bands spent the warmer months of the year in the forests. At that time the men made their trading expeditions to the Bay while their families fished and hunted along the shores of lakes and rivers in the forest land beyond the Shield. In late August, September, and October they hunted in the wooded areas adjacent to the prairies, taking moose and trapping beaver. From November to March they moved into the parkland belt proper where they [various Cree and select Assiniboine] often lived with the Assiniboine, hunting bison and trapping wolves and fox. In March, April, and May they reassembled along lakes and rivers to build their canoes, trap furs, fish, and hunt waterfowl.[49]

The Assiniboine groups who had only occasional interactions with the Cree and Assiniboine middlemen resided in the grasslands-parklands and presented a second cycle:

> [The portion of these bands] . . . in other cases . . . [were those] who traded principally with the French. These bands commonly resorted to the parklands in the winter season to seek shelter, hunt bison, and trap wolves. In the spring they often set up fishing weirs along principal rivers of the parklands, such as the Assiniboine, to take sturgeon. At this time, and often extending into the summer, raiding parties were sent into Siouan [Sioux] and Gros Ventre [Atsina] territory. In the middle and late summer, the tribal populations shifted to the open grasslands to prey on the large bison herds. Toward the end of the summer and into autumn, even into early winter in some instances,

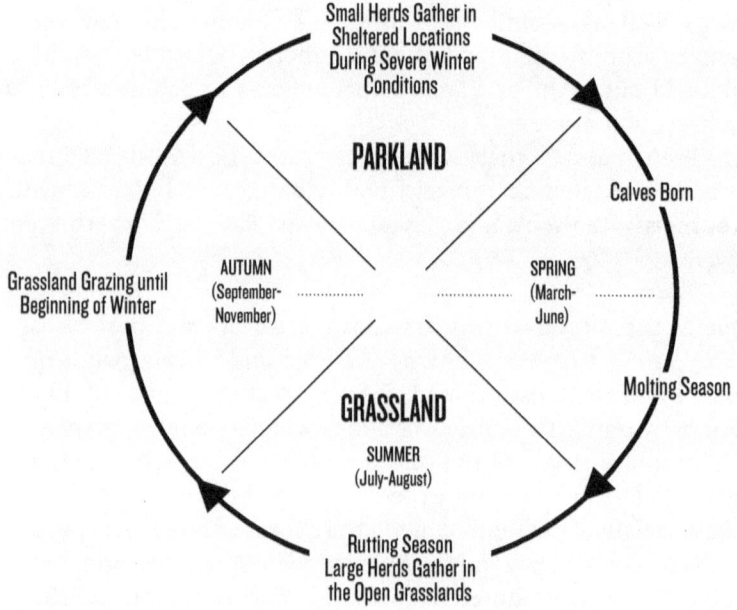

FIGURE 6: Assiniboine Early Annual Rounds
Reproduced from Ray, Indians in the Fur Trade, *33, Figure 13.*

the trading trip was made to the Mandan villages to obtain Indian corn. Upon completion of these expeditions the two groups returned to the parklands, except those who wintered in the scattered outliers of the forest zone, such as in the Turtle Mountains.[50]

Ray demonstrates that these two "overlapping economic systems" were utilized by "the tribes of the grasslands, forests, and parklands [that] came into contact with each other." He asserts that "these economic contacts encouraged inter-regional exchange of ideas. Through these exchanges, various bands pointed to the example of the Cree learning how to pound buffalo from the Assiniboine." Ray interprets his cycles as follows: "The ability to exploit all of these zones gave these groups a great deal of ecological flexibility. This flexibility permitted them to make rapid adjustments to changing economic conditions in the late eighteenth century. . . . It facilitated rapid inter-regional migration."[51]

CHAPTER 2

INITIAL FUR TRADE IMPLICATIONS

From the last half of the eighteenth century to the first decades of the nineteenth century, the fur trade brought further changes to the livelihood of the Assiniboine People. Smaller fur-bearing animals were continuously exploited to accommodate the increasing demands of the fur trade. Larger game animals were also exploited since the grease could be extracted from them, and the meat could be dried, pounded, and mixed with berries to make pemmican for the ever-growing provisions trade. The bison herds of the grasslands were a major source of the meat and grease used in making pemmican, traded as a commodity.[52] Later, the robe trade became profitable enough to transport robes.[53]

The 1770s were marked by other changes. The Assiniboine abandoned their role as middlemen in these years. The Canadians (Peddlers) had brought excessive amounts of liquor into the trade. Even though their trade goods were expensive, the profit was extracted by the liberal use of alcohol in exchanges. A number of posts for the Canadians and the HBC were situated to encourage the provisions trade. The flow of liquor was also accompanied by the increase in sexually transmitted diseases as relations with Indigenous women increased.[54] Consequently, violence and hardship in Indigenous communities increased, and by the end of the decade abuse and retribution were out of control. By the spring of 1779, the incidents of violence caused a number of relocations from areas considered too dangerous. Some Canadians began shipping furs at night.

The fur trade also brought widespread hunger. The HBC at Hudson's House sent dozens of its servants to spend the winter with Indigenous families. Periodic infusions of meat from occasional successful hunts did little to counter the effects of long-term malnutrition. By October 1781, there were reports that smallpox had spread from the Snakes (Shoshoni) and that it was widespread along the Saskatchewan River. "As had been the case decades earlier, disease spread along the Indigenous trade network that funnelled horses to the northern plains."[55] The epidemic with origins in Mexico City was continental in proportion, influencing even the outcome of the American revolutionary war.[56] The demographic upheaval that this represented must be understood regionally as well as beyond. "Mortality from [this] disease unleashed an unprecedented period of territorial and demographic change."[57]

The Shoshoni presence in southwestern Alberta ended, and they were pushed back to south of the Missouri River, allowing territorial expansion by the Blackfoot Confederacy. Along the North Saskatchewan River, the Assiniboine were hard hit, and survivors were few. Neighbouring Cree groups (Basquia, Pegogamy, and Cowinetow) in the vicinity of Cumberland House were decimated, and "the epidemic largely depopulated the lower Saskatchewan valley."[58] The demise of these groups "opened the lower Saskatchewan to immigrant groups closely attached to the fur trade, in particular the Muskego Cree and Anishinaabe."[59] By the summer of 1782, portions of Anishinaabe began their shift west to the Red and Assiniboine Rivers. "Equestrianism spread the disease quickly through the open country of the plains and parklands, but in the boreal forest, the contagion lingered for as long as two years."[60] The epidemic followed the networks and reached York Factory in 1782, brought by Bungi hunters, all of whom succumbed to it. The smallpox spread through much of northern Ontario, "significantly depopulating the Rainy River corridor and travelling the length of Albany River to James Bay."[61]

By the end of the 1780s, the "Indigenous occupation of western Canada" had changed because of the effects of smallpox. As many "cultural entities . . . ceased to exist," groups of survivors reorganized to create new communities, often characterized as a process of ethnogenesis.[62] Many newcomers were drawn to the region marked by so many vacated spaces. The impact of the epidemic on the extent and distribution of the region's fauna was not clear, but the fur resources were still considered bountiful apparently, and "the Muskego Cree and the Anishinaabe along with the Ottawa and Iroquois . . . came west as part of the ever-intensifying fur trade, which continued to grow despite the turmoil brought on by the loss of such a large portion of the Indigenous workforce."[63] A succession of territorial realignments occurred in response and "permanently changed the ethnic composition of western Canada":

> In the north, high mortality among the Cree, a consequence of their close relationship with traders, forced their retreat from land they had dominated in their role as fur trade middlemen. In Athabasca, the Dunneza (Beaver) people regained control of the region, and the Chipewyan Dene pushed the Cree south to the Churchill River. Muskego Cree trappers came west from the boreal forest of central Canada to exploit fur resources, as did several groups from the woodlands of the Great Lakes, including the Anishinaabe, Ottawa, and Iroquois.[64]

CHAPTER 2

Newcomers joined with survivors to create new social formations. Because of the labour shortages, many outsiders were recruited or encouraged to come into the region. Although many came, some did not care for the trade and returned to their home communities. However, others found new lives in the region and either joined existing social formations or founded their own.

The HBC had begun the building of inland fur trading posts and would continue this process, which would eventually eliminate the roles of the Assiniboine and Cree middlemen. The new market economy had changed the ecological balance.

The Basquia Cree, who occupied the Saskatchewan River Delta and were actively involved in the trade, suffered so many losses from the epidemic that their survivors joined the Swampy Cree who had moved onto the vacated Delta. Due to the violence and disease, Swampy Cree groups isolated themselves from the trade and from white traders, and except for seasonal visits to new inland posts, they no longer participated. The fur trade was changing.

South on the Northern Plains, the newcomers had emptied the region of game and fur animals—much of it within a decade, especially along the Saskatchewan River. "Extirpation of the species and adoption of equestrianism marked the end of an ecological relationship between humans and their environment that was thousands of years old."[65] Climate variability in the period 1780–1820 was marked by extreme summers and winters that "reduced game populations and threatened the humans who relied on them."[66] Many horses did not survive the winter weather. Throughout the 1790s, drought, the worst in 500 years, prevailed. Waterborne illness reduced human and animal populations. Many groups were under severe stress.[67] The Assiniboine were among these remnant groups, slowly reconstituting themselves, intermarrying, and creating new alliances. The epidemic meant a reconstitution of the fur trade as well. So many involved in the trade, including so many Indian producers, were swept away by the contagion.

The direct impact on the Assiniboine was a diminishment of the estimated population of 10,000 persons prior to the 1780–81 epidemic to less than a third.[68] However, redirecting their focus economically, many of the surviving Assiniboine were drawn to the south and the potential offered by the Missouri River country, initially for the winter seasons and then, for some of the bands, more permanently. With the Assiniboine homeland shifting (after a drift to the northwest from the epidemic), the survivors were predominantly part of what is known as "the southernmost bands." From 1808 to 1821, North West Company

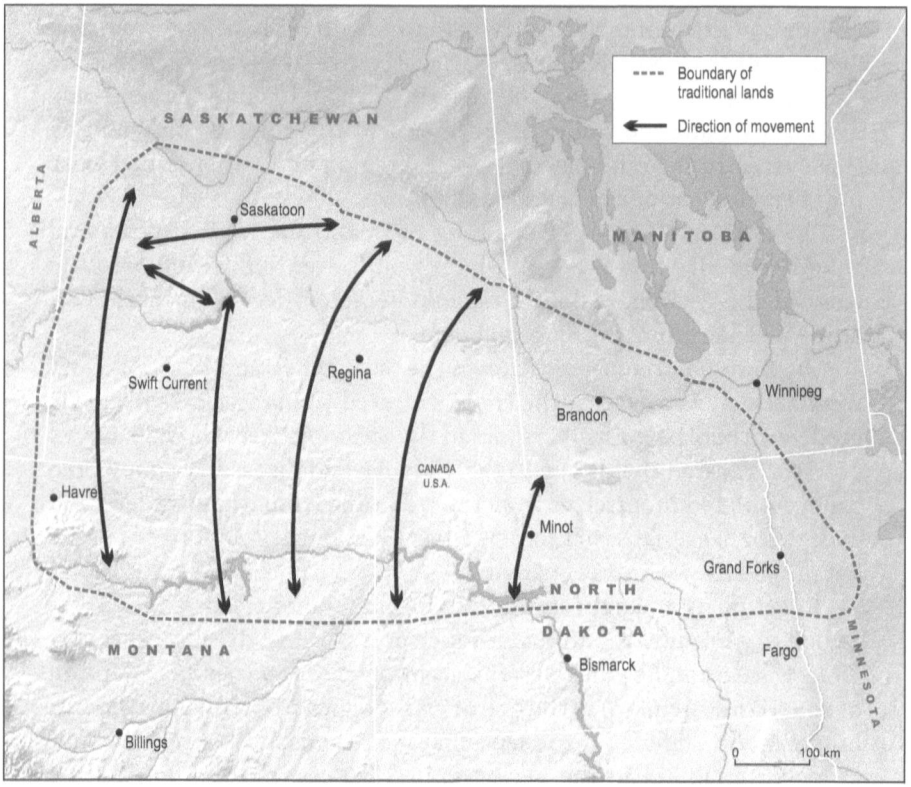

FIGURE 7: Annual Hunting Cycle of Assiniboine, c. 1821

employee Alexander Henry the Younger made observations of summer and winter camping locations for many of the bands, including the seasonal movements to the Missouri River.[69] Over half of the group's population continued to be concentrated in the Souris and Qu'Appelle Valleys. Another portion was located in territory between the South Saskatchewan River and the lower Battle River.[70]

In 1821, the merger of the interests of the HBC and its buyout of the North West Company reduced what had become a duopoly to a monopoly. The rising American trade was also a factor that made the Assiniboine groups and their potential contributions once again in demand. Much as their early role as middlemen was critical to the trade, once again they were positioned to play important new roles. Besides being a vector for diseases, the trade had negative influences. The use of "firewater" (liquor) in the trade was controversial and

CHAPTER 2

destructive, the system of credits and debits shaped the role of labour in the trade, and dependency was fostered in a number of practices. The Assiniboine were closely involved in the new formulations of the fur trade.

CHAPTER 3

Nakódabi 1799–1855 Čagúsam Makóče Missouri ičiyab

Upper Missouri Country and the Assiniboine, 1799–1855

The first European visitors to the plains observed millions of bison, possibly 70 million animals at their population height.¹ Eventually, settler society observed the bison migration cycles, of which there were two, a northern herd and a southern herd, maintaining different migration routes. The northern herd travelled in a huge loop through what became Saskatchewan, south of the Cypress Hills into Montana, back up beside the foothills of the Rockies, crossing the Old Man River, north across the Red Deer River, and up to the North Saskatchewan River, before bending back east and then south again. The Blackfoot Confederacy, the Assiniboine, and the middle and western divisions of the Sioux were among those Northern Plains tribal groups who lived primarily upon all that this bison herd gave them. Each group dominated their own region.

The Assiniboine, like other First Peoples, practised a seasonal harvest system based on the characteristics of the resources on which they relied. In the previous chapter, we discussed how the Assiniboine divided into more southern and northern bands, with different livelihood cycles, depending on the locations of the resources being harvested. Because of resource depletion, disease, and increased participation in the fur trade, the Assiniboine were also part of a westward shift, resulting in the increased wintering of select Assiniboine bands on the upper Missouri River, where the herds of bison were more reliably numerous. The effects of disease and the depletion of essential resources[2] also caused major dislocations in the ancient Traditional Territories of the First Peoples of the region.

EARLY 1800S: THE FUR TRADE AND FORT UNION

As the western regions of North America drew more attention from the markets of the eastern United States and British North America, the fur trade became even more significant in the livelihood of the First Peoples. The Missouri held the attraction of trade outlets and the capacity to seek commercial advantages. The Assiniboine saw these changes and adjusted their overall environment and resource use in response. However, the pressures on the Nakoda People would soon become intense.

After the Louisiana Purchase of 1803, the U.S. government commissioned the Lewis and Clark Expedition in an attempt to understand the boundaries and nature of the area that it had purchased from France. It is interesting to note that, after the boundaries of the Louisiana Purchase were finally identified, they extended into what is now Saskatchewan and Alberta. Before and after the purchase, these northern regions were the lands of the Nakoda and Blackfoot Peoples and remained their lands before and after the War of 1812 and the transfer of the lands from the United States to what is now Canada. Neither Lewis and Clark nor other officials of the United States or Canada met with the Nakoda or Blackfoot regarding the original disposition of their lands or the division of their lands between the two countries. Lewis and Clark made no contact with any Assiniboine either going or returning to this region, and they learned about the Assiniboine from the Mandan and Hidatsa in their visits and stays in their villages.[3]

The Missouri River villages of the Mandan and Hidatsa remained major trade centres, and Lewis and Clark were able to report that virtually all of the Indians whom they met were receptive to trade relations. The fur trade competition had been intensifying in the first decades of the nineteenth century and was expanding into the border regions between British North America and the United States from the Great Lakes and west to the Pacific coast. The North West Company was already supporting independent traders in the Mandan villages in the 1790s. In April 1808, the American Fur Company (AFC) was founded by John Jacob Astor, partly with the goal of challenging the other fur trade companies and their strategies, especially those coming from the north.

CHAPTER 3

The overall geographic influence of the Missouri River on the fur trade was significant because of the use of the river and its tributaries for transportation. Rafts and various river boats eventually gave way to the anticipated use of steamboats. St. Louis became a major trans-shipping point at the confluence of the Ohio, Mississippi, and Missouri Rivers. Much of the river traffic can be attributed to the developing fur trade. Consequently, various American-based fur companies were also operating out of St. Louis by the beginning of the nineteenth century.[4]

The movement of precious furs and beaver pelts, relatively light, had been the primary focus of the trade in the seventeenth and eighteenth centuries. The use of steel traps and beaver scent glands (castoreum) had allowed the taking of beaver, especially for "the barbed, fibrous under-hair which was 'pounded, mashed, stiffened, and rolled,' to make felting material for hats."[5] Bison hides continued to be processed and transformed into teepee covers and clothes, and bison were a source of many other traditional products and tools. Bison had been important in the production of pemmican to make the provisions vital to the fur trade when fresh meat or other food was not available. The parfleches of pemmican were lighter and easier to transport.[6]

A higher demand for bison hide began to develop in the fur trade, but the bulk and weight of the hides meant a scaling up of transportation logistics. The York boat, the Red River cart, and the steamboat made the transportation of the hides more possible logistically. The demand grew in the nineteenth century and became widespread as hides were made into industrial drive belts (bull bison hide), winter coats, sleigh and carriage blankets, and shoe leather. This increased demand for bison hides and robes further commodified the animal that was otherwise the staff of life for Plains Indians.

Between 1820 and 1824, there were transitions in the fur trade operations of the "Trans-Missouri West." Another era of trade began when William Ashley instituted the Rocky Mountain Trapping System and the American Fur Company extended its operations along the upper Missouri. "The intervening years were characterized by strenuous competition between a number of trading companies which were jostling for control of the fur trade on the Missouri River and competing for the furs of Blackfoot country."[7] By 1822, the AFC had absorbed several companies and established a western department in preparation for its upper Missouri trade in furs, and in 1826 it absorbed the Columbia Fur Company. In order to serve the Assiniboine trade, the AFC initially saw its most northern outpost as the Columbia Fur Company's White Earth River post, built along the Missouri by employee James Kipp in 1825–26.

Rafts, Equipment, and Supplies of the Fur Trappers and Traders
Illustration by William Macy; courtesy of the National Park Service Gallery, Jefferson National Expansion Memorial, VI07-000030.

CHAPTER 3

York Boat on the Nelson River, 1913

Photographer, O. Rolfson; courtesy of Library and Archives Canada, PA-020482.

Steamboats, St. Louis, Missouri, Levee, 1852

Credit: Photographer, Thomas Easterly; courtesy of the State Historical Society of Missouri.

By 1827, the AFC had acquired a network of trading posts throughout the Missouri Valley, equipped with experienced groups of traders. This was the foundation "for a production system that would endure until the 1860s."[8]

Concerned about controlling trade with the Assiniboine, the AFC saw the need for a major post at the confluence of the Missouri and Yellowstone Rivers. Kenneth McKenzie and his crew built Fort Union on the high north bank of the Missouri in the fall of 1829—just above the confluence of the two rivers. Consequently, an important consideration beyond the obvious goal of trans-shipment was the number of Assiniboine in the immediate vicinity eager for a trade centre and the abundance of fur animals and bison in the region.[9] One source says that the site was recommended by the leader of the Assiniboine Rock Band.[10]

In 1830, Tchatka (or Le Gaucher), an Assiniboine leader, visited Fort Union, testing the resolve of the AFC traders and McKenzie in particular. Having lost face with his almost 200 followers in a foray against the Blackfoot, Tchatka planned an attack on the new trade establishment. Upon their arrival at Fort Union, he told McKenzie that they were on their way to attack the Minnitarees and asked for powder. Friendly Indians were often allowed to sleep inside the fort, and Tchatka and his delegation were assigned rooms, waiting to execute their plan. However, one of McKenzie's employees, married to an Assiniboine woman, learned about the planned attack from her brother, among Tchatka's group. After the word got to McKenzie, he acted as if he knew nothing. He armed his employees and positioned them throughout the post. He then summoned Tchatka and told him that he knew of their plan and would allow the Assiniboine to leave peacefully, which they did. The relations with the Assiniboine were maintained, and the role of Fort Union was emphasized.[11]

To open the Blackfoot trade, Fort McKenzie was established in 1831 near the mouth of the Marias River, west of Fort Union along the Missouri River. The Assiniboine were not enthusiastic about this development or the initiative in 1832 to build Fort Cass at the mouth of the Big Horn River on the Yellowstone River to trade with their other enemies, the Crow. "This made Fort Union the pivot point for the upper reaches of both rivers; its storerooms supplied the goods and stored the furs and robes" awaiting shipment to St. Louis.[12]

Although the AFC had complete control of the upper Missouri and its various tributaries by the 1830s, other ventures were also formed in an effort to compete. Among the various companies were employees who would go to nearby Indian camps, no matter the weather, to

CHAPTER 3

Fort Union on the Missouri River, 1833
Artist, Karl Bodmer; courtesy of the National Park Service Gallery, FOUS 2761.

pick up furs and robes, especially from anyone who had been advanced credits and taken goods in the previous season. With the arrival of so many American traders, the Mandan and Hidatsa no longer needed the English-sourced goods brought south to them by various groups of Assiniboine. The Assiniboine and other upper Missouri tribal groups concentrated on creating a surplus—beyond their immediate needs for survival—that they could trade.

Ventures such as the Campbell and Sublette Company sought to take the Indian trade away from other traders and used alcohol in their interactions, forcing other traders also to use alcohol in the trade in an effort to hold sway over their particular clients. Competition resulted in traders giving away large quantities of alcohol to ruin the exchange value of alcohol offered by others.[13] Although liquor had long been used in the trade, it now reinforced loyalty and undermined competitors since there was no restriction posed by the HBC and independents based north of the international boundary. This use of alcohol had an

Assiniboine Woman and Child, Fort Union, 1832
Artist, George Catlin; courtesy of the Smithsonian American Art Museum, Gift of Mrs. Joseph Harrison Jr., 1985.66.181.

insidious influence on all Indians, including the Assiniboine, eroding values and authority structures within the immediate region.

In 1831, artist George Catlin, fascinated to represent Indian life and people, made his way upriver to Fort Union. During his visit, Catlin

CHAPTER 3

Buffalo Chase with Bows and Lances, 1832–33
Artist, George Catlin; courtesy of the Smithsonian American Art Museum, Gift of Mrs. Joseph Harrison Jr., 1985.66.410.

produced the first of many images of the Assiniboine, both individual portraits and scenes from their daily lives. During his eighty-six days along the upper Missouri River, much of it at Fort Union, Catlin produced 136 paintings. He set up a studio in one of the fort's bastions, where he interacted with many of his subjects or those who wanted to watch him paint. While at Fort Union, Catlin was also able to observe and paint small groups of Blackfoot and Cree. When the Indians came to trade, McKenzie took great care to keep the groups away from each other, assigning them camping areas on opposite sides of the fort out on the prairie. He disarmed them for the duration of their stays.[14]

Sub-Indian Agent John Sanford arranged a delegation to Washington, DC, in the fall of 1831. The Assiniboine representative, Wi-jún-jon—The Light (meaning "the light as seen through the bottom of a bottle of thick glass"), also known as Pigeon's Egg Head, was the eldest son of Iron Arrow Point, the leader of the Rock Band of

Wi-jún-jon, Pigeon's Egg Head (The Light) Going to and Returning from Washington, 1837–39
Artist, George Catlin; courtesy of the Smithsonian American Art Museum, Gift of Mrs. Joseph Harrison Jr., 1985.66.474.

Assiniboine, one of the Lower Assiniboine groups on the Missouri. He was renowned as a hunter and warrior, and he was in favour among the trade hierarchy at Fort Union, where he was considered a "soldier" on behalf of the AFC, responsible for keeping order among the Indians who came to trade and especially any actions perpetrated by "brash young Assiniboin braves."[15]

Upon reaching St. Louis, all were vaccinated and the subjects of portraits painted by George Catlin, there at the time. They left for Washington on January 1, 1832, by stagecoach and finally by train, arriving in Washington by January 15. Besides many tours through cities and military sites, the foremost event was an audience with President Andrew Jackson. The Light suggested that they exchange names and clothes—a general's uniform and the name Jackson were meaningful to the Assiniboine. They travelled back in the spring of 1832, and The Light was dead within several years of his return. His descendants carry the surname Jackson and reside on the Fort Peck Reservation.

Another guest and important observer at Fort Union in 1833 was German Prince Maximilian of Weid, accompanied by his employees: hunter-taxidermist David Dreidoppel and Swiss artist Karl Bodmer.[16]

Prince Maximilian kept a detailed journal, recording encounters with groups, their material cultures, personalities with whom he interacted, and all the information learned from them. Through his hunting and taxidermy skills, Dreidoppel assembled a representative collection of animals, with illustrations and descriptions. Bodmer then painted images that gave a naturalistic, almost photographic, realism to his renderings, especially his portraits. The Assiniboine and their relationship with their lands and resources were vividly portrayed.

In his journal, Maximilian summarized the extent of the trade flowing from Fort Union and noted that, whereas the annual number of beaver pelts was 25,000, the number of bison hides was between 40,000 and 50,000 per year. Other skins received in trade included otter, weasel, marten, lynx, red fox, cross fox, silver fox, mink, muskrat, and deer. The workforce at Fort Union was estimated to consume from 600 to 800 bison annually. Although vegetables were not easily grown without special attention, corn was traded from the groups downriver—much of which was thought to have been used by McKenzie in his still. Maximilian listed all the birds and animals that he observed, and he gave estimates of the populations of the Indian groups served by Fort Union. His estimated census of the Assiniboine in the vicinity was 28,000, living in 3,000 teepees. Of this population, 7,000 were warriors. Within days of his arrival, Maximilian reported that a large number of Assiniboine had come in:

> Towards the northwest, the whole prairie was covered with scattered Indians, whose numerous dogs drew the sledges

with the baggage; a close body of warriors, about 250 or 300 in number, had formed themselves in the center, in the manner of two bodies of infantry, and advanced in quick time towards the fort. The Indian warriors marched in close ranks, three or four men deep, not keeping their file very regularly, yet in pretty good order, and formed a considerable line. Before the center . . . three or four chiefs advanced, arm in arm, from the ranks. . . . Loud musket-shots were heard. The whole troop of these warriors now commenced their original song . . . [with] many abrupt, broken tones. . . . The loaded dogs guided by women and children, surrounded the nucleus of warriors.

They advanced to within about sixty paces then halted at a fosse [a ditch or small ravine] running from the Missouri past the fort, and waited, the chief standing in front, for our welcome.[17]

An important turning point came at the end of the summer of 1832 when the rise of silk hats became the fashion of the day over those made from beaver felt. AFC founder Jacob Astor recognized that the end of the beaver trade had finally come. Effective June 1, 1834, he sold his interest in the company. Bison had become the commodity most sought; although bison hide was already an important aspect of the fur trade, it would become the major item of production and trade.

DISEASE, POPULATION DECLINE, AND RECONFIGURATION

In June 1833, when Maximilian and his party were dropped off at Fort Pierre, the steamboat *Yellowstone* went upriver again, and onboard was the cholera bacterium. "Cholera's symptoms are fearsome, the most infamous being an acute diarrhea that can dehydrate and kill a victim in hours. Contaminated food and water spread the infection."[18] Outbreaks of disease and episodes of ruthless trade sparked a period of intensified warfare among groups, which led to even more casualties. Next came smallpox—again. The *St. Peter's* was "a wide-ranging ship of death. It dropped smallpox from Council Bluffs all the way to Fort Union on its upstream journey in [the] spring of 1837. And it may have reintroduced the infection as it steamed back down the river later in the summer."[19]

At Fort Union and its hinterland, Assiniboines, Plains Crees, Blackfeet, Piegans, Bloods, and Atsinas sickened and died. By one estimate, the smallpox killed "not less than 10,000" people. By another, the total loss was "near to 15,000." The commissioner of Indian Affairs calculated some 17,200 Mandans, Hidatsas, Arikaras, Assiniboines, and Blackfeet had "sunk under the smallpox." Joshua Pilcher, the U.S. Indian Agent, was less precise but more graphic. "The upper-Missouri country" he said was "one great grave yard."[20]

People at Fort Union sent messages to their long-time Assiniboine trading partners to stay away, but a good number of them were still exposed. "A party of more than 1,000 Indians ignored warnings to stay away from the fort and they contracted smallpox soon after their arrival. Only 150 survived."[21] The dispersion of the epidemic among the Assiniboine and the Blackfoot meant that their affiliated groups to the north were also vulnerable. News of the epidemic spread among the HBC posts, word often coming from individuals and groups already exposed. William Todd, the chief factor at the Swan River district, was among the first to hear and "to take measures to protect the health of his men and the local Indians."[22] Todd was also a medical doctor, and consequently he began to vaccinate as many as possible. He soon discovered, however, that the active pox vaccine that had been distributed to a number of posts was sterile and had to be replaced before effectiveness could be assessed.[23] "Infected Assiniboines fled north, but they could not outrun the disease; an estimated two-thirds of southern Assiniboines died. Two decades later, the southern Assiniboine population had increased by only 100 lodges, bringing their population by the mid-1850s to 500 lodges—one half [of] their pre-epidemic population."[24]

The overall depopulation of the Assiniboine People further threatened their security in that it made the nation more vulnerable to its many tribal neighbours: "This included Peigans (the easternmost of the three Blackfoot tribes) and Gros Ventres [Atsinas] to the west, Crows to the south, and Hidatsa, Upper Yanktonai and Lakotas to the east. In 1844, Assiniboines established peaceful relations with both the Crows and Hidatsas (two closely related tribes). This was surely an equitable arrangement for the Hidatsa, an earth-lodge village people who lost one-half [of] their population during the 1837–38 smallpox epidemic."[25] The reconstitution of their families and society often meant intertribal marriages and more dependence on interethnic relations in their domestic and civil affairs. Although there had been a disposition to marriages with Cree and Saulteaux allies, the degree to which such marriages and alliances became necessary resulted in many more changes for the Assiniboine People.

Charles Larpenteur went upriver and worked for Campbell and Sublette and their Rocky Mountain Fur Company. Once the company was bought and amalgamated with the AFC, he entered the service of the AFC in 1834 and served until the 1850s before becoming an independent. His first two wives were Assiniboine. His first wife died of smallpox in 1837, and his second wife was the mother of six of his children. He described how the buildings of old Fort William were turned into a primitive hospital to keep those ill and dying away from Fort Union, and the bodies of the dead were dumped into the nearby marsh since there were too many to be buried immediately. By the spring of 1838, Larpenteur estimated that Assiniboines in the area had been reduced by half.[26]

Larpenteur kept journals throughout his career and had much to say about the Assiniboine with whom he interacted. He described how, following the terrible epidemic, the challenges of status and role dominated how the Assiniboine interacted with each other and other Indian groups. He described in detail the orientation of Assiniboine camps that secured products of the hunted bison: the meat, the tallow fat for grease, and the processed or unprocessed hides. This compelled many families to take on the role of producers, which became a year-round occupation and orientation, sometimes in conflict with their very survival needs.[27]

Another person who would become instrumental in describing the role of the Assiniboine in relation to Fort Union was Edwin Thompson Denig. He signed on with the AFC for his first contract on April 10, 1833, and was assigned to duties as a clerk at Fort Pierre, spending one winter running a trading house at Cherry Creek on the Cheyenne River. His value to the company recognized, he was transferred to Fort Union in 1837 while the epidemic was taking its toll. In 1843, Denig was promoted to head clerk, and in 1848 he was appointed bourgeois, in command of Fort Union and its operations: "Denig's situation at Fort Union put him in a position to become an authority on the Assiniboine and other Indians in the region. The knowledge, both cultural and linguistic, that he acquired in his role as a trader allowed him to understand Indians as producers and consumers."[28]

In his tenure at Fort Union from 1837 to 1855, Denig was married twice—both times to Assiniboine women—and observed many changes among the company's clientele, providing a unique set of observations. Fort Union continued to draw early scientists-travellers, made easier by regular steamboat traffic. There were visits from John James Audubon

CHAPTER 3

in the summer of 1843, naturalist Thaddeus Culbertson in 1850 on behalf of the recently established Smithsonian Institution, and Father Pierre-Jean De Smet, first in the 1840s and again in 1851, just prior to the treaty gathering at Fort Laramie. Crazy Bear and First to Fly went south to the negotiation to represent the Assiniboine; the purpose of the great meeting was to put an end to intertribal warfare by assigning specific lands to specific tribes, some cooperative but others not.[29]

However, Father De Smet encouraged Denig, clearly very knowledgeable about the Assiniboine and other upper Missouri River tribal groups, to write a series of cultural descriptions. De Smet received Denig's first account in September 1852 and incorporated it into his published letters in *Western Missions and Missionaries* (1863).[30]

The Swiss artist Rudolph Frederich Kurz spent seven months visiting Fort Union, from September 1851 to April 1852, keeping a journal, working as a secretary/clerk, and making a series of sketches. Kurz referred to Denig reading to him from a manuscript that he was writing for De Smet. Kurz was interested in Denig's collection of animal specimens, natural history, and ethnographic objects, many of which Kurz sketched.[31]

Denig's next assignment was a much larger project. Governor Isaac Stevens of Washington Territory stopped at Fort Union for eight days in August 1853 and asked Denig to answer a Schoolcraft questionnaire consisting of 348 questions. Denig took this assignment seriously; many of the questions he could answer from what he already knew, and for those that he could not answer he asked his friends and relatives among the Assiniboine. He forwarded his completed report to Stevens in 1855, just prior to his retirement from his post at Fort Union.[32]

In his lengthy answers, Denig addressed a variety of issues associated with Assiniboine land use. He explained that the "Da-co-tah" called the Assiniboine "Ho'-hai" or "fish eaters" since Indians from the north lived on fish. "By the Cree and Chippewa they are called 'As-see-nee-poi-tuc' or Stone Indians," giving rise to the anglicized "Assiniboine." He continued thus:

> At the earliest date known they roved about the head of St. Peters, Des Moines, Lac du Diable, and Lac qui Parle; and then they joined the Sioux Indians, who inhabited and claimed all the lands between the Mississippi and the Missouri as low as Big Sioux River and as high as the head of Rivier à Jacque, thence northward towards Lac du Diable, other bands of Sioux (Teton) residing west of the Missouri.

The number of Assiniboines when they separated must have been at least 1,500 lodges, averaging six souls to a lodge [or about 9,000 people]. Their migration has been referred to and the extent of land they occupied in the British territory on the Saskatchewan, etc., was very large, but at present their habitat is entirely different and it may be as well to state it here. The northern Assiniboine, 250 or 300 lodges, rove the country from the west banks of the Saskatchewan, Assiniboine, and Red Rivers in a westerly direction to the Woody Mountains north and west among small spurs of the Rocky Mountains east of the Missouri, and among chains of small lakes through this immense region.

The rest of the Assiniboine, say 500 to 520 lodges [who may be called the southern Assiniboine], occupy the following district, commencing at the mouth of the White Earth River on the east, extending up that river to its head, thence northwest along the Coteau de Prairie or Divide, as far west as the Cyprus [sic] Mountains on the north Fork of the Milk River, thence, down the Milk River to its junction with the Missouri River, thence down the Missouri River to the mouth of the White Earth River, or the starting point.

Formerly they inhabited a portion of country on the south side of the Missouri River along the Yellowstone River, but of late years, having met with great losses by Blackfeet, Sioux, and Crow war parties, they have been obliged to abandon this region and now they never go there. As before remarked, the Assiniboine still numbered 1,000 to 1,200 lodges, trading on the Missouri until the year 1838, when smallpox reduced their numbers to less than 400 lodges. Also being surrounded by large and hostile tribes, war has had its share in their destruction, though now they are increasing slowly.[33]

The Assiniboine population as a whole was severely reduced by widespread European diseases, notably smallpox: "In the early nineteenth century, before being devastated by smallpox, they were thought to have numbered 80,000, and some estimates suggest their numbers were much higher."[34] In an interview contained within the Carry The Kettle archives, Chief Talks Differently explained that at one time the Nakoda, when gathered, had 7,700 lodges with ten to twelve people per lodge. After continuous European contact, however, the population declined drastically. According to Nick Alvares in September 1929, my father told me that . . . there were about 3,000 families of Assiniboine's. . . . What the real old members who lived at that time told me and also what my father told me was that somebody had smallpox and his blanket was shipped up in this country, and that is how the epidemic spread. . . . My father told me that on account of an epidemic, a band of them ran away from Fort Union. . . . I understand we called the far-away Indians, away off here, the Assiniboine's of the Meadows, but those in Canada belonged to this tribe here.

CTK Elder Garry Whitecap observed in July 2015 that

we controlled a big territory. The reason they lost it is because of disease, smallpox, measles, TB, and all that there reduced the population, and in turn it shrunk. Now we're only on this reserve, and there's a lot of Assiniboine reserves in Alberta, like I said, Alexis, Mosquito, Morley, Grizzly Bear, but they're just scattered. But it was once a huge territory. But now there's only a few reserves left. But that was a big land base.

That "big land base," according to Denig, did not come to the Assiniboine by conquering other Indigenous groups: "The Assiniboine conquered nothing to come into possession of their habitat, they had their difficulties with surrounding tribes and still have, as others have, and continue as they commenced, fighting and hunting alternatively."[35] Denig continued on to the topic of "Ancient and Modern Habitat" and described the Assiniboine orientation:

They do not think that the Great Spirit created them on or for a particular portion of country, but that he made the whole prairie for the sole use of the Indian, and the Indian to suit the prairie, giving among other reasons the fact that the buffalo is so well adapted to their wants as to meat and clothing, even for their lodges and bowstrings. To the Indian, he is allotted legs to run, eyes to see far, bravery, instinct, watchfulness, and other capacities not developed in the same degree in the whites. The Indian, therefore, occupies any section of prairie where game is plentiful and he can protect himself from enemies. With regard to any other kind of right than that of possession and ability to defend, besides the general right granted by the Great Spirit, they have not the most distant idea.[36]

The Assiniboine in this era experienced many changes as the fur trade became the robe trade and as their contact with non-Indians increased. Disease for which there was little or no immunity was only part of the larger story. The use of "firewater" in the trade was corrosive and debilitating. The system of credits and debits atomized the trade to individuals and overstepped the importance of community formations. This system also fostered dependencies that narrowed options and flexibility for individuals. Denig, in the conclusion to his report for Stevens, saw the end of the bison and consequently cashed out for retirement, but that was short lived. His travel downriver to St. Louis and Ohio allowed him to feel the rising sentiments that would collide in the impending Civil War. The Assiniboine, though initially isolated, would feel the effects of changes in the Montana territory, and they found it increasingly difficult to sustain their economic and political autonomy. The international boundary would begin to play a part in their lives in terms of what they could do to live on the lands of this border region.

CHAPTER 4

Wiyóȟpeyadagiya Knaškíŋyaŋbi

The Wild West

The Assiniboine moved westward to exploit the bison trade, which again took them farther from their original home in the parklands of current-day western Ontario, southern Manitoba, Saskatchewan, and Minnesota to the plains of Saskatchewan, North Dakota, and Montana, where they had previously adapted to a nineteenth-century plains livelihood. However, this time many Indigenous groups were also migrating westward in response to eastern pressures, bringing the Assiniboine closer to other Indigenous Peoples and forcing them to compete for the dwindling bison resources. Carry The Kettle First Nation Traditional Knowledge also addresses the Assiniboine moving northwest from centres of disease to avoid sicknesses, and this is one explanation of the more recent northern Assiniboine separation.

DISEASE AND ALCOHOL

Waves of European diseases such as cholera, influenza, and smallpox spread throughout the prairie Indigenous populations. Each epidemic reduced tribal populations by as much as half, forcing survivors to adapt by forming alliances with other tribes. During this period, the Assiniboine were hit with two devastating smallpox outbreaks, one in 1859 and another near the Milk River Agency in September 1869. The Gros Ventres were also hit by the disease, and by that summer the Upper

Assiniboine married a hundred of their women to the diminished Gros Ventres. This appears to have been an adaptation used specifically by the Assiniboine to build up their population more quickly than other tribes after an epidemic.

On top of the effects of diseases, Indigenous Peoples were plied with alcohol by hide traders, who used it to take financial advantage of the Indigenous trappers and traders. Overconsumption of alcohol regularly resulted in death, loss of cultural standards, and disintegration of life-supporting relationships. We describe these problems in more detail later in the chapter in our discussion of the Whoop-Up escapades.

DEVELOPMENT OF THE AMERICAN NORTHWEST

The Missouri River became the most important transportation route for heavy bison hides from the northwestern plains. The American trade expanded quickly as the west opened up. After the Louisiana Purchase of 1803, the American government adopted a policy of settlement in the northwest region. To clear the way for settlement, the government made efforts to reduce the bison herds and confine the Indigenous Peoples to reserves.

The establishment of the American border after the War of 1812, and the eventual enforcement of border traffic, had significant effects on those Indigenous Peoples who had regularly used their lands on both sides of this new boundary. The Assiniboine (Nakoda) People had migrated westward and followed the bison and other game wherever they could be found on both sides of this new boundary from east to west. The boundary was surveyed in 1872. According to CTK Traditional Knowledge, it had always been common for the so-called northern Nakoda group to live both north and south of the "medicine line."

Although the American authorities invited all the tribes, the northern Assiniboine did not attend the great treaty made at Fort Laramie during the summer of 1851. With this treaty, the American government attempted to recognize most of the tribes of the upper Missouri River. The process involved government agents defining territories that they said belonged to specific tribes. According to this new policy, each tribe was to stay and sustain itself within its assigned "hunting grounds." The southern Assiniboine were represented at this gathering by the headmen Crazy Bear and First to Fly. During this treaty, annuities were promised over a fifty-year period, but upon ratification of the treaty this time period was unilaterally shortened to a decade by the U.S. Senate.

CHAPTER 4

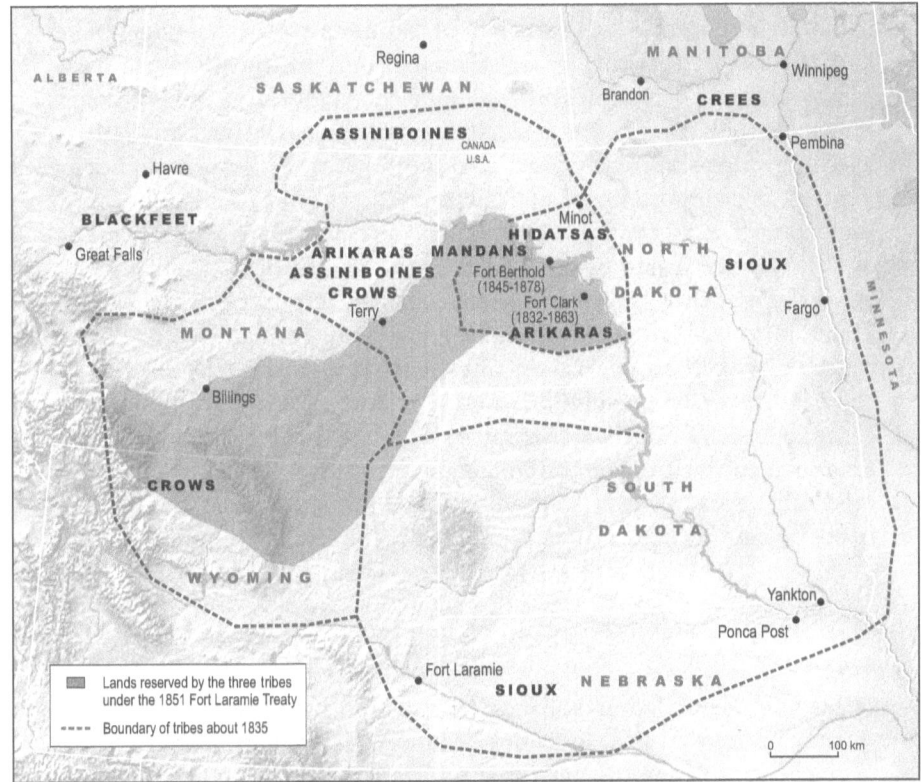

FIGURE 8: Lands Reserved by the Mandan, Hidatsa, and Arikara under the 1851 Fort Laramie Treaty

The next round of encounters with Indigenous Peoples was during the travels of Governor Isaac Stevens (Washington Territory, 1853–55) across the vast territory that was his charge. Stevens served as the ex-officio superintendent of Indian Affairs and therefore had the authority to negotiate treaties with numerous Indian Nations across the Washington Territory, which included current-day Montana, Wyoming, Idaho, Washington, and Oregon. When Stevens reached Fort Benton in the fall of 1853 to begin negotiations on what would become the Stevens Treaty of 1855, he was not able to find the Blackfoot and therefore began treaty negotiations with the Salish and Sahaptan groups. During their talks, he agreed to terms that gave these groups full access to lands and bison herds in the foothills east of the Rockies—lands that have long been considered Blackfoot territory. Consequently, when negotiating later with the Blackfoot, Stevens proposed creation of the "Great Blackfoot Hunting Ground," which would run from Fort Benton to the Rockies and then north to the international boundary, including the entire northern tier of Montana to the boundary line, with the Dakota Territory bounded on the south by the Missouri River.

Stevens proposed that this region be shared by all those promised hunting access from the west, including the Flatheads (Eastern Salish), and all groups sharing the northern tier: Mountain Crow, Atsina Gros Ventres, growing numbers of Yanktonai Sioux, and Assiniboine. It is important to note that the Assiniboine were not invited to or present at the Stevens Treaty of 1855, held at the mouth of the Judith River. Nevertheless, this American-style treaty had implications for all the Assiniboine and others, especially since they were allocated lands together with their mortal enemies. Little or no attempt was made to coordinate the stipulations of the Stevens Treaty with the Fort Laramie Treaty of 1851 made through William Farr.[1] Clearly, neither the American authorities nor the Canadian authorities were aware, or bothered to become aware, of the traditional hunting grounds of the various tribes or peoples before allocating them within treaty boundaries.

SIOUX CONFLICTS

The Americans had established forts along the Missouri River, and they became central locations around which the rapidly changing livelihoods of the Indigenous Peoples revolved. Fort Union was the fort at which the Assiniboine primarily traded. James Kipp assumed command of Fort Union in the fall of 1856 and reported the smallpox epidemic that began among the Assiniboine in November and a Sioux raid for horses in December.[2] Observers William H. Schieffelin, William M. Cary (artist), and Emlen N. Lawrence became stranded for six weeks in Fort Union, and during their stay they reported that a large band of Assiniboine came in and camped nearby. They also reported increased harassment from Sioux groups raiding in the area. Even by 1856 it had become clear that the Sioux would play a pivotal role in the disintegration of the regional situation.[3]

James Harkness, a competitor, visited Fort Union in June 1862 and noted that the previous winter had been extremely cold and that the Indians in the vicinity had lost over 500 horses because of the weather. Harkness reported that portions of the fort were decaying and that the menace of the Sioux was putting everyone on edge.[4] The effects of the conflict between the Dakota Sioux and the American settler society—which had erupted in 1862 in Minnesota—cast a dark shadow over the northwest thereafter. Henry A. Boller witnessed first-hand a

CHAPTER 4

Lakota Sioux raid on the fort, suggesting that groups of Lakota Sioux were increasingly moving westward as they tried to maintain their livelihood. The location of Fort Union was less viable as conflict among Indians increased. Access to bison was diminishing east of the Missouri, and the Yanktonai (western Dakota) were following a western flow of Lakota moving into areas that had been set aside for the Assiniboine by the Fort Laramie Treaty of 1851. Consequently, by the late 1850s and early 1860s, various Sioux were hunting and living in lands in Montana, and growing numbers were operating in the area of Fort Union.[5]

Competition for hunting lands was complicated by settler traffic moving westward along the Oregon Trail, various silver and gold rushes, and the building of forts along the Bozeman Trail and other trails. The settler activities continued to disrupt the bison and other game herds, and groups among the Lakota and the middle division of the Dakota continued to feel cramped in the east and began breaking out to the west and northwest. The anger among the Sioux toward the American federal government regarding "disturbances inflicted by white overland and Missouri River steamboat travellers" was rising. Upper Missouri Indian Agent Samuel N. Latta met in May 1862 at Fort Pierre with Lakota and Yanktonai, where many of the friendly chiefs were candid in their assessments of the problems of sustaining their ways of life. When Latta travelled to Fort Union in late June to meet with the Assiniboine, they confirmed their continued peace with whites and dedication to the terms of the 1851 treaty. However, without effective use of their designated lands, now occupied by the Lakota and Yanktonai, they were forced to hunt north of the border in British North America. As a result of this situation, the request was made for a military post "to keep back the Sioux."[6]

In the months after the 1862 Dakota outbreak in Minnesota, the U.S. Army pursued the eastern Dakota (Santee) Sioux, who fled to the prairies, including groups crossing the Missouri and taking refuge among their western kinsmen. Leading several thousand Minnesota militiamen, Brigadier General Alfred Sully crossed the Little Missouri badlands in the direction of the Yellowstone in the summer of 1864 in order to punish perpetrators of the outbreak. He intended to build a permanent post along the Yellowstone, but his supplies continued up the Missouri and were stored at Fort Union. His force was worn out and dispirited by the time they reached the Yellowstone on August 12, and when Sully saw the state of Fort Union, he chose instead a location directly at the confluence of the rivers for a new military fort. This is where Fort Buford was built two years later.[7]

In the spring of 1864, after thirty years in the service, Charles Larpenteur became the bourgeois of Fort Union. That June many Assiniboine arrived for trade, as in the "old days," and performed fine dancing for the occupants of the fort. Indian Agent Mahlon Wilkinson issued the Assiniboine their annuities at a council held on June 11, and in mid-June Company I, 30th Wisconsin Infantry, arrived to guard military supplies. As a civilian establishment, Fort Union observed the 4th of July, and the celebration by the army unit included six cannons fired in the morning and other firings later in the day. Despite this military display, on July 23, Larpenteur reported that twenty-five Sioux raided the horse guard and successfully made off with all seventeen horses. Although two detachments of soldiers tried to pursue them, it was to no avail. In the middle of September, the Crows came for their annuities, and a second council was held.[8] However, the AFC and Fort Union were entering the twilight of their influence economically and politically.

The displacement of the eastern Dakota Sioux from their homelands in Minnesota continued to have effects on the development of the Northern Plains. Henry Hastings Sibley pursued the Dakota over a two-year period in an attempt to punish them. Many Lakota were also drawn into a series of fights. It was like stirring up bees in a swarm. Beginning in the summer of 1862, Lakota began firing on steamboats. A military post was built at Fort Buford in 1866, as the Assiniboine had requested, but skirmishes between the Lakota and the U.S. Army continued and escalated as attempts were made to build military forts along the Bozeman Trail. These armed conflicts reached such a high level that they were labelled the Great Sioux War of 1865 to 1868.

President Andrew Johnson appointed a Peace Commission that travelled to the Northern Plains every year from 1865 to 1868 in an effort to cease fighting and establish a series of reservations that would result in the isolation of Indians from the transportation corridors.[9]

The Treaty Commission would oversee the negotiation of the Fort Laramie Treaty in 1868, which reflected a division between Indigenous Peoples willing to live on rations and reservations and those who wanted to fight for their traditional ways. As the commissioners continued treaty making, they anchored off Fort Union and met with various Indians in the vicinity, including select Assiniboine as well as Crows and Atsina Gros Ventres. None of the treaties negotiated during that period was ratified by the Senate, only those for 1865.[10]

Canadian Confederation in 1867 initiated the Dominion of Canada, enabled by the *British North America Act*. Shortly thereafter, the purchase of Rupert's Land in 1868 doubled the size of the young country. In the agreement with the Hudson's Bay Company for the purchase, Canada was to settle any outstanding issues with the Indigenous Peoples of this vast territory, and this commitment led directly to Canadian treaty making.[11]

THE MILK RIVER AGENCY

The central and eastern portions of the Great Blackfoot Hunting Ground were in desperate need of order. By the mid-1860s, the Atsina Gros Ventres were again enemies with the Blackfoot and asked for their own agency as early as 1866. Construction of the new Milk River Agency began in August and was completed by October 1868. It was located on the Big Bend of the Milk River, about ninety miles upstream from the Missouri River, near present-day Dodson, Montana, and near the Fort Browning Trading Post, owned by Durfee, Peck, and Company.[12]

Reorganization of the Indian Department led to a proposal in the fall of 1869 that the Assiniboine be included in this new Milk River Agency. The encroachments by the Sioux necessitated the inclusion of the Lower Assiniboine, partly as a security measure. This was the first time that the Assiniboine were incorporated into an agency—they had not been a party in the Stevens Treaty and the Great Blackfoot Hunting Ground. The lands east of the mouth of the Milk on the Missouri extending east to the Dakota territorial line where the Assiniboine resided were treated as if they were in the treaty hunting ground even though they were not actually there. Then an executive order in 1873 absorbed these lands into the Blackfoot Reservation of the Stevens Treaty.[13]

The Atsina Gros Ventres had a developing relationship with the Upper Assiniboine, the name for the Assiniboine farther west upstream on the Missouri River. These Upper Assiniboine groups were on the lower Milk River and were led by Chiefs Long Hair and Whirlwind. Their counterparts, the Lower Assiniboine, were located between Milk River and White Earth River in eastern North Dakota, all along the Missouri River. They were primarily the Canoe Paddlers Band, led by Chiefs Red Stone and Broken Arm: "In contrast to their Upper Assiniboine brethren, Lower Assiniboines had generally more strained relations with Gros Ventres. Assiniboines at the time of the agency creation in 1868 also had unfriendly relations with the River Crows. It is unclear if the Upper Assiniboine, because of their alliance with Gros Ventres, had more friendly River Crow relations. Lower Assiniboines and River Crows had hostile relations when the agency was founded."[14]

Lower Assiniboine were forging more amicable relations with Cuthead Yanktonai of Medicine Bear, including camping more frequently together and even hunting together. This led to intermarriages between the two groups, even though they had been hostile to each other in earlier times. This development strongly affected relations with Gros Ventres at the new agency because the Gros Ventres and the Sioux were "unequivocal enemies."[15]

Defining the affairs of the agency, and especially affecting the Assiniboine, was the speed of the arrival of many more Sioux to Fort Buford. In September 1869, approximately 1,000 Yanktonai arrived at Fort Buford and demanded a reservation of their own, and many of the leaders of the Cuthead Yanktonai and Upper Yanktonai were present. A week later, leaders of the Takini Band of the Upper Yanktonai went to Fort Buford to ask for a treaty as well. Promising to feed them for the winter, the commander at Fort Buford noted that Red Stone's Assiniboine came later and camped near the Yanktonai. A group of Hunkpapa (Sioux) were camped upriver, conducting raids on the Crows.[16] Most unsettling was the extent to which many groups of Sioux warriors carried out raids throughout the agency.

Andrew J. Simmons assumed authority of the agency in January 1871 and kept extremely detailed accounts of his administration. In April that year, Sisseton Chief Standing Buffalo arrived with 260 lodges with as many as 2,500 people and made overtures to Assiniboine leaders Red Stone and Little Bull that his group be allowed to stay in the area. Simmons sent gifts and food to facilitate the interaction.[17] The Assiniboine helped to broker the peace with Standing Buffalo, but this was not easily done with the other Sioux groups who had now taken up residence. Goaded by various (Sioux) Yanktonai, Standing Buffalo died in June 1871, throwing his life away in battle with Upper Assiniboine and Atsina Gros Ventres. A portion of his people later made their home in Canada.

In the three years since the founding of the new agency, the configuration of tribal groups had shifted. The bison had been the focus of Assiniboine, but the immigration of the various Sioux groups confounded their hunting opportunities. "Assiniboines had long historic roots in the Missouri and Milk River areas, and in the short period from 1869 to 1871, an extraordinary number of Sioux settled in the region. These changes would result in the dissolution of the Milk River Agency by 1872 and the creation of two new agencies."[18] These agencies redefined the Upper and Lower Assiniboine.

CHAPTER 4

FORT PECK AND FORT BELKNAP AGENCIES

The management crisis caused by the influx of the Yanktonai and assorted other Lakota groups strained supplies of goods intended to keep order among various groups. This was coupled with the isolation of the region from any substantial military presence and left American authorities scrambling to seek a pragmatic solution. All of this put stress on the Assiniboine for several reasons, including the fact that their annuities were shared with the various Sioux groups until replacement supplies could be received. The Cowen Treaty Commission recommended the establishment of two agencies: the Milk River Agency became the Fort Peck Agency, and the Fort Belknap Agency was created. These changes were implemented in the late spring of 1873.

The baseline population of the new Fort Peck Agency consisted of 4,600 individuals.[19] This constituted the transfer of the Lower Assiniboine and Sioux, to be joined by the "new agency Lakotas." The Lower Assiniboine totalled 2,216 and the Sioux 2,744: "For the Canoe Paddler Band of Lower Assiniboines, Simmons reported 648 persons under Red Stone's Band, 416 under Broken Arm, 480 with Bobtail Bear, 272 with Little Bull, and 400 followers of Red Snow. Concerning the Sioux, Simmons listed Long Sioux's Band of mixed Assiniboine and Sioux as 208 members. The primarily Sissetons and Wahpetons of Standing Buffalo's brother totaled 1,236 persons, and Struck by the Ree's (son) Yanktons numbered 1,300."[20] The baseline population of the new Fort Belknap Agency consisted of 5,090 individuals.[21] Based on a census, Simmons reported in May 1873 "that the Upper Assiniboine totaled 2,605 persons, which included 1,110 North Band, 1,070 Stone (or Rock) Band, and 425 Dogtail Band members." Also contributing to the population of the new agency were 1,321 Atsina Gros Ventres and 1,162 River Crows.[22]

In his attempts to maintain a semblance of harmony, Simmons had tried to assess areas of use for the various groups within the agency and indicated that "the Upper Assiniboine preferred hunting in the Upper Milk River as far north as the Cypress Hills (present-day southwestern Saskatchewan and southeastern Alberta), where they associated with other Southern Canadian Assiniboines."[23] Testimony of Elders for the Assiniboine land claim in 1929 before the U.S. Court of Claims indicated that the Upper Assiniboine regularly hunted as far north as the plains and parklands of Saskatchewan. We should note that the Assiniboine did not categorize themselves as "Lower" or "Southern" or as "Upper" or "Canadian" but considered themselves to be part of the same group.

Assiniboine and Gros Ventre Indian Chiefs at Fort Belknap Ready for Grass Dance
Courtesy of the Milwaukee Public Museum, Catalogue Number 43782.

The division of Assiniboine between Canada and the United States was not easily distinguished by outsiders.

ASSINIBOINE TRADITIONAL BOUNDARIES

In spite of "white man's law," treaties, and the international border, the Assiniboine Traditional Territories had always been vast, and when the border became an issue, those territories included a large portion of the northwestern plains of the United States and the southwestern plains of Canada, including major portions of the American states of Montana and North Dakota and the Canadian provinces of Alberta, Saskatchewan, and Manitoba. The Assiniboine People continued their traditional livelihood for as long as they could. In interviews conducted in 1929 at Wolf Point, Montana,[24] the Assiniboine Tribe of Indians—ancestors and relatives of Carry The Kettle members—outlined the seasonal activities and Traditional Territories of themselves and their grandfathers, clearly including Canada as an important harvesting region. In his interview, The Man noted that

CHAPTER 4

the east boundary is White Earth Creek, Minnesota and goes up to the Yellowstone,[25] clear to the mouth of the Powder River[26] on the south and I myself joined in 10 different hunting expeditions across the Missouri River. . . . The west boundary was the Musselshell River.[27] I was present at one time when other Assiniboine's were over there. (Northwest) a little beyond Little Rocky Mountains,[28] north of the Missouri, and due north from there to the Cypress Hills. . . .[29] We would go clear into Canada, clear up to the mountains into Canada.

Bear Cub indicated that

> when I was a boy I remember the Assiniboine's roamed around White Earth country in North Dakota. . . . Our territory was bounded by the White Earth Creek on the east, up to Turtle Mountain[30] on the north, and west from there. Cypress Hills, that was the north boundary, then on the south boundary, on the Yellowstone from its mouth west to the mouth of Powder River and up to the headwaters of Musselshell, following that stream down to its mouth, and from there to the Bears Paw[31] west, and north there to the Cypress Hills.

And Blue Cloud mentioned that from

> my experiences I know, in North Dakota near the Fort Berthold Reservation,[32] a place we called Deep Water—now Little Missouri Creek. From there north over to Devils Lake[33] and then out north into Canada. That is as far as I know in that section as to the eastern boundaries. On the west side, I remember one time when we roamed up the Yellowstone River, clear up west near its source, clear up to Great Falls of the Missouri River and then up to the Sweet Grass Hills and to the Cypress Hills. That is what I know from my experiences.

Gabriel Beauchman, a member of the Assiniboine Tribe of Indians, stated that the Assiniboine usually stayed on the north side of the Missouri River and travelled up from Fort Union toward the Cypress Hills. Moreover, "by personal experience," Red Feather noted that "I have been over this ground and know about half of it myself. I traveled east here from the Turtle Mountain to Moose Mountain[34] over into Canada, and going west from there to the Cypress Hills, to the Sweet

Assiniboine Camp in the Cypress Hills, c. 1878
Courtesy of Glenbow Archives, NA-790-4.

Grass Hills."[35] And Bear Cub mentioned that, "when I was about eight years old, we went up to the Sweet Grass Hills and over into Canada."

These Canadian traditional use boundaries were elaborated by Iron Horn of the Assiniboine Tribe of Indians:

> Following the Missouri up west and then opposite the Little Rockies it leads out and west around the Little Rockies clear around to the Sweet Grass Hills; then it runs due north clear up to Battleford[36] in Canada and it goes up into Canada over in the timberlands there; then goes east from there to the Turtle Mountains; from there it goes to the Missouri River. That is the boundary that my grandfather told me belonged to the Assiniboine's.

Talks Differently also explained the Assiniboine boundaries within which he harvested: "And from there to Sweet Grass Hills and from there to the Canadian border to a place they call Medicine Hat[37] and from there along the limits of the wooded country back to the place of

CHAPTER 4

Indian Dog Travois at Fort Walsh Settlement, Saskatchewan, c. 1879
Courtesy of Glenbow Archives, NA-354-24.

beginning." Similarly, Mrs. Medicine Bear/Iron Cradle indicated "also up to Sweet Grass Hills, and to Cypress Hills in the north and back along the same route, going back east.... They roamed far east of Fort Union, up around White Earth and also farther east. People lived down there, the Assiniboine's, and they died of old age and the new generation still used the same territory." According to Speaks Thunder, the Traditional Territories went

> west along the river to Earth House, they called Fort Benton the Earth House in those days. And from there to Cypress Hills and from there is a place they called Big Lake,[38] and on the other side of Big Lake there was the Assiniboine territory, and up into the Cypress Hills, and then to the limits of a wooded country, back east to the place of beginning.... My grandfathers ... the real old Indians told me that.

Night indicated that

when I was a boy I recollect that I travelled with my grandfather over Woody Mountains, beginning at Woody Mountains[39] along the line over into North Dakota; east into the Gros Ventres territory; then going back into Canada, out north clear over into the timberlands, and traveled west over to Cypress Hills and west clear up to the foothills of the Rocky Mountains. I traveled in a travois when I was small and traveled all over that country. I saw these territories with my own eyes.

As Last recalled,

the Assiniboine's roamed at the Mouse River,[40] from there south to Fort Berthold, and up the river, following the Yellowstone, up the Yellowstone River, up the mouth of Powder River, and from there north to the headwaters of the Musselshell, down its mouth. From there, in a circular route around to the Little Rocky Mountains. From there to the Sweet Grass Hills and up to the Cypress Hills into Canada, crossing over the Swift Current River.[41] Within that territory the Assiniboine's roamed.... This I know. I have been all in that territory and I have been told by my grandfathers.

Mrs. Medicine Bear/Iron Cradle was born in Canada near White Earth:

I was born north of Fort Union at a place they call a ridge or bench land.... It was north of the place where they always received annuities, Fort Union. My mother didn't know any better, she never told me just the very spot where I was born.... I was married to an Indian and went up north and stayed around Woody Mountain. I was married to another man by the name of Medicine Bear, and we were roaming around all that time; roamed around Cypress Hills and up around Bear Paw mountains, traveling back and forth at that time.... I occupied and roamed all the western part of the Assiniboine territory and my children were brought up and raised there and I never had a chance to even go down as far as where the Canoe Indians are now at Fort Peck Reservation.

The Assiniboine were a large and powerful people with a horse and warrior culture centred on the vast number of bison spanning the border. As Gabriel Beauchman noted, "they travelled clear to the Cypress

CHAPTER 4

Hills, all over. The country was free then, open, no line those days. They travelled all over." By 1840, however, the American-Canadian border was having a negative effect on the traditional harvesting practices of the Assiniboine: "We would go clear into Canada," The Man indicated, "clear up to the mountains into Canada, but after the international boundary was laid across, we were held on this side of the line by the white people."

Carry The Kettle Elder Delmar Runs mentioned in 2015 that

> most of them moved across the line, but there was no line at that time—no international line. . . . And then in the fall the cold weather was coming, and most of the tribes from the States went back because it was warmer over there. So that's where they stayed. And then in the spring they all come back (to Canada). . . . Take the Coat, Mountain Lodge, Carry The Kettle, that essentially is three families, they are brothers, . . . [and] they winter in the States. In the spring, they all come back. That's what my dad told me.

Runs also talked of his grandparents, who crossed the "international line" into the United States to Wolf Point, Montana, "because that's where all the Nakoda People are. A lot of their relations are there—their brothers and sisters—and that's where they went."

Back in 1929 in the United States, Looking mentioned that "there were quite a large number of Assiniboine's at that time . . . a great number of them, I could not even make a guess. My father-in-law and my mother-in-law were buried there (Cypress Hills) and also my grand-father."

Carry The Kettle Elder Myrtle Hassler's grandparents lived in the Cypress Hills, but her grandfather's family all lived south of the border. As Hassler noted in 2015, "they were given rations there [Cypress Hills], that's the first place I know they got together. . . . I don't know where they got married. . . . And they came on this side, instead of from my grandfather's side in the United States. . . . They came from Cypress." Kurt Ryder's grandparents traditionally hunted, trapped, and fished in the Cypress Hills. As Ryder mentioned in his interview, "around the Cypress Hills area . . . all through there and Montana . . . all around there until they moved here [Indian Head Reserve]. . . . My grandfather was born in the Cypress Hills, and my great-grandfather, he was born there too, . . . and my grandmother was from Opaten, South Dakota." Keith Prettyshield said that his grandfather also hunted in that area:

> Standing Buffalo, Cypress, here, all over, even Manitoba and the States. . . . Well, he'd go down there . . . stay for a while . . . just basically for moose or elk. . . . He had family down there on my dad's side. My grandfather on my dad's side. . . . I don't know the name of the reserve. . . . It was Assiniboine. Wherever there's Sioux down there, there's relatives. So there's quite a few reserves.

Elder Garry Whitecap noted that "Carry The Kettle, we're Nakoda, they're part of a group that's called the Assiniboine Nation, and our territory once stretched from—like in the States, South Dakota up through Manitoba. There's even towns with Sioux names, like Mikato, Pipestone, it goes all the way north . . . all the way up to Alexis, close to Edmonton. That's all Assiniboine, Nakoda territory."

Elder James O'Watch, interviewed in 2015 in the Cypress Hills Group Interview, clarified that

> the Assiniboine People inhabited right up to the treaty line which is around Prince Albert, right into Manitoba, right into the Missouri River, Montana, all this way, right into Alberta to the Rocky Mountains. Our tribe used to move back and forth from Winnipeg to the Rocky Mountains. In the wintertime, this is where they stayed because of the chinooks—there was a lot of trees, there was a lot of animals, there was a lot of medicines. Everything was here for them, so we stayed here. And then, when the summer came, they followed the buffalo and travelled back and forth. . . . We have a wealth of information about the history of our people going right back to the Mouth [Mouse] River into the United States, Montana.

The Cypress Hills region was a source for lodgepole pine, as well as occasional hunting grounds. Lodgepoles were an important traditional aspect of the Assiniboine lifestyle, used for rafts when travelling waterways, for both dog and horse travois, as well as for teepee and lodging needs. These trees are a unique feature of the ecosystem of the plains, and the only other place that these tall straight pines can be found is in the Rocky Mountains.[42]

Assiniboine ancestors explained in 1929 that the best place to harvest their teepee and travois poles was always in the Cypress Hills. "I used to go up there to secure lodgepole pine," Looking recalled, and Sam King mentioned that "we made rafts out of lodgepoles there." "Pine. Over

CHAPTER 4

in Canada," Red Feather said. "There are timberlands and all kinds of pine." And Night confirmed that "the Assiniboine Tribe grew up in this territory and this is all we roamed [and] we would go clear up to the Cypress Hills and away beyond north of the Cypress Hills. We even wintered below the Sweet Grass Hills, and we used to timber on the hills as we traveled along. That was our territory and that is where we secured lodgepoles many a time."

THE WHOOP-UP TRAIL

The immigration of Sioux to Fort Benton, the creation of the "liquor trade" and Whoop-Up Trail, the destabilizing effects of disease, and the starvation brought on by the destruction of the bison created chaos for the tribal groups close to the international boundary.

Historian Hugh Dempsey related what the new traders witnessed as the Blackfoot, Cree, and Assiniboine engaged in intertribal warfare—fighting for the last of the bison in "the last great Indian battle on the Canadian frontier."[43]

> The trouble arose because of a fight six months earlier, in which Peigans had roundly defeated a large group of Assiniboines near the Cypress Hills. When it was over, seventy Assiniboines had been slain while the Peigans lost only one man.
>
> Later in the season the Assiniboines called their allies together to attack the Blackfoot tribes in a force. Piapot, leader of the Young Dogs (a group of mixed Assiniboine-Cree warriors), and Cree chiefs Big Bear and Little Pine joined Little Mountain and set out from Fort Qu'Appelle Valley for Blackfoot country. They gathered at the Red Ochre Hills on the South Saskatchewan River in late October, then travelled westward, passing the Cypress Hills and making a war camp at the mouth of the Little Bow River. From there, scouts were sent out to find their enemies somewhere in the vicinity of Fort Whoop-Up. They expected to locate a few Blood camps and had no way of knowing that Mountain Chief and the other south Peigans were wintering near the fort. After discovering a Blood camp on the river bottom about 3 miles upstream from Whoop-Up, the scouts reported that it would be an easy prey and an appropriate target for their revenge.

Just before dawn on or about 1 November 1870, the Assiniboines and Crees arrived at the brow of the hill overlooking the river. Below them, in the semi-darkness, was a camp of eleven Blood teepees under the leadership of Chief Mountain. When the attack began, a larger camp across the river heard the gunfire and quickly raced to the defence of their beleaguered comrades. At dawn, each side made a discovery: the Bloods became aware of the huge size of the revenge party they were facing, and the Assiniboines and Crees saw that their enemies were not in the numbers they had expected. . . .

As soon as the fight began, a Blood messenger was sent to the south Peigans for help. . . . The south Peigans were quickly roused to action when they heard of the big fight. . . .

When the Assiniboines and Crees saw how they had misjudged their enemy's strength, they tried to flee. They moved out of the valley onto the tableland that stretched four miles across a wide bend in the Oldman River. They retreated to the northeast, fighting a rear guard action against the Bloods, who were now streaming up from their camps along the river, and fleeing from the Peigans, who were coming from the south. The Assiniboines and Crees finally reached a long coulee that extended out from the Oldman River and each group took up a strong defensive position. Some of the Bloods occupied a short coulee to the south of the Crees, and these two coulees became the main focus of the battle for the next four hours.[44]

As the Assiniboine and Cree fighters began to slip away, the Blackfoot charged the coulees, and the "withdrawal became a rout." "The Assiniboines and Crees rushed into the river by the score, and the Peigans and Bloods stood on the banks, firing on them with their Winchester and Spencer repeating rifles until the river ran red with their blood. The battle had become a slaughter."[45]

Although many of the fleeing Indians reached the opposite bank of the river, they did not escape the fury of their enemies. Warriors rode across the stream and continued the slaughter. During the melee, a party of Assiniboines and Crees tried to make a stand but they were surrounded and about fifty of them were killed. Another group of ten took refuge in a grove of trees where they dug trenches; they would have been annihilated

CHAPTER 4

except that Chief Mountain said there had been enough killing and it was time to go home.[46]

The role of traders and smugglers in this kind of warfare was scrutinized by both American and Canadian authorities, for this type of battle was made more serious by the crowding of tribes and their displacement and immigration from other regions.

MASSACRES

The "devastating traffic"—the influx of Whoop-Up perpetrators—penetrated the "Indian Country" of the border region. This escalation reached a new intensity the winter of 1871–72 when mostly Montana-based wolfers joined the whiskey traders, paying no attention to the international boundary. One group of wolfers was led by Thomas Hartwick, a Civil War rebel who had already fought against a Sioux and Lower Assiniboine war party near the Little Rocky Mountains in October 1870. In the fall of 1871, they went on to tangle with Crow and Peigan warriors and operated in the vicinity of the Sweet Grass Hills, which straddle the border.

Hartwick had lost a number of horses to Sioux raids, and though many were restored to him by Agent Simmons the concern about horse stealing and the punishment of perpetrators were front and centre for Hartwick. In April 1872, a party of Indians was spotted near the Sweet Grass Hills whiskey fort of Abel Farwell. Mistaken as Blackfoot, they were fired on, and four Assiniboine were killed. This incident came to be called the Sweet Grass Hills Massacre.[47]

The next season a new whiskey fort was built by Farwell in the Cypress Hills. In the first days of June 1873, Hartwick and his group, seeking another group of Indigenous horse thieves, fell indiscriminately on a band of Assiniboine led by Little Soldier. They were camped nearby but knew nothing about the missing horses. Having fewer guns and less ammunition than their attackers, many Assiniboine lay dead after the shooting had finally stopped. This incident was soon known as the Cypress Hills Massacre.[48]

Carry The Kettle Elders had a difficult time sharing the details of this event, passed down to them through the generations. "They talked about being in Cypress Hills and coming from Cypress Hills," Elder Myrtle Hassler observed in 2015. "But a lot of them didn't want to talk about it because, you know, a lot of them had bad experiences. Like these wolfers coming and attacking them . . . [and] their parents and their brothers getting slaughtered out there. So a lot of them just didn't want to talk about it. It's just too painful for them."

In his book *Recollections of an Assiniboine Chief*, published in 1972, Chief Dan Kennedy spoke of his first-hand experience of the massacre:

> In the morning of that fateful day, my father had just returned from his visit to the Whiskey Traders, with the news of the arrival of the ten American horsemen and the warning he had received that these men were looking for trouble. Immediately he instructed his followers to break camp, but 'Wincanahe.' An outspoken Indian, ridiculed and scoffed at their panic, and he bluffed them into staying encamped.
>
> That morning whisky flowed like water in the camps and by mid-day the tribesmen were all hopelessly drunk. Inside of our tent my father lay in a stupor, and we employed every artifice, including herbs, to revive him to consciousness.
>
> I know the other camps were also in the same predicament, working frantically over their men, but it was hopeless; we were doomed. We were left defenceless.[49]

In the year 2000, Elder Kaye Thompson testified to the Indian Claims Commission about the massacre:

> The massacre's onslaught occurred when our people were given poisoned whisky. Our people were slaughtered and killed like wild animals. The children had been abducted from their teepees, and then clutching them by their feet, they were beaten savagely upon the ground. The women were brutally raped throughout the night, used and cast off. It has been told that a group of men had continuously raped women all night in a camp near the massacre site. Our old people were beaten and left to die. The bones of our dead ancestors were left scorching the prairies, instilling antagonizing threats of fear into our forefathers of the white man's bitterness.[50]

Elder Nancy Eashappie relayed what she had been told by her grandfather, a boy at the time who had witnessed this massacre, and explained that it was not even their people who had stolen the horses and caused this brutal retaliation by the wolfers:

CHAPTER 4

So that one early morning—this is not right after but a few days after—that's when they came with a barrel of whiskey, and then they had it out there, and they invite some of the people.... About three or four from this group, Assiniboine, went over and had the whiskey with them. From there, the leaders went to see what their people are doing. And they saw them all in a circle having whiskey.... He sat down with them.... And, as every one of them are getting drunk, some of the people—the wolfers—were looking over the hill.... His little son, my grandfather, ... told his dad "You better stop drinking because, look, there's some guys peeping out there. That means there's trouble."... So he got up, and he told his friend not to bring his group, keep them back. "Let's go home," he said, because these ones are already drunk, and so were the others, "there's somebody out there that's going to come and hurt the people."

So they went back to their group, and they told them "Take all your belongings, what is important to you, and go down east—down that way—because there's gonna be trouble over the horses," he said.... They brought their horses up with them, but just then, when they got back, the battle was on already. Clubbing them. They were trying to fight back, but they couldn't do it. So my grandfather took some of the boys—they're sober—and they went back, and that's when they returned to the hitting battle, and they chased them out. But already ... they killed Rattle Snake's father, and Rattle Snake is from here. He's just a little boy, he was from the camp with his mom when his dad got killed by those wolfers.... And already they know three or four of theirs was killed.... They tried to sober those other people, ... so they told their boss to come and look after them.... So they took the bodies from there, and they buried them, while the others were running away, ... and that's how it happened.... The whole story was in history as told by my grandfather how it was. How it all went that day.

Elder Bernice Saulteaux was also interviewed in 2015 as part of the Cypress Hills Group Interview:

My great-grandmother—my mom's grandma—she was stabbed in the massacre area.... My mom told us this story. Her grandmother's name was Stabbed Many Times. She was out in the massacre area.... She had a dream. In this dream, she was told

OWÓKNAGE / CARRY THE KETTLE NAKODA FIRST NATION

Stabbed Many Times
Photo provided by Carry The Kettle Nakoda First Nation.

CHAPTER 4

she was going to be attacked: "You have to go tell the grandmothers, tell the aunties, to go prepare the medicines and get everything ready because this is what's going to happen to you." This was her dream. So she goes and tells the grandmas, aunties, and her mother that she dreamt this.... So they had the medicines ready, but she was down by the massacre area getting kindling wood for the campfire.... All the men were out hunting; this was her job to go get the wood so they could have the fire to cook.... And when she was doing that she was attacked, and she was stabbed thirteen times in her body.

And then somehow somebody found her and had taken her back to the camp. So when they arrived at the camp, already the grandmother, the aunties, and her mother knew that was her dream. So they got the medicines ready and looked after her. And they said her kidney was sticking out, so what they did was sew it up with sinew—long ago that's what they had—and then they gave her all this medicine that they had prepared to give her.... She survived and lived.

So then from there they were moved from Cypress Hills to CTK, and my mom and her sisters... there were three of them—their grandma showed them the stab wounds in her body, and she let them count them. Mom said there were thirteen stabs. They were all the scars... from where she was stabbed.... She was just a little girl (at that time), so she was able to share that story with us.... She's buried there on CTK—Stabbed Many Times.

By 1873, the Nakoda people had experienced the effects of a genocide of neglect. Most of the hunting territories below the new border were crowded by other Indigenous groups or under siege by the American military. They fought for remaining lands north of the border and were attacked by disease, whiskey traders, and wolfers from the south. Their game was almost depleted by commercial impacts, and they had retreated to the Cypress Hills for refuge. Even there they were massacred.

Based on the reports of Lieutenant William Butler and others, the government of Sir John A. Macdonald introduced legislation on May 23, 1873, to bring order to the Canadian west. This initiative gained political momentum once the news was received of the massacres that had occurred in Whoop-Up country and the desperate need for immediate law and order.[51] The force was recruited, trained, and mobilized

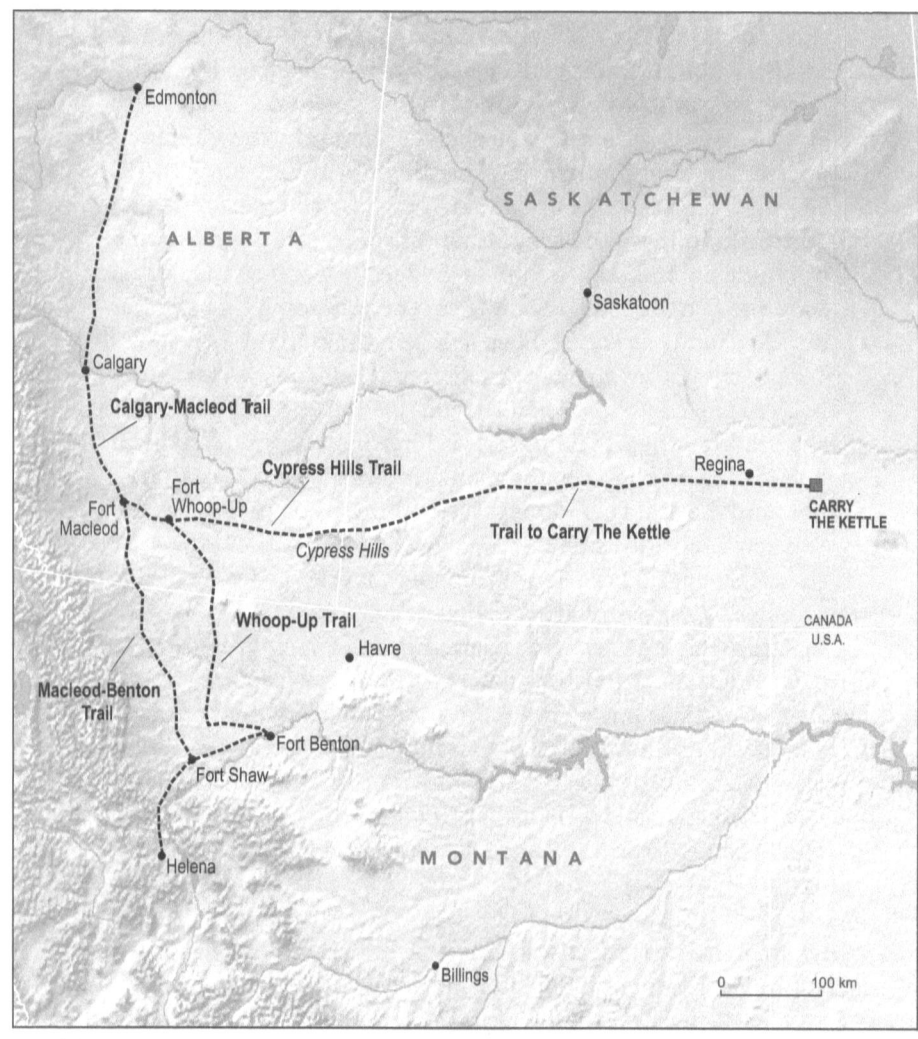

FIGURE 9: Trails Used by First Nations People for Migration and Trades

by the summer of 1874, and a substantial contingent was dispatched to Whoop-Up country via an overland march. The initial force of the North West Mounted Police arrived and built Fort Walsh in the same valley near the site of the Cypress Hills massacre, raising a Union Jack flag above the post to symbolize the beginning of a new regime. Meanwhile, other posts were built strategically to interdict and end the alcohol-based trade.[52]

CHAPTER 5

Oyáde Wowábiyutaŋibi hiŋkda Makóče Wokšúbi

Treaty 4 and Reserve Farming

After 1867, the Canadian government was immediately challenged with the task of nation building, which included obtaining proper title to HBC lands and Indigenous lands and protecting the border from the expansionist inclinations of the United States. In the 1870s, soon after Confederation, the government began the Numbered Treaties.

In September 1874 at Fort Qu'Appelle, not long after the Cypress Hills Massacre, a meeting with Indigenous Peoples was held to negotiate Treaty 4, but no Assiniboine leaders were present. The boundaries chosen by the government for Treaty 4 included Assiniboine, Saulteaux, and Cree Traditional Territories and consisted of 194,000 square kilometres (75,000 square miles). However, this area was not defined with a clear understanding of all the lands used by these groups. Besides leaving out large areas of Assiniboine land, Treaty 4 included many other bands and peoples who had fairly recently migrated into primarily Assiniboine lands and whose claims to the lands were tenuous, relative to the history of the Assiniboine People.[1]

In the previous chapters, we thoroughly reviewed the prehistorical and historical information on land use of the Nakoda People, which can be compared with treaty boundaries. The Nakoda People who eventually became Carry The Kettle First Nation roamed across the territorial/American border, moving as far north as the Battlefords area in Saskatchewan. The two bands, Man Who Took the Coat and Long Lodge, had close ties with the Milk River, Montana, Nakoda, who eventually settled around Fort Belknap and Fort Peck Agencies. Together with these and other bands, the Nakoda People used the Cypress Hills as a winter camp and spiritual centre, part of a northern cycle including Wood Mountain and other wooded areas of Saskatchewan, and then they would hunt bison to the south on both sides of the eventual border down to the Yellowstone and Missouri Rivers.

By the 1870s, their cycles of life were increasingly disrupted as the Sioux moved farther into the American west and the bison declined. As American military occupation, settlement, and trade increased, conflict also increased, and the bison herds were further diminished. By 1874, the bison were gone from the Souris plains and scarce even in southern Saskatchewan: "After 1873, no large numbers of buffalo were seen in the Wood Mountain District. In 1875–76, only straggling herds were found east of the Cypress Hills. For the Aboriginal peoples of the area, travelling from southwestern Saskatchewan to hunt buffalo in Montana around the Milk River was a necessary and often futile search for food."[2]

The herds in Montana were completely eliminated by 1883, but north of the border they were eliminated by 1879.[3] By 1877, with the impact of fires intended to stop the bison and the first railway lines in North Dakota, bison hunts into the United States were becoming futile. By 1877, Indigenous Peoples of the Northern Plains were beginning to starve.[4] They began to congregate in areas where they thought that they would have the easiest access to game and wild foods, as well as trade items. They would visit the posts at Milk River in the United States or Maple Creek in Canada in search of food.

On September 12, 1876, Inspector J.M. Walsh reported from the new Fort Walsh post that he had told the Assiniboine that only "British Indians," which had never signed treaties in the United States, would be allowed to take payments and adhere to Treaty 4. That treaty had been negotiated and signed at Fort Qu'Appelle in 1874, and annuity payments were made at Fort Walsh or at nearby Maple Creek starting the following year. After he completed payments, Walsh learned that ninety more lodges were on their way from the United States, where they had been hunting, but they claimed that they were from the area between the Assiniboine and South Saskatchewan Rivers. But Walsh was out of money, so he sent word that they would be paid the following year.[5] Most of them did return the next fall. The payment of annuities to the "Assiniboine Band" was made from 1877 to 1882. Long Lodge was paid an annuity for 1876, a year in which Walsh had refused to allow

CHAPTER 5

Assiniboine Chief Little Chief Consecrating Tobacco and Herbs to Be Smoked about Sacred Lodge Pole Tree, Fort Belknap Reservation, c. 1904–06
Photographer, John G. Carter, Series 5; courtesy of Montana State University/Archives West: Orbis Cascade Alliance.

him to take his adhesion without seeking permission of the superintendent general of Indian Affairs.[6]

Inspector Walsh reported on May 27, 1877, that there were 250 Assiniboine lodges camped at the Cypress Hills, led by Little Chief, Shell, King, and Long Lodge, all "British Indians." Little Child's Saulteaux band was nearby, and the various bands began to assert an active interest in remaining in the area. On October 28 that year, Walsh wrote a long report to the deputy minister of the interior about the situation at Fort Walsh. There were 145 Assiniboine lodges there that had never adhered to a treaty or received a payment. He believed that most were entitled to be paid as "British Indians." It was his task to sort out who belonged to that group: "Two years ago when Long Lodge, Little Mountain, and the Poor Man refused to go to the Agency [Belknap] to receive annuities, both Little Chief and Shell went. Little Chief, Shell, and King numbered from 80 to 90 lodges, all originally British Indians."[7]

Walsh got the books from the Belknap Agency and sent Indian Agent Edwin Allen to Wolf Point to see who had been paid there. He determined that Little Chief, Poor Man, and Long Lodge should be paid annuities, though various members of these bands appear to have deserted to the other side of the border or were refused payment for that reason, leaving the bands much smaller. The Man Who Took the Coat, a young man of twenty-two in Little Black Bear's band, was chosen as Chief by the Assiniboine of Little Black Bear, and he formed his own band with forty-four lodges from that band and sixty-nine lodges of non-treaty Indians. Most of the bands signed a formal adhesion to Treaty 4 in 1877, but Little Chief apparently did not. He and his people appear to have been paid first in 1879, in a group with Long Lodge, The Man Who Took the Coat, and Poor Man. Many of the followers of Long Lodge and Poor Man were rejected because of an American annuity affiliation; the creation of the international border was strange to the Assiniboine, and they would continue to cross it for many years. Walsh also said of the Assiniboine, in the same October letter, that they "must be paid here, this being their country, and the majority of them could not be induced to go elsewhere."[8]

After some discussion of the content of the treaty, Assiniboine leaders made adhesion to Treaty 4 on September 25, 1877, at Fort Walsh in the Cypress Hills, where most of the Assiniboine were then staying.[9] The leaders who signed the adhesion were The Man Who Took the Coat, Long Lodge, Wich-a-wos-taka, and Poor Man. The adhesion was taken by NWMP Inspector Walsh and other officers. A census was taken between September 19 and 23 that named the bands that had assembled at Fort Walsh. In total, there were 296 lodges: "189 Assiniboine, 60 Saulteaux, and 47 Cree at Fort Walsh that September."[10] In a letter to the deputy minister of the interior, Walsh provided context for how the leaders of the Assiniboine bands were constituted, with insight that he had clearly learned from them:

> After Mr. Allen had completed taking the census I found more treaty Indians divided into three bands, sixty-nine (69) lodges under the "Man Who Took the Coat," forty-two (42) under "Long Lodge," and thirty-four (34) lodges under the "Poorman." The "Man Who Took the Coat" has been a treaty Indian since 1875, and a head soldier to the "Little Black Bear" (Cree). He is a young man of twenty-two (22) years of age, and at the present time the most influential Indian in this section. He is an exceedingly good man and very obedient to the law.

CHAPTER 5

NWMP Band Concert at Fort Walsh, 1878
Library and Archives Canada / Royal Canadian Mounted Police fonds/e011184434. © Government of Canada. Reproduced with the permission of Library and Archives Canada (2021).

The forty-four (44) lodges of Assiniboine who had drawn annuities previously with the "Little Black Bear" told me they wanted a chief of their tribe added to this number: there were sixty-nine (69) lodges of non-treaty Indians who made a similar request. At the solicitation of such a large number of persons I consented to allow the Assiniboine who had formerly gone with "Little Black Bear" to withdraw from the latter's band, and knowing the "Man Who Took the Coat" to be a good man, and one on whom the government could depend, I consented to their request, and allowed them to elect him their chief. I then allowed him to appoint two (2) headmen. "Long Lodge," an old and recognized chief of the Assiniboine for a great many years had only forty-two (42) lodges. This number said they did not want to see him thrown to one side and not admitted by the "White Mother" as a chief, that he was now getting old and had always been a good friend to his people and the whites.

Since my arrival here "Long Lodge" and camp (altogether considered notorious before the arrival of the police) have been most obedient to the law. The "Poor Man" much the same as "Long Lodge's" camp, is very much reduced owing to the objections that many of his followers were American Indians; he has at present thirty-four (34) lodges; he is a good man and very friendly to the whites; his people said they would not join any other chief, and if I could not admit him as such, to pay them by themselves. As the Act states that every band composed of thirty (30) Indians was entitled to a chief, I allowed them to elect him as such.[11]

In 1877 on treaty adhesion, there were 550 people paid from Man Who Took the Coat Band and Long Lodge, and Headman Little Mountain had 133 people, which totalled 683 people.

THE YEAR 1879

An affidavit included in the Assiniboine land claim taken to the U.S. Court of Claims in 1929 declared that Long Lodge, in his later years, was considered the paramount Chief of the entire Assiniboine Nation.[12] This naturally brings up the question of how to assign a nationality (American or Canadian) to an Indigenous group that seasonally used both sides of the new border. If Long Lodge was considered the paramount Chief of the Assiniboine, then it leads one to understand that they were one people living on lands through which settlers had drawn an imaginary line. Clearly, such a boundary was foreign to their land use practices and culture, and even the divisions among different Indigenous groups' lands included broad overlapping areas.

The bands were not paid at Fort Walsh in 1878 but appeared again in 1879. Most likely they were hunting during this period, roaming down to the Milk River and east to Wood Mountain in search of game. There are references in the diary of J.H. McIlree regarding Little Chief and Little Black Bear, with Jack, in the area in the spring.[13]

The year 1879 was pivotal. It was considered the year when the bison herds were finally eliminated from the southern part of the British territories, primarily because they were kept south of the line by the American military and guarded by "American Indians." Only occasional herd sightings were made north of the boundary after that, with the bulk of the remaining bison down at the Bear Paw Mountains. Prairie fires were used to control their movement and prevent a migration north.[14] The Cypress Hills, where the Fort Walsh NWMP post was

CHAPTER 5

located, was where people gathered for hunts into the Milk River area. When those hunts failed, they asked the police for food or showed up for annuities. Deputy Superintendent-General Lawrence Vankoughnet wrote at the end of that year that

> the scarcity of buffalo in the Territories reduced the Indians to great straits, and a number of deaths from actual starvation ensued.

...

> The suffering was principally confined to the Indians of the south-western portion of the Territories; although, even as far east as Qu'Appelle, much suffering was endured. The Indians were reduced to such extremities that they eat mice, their dogs, and some of them even their buffalo skins, and they greedily devoured meat raw when given to them.[15]

The NWMP assistant commissioner reported that

> during the spring and early summer the condition of our Indians was deplorable in the extreme. Buffalo, their only source of supply, had moved south, and their horses were too weak to follow. The flour and beef supplied by the Government was sufficient for a time, to ward off the impending famine, and to supply a large number with enough to take them to the Milk River country.... The Assiniboines and other Indians about the Cypress, pursued the course as soon as they were supplied with food to take them to where the buffalo were.... I think it advisable, on account of the large number of Indians who will undoubtedly flock back in the spring to both Cypress Hills and the Bow River country, that the force I have mentioned should be kept at these posts. It will be some time before these people can be settled down on their reserves, and there will be a great deal of trouble making them do so.[16]

The minister of the interior said that

> one of the first matters which forced itself upon my attention, on becoming Minister of the Interior, and which has since

received earnest consideration by the Government, was the gravity of the situation as regards the Indians of the great plains of the North West. Their principal means of subsistence—the buffalo—had for years been gradually disappearing, and, even had nothing happened to hasten the event, the complete extinction of these animals has become, according to the best authorities, a matter of comparatively few years at most. But the continued presence in the neighbourhood of Fort Walsh, Wood Mountain and elsewhere along the boundary, near to and within the territory covered by Treaty No. 7, of a large number of United States Indians who took refuge in Canada from United States troops some three years ago, rendered the greatest possible product of the hunt so disproportioned to the wants of the population, and accelerated so much the approach of the time when the Indians could no longer obtain from that source the necessaries of life, that it became imperative at once to devise means for the prevention of the famine which, not immediately, but yet not very remotely, must ensue.[17]

The treaty annuity pay lists in that year reflect the beginning of chaotic times when bands split and reformed. Tribal boundaries had softened, and alliances had reformed. "All turned upon the slightest impulse towards the little citadel and trading centre in the Cypress Hills."[18] Some leaders were able to keep their peoples together, and some were not; others promised success in the hunt and continuing autonomy. There were rumours of alliances for reasons of war, including large forces to be amassed by Louis Riel. Sitting Bull and his people, moving back and forth to find food, ramped up intergovernmental tensions as the Americans demanded that the British keep him. "Half-breeds" involved in the bison trade were forced north perhaps to avoid horse-stealing skirmishes while the bison, the primary source of food, were restrained from going north.[19] About 300 families of Canadian "half-breeds" were apprehended by General Nelson Miles of the American military in the summer of 1879. Miles also forced Sitting Bull's band back north after a skirmish south of Milk River and met with Inspector Walsh of Wood Mountain to reinforce the American desire that all "troublemakers" be kept north of the border.[20]

On May 9, 1879, Colonel Acheson Irvine wrote in his journal from Fort Walsh that he should increase his force by 200 men to prevent trouble. "I have had a fearfully busy week of it, thousands of starving Indians at me from morning 'til night. A good many have moved off south east of this across the line in search of buffalo."[21] On June 7, he said that

> there are any number of Indians here now, *in a starving condition*, the fort is just crowded with them. I have been powwowing with them all morning. I suppose we will have a busy summer with them. There are so many different kinds of Indians here together that it keeps me busy talking to them to keep everything alright. To give you an idea of the mixture today, there are . . . Blackfoot, Blood, Piegan, Cree, Saulteaux, Assiniboine, Sioux, and Nez Perce. The windows are dark with people pressing against them, wanting food.[22]

Walsh wrote of the dilemma in June. Irvine reported on July 30, 1879, that Indian Commissioner Edgar Dewdney was at Fort Walsh.[23] Dewdney had only recently been appointed as commissioner and was ordered to Forts Macleod and Walsh to assess the situation and distribute rations.[24] He would come away from this trip convinced that the Indigenous Peoples needed help, but he had more trouble convincing people in Ottawa that appropriate expenditures be made.

A report from the reopened Fort Belknap, made August 1, 1879, by Agent W.L. Lincoln, stated that some of the Assiniboine were scattered between the Missouri River and the Cypress Hills and that they were demoralized and destitute. Some of them had joined the "British Indians" after the closure of Fort Belknap in 1874. However, when the post reopened, as many as 2,000 returned in the spring and summer in the hope of receiving rations. When Agent Lincoln refused them, they headed back to the Cypress Hills.[25]

Slightly more than half of those who originally signed a treaty returned with their Chiefs. The Man Who Took the Coat had far fewer people with him in the early fall of 1879 when annuity payments were issued. The band numbered 229, whereas Long Lodge had 107 people.

Some might have returned to the United States, where reserve settlement was already well under way. Others might have joined larger aggregates, and some undoubtedly had died, though this information was not captured on the pay sheets. Some were paid arrears for 1878. Dewdney asked them about taking a reserve when he visited in the summer of 1879, and they asked for a site in the Cypress Hills. Walsh said to Dewdney that keeping the Assiniboine in the area placed them near the Wolf Point people, who were "advanced" in agriculture and might provide a good example to their northern kin.[26]

Little Chief and Poor Man brought an additional 380 Nakoda People into the area. There were a few small Cree bands and some larger aggregations under Piapot (311), Cowessess (323), Little Pine (324), and Lucky Man (467). Little Pine was a Plains Cree Chief who had led raids on the Blackfoot to the west; he collaborated with Big Bear and Piapot to push the Blackfoot out of the Cypress Hills. Both Little Pine and Big Bear resisted taking treaty until their members, starving, began to split away to get annuity payments. Little Pine conceded and took treaty in 1879. Lucky Man, another charismatic individual, headed a group of people under Big Bear who broke with the latter in order to take treaty that year.

Little Black Bear's band was split, with some taking treaty at Qu'Appelle. The same was true of Cowessess, Cheechuk, and Star Blanket. There were more than 3,000 people in the area ready to hunt but relying on fish, game, berries, and rations. Some of the southern Alberta tribes came in for food as well. The large Plains Cree bands went south from late 1879 to early 1880, when they returned, starving, from a poor hunt.[27] Mountain fever plagued them, killing the young and weak.[28]

It was clear that starvation had become an issue before 1877, when the Assiniboine adhered to treaty. In 1876, Treaty 6 included a famine and pestilence clause, as well as a provision for a medicine chest on new reserves, both based on the feelings of insecurity among most Indigenous groups since there were no more bison. But the signing of treaties did not alleviate the hunger and starvation that followed:

> By the time of Dewdney's appointment (1879) Indians had already starved to death at Fort Qu'Appelle, Fort Walsh, Fort Macleod, Battleford, Carlton, Fort Pitt, Fort Saskatchewan, Edmonton, Touchwood Hills, Fort Ellice, Moose Mountain, Fort Calgary, and elsewhere. Despite the Indians' perilous circumstances, relief was meted out by the DSGIA, Lawrence Vankoughnet, on the condition that his Indian agents "require labor from able-bodied Indians for any supplies given them" so they would learn "they must give something in return of what they receive."[29]

Internal government correspondence of the day supports a Eurocentric policy aimed at destroying Indigenous cultures and practices and forcing Indigenous Peoples to adopt farming to survive. By limiting rations, this policy resulted in genocidal conditions that forced Indigenous groups to search for bison south of the international border,

CHAPTER 5

naturally pursuing their right to survive. It was the government's policy on rations, contradicting its insistence that the Assiniboine People remain in the Cypress Hills, that forced them to search for food across the border.

Changes in policy on treaty Indians were embodied by the appointment of Indian Commissioner of the North West Territories Edgar Dewdney in May 1879. He communicated directly with Prime Minister Sir John A. Macdonald, who was also the minister of the interior and consequently had considerable discretionary power to administer Indigenous matters in the west, especially the establishment of "farming agencies" designed to discourage Indigenous Peoples from hunting and encouraging them to settle on reserves and accept an agricultural way of life. The latter policy seemed to be ineffective and expensive, and it was put aside after several years of attempted implementation.[30]

Upon his arrival at Fort Walsh in the last days of June 1879, Dewdney found that the earlier assessment of destitution was not an exaggeration. Some groups were begging for provisions to carry them south to the boundary line to search for bison. Dewdney met with leaders of bands to explain the need for them to select lands and settle on them so that crops could be planted and raised. Fields would need to be prepared, so the relocations should be planned and implemented as soon as feasible. The Man Who Took the Coat (Assiniboine) and Cowessess (Little Child, Cree) immediately requested to select their lands and settle down.[31]

Planning began for an Assiniboine reserve to be established in the Cypress Hills. After meeting with Dewdney in June 1879, 747 Assiniboine were paid treaty annuities at Fort Walsh in September. Then, on October 26, Dewdney was back at Fort Walsh and able to visit the land that The Man Who Took the Coat had chosen for his reserve. Dewdney appointed J.J. English as a farm instructor and ordered him to start a farm on the reserve land. The site was 32 kilometres (20 miles) west of Fort Walsh, and Dewdney was concerned about the susceptibility to frost. The following description appeared in the Annual Report of the Department of Indian Affairs for 1880:

> It is situated on the north-west end of Cypress Mountains, and is well located for farming, provided early summer frosts are not prevalent.
> As no crop of any kind has ever been put in this locality, it is difficult to say how it may turn out.

It has been a favorite wintering place for Half-breeds for several years, and there are a number of abandoned houses, which will be made use of by the Indian instructor sent there, as well as by the Indians themselves.[32]

The Home Farm program began as a Conservative policy experiment. Political appointees were sent west to set up farms merely to show Indigenous people how to farm—not to supply them with food. Cattle were brought into Fort Walsh to provide food. Dewdney had with him the two farmers who would work with the Assiniboine and Cree at the Cypress Hills when he met with The Man Who Took the Coat, instructors J.J. English for the Assiniboine and John Setter for the Cree. The success of this program was varied.

The irony of Dewdney's rhetoric about self-sufficiency was that, in fact, Indigenous Peoples had only just lost it and now were forced to ask for help. The last resort, it was thought, was to issue rations to those facing starvation. The North West Mounted Police, faced with the reality of camps of people who were ill, poorly clothed, and starving, wanted to be more generous with rations than the Department of Indian Affairs allowed. Deputy Superintendent General Vankoughnet and Indian Commissioner Dewdney believed that rations should be used for two purposes: to force Indigenous people into a labour-for-pay system and to force them to move to alternative locations. This policy appears to have violated the spirit and intent of the treaties and was an odd requirement in a place where there was no or little labour opportunity.

In 1879, there were so many reports of starvation in the west, as noted above, that a conference was held at Battleford in late August. It included Indian Commissioner Dewdney, still in the west, NWMP Commissioner Macleod, the lieutenant governor, members of the North West Council, and Indian Agents. The purpose was to create a plan to offset starvation during the winter. In his journal, Dewdney said that a resolution was passed on the second day, August 27, supporting a motion by Colonel Macleod recommending an increase in rations for Treaty 6 of flour and beef.[33] Members agreed that supplies were to be sent to various points, but instructions were given that any able-bodied Indigenous people were to work in return for rations: "Strict instructions have been given to the agents to require labor from able-bodied Indians for any supplies given [to] them. This principle was laid down for the sake of the moral effect that it would have upon the Indians in showing them that they must give something in return for what they

CHAPTER 5

receive, and also for the purpose of preventing them from hereafter expecting gratuitous assistance from the government."[34]

STARVATION CRISIS IN 1880

Despite the conference on starvation and the plans made to deal with the situation, food riots broke out among the Cree at Fort Walsh after a hard winter. Leaders such as Little Pine and Lucky Man began to attract followers in large numbers, mostly from Big Bear's band, simply with the promise of keeping them alive by hunting, but there was little game to be obtained. The population in the Walsh–Cypress Hills area swelled to 5,000, with people taking treaty for the first time or leaving bands based at Qu'Appelle or Battleford because they were starving there with minimal rations.[35] The Cypress Hills were one of the few areas that at least held out the hope of wild game such as bison. By not providing adequate rations even to those farther east or north, the government created a crisis in the Cypress Hills. Dewdney wrote to Macdonald that the amount of food required at the Cypress Hills to feed the Indigenous Peoples there would astonish the government:

> I am sorry to say that matters generally are not as satisfactory as I hoped they would be. Our farmers on the whole have done well, they put in large crops both on their locations and on the Indian reserves, but the territories both north and south have been visited with early frosts which in some localities have entirely ruined the crops and in others partially.... At Cypress on the reservations the potato crop is good but it is feared they are not ripe enough to keep over the winter so I have ordered them to be issued instead of flour at once. At Cypress on two reservations about 1500 have been receiving rations and 2000 other Indians who are unsettled have been fed at Fort Walsh for the last five weeks. There has been some trouble with them, they are the refuse of the Cree Nations and old followers of Big Bear.... The only Indians belonging to us who are now on the American side are about 2/3 of the Blackfeet and a little more than half the Blood with a few Crees, they have been reported coming in but I am in hopes that they will continue with the buffalo although I hear strong inducement[s] are being held out to them by some traders to come in and be paid. Should they do so and be on our hands this winter we will have no

less than 10,000 Indians in this southern country and they will require to be fed and how we will be able to get food for them I don't know for there is not transport in the country to do the work. Cattle can be obtained but not enough flour. The expenditure will be very heavy and far exceeding the appropriations.... The visit below the line after buffalo this year has done the Indians no good and they return quite demoralized, they have been at constant war with the American Indians and have lost a number of lives. Whisky traders have been among them and anything in the shape of robes or dryed [sic] meat and horses have been bartered and they return to us worse off than when they left.[36]

Little Pine drew 385 people and Lucky Man 754. Piapot had 200 hunting followers, and many small bands or factions, under 100 people, maintained hunting camps. These people had been unable to follow their traditional annual rounds and were searching for harvest opportunities, like Big Bear and Thunderchild, who came into and went out of the area but were paid elsewhere.

In June, Colonel Macleod wrote to his wife from Fort Walsh:

The poor creatures have been living on fish for some time back as the supplies here are about exhausted, but that source is now failing them, as the fish are going back from the creeks into the lakes where the Indians cannot catch them with their nets. I am not at all satisfied with the arrangements the Government has made about the supplies for the Indians. Indeed, they do not appear to appreciate in the least the calls that will be made upon them this summer. They appear still to think that the poor creatures can gain their livelihood by hunting, as if everyone didn't know that there is nothing for them to hunt. The fact is they are not half doing the thing and the result will be that the Indians will be less satisfied and what the Government spends will be thrown away.[37]

It is important to distinguish the large hunting bands from those who, in the spring of 1880, established themselves on reserves in Cypress Hills. Two of the Home Farms were set up, one for the Cree and Saulteaux near Maple Creek, a settlement just north of the Cypress Hills. This group included 260 of Piapot's people, 352 of the followers of Cowessess, and 215 of the Muscowequan People. The other Home Farm,

CHAPTER 5

Members of the Kainai First Nation at Fort Whoop-Up, Alberta, 1881. [Original title: Blood Indians at Fort Whoop-Up].
Photo by George M. Dawson. Library and Archives Canada/Natural Resources Canada fonds/a051156.

headed by J.J. English, was set up for the benefit of the Assiniboine People (670), whose reserve was surveyed in the summer of 1880 at the Head of the Mountain.

The bands of Long Lodge, Poor Man, The Man Who Took the Coat, and Little Chief were there, and they were paid on reserve in August 1880. The Man Who Took the Coat had 280 people, more than the year before, with 50 men, 69 women, and 161 children. Long Lodge had 100 people, with 16 men and 28 women. Little Chief had 151, and Poor Man 100, making a total of 631. The bands asked for lands rich in timber, fowl, and fish and thus were able, for a time, to feed themselves before game ran out.[38] Others, however, were struggling.

A newspaper correspondent for Toronto's the *Globe* spent some time with the Assiniboine at Fort Walsh and later at the Head of the Mountain reserve. He reported in May 1880 that people were boiling grass and eating gophers. He noted the work-for-rations policy and that the cattle brought from Montana to Fort Walsh were too wild for ploughing. People clung to their horses and would eat them only in extreme circumstances.[39] By June, people were on reserve, but farming was difficult. They were being rationed one pound of flour and one pound of meat per day, and farmer J.J. English treated them well. He suggested, however, that only 400 people were on reserve, far fewer than the combined total of the Assiniboine bands.[40] Some, like Long Lodge, were recorded to have been frequently away hunting.

Fort Qu'Appelle Indian Agent McDonald wrote on September 12, 1880, that "on my return from making the payments of annuities at the Cypress Hills, I found nearly all the Indians I had paid here, still camped about the Qu'Appelle Lakes, and every few days calling at the office for relief. They were quite bewildered, not knowing what to do; to return to the plains was pure starvation, and every likelihood of the few horses they had being stolen from them."[41] McDonald said that during the winters women and children had been left on reserves while the men had attempted to hunt. Indian Agent Edwin Allen reported from Fort Walsh that the people coming in from the plains had few horses and almost no clothing, and they were bunking fifteen to twenty per lodge. There were 2,500 people, mostly Cree and Assiniboine, who needed rations, plus others in temporary camps.[42]

The farm instructor had a farm taking shape on the "Assiniboine reserve" in the summer of 1880 that was ready to be surveyed. Allan Poyntz Patrick was assigned to conduct the survey upon Dewdney's instructions. Dewdney had an indication that the "North Assiniboine" wanted a location near Wood Mountain in contrast to the "South Assiniboine" wishing to settle in the Cypress Hills. In January 1880, the Assiniboine had not taken up residence on these reserves.[43] Also that month Dewdney recommended that a Fort Walsh Indian Agency be formed and its own agent be named. There was an agent for the eastern part of Treaty 4 territory, and in September 1880 Edwin Allen was named the Indian Agent to be based at Fort Walsh. He did not arrive there until October.[44] English, the farming instructor, left a memoir speaking of his responsibilities for the Assiniboine as their caretaker:

> Have thirty acres under crop, broken this spring with one team, out of sod. The crop consists of six acres of wheat, eight of potatoes, seven of oats, and seven of barley, with two acres of turnips and carrots and about two of garden vegetables, which took well for this high climate, we have lots of very cold weather, being over 4200 feet above the level of the sea.
>
> I have at present about eight hundred Indians on the reservations to whom I issue rations every morning, namely half a

CHAPTER 5

pound of flour and half a pound of beef for each member of the family. The beef cattle are driven up from the government herd at the fort, and killed on the reservation.

I have forty Indians at work, for which they receive extra rations. They work well and I have very little trouble with them. They are very kind to me and often make me presents, but at the same time, as is natural with Indians, expect double the value in return.

I intend to have a jollification for them as soon as I get my new house, which I think will be about the 12 inst. I invited some of my friends up from the fort and have purchased some articles for prizes, as I intend to have races, shooting, sack races, squaw races and a lot of other amusements, and also give them a big feed, as I promised it to them when I got my new house.

I expect about 1500 Indians on the 25th inst., as that is about the time the payments are being made, and all Indians this year have to be paid on the reservations.[45]

Dewdney's support for "farming agencies" came down to three points. First, the crops produced in the first efforts were the results of their own labour and were theirs. Second, farm instructors would have both independence and flexibility to assist their clients. Third, any surplus could be sent to a central depot to be sent on to the less successful.[46]

The survey of the Assiniboine reserve in the Cypress Hills apparently was planned when Patrick was at Fort Walsh in January 1880 in a communication that Dewdney had with Surveyor General Lindsay Russell.[47] This was also the time of the major reorganization and the establishment of a separate Department of Indian Affairs (DIA) within the Department of the Interior, including a Survey Branch. Therefore, this was a period about which there remains some confusion regarding who was ordering surveys and who was implementing them.[48] Consequently, in the spring of 1880, instructed by Assistant Commissioner Elliot T. Galt, Allan Patrick made the actual survey. "The area he marked off during the summer of 1880, in consultation with the Assiniboine chiefs, encompassed 340 square miles, including the model farm at the west end of the Cypress Hills and, to the north at the lower elevation, prairie and a lake." The reserve was generally described as an area that "included timber, fish, fowl, rich pasture, and rich soil as barren plains, alkaline soil, and sparsely timbered coulees."[49]

Down in Fort Belknap, the agent reported on August 11, 1880, that the Assiniboine alternated time between there and Wolf Point to the east, where they had relatives, and that they were kept from the remaining bison by their enemies, the Sioux, and by the presence of "half-breeds" and "foreign" Indians in the area.[50]

In October 1880, after annuity payments, many of the Indigenous Peoples around Fort Walsh left to go south to look for bison. They did not get far before an outbreak of scarlet fever afflicted many of them, and the police sent Dr. George A. Kennedy from the post to their camp to tend to them. The disease was especially debilitating in their weakened state. Some stayed around Fort Walsh, and some wintered farther south.[51] Meanwhile, with regard to the Assiniboine reserve, Commissioner Dewdney reported to the superintendent general that crops had been poor, hampered by rain and frost, though the Indigenous workers had done their best. He suggested a move north for the Assiniboine bands.[52]

It should have been clear to the Canadian government that a crisis was under way. The bison had been eliminated from the "British" territories, and with limited rations the Indigenous Peoples had no choice but to venture south to survive. However, the American government wanted Canada to keep them in the western territories north of the border. The American authorities feared horse raids, and further depredation of bison herds, but at the same time they were preventing the bison from venturing north in their natural cycle. The meagre rations policy of the Canadian government aggravated a serious situation.

The reserve size of 340 square miles, taking the treaty formula into account, could accommodate approximately 1,750 individuals.[53] Patrick's plans for his survey of a number of reserves were forwarded to Deputy Superintendent General Vankoughnet, and then to Dewdney, who approved them on July 4, 1881. Still, as described in his December 1880 report, no plan for the Assiniboine reserve was approved, as had been done for the other surveys by Patrick.[54] However, references made in the Annual Report of the Department of Indian Affairs for 1880 show that the NWMP officials at Fort Walsh and DIA employees continued to recognize the Assiniboine reserve as an entity.[55]

John Macoun, a botanist and geologist, visited the Cypress Hills in the summer of 1880. While there, he went to English's farm and made several observations. Although he pronounced that the soil on the farm was of superior quality at the Head of the Mountain, he also declared that the altitude, using the word *climate*, would doom any agricultural endeavour to failure. Agent Edwin Allen, in his report for 1880, declared a similar sentiment:

> I next visited the Assiniboine reservation at the head of the Cypress Mountain. The reserve is situated in an excellent locality, for wood and water, but the climate is such that it is useless to think of continuing agriculture in that locality owing to the early frosts and snow storms that are so prevalent.... It is very much regretted the crops were not a success as the Assiniboines took every interest in the advancement of their agricultural pursuits, and displayed great willingness to do any work they were called upon to perform. I trust that they will meet with better success next year, as their conduct during the past season has been most commendable and really merits better success than has attended them this year. Although their crops were a failure they appear in no way discouraged, on the contrary, they speak of looking for a better location for their reserve next year.[56]

In a communication to Macdonald in November 1880, Dewdney suggested that "costs associated with anticipated crop failures at the 'Assiniboine Reserve' were a reason to move the Assiniboine to the lower elevation of Maple Creek." He described the crop failure in detail:

> The grain was all frozen and had to be cut for hay, the potatoes were all infused by the frost but the yield was considerable, fearing however that they had not ripened sufficiently to keep over the winter, I directed they should be fed, thus saving our flour.
>
> I am not at all sure whether in most seasons both potatoes and barley could not be raised here, but as a failure of a crop on a reserve where so many Indians would eventually reside and depend on for food would be a very serious matter, I thought it better to advise a change of location for the Assiniboine Indians.[57]

Dewdney then suggested that the Cree at the Maple Creek reserve be relocated farther north and that the Assiniboine then be relocated to Maple Creek.

However, CTK Elder Delmar Runs explained in his interview in 2015 that the farming the Assiniboine People did in the Cypress Hills had been successful, and it seemed more like the government was making excuses for moving the Assiniboine People from their homelands:

> They farmed there . . . [and] had some houses built here. . . . They had potatoes by the tonnes, they had carrots, they had everything. But yet . . . the one report to the government . . . says they had a frost. That was a lie. . . . They wanted to move them. But according to the *Indian Act*, wherever the reserve is surveyed, it cannot be moved. . . . They lied, and at that time they told [The] Chief Who Took the Coat . . . to move, but he didn't want to move . . . because they made a promise when they sat down in Cypress Hills and they smoked that pipe. . . . When Edgar [Dewdney] got the report, he turned around and told Macdonald, and they agreed, and the agreement was to remove all Indians from Cypress Hills. . . . How come they made that policy? See, they lied, which is not right.

Meanwhile, a minority of Assiniboine and Blackfoot were still trying to conduct their seasonal rounds south of the border in search of bison and smaller game to hunt. This was evidence of how much these groups needed to continue their traditional livelihoods and remain in their Traditional Territories, in spite of the risk of encounters with U.S. Army border patrols, hostile Indian enemies, horse thieves, and what was left of the whiskey peddlers.

Authorities in Ottawa "wanted to avoid any untoward incidents with the Americans. Especially since any violence on the frontier was contrary to Canada's plan for the opening of the North-West to agricultural settlers."[58] Fearful of international implications, Prime Minister Macdonald addressed these "border crossing" concerns in 1882: "Apart from considerations of an economical nature, the presence of these Indians in the vicinity of Fort Walsh is objectionable from an international point of view."[59] "Consequently, a pass system was proposed to curtail the movement of Indians across the border."[60]

Several factors contributed to the decision to relocate Indigenous Peoples away from the border. The managed exile of various Sioux in the vicinity of Wood Mountain from 1876 to 1881 required constant vigilance by the NWMP and took considerable diplomatic efforts internationally. There were also concerns pertaining to the Macdonald government's National Policy: "Three weeks before Dewdney wrote [to] Macdonald proposing a relocation of the Assiniboine Band, the Macdonald government signed, on October 21, 1880, the controversial and costly contract for constructing the Canadian National Railway. Regardless of whether farming or ranching would have provided a feasible livelihood for the Assiniboine Band in the Cypress Hills, larger political and economic factors were at work."[61]

During the winter of 1880–81, the numbers of Indigenous Peoples increased significantly in the general area of Fort Walsh and the Cypress Hills. They were unable to subsist by hunting, farming, or selling their labour, and rations were not adequate to sustain all the mouths that needed to be fed. One account mentions the Assiniboine eating their horses.[62] As dependency on rations increased, so did the numbers of Indigenous Peoples arriving at Fort Walsh from the Missouri River and the Qu'Appelle River areas. Assistant Commissioner Galt continued to suggest cutting the amount of rations and downgrading the quality of meat. He tried to devise the cheapest way of feeding those who refused to go to their designated reserves. Agent Allen tried to put Indigenous people who were not working on half rations. The NWMP thought this tactic unwise considering the number of people around Fort Walsh and the potential for further food riots. Later in 1881, a request was made to increase the number of police from 300 to 500 distributed across the thirteen posts in the North West Territories.[63]

THE BORDER CRISIS

The refugee Sitting Bull was a threat to the peace of the area, and neither the American government nor the Canadian government was willing to accept him and his people. Leaders such as Big Bear were wary of government policies and actions, unwilling to give away his rights under treaty and determined to provide for his band through hunting on either side of the border. The government was also concerned about "half-breeds" who had been participating in the bison hide trade and were unsatisfied with their exclusion from their lands in Canada. Correspondence between the two governments emphasized the need for each to keep "hostiles" on its own side. From time to time, the Americans threatened military force to accomplish this goal. Canada could not respond, having only the one western police post. After the Civil War, the American side had been developing and encouraging immigration at a faster rate and was crowded by many dispossessed Indigenous Peoples. The American authorities also had a propensity to export their problems to the Canadian side while retaining the remaining bison on their side.

The NWMP cultivated a better, more cooperative relationship with the First Nations camped in the Cypress Hills, directed by men such as Major Walsh. But he was censured by the Canadian government in late 1879 for writing directly to an agent at Fort Buford about the trespass of "half-breeds" on the reservations there and the danger of Riel and others building a strong military alliance and, further, blocking the northern migration of the bison. Walsh was told that he had no right to make policy decisions, yet he was working from information obtained directly and locally.[64] The police stored and disbursed rations and tried to convince the Indigenous Peoples to leave for their own welfare. Superintendent Leif N.F. Crozier, in charge of a small post at Wood Mountain, where the Lakota Sioux were based in Canada, wrote that

> the strength of the force necessary to be permanently maintained here will depend to a great extent upon the location of the Indian reservations upon both sides of the line, as well as the actions of the Indians themselves. If Indian reservations are situated close to the line, it is only to be expected that a strong force will have to be maintained on both sides, not only to prevent trouble between Indians of the two countries, which for some years at least would be very apt to occur, but to give a sense of safety and security to settlers. On the other hand, if the Indians are placed on reservations and settled down a considerable distance from the border, it does not seem to me that there would be the same reason for maintaining a large force along the frontier. During the present unsettled state of affairs a force of at least 50 men should be stationed here (Wood Mountain) until the surrendered hostile Sioux are settled upon their reservations, and even afterwards. Unless they are placed far from the border and well watched, and as they will not have the same interests in behaving themselves as when this country was their home, it is only natural to suppose that they will not restrain their mischievous inclinations. In fact, should they come, they would do so in all probability as "war parties," which means horse stealing, or when necessary or convenient, killing people as well. Threats to that effect have, I understand, been already made by those who have gone to the American agencies.[65]

In late 1880, Commissioner Dewdney expressed his concerns about "American Indians" attacking and killing "British Indians";

CHAPTER 5

"straggling" parties were being attacked and robbed, and one attack at Moose Mountain resulted in many casualties.[66] A memo from Deputy Superintendent General Lawrence Vankoughnet on January 30, 1882, indicates that "American Indians" actually raided a Cree camp at Fort Walsh and took all the horses.[67] There were constant tensions as both the Canadians and the Americans tried to keep Indigenous groups from crossing the line. The police, however, were not a military force, only a peacekeeping one. They were already considering closing the post to induce the Indigenous Peoples to move farther away.

Brian Hubner undertook an analysis of horse stealing, via raids, during this period. As "Canadian/British Indians" went south to the Milk and Missouri Rivers to find bison, they also engaged in the culturally and economically valuable activity of horse raiding. Hubner details the expansion of the American military presence in outposts such as Fort Assinniboine (spelled thus) in Montana, set up to use force, as necessary, to push Indians back north. For instance, Big Bear raided the Crow in 1881, and both army militia and local ranchers organized into troops to drive him back: "The NWMP and DIA officials increasingly believed that these movements south were actually intended to steal horses or 'lift scalps' and would soon result in more serious incidents with the United States military. This was an important factor in the decision to refuse several Indian bands, including those under Big Bear and Piapot, reserves in the Cypress Hills in 1881–83."[68] After 1880, Hubner states, the NWMP began to use harsher sentences in the prosecution of horse thieves, including those bringing horses back over the line. They also began to cooperate with U.S. authorities, rather than antagonize them, in returning property on both sides of the border. This was a major shift in relationships since horse raids had never been considered a crime by any of the First Nations.[69]

Colonel Macleod, writing to his wife from Fort Walsh on May 29, 1880, said,

> I find [Assistant Indian Commissioner] Galt a very pleasant travelling companion. He is in an awful funk about Indian matters. There are about 4000 Indians here and in the neighbourhood and the authorities at Ottawa appear to have overlooked the necessity which *has been pointed out to them over and over again, that they would require to be fed or they would starve*.[70]

THE YEAR 1881

The first report on the Assiniboine in 1881 came from Dr. George Kennedy, a surgeon who visited the reserve in January. On February 1, he reported to Commissioner Dewdney that there was considerable illness among the people, which he attributed to a lack of clean housing. He asked the farmer's wife, Mrs. English, to track the "decrease" in population.[71] That month newly appointed Indian Agency Inspector T.P. Wadsworth was asked by Dewdney to inquire if, as he was hearing, the Assiniboine wanted to move north, possibly to the Touchwood Hills. This comment is interesting since it was Dewdney who seems to have suggested the move north a few months earlier. He said that, if they did not move north, he would ask Agent McDonald at Fort Qu'Appelle to select and plow a reserve site there. Thus, already, there was a plan to move them out of a place that Major Walsh had just recently identified as their home.[72] Indian Agent Edwin Allen accompanied Inspector Wadsworth and said that the Assiniboine showed no interest in moving. Allen attributed this recalcitrance to a "secret power" acting among the chiefs but did not say what it was.[73]

Almost 6,000 Indigenous Peoples were camped near the police post. Chief Piapot had drawn people from other bands and had 1,400 members at the July payments at Fort Walsh. There were almost 1,000 people under Little Pine and Lucky Man, many of whom had come from other bands; some new adherents had come from the "Missouri" in the United States. Another 800 people, leaderless, were paid as stragglers. Foremost Man, or Nekaneet, was gathering a band drawn from Fort Qu'Appelle and Battleford reserves. Some of the stragglers were Assiniboine but mostly from the more easterly Pheasant Rump Band (Duck's Head Necklace); they wanted to settle at Wood Mountain. Some of the Little Black Bear people were with Little Child and Muscowequan and various stragglers at the Maple Creek reserve, a total of 330 people, considerably fewer than in 1880. However, Piapot chose a reserve site ten miles north of the Maple Creek farm.[74]

The Assiniboine continued with farming, fishing, and hunting. The reporter from the *Globe*, however, said that English's farm at the Head of the Mountain was closed and that only one remained viable, probably the Setter farm where the Cree were, thirty miles east of the Fort. He reported that there were only 300 to 400 Indigenous people combined working at the farm, but it is not clear whether the reserve at the Head of the Mountain, as opposed to the farm, was also closed.[75] The farms were set up partly to grow food and partly to "demonstrate" farming to

CHAPTER 5

the Indigenous people. There is further evidence that the Assiniboine were in Maple Creek in the summer report of surgeon George Kennedy. He treated two Assiniboine for scrofula and Long Lodge for a tumour.[76]

Poor Man (138) and Bear's Head (286) were there and a few from Duck's Head Necklace (13). The Man Who Took the Coat had 46 men, 76 women, and 135 children, totalling 257. This was consistent with the year before, suggesting little movement. There were four headmen: Not a Young Man, Grunting Calf, Yellow Leg, and Bend the Stick. Five deaths were recorded in the notes. Long Lodge had 102, with 17 men, 33 women, and 52 children. He had three headmen in that year, Crooked Arm, Little Mountain, and Bisobbe. His membership had grown slightly over the period.

The large number of people, and their poor condition, reflected the loss of the bison-based economy. Those who remained on the two reserves and set about farming might have received more rations than those in hunting camps, simply because there was now a need for labour on the farms. In late 1880, Commissioner Dewdney recommended that Indigenous people be hired as labourers on the Canadian Pacific Railway (CPR) cutting ties and doing other basic labour, but apparently this idea was not accepted.[77] Certainly, the game in the hills was quickly obliterated; at best, fish and beef rations provided some protein. After the late-summer treaty payments, many left for the hunt but soon returned.[78] Mounted police and Ottawa officials continued to worry about the concentration of people in the Cypress Hills, especially as CPR construction approached. It would be this railway, built just north of the Cypress Hills in 1882, that would herald the "opening of the west" to settlers. The U.S. government wanted the "British Indians" moved away from the border and began to use soldiers to drive them back, thinking that all of them should be moved north of the new rail line. The hunting bands stayed just north of the border, but there was little left to hunt.[79]

In May 1881, Indian Agent Allen wrote to Commissioner Dewdney about the "unruly" concentrations of Indigenous Peoples at Fort Walsh, augmented by "British Indians" driven back north by the Americans. The newspaper man at Fort Walsh noted that they were starving.[80] People who had already moved to the Qu'Appelle River area to reserves were also starving there and coming back. The reply that Allen got was from Assistant Commissioner Galt, who took a strict line about the need to have Indigenous Peoples return to reserves and work before getting rations. No reserves were to be surveyed in the Cypress Hills region, he said. Galt then wrote to Superintendent General John A.

Macdonald detailing an argument for bacon rather than beef as rations. It was cheaper and easier to transport, and the Indigenous Peoples did not like it as well. Galt also pointed out that stockmen in Montana were pressuring the American government to move "British Indians" by force back across the line to British territories.[81] In a private letter to D.L. McPherson of the Department of the Interior on June 6, 1881, Galt assured him that, though feeding "thousands" of Indians would be expensive, he could provide some controls: "I can assure you that everything will be done to keep it down as much as possible."[82]

Dewdney did get rations, acknowledging that most of the Indians were forced to "eke out an existence." Still, he thought that they should work for rations if possible. "The whole question of getting work to any large extent is beset with difficulties." He also requisitioned clothing but found that the Privy Council would not approve this expenditure. In another private letter to Macdonald, Dewdney said that he regretted this since clothing was not only necessary for work but also an inducement. Men and women were going out mid-winter to cut wood wearing only flour sacks.[83] Dewdney went on to say that there was continuing fear of Indigenous discontent—particularly a Cree-Blackfoot alliance—if food and clothing were not provided. Finally, he said that he was ordering that hunting parties be supplied with provisions and ammunition so that people could feed themselves. He said that he had sleepless nights worrying about how to handle matters. The only solution to feeding and clothing the starving people, and saving money, was to order provisions well in advance and not rely on local contractors.[84] Soon after, McPherson wrote that clothing and provisions would be sent and that hunting parties should be encouraged to go below the line.[85]

There was clearly tension building between the police and the department. The cost-cutting measures that made sense to officials in the east had to be carried out by the force, and they understood the consequences. In his journal, Colonel Acheson Irvine wrote about the unsettled conditions prevailing at Fort Walsh. On July 23, he wrote that

> the Indians here are in a very unsettled state. I am afraid I will not be able to leave this place at present much as I should like to meet His Excellency [governor general]. It is really too bad. It is a great mistake ever taking the management of Indians out of the hands of the police. The Inspector of Indian Agencies [T.P. Wadsworth] is here now and he had found things in a beautiful mess. The Indian Agent here is a son of Dr. Allen of

CHAPTER 5

Cornwall and a great friend of Major Walsh. He and Walsh are both tarred with the same brush. The Inspector is now staying with me. I have made him go fully into the inspection of the Indian Agency here, for if we ever have trouble with the Indians it will be through the mismanagement of these agents. The head chief of the Indians came to me yesterday. He said, I hear of you going away to meet with the big chief that is coming up to Canada. I have come to tell you that if you go away there will be trouble. There is no use my telling you, you know you are the only man that keeps us from having trouble.[86]

Irvine went on to state on July 28, 1881, that Indigenous Peoples had no trust in the Indian Agents and that the inspector himself talked too much and had no tact.[87] Meanwhile, Galt was directing that Indigenous Peoples who did not "belong" in the Cypress Hills were not to be paid there or otherwise supported:

It is the policy of the government to keep the Indians on their reservations as much as possible, and to that end to feed there only—and if they choose to roam about the country they must not be permitted to think that they can go to any post and receive a similar ration to those Indians who belong there. . . . Before you leave Walsh, establish a fixed ration for those who are settled on their reservations and also a meagre ration for those who don't belong to the district and who won't go home. Stop the issuing of anything but flour and bacon or beef as the case may be, except when it is considered advisable to issue a little tea now and again to sick people or to Indians who are really doing well on their reserves—and even then in lieu of a certain portion of the staples. You must use your discretion in these matters, keeping down the expenditure as much as possible, while at the same time making sure that peace and order will be preserved.[88]

Wadsworth wrote a private missive: "I cannot see what particular good I would be here at the treaty. These Indians have been in the habit of being fed and no one man can introduce a policy of non-feeding. I cannot take the responsibility of feeding them in the face of these instructions. I therefore think that as I telegraphed—that the commissioner himself should come here and put the whole matter on a working basis."[89]

According to historian James Daschuk, once Commissioner Dewdney did investigate the relationship between contractor I.G. Baker Co. and Agent Allen's friends, Allen was discovered to have double-billed the department by issuing invoices for twice the quantity of rations received. He had fed carrion to people and inflated the rations. Soon after this exchange, Allen was suspended by Wadsworth for alleged theft, mismanaging the delivery of rations to Fort Walsh, and double-billing. He was fired in September, an act confirmed by an order in council in November 1881.[90]

Those in the Cypress Hills were not receiving the rations paid for, and Assistant Commissioner E.T. Galt continued to recommend withholding rations to those without reserves. Meanwhile, Inspector Wadsworth restated his concerns about the policy of withholding rations, expressing concern about his own safety, and he recommended abandoning the fort. Another complication of this volatile situation was the complicity of I.G. Baker from Montana with the food scams of Allen. Not only was Baker fraudulent, but also he was making efforts to continue supplying rations to the area forts by meddling with the groups.

Agent Allen was replaced by Cecil E. Denny, who continued the policy of meagre rations. He was also asked to attempt to persuade the Assiniboine to move north. It is interesting to note that Allen was a relative of Vankoughnet, and Galt was the son of the prominent Galt of Canadian Confederation. Both Galt and Allen were suspected of over-billing and worse, and they left the service of the government during this crisis.

Essentially, the policy of meagre rations had created an enormous crisis. Out of desperation and fear, various civil servants recommended closing Fort Walsh. Irvine was concerned that issuing firearms and ammunition should be strictly prohibited, even for hunting, as he believed that the Indigenous people would be more dangerous if armed. The authorities could not agree on whether or not to issue ammunition; neither could they agree on the level of rations or whether or not the fort should be closed. In the midst of this indecision, the agent and contractors were fraudulently bilking the government for supplying poor-quality foods. The result of all this incompetence was the starvation of those Indigenous Peoples whose lives were in the hands of those who had destroyed the bison and taken their lands.

The agent at Fort Belknap reported in the summer of 1881 that there was still some movement of Assiniboine from that post to Wolf Point and back to the Cypress Hills to "take their money, thus becoming British Indians." (There is no indication from the pay sheets for

CHAPTER 5

The Man Who Took the Coat and Long Lodge that their numbers increased, but these people could have been paid as stragglers.) The agent went on to blame the "half-breeds," most of whom were also traders, and allegedly from Canada, for keeping the Indians away from the bison by "falsehoods, threats, and by forming combinations to drive the buffalo away from this part of the country. Buffalo are now within 50 miles of this post, but the half-breeds and northern Indians are moving in such numbers that they will soon be slaughtered and driven out."[91]

As 1881 passed, the government continued to plan to move Indigenous Peoples out of the Cypress Hills. Farming results had not been great, timber was scarce in some areas, and game had been virtually hunted out. In the fall, Wadsworth continued to try to convince the bands to settle elsewhere, but he concluded that people were leaving reserves to return to Fort Walsh because there was no work for them to do, leading them to conclude that they would not have to work for rations, as they did on reserves.[92] As winter came, all four of the Assiniboine bands left the reserve periodically to hunt, and some came into Fort Walsh so that the old and sick could get rations while the rest were away. They had few horses and asked for ammunition for the hunt.[93]

The Cypress Hills farm was considered closed, and farm instructor J.J. English was transferred to the Maple Creek farm to replace farm instructor John Setter, transferred to the Crooked Lake Agency.[94] Confusion prevailed among DIA authorities regarding the rivalry between Piapot and the leaders of the Assiniboine band and the selection of reserve sites for the groups since the 1881 report declared that "all of the members of the bands of Man Who Took the Coat (278), Long Lodge (123), Poor Man (137), Chic-ne-na-bais (286), and Duck Head Necklace (13), plus 74 'Stragglers,' are shown as absent and 'Hunting Buffalo, Fort Walsh District.'"[95] In the fall of 1881, Indian Agent Cecil E. Denny, who had replaced Allen at Fort Walsh, reported that "I succeeded after tedious negotiations in persuading them to their different reservations, the Crees to the north and the Assiniboine to the east."[96] Directions were received from Ottawa in July 1881 to prepare for the abandonment of Fort Walsh.

In an evaluation of the Maple Creek reserve location, Inspector Wadsworth and Colonel Irvine agreed that it was too far from timber needed to develop the reserve.[97] However, English had paid some Indigenous people to help him and had a successful potato crop at Maple Creek, with 10,000 pounds set aside for seed and the remaining 60,000 pounds turned over to the police. Denny reported that the Cree and Assiniboine who had gone south to hunt along the Missouri River in late summer 1881 had returned starving, some without horses.[98] He increased the amount of rations issued.[99] The majority of the bands of The Man Who Took the Coat, Poor Man, and Long Lodge were toward the foot of the Cypress Hills and expected to come to the fort. Denny gave ammunition to the most able among the destitute and encouraged them to continue hunting. Meanwhile, he continued to address the problem of how to get the Assiniboine to relocate: "I have been talking to Bear's Head and the Poor Man (Assiniboine chiefs) about their moving to Qu'Appelle but can get no answer out of them as yet. Mr. English seems to be liked by the Assiniboines and I think that if he could go with them in the spring to Qu'Appelle, it would be hard to get them off. With your permission I would speak to Mr. English about going with them."[100]

CHAPTER 6

Wazi Ȟe Makóče Žedáhaŋ Nakódabi Baȟeyam iyéya hiŋkda ne Canadian's Išta Mneǧá Hiyúbi Ičíyabi

The Assiniboine Removal from Cypress Hills and the "Canadian" Trail of Tears, 1883

On January 18, 1882, the minister of the interior reported to the government that there were considerable concerns about the changed condition of the Indigenous Peoples "since the almost total disappearance of the buffalo and the rapid development of the country by white settlers."[1] In response, the commissioner of the North West Mounted Police recommended an increase in the size of the force to be stationed at Fort Walsh—from 300 to 500. The Blackfoot had recently returned from south of the boundary line and were "assuming a threatening attitude." Leif N.F. Crozier thought that hundreds would have starved had the police not fed them through the winter. Fish ran at the Assiniboine reserve in the spring, and that helped to feed all the Indigenous Peoples camped on and off reserve.[2]

The strategy changed as spring came in 1882. The Home Farms in the hills were shut down. A final decision was made to close the Fort Walsh Mounted Police post and to discontinue rations until all the Indigenous Peoples left the hills for reserves in the Fort Qu'Appelle and Battlefords areas. None of this came to pass as quickly as planned, and Agent Cecil E. Denny reported on January 17, 1882, that some Assiniboine had gone south of the line on the rumour of bison amassing there, but he thought that they would go to the Qu'Appelle Valley in the spring.[3] He had to leave just after that, and Acting Indian Agent McIlree wrote on February 1 asking for more rations since the Assiniboine were starving for lack of bison and freezing for lack of clothing. Their horses were being stolen, and they had no way to leave to go north or east. The Assiniboine south of the line were returning since, allegedly, American troops were in pursuit.[4]

Authorities at Fort Walsh and Maple Creek recognized that the Assiniboine would have to consent to any relocation since the Cypress Hills were considered their lands.[5] However, consent was far from possible given the health condition of the Assiniboine People. Despite this obvious fact, Dewdney asked McIlree, who was also an inspector for the NWMP, to consult with the Assiniboine about their wishes.[6]

Dewdney received a long answer on February 15, 1882. McIlree met with The Man Who Took the Coat, Bear's Head, and Poor Man. Long Lodge was still south of the line. The Chiefs listened to McIlree's argument and returned two days later to say that they wished to stay and settle permanently on their reserve. They said that they had been brought up in that country, and though they had given up their country to the queen she had promised to give them a reserve where they wished. They did not want to live with the northern Indigenous Peoples.[7] Dewdney responded to McIlree by saying that the Assiniboine could stay where they were as long as they agreed to farm individual gardens.[8] This promise would not last. A food shortage was created as an incentive to get groups to move on to their new reserves.

Long Lodge was reported to have been south of the line all this time, but there is an NWMP requisition for food and other supplies on record from Fort Qu'Appelle in February 1882 with a note from a J.A. Fraser. Major Walsh ordered the release of supplies from the Fort Qu'Appelle detachment after meeting Long Lodge and his people on the nearby trail. Because Agent McDonald was away at the time, no supplies were released. Fraser later left the force and joined the Department of Indian Affairs, where he was finally able to release provisions. Long Lodge and his people were described as destitute, nearly starving, but it is not clear if the encounter with Walsh took place in the fall of 1881 or in fact during the harsh winter.[9]

Commissioner Dewdney sent Métis trader Peter Erasmus to the Cypress Hills to talk to the Indigenous Peoples there and provide intelligence, particularly of people not with their proper bands. Erasmus was to explain to them that they *must* move out of the area. This was affirmed in a letter to NWMP Commissioner Colonel Irvine. The Indigenous Peoples were to be told that when they came in from their hunts they must immediately go to reserves, for they would not get assistance at Fort Walsh.[10] On March 2, 1882, Inspector McIlree met with The Man Who Took the Coat about leaving, followed by a meeting on March 3, at which the Chief said that he would go to Battleford but not Fort Qu'Appelle. On March 4, they were rewarded with rations of flour and meat.

The next day The Man Who Took the Coat's brother poisoned himself, and on March 6, after a five-hour discussion, the Chief agreed to go to Fort Qu'Appelle. Long Lodge did not agree until April 20, 1882.[11] An interview with Elder Charles Ryder of Carry The Kettle First Nation adds to this account of poisoning. Ryder said that the man in question was a nephew, Runner. He had shot a man over a love dispute, then poisoned himself with meat laced with coyote poison. He did not die, however, and was later tried in court and sentenced to hang; he survived that as well. Elder Ryder said that the incident propelled the Chief to make the move, though it is not entirely clear why from his comments.

In April 1882, The Man Who Took the Coat and his camp were prepared to leave for Fort Qu'Appelle. On May 7, after transport had finally been arranged, the bands were ready to begin their journeys. With great regret, Chiefs Long Lodge, Jack, Little Child, and Sparrow Hawk and their bands, and "some independent bodies of Indians going to join their respective chiefs," left the Cypress Hills.[12] In 2015, Carry The Kettle Elder Delmar Runs explained this event as relayed to him through his ancestors:

> When they were forced to move, they already gathered all the people at Fort Walsh. They were all gathered there, and that's where they had their rations. . . . And when they told them to move, they said "No. We don't want to move. Cypress Hills is our homeland. And all our loved ones that have gone are buried here. Why should we move?" . . . Before that move, they were cut off on rations. It was one of the government's policies, so they went to Maple Creek on the reserve there, but they needed lodging. They wanted to go back to their homeland. But the first move they walked to Indian Head. And dad said there were many who were sick, and many of them died on the road. Because when they came back they numbered the people, and there was a little over 336 I think. On that map, it is written on the map, the population. So we lost what, 1,200 people, 1,100 and something, just travelling back and forth. That was the government's policy—to remove Indians, but the reserve is still there yet. And that reserve was surveyed under Take the Coat.

Thus, the spring of 1882 was the time of forced marches and transport to these new sites. A telegram to Captain McIlree on March 14 commanded him to move Indigenous Peoples out of the Cypress Hills as "economically" as possible. Able-bodied people were to walk, and carts could be provided for lodges and provisions.[13] Colonel Irvine met with the Assiniboine to negotiate a transfer in April, only a few months after they had stated their interest in staying put. We quote at length his letter to his superior, Fred White, of May 20, because of the significance of the message in the context of the times. According to a marginal note, the letter was forwarded to Commissioner Dewdney:

> I have the honour to inform you, that I will have the treaty Indians at present in the Cypress Hills systematically divided into separate camps. These Indians are now ready, in fact, anxious to move Northward, the only cause of delay is want of provisions and transport. I cannot understand why I.G. Baker and Co. have failed to supply provisions ordered by the acting Indian Agent some time ago. . . . Now that the Indians have fully agreed to go North, I venture, most respectfully to impress upon the Government the importance of their being well received in the North, also the fulfilling of treaty obligations. It should be borne in mind that in many cases the mode of life, and particularly the surroundings will be some[what] different, from that, to which the Indians have been accustomed, for this some little allowance should be made and the treatment they receive, particularly on arrival, should be kind. If these recommendations are not acted on, I feel that I am not far astray in predicting a general stampede Southwards, should this once occur, the final settlement of the Indians on allotted reservations will be materially retarded. The experience of our neighbours the Americans, cannot be without its lesson to us, in their case the non-fulfilment of treaty obligations gave rise to much of the trouble, and expense they have been put to in the governance of their Indians. It is worthy of note, that even with a very strong force at their command, it has not been found practical to force Indians to remain on a particular reservation. Already several of "Big Bear's" followers, non-treaty Indians, was here, have surreptitiously stated to our treaty chiefs that they will find on going North, that a disregard will be paid to the conditions set forth in the treaties with the government.[14]

CHAPTER 6

Poor Man (Lean Man) and Grizzly Bear's Head went north to new reserves beside that of Mosquito, in the Eagle Hills. The Man Who Took the Coat and Long Lodge journeyed east to the Skull Mountains, near the railway settlement of Indian Head. Instructor J.J. English went with them, and the journey took from May 8 to June 9. The people departed from the Maple Creek farm, and the trip was made on foot, by wagon, and on horseback, with dogs in tow. Other Qu'Appelle Valley groups were with them, a party of 453, of which only 254 were Assiniboine. A few were headed to Ocean Man at Moose Mountain. Agent McDonald wrote a detailed account of their arrival, noting that there were no "incidents" on the way; Corporal Hamilton of the police travelled with them, he said, and looked after young and old.[15] There were Indigenous people from Little Child, Kakewistahaw, and Peepeekesis.

Piapot left the Cypress Hills in June with 500 people in "wretched" condition and without horses. The police used their own horses and wagons for transport. Colonel Irvine opined that it had been most difficult to get everyone out of the Cypress Hills, especially since the American traders were sending emissaries to the camps to persuade the Indigenous Peoples to stay, hopeful of spending their annuities. He had also learned that 200 troops were amassed at the Big Bend of the Milk River, ready to attack any "British Indians" coming in search of bison.[16] The herds would be gone by 1883.

Dewdney made plans to be present at Fort Qu'Appelle to greet the arriving Indigenous Peoples, and he reassured Indian Agent Alan McDonald in a communication dated April 26, 1882, that he would make sure that they were satisfied with their relocation. Dewdney instructed McDonald that sod had been broken and plowed on two reserves, one of them at the location of the new Assiniboine Agency near Indian Head.[17] Irvine warned of the importance of a proper reception at Fort Qu'Appelle, or there might be a "stampede southward" for those dissatisfied. The American experience of reactions by Indians not satisfied with the fulfillment of treaties had proven to be expensive in many ways.

Access to adequate amounts of food might seem to have been a proper incentive, but the challenge remained to fulfill promises at the new agencies and reserves. Having the proper amounts distributed to all the necessary locations was far from accomplished.[18] Commissioner Dewdney and Major Walsh promised the Chiefs oxen and wagons if they would at least view their new reserves. The following day Dewdney and McDonald provided them with three days of rations of flour and bacon "together with some tea, tobacco, [and] pemmican as presents from the commissioner."[19] On June 12, 1882, a meeting was held with Dewdney in

Walsh's tent, with McDonald noting "signs of discontent" and a general "unwillingness to go to their reserve." At subsequent meetings, the commissioner and the agent read the terms of Treaty 4 to the Chiefs and headmen, explaining the contents.

Before they arrived, Qu'Appelle Agent McDonald had engaged men to plant potatoes and turnips on the Assiniboine reserve site and had secured rations of bacon and flour. This was to be the new diet of the bison hunters. McDonald planned to get the Assiniboine People engaged immediately in cutting wood for housing and fencing. He expected that, given their proximity to settlers, they would quickly learn to farm and no longer be a burden on the government.[20]

The two bands did go to see the reserve surveyed by John Nelson; the land area was big enough to accommodate Piapot, who, with his people, was moved from a reserve near Maple Creek. Piapot and 358 band members arrived on July 29, 1882. They showed considerable disdain for the site and later chose one northwest of there, along the Qu'Appelle Valley.[21]

The two Assiniboine bands camped there, allegedly satisfied with the location, large and timbered, but also littered with skulls from an epidemic disaster years before. Long Lodge tried to get annuities so that his people could go to Wood Mountain to trade, but McDonald told them that annuities would not be paid until September. He told them that they would get three-quarters of a pound of flour and one-quarter of a pound of bacon at each issuance, and they asked for more. They argued that, if they were paid for working, then they would like clothing, tobacco, and tea. The agent also agreed to pay them for building two government buildings, and twenty-four houses for The Man Who Took the Coat and eighteen for Long Lodge, at the rate of ten dollars a house plus additions. Tea would be issued for shingling.[22] McDonald continued, "I however have no doubt that time will heal all old wounds, and they will turn out as well for roofing and thatching, paid in clothing and tea."[23] But McDonald's actions were questioned in a letter from Deputy Superintendent General of Indian Affairs Lawrence Vankoughnet to E.T. Galt, and presumably the doubts were to be passed on: able-bodied people were to receive as little as possible in rations, and McDonald was told that he had no authority to pay people to build houses.[24] Thus, they were to have no food and no money to feed, house, and clothe themselves in the new location.

People were soon unhappy with the rations and the root crops and continued to try to hunt. The Indian Agent quickly reported that the change from fresh meat on their previous reserve to bacon rations led

CHAPTER 6

Chief Pi-a-pot (Piapot), 1884
Photo by J.A. Brock; courtesy of Library and Archives Canada/Canadian Intellectual Property Office fonds/c003863.

to outbreaks of diarrhea, with some deaths. He said that The Man Who Took the Coat, or Jack, was very cooperative, but Long Lodge's people were not:

> I regret to say that in the case of Long Lodge and his band, they do not, with the exception of two families, appear to be as contented as their neighbours, Jack and his band. This . . . is no doubt due to the loss of *several of their numbers by death, immediately to their departure north to here.* I however . . . have no doubt that time will heal all old wounds, and that they will turn out as well as those under Jack. Of course you are fully acquainted with the veneration and love that Indians all exhibit towards the spots where their parents or relations lie buried, as there is some excuse for Long Lodge's party not appearing as contented as might be desired by us.[25]

McDonald went on to say that the building of storehouses was delayed by the lack of nails and that dogs were eating the bacon. In a letter on July 29, 1882, the Indian Agent, describing a speech by the newly arrived Chief Piapot, referred to "lies" about starvation at Fort Qu'Appelle being spread by Chief Cha-ca-chas.[26] The agent also spoke of diet and starvation, with reference to a conversation with Piapot:

> I told him that it was needless all this display of eloquence in asking for fresh meat, as all that I had power to give my Indians was flour and bacon and of this they would have daily rations as heretofore, but that the commissioner when here had purchased and set aside a few bags of pemmican and dried meat for him when he arrived—and that would be given [to] him—power to buy fresh meat or anything whatsoever were denied me so I could not consider the request for a change of diet. That I was sorry to hear of the death of the old woman that morning.[27]

Two days later McDonald wrote to Galt again saying that Long Lodge was getting ready to return to the plains in search of fresh meat, dissatisfied, as were the other Chiefs, with bacon. The agent made a desperate plea for beef to prevent the Indigenous Peoples from returning to Fort Walsh for it, but it appears not to have been heeded:

> Mr. Provost arrived in from Indian Head with Chief "Jack" and reported the out of Long Lodge's party and the reasons. There

is no doubt that an alarming amount of sickness of the type of diarrhoea has been prevailing among these Assiniboines and which . . . there is also no doubt has arisen from the change from fresh meat to that of bacon. The same unfortunate state of things is met within Piepot's [sic] camp where some deaths have occurred. Added to this is the suicide of an old blind man of Piepot's [sic] band whose grand-daughter had died two days ago from diarrhoea.[28]

McDonald killed one of his own oxen to feed people and criticized restrictive government policies—a rare action for an agent during those times.[29]

The replacement for Galt, Assistant Commissioner Hayter Reed, and NWMP Colonel Irvine toured the reserves near Indian Head, where they urged The Man Who Took the Coat to remain on his new reserve. However, Irvine reported that both Piapot and Long Lodge with their bands had "grievances" that resulted in their being off their reserves.

Long Lodge and his followers were also full of discontent. They complained of the lack of fresh meat and vegetables, which had resulted in illness. This contributed to the overall morale of a place that had to be literally built from the ground up,[30] and McDonald still had instructions to reduce rations further to individuals who did not do the development work.[31] He was well aware that the restrictions on his purchasing power and his capability to provide quality rations "could jeopardize the efforts to settle the Indians on the northern reserves."[32]

Long Lodge (eighteen lodges) was the first to leave the Indian Head reserve in August 1882, and his group departed for Wood Mountain, and they were reported to have spent the winter of 1882–83 south of the border. Subsequently, The Man Who Took the Coat, reflecting the sentiment of his band, made apologies and departed in an attempt to return to the Cypress Hills, where his group really wanted to have a reserve. They could not live on bacon when they preferred fresh beef. CTK Elder Delmar Runs explained in 2015 that the government never really followed through on promises made at the time of Treaty 4, and the minimal rations that it did provide were not enough to help the Assiniboine live healthy lives as before: "They got some rations, they said it was pork—salted pork. But when they ate the salted pork, many of the people died because they were not used to that. They were used to fresh meat. That was their diet. That's how they lived." Some left before the September annuity payments; 200 were paid, but later 140 received arrears for 1882 for the two bands combined. Only 37 men and

56 women were paid in September as The Man Who Took the Coat Band, with 77 children—a loss of 30 adults from 1881—some or all of whom were paid later at Fort Walsh. Within the "other person" category, 177 people were paid. Three deaths of children were recorded. A few people had come into the band from Piapot, Little Child, and Bear's Head. Comments about arrears, however, indicate that the band was very unsettled, with numbers of people south of the line.

Meanwhile, many Indigenous Peoples remained at Fort Walsh. Colonel Irvine wrote to Police Headquarters on September 20, 1882, saying that 2,000 were still there and starving, and he had supplies for only three weeks. Frank Norman, a police inspector, had taken over from McIlree as Acting Indian Agent. He confirmed that they had little food left. NWMP Comptroller Fred White went west and wrote to Dewdney on October 17:

> I arrived here on the night of the 14th inst. And since then have devoted myself closely to the Indian situation. There are about 260 lodges in this vicinity, and a more wretched half-starved camp could not be imagined. The provisions issued to them have averaged about 4 oz. of flour and 2 oz. of dried meat per day. . . . They are huddled together two or three families to a lodge; the lodges are old and dilapidated and the women and children are suffering from want of food and clothing, in fact many of the children are quite naked. It has snowed every day since I arrived and unless something is done for them without delay the old people and young children who are now lying prostrate from starvation must succumb. Moving north or east is out of the question as many of them have sold their ponies for provisions. Dr. Jukes accompanied me through the camp and the enclosed letter from him speaks for itself. Of course they have asked again to have reservations here and say they may as well starve to death [at Fort Walsh] as on the reservations north and east, but many of them are in such a desperate condition that I fear hunger may impel them to commit illegal acts, and as large working parties are now grading the CPR north of here it would be a pity to risk trouble this winter.
>
> Limited rations, absence of game, scarcity of clothing and the suffering they must endure this winter owing to the tattered condition of their lodges . . . will I hope bring them to their senses by next spring. . . . Under all circumstances, though with great reluctance, I have telegraphed asking you

CHAPTER 6

Assiniboine Camp, Lac de Marons, Manitoba, July 17, 1874
Library and Archives Canada/George M. Dawson fonds/e011156511.

to send [Indian Agent] McDonald from [Fort] Qu'Appelle to pay them. He knows who have been paid and who are entitled to pay and for other reasons it is better that the payments should not be made by the police.[33]

Commissioner Dewdney then wrote to Colonel Irvine asking why the fort had not been closed as planned, and, though he agreed to pay treaty annuities, he asked officers there to remind the Indigenous Peoples that their wretched condition was their own fault.[34] Vankoughnet in turn wrote to the prime minister on November 2, 1882, saying that Irvine's concerns were misguided; they should not have acceded to his views.[35]

A later annuity payment, in November 1882, was made there to people who had not yet left the Cypress Hills. Little Pine had over 1,000 people, and Lucky Man had 872. Piapot had almost 900. Some of Big Bear's people and various "stragglers" were paid, another 1,000 souls. Cowessess and Front Man headed large temporary bands of people who "belonged" on the Qu'Appelle River area reserves. People from both the Indian Head Assiniboine bands went back to the Fort Walsh area after the September 1882 payment, where they remained with Piapot and his people. Thirty people from The Man Who Took the Coat and 19 from Long Lodge were paid at the fort. There were more than 4,000 people being fed in the fall of 1882 by a small staff at Fort Walsh. NWMP Inspector Norman reported that there was extreme misery in the camps, with multiple families in cotton lodges and little clothing. The people were deliberately being kept on a starvation allowance. Irvine wrote that they were going to starve to death if nothing more were done.[36]

In mid-October, Peter Hourie, an interpreter at Fort Walsh, wrote to Agent McDonald stating that he would stay there for the winter since 290 Assiniboine lodges were camped there. He said that Piapot Cree (Cree-speaking Assiniboine), some Assiniboine who had returned from Fort Qu'Appelle (not identifying bands), and some Cree from elsewhere were ensconced. He also reported that the Assiniboine with The Man Who Took the Coat had come in from Wood Mountain. Bison were reported near the international border, and the U.S. Army patrols were keeping the Indigenous groups from the north from hunting. This also contributed to the condition of those camped about Fort Walsh.[37]

The winter of 1882–83 at the fort was a bitter one, with ration distributions meagre:

> Faced with "sometimes over four thousand Indians in the immediate vicinity of Fort Walsh . . . in a very deplorable and starving condition," Norman refused to further reduce the food allowance as instructed. As it was, for every seven days he was issuing each Indian sufficient flour and meat to last just two days. In January 1883, Norman had to borrow from the NWMP stores to meet the demand for rations. By the beginning of February, supplies were running out entirely. Deep snow made it impossible to travel the 43 miles to the end of the CPR track to pick up the flour available there. Nor could supplies be obtained from Fort Benton, which was 200 kilometres south of Fort Walsh.[38]

During the final winter in Cypress Hills, the Nakoda experienced a desperate existence of starvation and minimal shelter, and they realized that there would no longer be rations distributed to them at Fort Walsh. The government officials had failed to move the Assiniboine and were now attempting to punish them for the failure of government policies. The officials effectively sentenced some of the Assiniboine to death by starvation. But it was not finished.

CHAPTER 6

THE YEAR 1883

Turmoil persisted in the Cypress Hills. On May 7, 1883, the commander of Fort Assiniboine, Montana, wrote to the commanding officer at Fort Walsh, still operational with a small detachment. The Americans had intelligence that a large camp of Cree under Little Pine, Lucky Man, and Big Bear, twenty-two miles east of Fort Walsh, was preparing to cross the line, a day's ride away, to attack the Gros Ventres and Assiniboine at Milk River. The raid was to be in revenge for the killing of some Cree in April by the American military at Wild Horse Lake. Already small raiding parties were coming across the boundary line to steal horses. The American commander asked the NWMP to look into matters and try to prevent further violence.[39] The Assiniboine at Milk River were most likely the relatives of the Assiniboine massed over the winter of 1882–83 in the Cypress Hills; there is some notation in the pay sheets of men killed in raids.

The government representatives set out once more to convince the Assiniboine and others to return to the eastern reserves. However, there was still much consternation. When Piapot originally rejected the Indian Head reserve, he was reported to have complained about the "stench that emanated from the dead bodies of unburied Indians then lying on the ground."[40] The reserves were on lands that had been places of the dead where scaffold burials were performed, and once the carrion eaters had done their work the bones would fall down awaiting the return of family members to perform the last act of reburial of the bones of their deceased relatives. In some cases, the remains belonged to no living relatives and just remained as nature took its course. Irvine referred to the conditions of the location in his report on May 18, 1883, about his interactions with Piapot:

> These bodies had, in accordance with their usual custom in that respect, been placed in small trees which having been burned down by fire, caused the bodies to drop upon the ground where they remained. He also told me that he was going with this people to some place where they would be able to catch fish sufficient to live upon. I explained to him fully that the government would not permit in the present settled state of the country, armed parties of either whites or Indians moving to different parts of the territories, such a [illegible] being contrary to law and that he had better carefully consider his movements.[41]

Not only were the authorities attempting to starve the Assiniboine People into submission and force them to comply with the move, but also when Piapot rejected the reserve Irvine tried to threaten him that, if he took his people off the reserve—a sacred burial ground of the Cree, with scattered rotting bodies—and left with weapons, he would be breaking the law and could be arrested or perhaps worse.

Being settled on a vast rise of land equivalent to a graveyard added difficulty to the second beginning of the Assiniboine in basically the same location as the year before. Chief Dan Kennedy noted in 1972 that "we left Cypress Hills, our favourite hunting territory—the land of the evergreens, chinook winds and running brooks—and moved to our reserve, the Skull Mountainettes—the land of the dead—where two epidemics of smallpox wiped out two large tribes of Crees in the forties of the last century."[42] And CTK Elder Delmar Runs mentioned in 2015 that

> a tribe was there before, a Cree tribe, and when they came here they called it the Heritage Hills. . . . All you could see was skeletons. The Cree tribe that came here was struck by a disease . . . smallpox. . . . It came and struck all the people in that Cree tribe. And this is where they put the Assiniboines, and they didn't like it. . . . When they first came here, and when they look at this land, what they seen was something like a graveyard. They said there was a lot of skeletons all over, and they didn't like that. But there was plenty here to survive on as for wild meat. It was good, so they stayed here. But they didn't like this place. . . . Dad said many were homesick. They were lonely. They wanted to go back to the other land where they came from. They were always there—happy. There was joy.

In his December 1882 report to Dewdney, McIlree noted his difficulty getting all the groups to agree to leave the Cypress Hills again and return to their new reserves. After days of discussion and negotiation, the following agreements were made:

> The Assiniboine first, though they felt it really hard to leave Cypress Hills. Then Piapot said he would go and these were really the only two bodies of Indians who had any claim to call the Cypress Hills their own. The remainder belonged to the Saskatchewan valley mostly. The Assiniboine and Piapot's band being very poor and owning no horses, it was agreed that transport should be furnished them. . . . As it was impossible to

CHAPTER 6

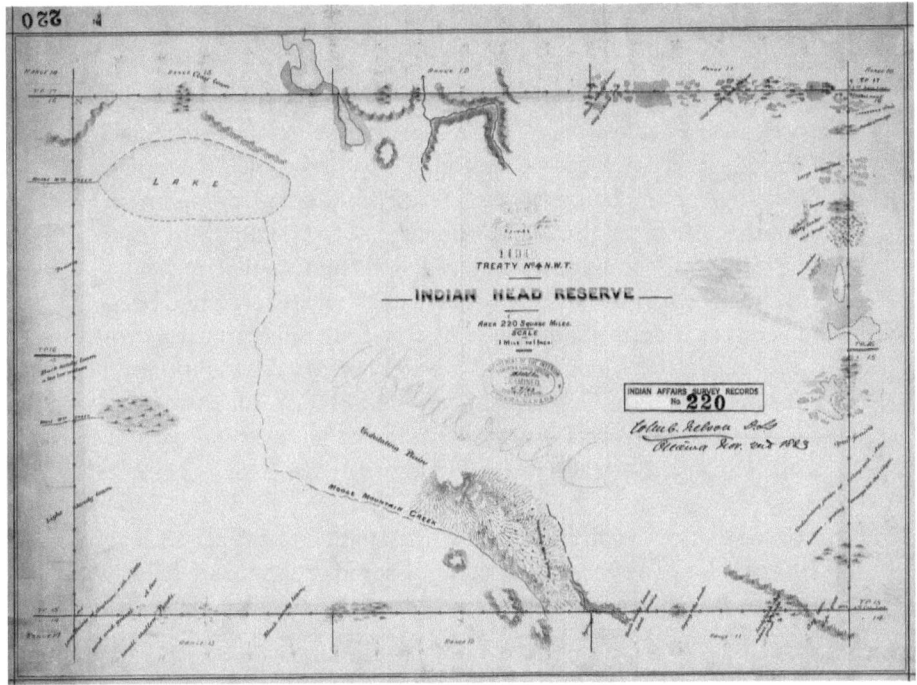

FIGURE 10: Original Indian Head Reserve Map
Treaty No. 4, NWT Indian Head Reserve. John C. Nelson, DLS, Ottawa, Nov. 2, 1883.
Source: Library and Archives Canada/Department of Indian Affairs and Northern Development fonds/Item 2197.

> [illegible] transport at that time the Assiniboine were sent to Maple Creek Farm and the Crees [Cree-speaking Assiniboine] to David Lake, where Piapot had been camped all winter. . . . On the 12th Long Lodge, head chief of the Assiniboine, got in. He after numerous interviews with Col. Irvine said he would go to Qu'Appelle and was sent out to Maple Creek Farm to the fishing ground.[43]

In his January 1883 report, Irvine outlined the agreements and meeting results as follows:

> "The Man That Took The Coat" or "Jack" was the first Assiniboine chief who consented to proceed to the reservation allotted him by the government. . . . I afterwards secured a promise from "Long Lodge," "The Poor Man," "Bear's Head" that they and their people would accept the new reservations as allotted

by the Indian Department. "Long Lodge's" reservation near Qu'Appelle, "The Poor Man," and "Bear's Head," in the vicinity of Battleford, their previous reservations having been at Maple Creek near Fort Walsh. . . . The Assiniboine chiefs "Jack" and "Long Lodge" left Maple Creek farm in charge of Mr. English, farm instructor, being accompanied by a small detachment of police and straggling Crees belonging to "Little Child" and "Sparrow Hawk's" bands. They reached Qu'Appelle on the 1st of June. I was afterwards informed that their reserve had been selected at Indian Head, about twenty-four miles southeast of Qu'Appelle. . . . "Bear's Head" and "Poor Man" (Assiniboine) left Fort Walsh on the 23rd of May for Battleford, they were accompanied by a constable of the force who issued rations while enroute. They arrived at Battleford on the 17th [of] June.[44]

Little was said initially about the fact that the first removal to the new reserves had not been successful for some groups, particularly the Assiniboine. Their attachment to the Cypress Hills was more substantial than originally anticipated.

The next removal from the Cypress Hills was facilitated by the CPR tracks that then ran from Maple Creek eastward, which theoretically enabled the bands of The Man Who Took the Coat, Long Lodge, and Piapot to be transported more efficiently. However, there was a derailment enroute to Qu'Appelle that left some Assiniboine injured.[45] The Indian commissioner reporting to Ottawa on May 25, 1883, gave a progress report about the relocation of various Indigenous groups:

> Great difficulty has been experienced in inducing the Walsh Indians to go to their various reserves, influence[s] from many sources were strongly bearing upon those who were deciding to go north to change their minds, and not go. The railway accident which happened to those who were on their way to Qu'Appelle did a great deal towards upsetting their minds and it was with great persuasion that they were induced to go further, nothing would encourage them to take the cars again, so cart[s] had to be engaged to do the carrying of those unable to walk.[46]

In 2015, CTK Elder James O'Watch recounted the devastation that his people endured during those times of uncertainty:

CHAPTER 6

> I think that was the last year they brought them back—by railcar—and the story is that they (the government) did stage a derailment, or they planned a derailment . . . of our Assiniboine people. And it did happen. Bernice talks about her grandmother. She had a broken arm. . . . And Wilma Kennedy . . . she's got stories about someone else getting injured during that derailment. One of her relatives.

Indian Agent McDonald at Fort Qu'Appelle wrote that

> the Assiniboines are located at the Indian Head reserve, under the charge of Instructor Provost. They went on their reserve last summer, but owing to the lateness of the season, only a few bushels of potatoes were planted. Long Lodge and his followers set out immediately after receiving their annuities for the Wood Mountains, and from there went south of the line, where, I believe, they now are. The Man Who Took the Coat left shortly after; he went to Fort Walsh at which place he wintered. He and eighty of his followers, and Little Mountain, one of Long Lodge's head men, came east this spring and are now on the reserve. We have managed to put thirty-seven acres under crop for them.[47]

Upon their return to Indian Head, the bands set up camps and began to cultivate root crops to keep them alive. A local doctor attending the camps reported consumption and starvation and the loss of thirty-three people over the winter. "Many of those who have died this winter have died from absolute starvation. They were ill and could not eat the bacon and flour and having nothing else died."[48] The pay sheets reveal that some had gone to Milk River to stay with family members there. Two families had moved in from Poor Man's band. There remained 46 men, 68 women, 61 boys, and 72 girls with The Man Who Took the Coat, or 247 people, but there are notes of eight children having died. Long Lodge's band had seven deaths, mostly children. There were 18 men, 21 women, and 37 children paid, totalling 76.

Elder O'Watch also noted in his Cypress Hills Group Interview that

> we all talk about this land (Cypress Hills) being ours. They took us and moved us three times. Took us over there, came back, took us over there, came back, the third time we stayed. And everything was forced on us as Assiniboine people. Everything

that was done to us was forced, we never agreed to do anything. We never agreed to give this land up, we never agreed to move.... Lots of devastation. We went through lots. We went through hell as Assiniboine People.

The 1884 pay sheets, prepared in August, reveal a dramatic loss in The Man Who Took the Coat's band, down to 231 people, with twenty-one recorded deaths of children. Long Lodge's band had 91 people, including the Chief, perhaps back for a time from the south, but he would leave again.

The documentation provided above describes one of the most repugnant periods in Canadian history as Indigenous Peoples were subjected to purposeful neglect, forced labour, genocidal rationing policies, and forced relocation to unfavourable locations. This period in the history of the Nakoda People was prefaced by two massacres: one at the Sweet Grass Hills and one known as the Cypress Hills Massacre, in which Nakoda People were murdered by American wolfers and liquor traders. These massacres, however, were minor compared with the anguish and devastation created by government rationing and forced relocation policies.

According to some information, the basis of the Nakoda livelihood, the bison, was annihilated from southwestern Canada around 1877, the year when The Man Who Took the Coat and Long Lodge took treaty. Before this time, there were still bison, which gave hope and some opportunity to the various groups who traditionally relied on the bison for their livelihood. But once they were gone, great pressures were placed on these Indigenous Peoples to survive, which created increased incentives to sign treaties in which they were promised that the queen would take care of them. People cannot survive long without eating, and it was not long before great masses of people congregated in areas where they hoped that they could find bison or other game and plants to eat or receive rations and support from agencies or posts.

The Canadian government seemed to be concerned not only about the effects of intrusions into its territory by American wolfers and liquor traders but also about the possibility of American military intervention on Canadian soil. The government was not as concerned when the bison were unable to migrate north to Canada to feed the starving Indigenous Peoples, nor was it interested in adequately feeding those who had no more game to support them. To the contrary, the Canadian government acquiesced to American threats by attempting to move all the Indigenous Peoples north of the CPR line to reduce the potential for international incidents.

CHAPTER 6

The government proceeded to starve the Indigenous Peoples out of the Cypress Hills, even those who belonged there, such as the Nakoda. The policies of starvation were deliberate rather than neglectful. Even when government officials were told that people were starving, they did very little. Instead, they continued to pursue a policy of work for rations even when there was no work to be done.

Then, when the Assiniboine refused to leave the Cypress Hills, officials cut rations further and approached Chiefs at a weak moment to coerce them into moving. The people were weak from a starvation diet, and some died during the trip—a fact not recorded except in one report explaining why the Assiniboine were reluctant to stay at the new reserve. While the Assiniboine were at the new reserve, despite other attempts to encourage them, the cost-cutting, ration-reducing bureaucrats fed them bacon and flour, which not only made them sick but also caused several deaths.

This action forced the people to flee, and desperately looking for game they moved south and west toward possible game locations. Their possessions and their physical and mental health had been ravaged by the government's policies on rations for at least two years, and they were forced to relocate. They were ill-equipped to survive another winter for which they had little time to prepare. Rations continued to be meagre when they returned to the Cypress Hills, and Dewdney told them that it was their own fault for leaving the bald prairie reserves that he had designated. More starvation and goading followed, and the Chiefs grudgingly agreed to move back to the prairie. More deaths followed, and when the next census was taken the band populations had declined significantly. According to an attending doctor, many of the deaths had been caused directly by eating bacon in their weakened condition.

These issues raise the question of the validity of the treaty itself. As a result of the slaughter of bison and other important species, the exposure to massacres, starvation, and waves of disease, the signing of treaties by the Assiniboine and other Indigenous Peoples must have involved a certain amount of desperation and even panic. Furthermore, if rations were withheld once the bison were eliminated, then signing likely involved coercion, which would have been entirely contrary to the provisions of the proclamation under which the treaties were required.

Information about the signing of Treaty 4 by the Cree in 1874 at Fort Qu'Appelle identifies the impetus as the shortages of game, particularly bison, and the treaty promises made to care for them. This also contributed to the incentive for the Assiniboine to sign the treaty. They were aware of the possible treachery of white men. Within the lifetimes of those Nakoda (Assiniboine) asked to sign Treaty 4, they had witnessed or were told of the Sioux and Cheyenne Wars in the United States, and they had experienced several waves of devastating diseases. They had directly experienced several massacres at the hands of lawless white men who were not punished for their murders of Assiniboine People. They were well aware that their way of life and very existence were threatened and would be even more so if they did not agree to submit to the onslaught of European will.

Elders Victoria, Joyce, and Gladys Prettyshield commented in 2015 that

> we were all young then. . . . Charlie Ryder, he said, "Sit down, and I want tea and some bannock, and I want to tell you." . . . He pointed at all of us, and he said, "Someday, if you want to, you go back to Cypress Hills. That's your land, you go down there and live over there." . . . That's where we signed treaties, and that's where we come from. "You go back there," he told us. . . . We were small, but I remember that, I'll never forget that. All the old people said that. "Go back there. That's your land."

CHAPTER 7

Nakóda Makóče En Piyábi Dagu Wičóni nagu T'abi Owóknága

Life and Death on the New Reserve

The final movement of Carry The Kettle First Nation ancestors from the Cypress Hills to the reserve south of Sintaluta (southeast of Indian Head), Saskatchewan, marked the beginning of the era of reserve life. The reserve lands had been surveyed, and a few buildings were erected in 1882, but upon arrival most of the people had to continue to live in teepees. Prior to the relocation in 1882 to this new reserve, some initial ground had been plowed, and a small amount of potatoes was planted.

POLICE SUPERVISION AND STARVATION AT THE NEW RESERVE

Government correspondence indicates that Commissioner Acheson Irvine reported that police were present and conspicuous in the areas of the new reserves and among the new settlers taking up lands in the vicinity of the reserves. The government was conscious of preventing any difficulties from arising.[1] Indian Agent Alan McDonald reported that there were eighty-six people in the band of The Man Who Took the Coat, and the headman of Long Lodge, Little Mountain, was with him. By the end of the summer in 1883, the agent's office was relocated from Fort Qu'Appelle to Indian Head. McDonald noted in his report that, "since spring, Indians have been coming from the vicinity of Cypress Hills and going on their reserve."[2] Piapot and his band

Sioux and Cree at Carry The Kettle Reserve, Saskatchewan, 1912
Courtesy of Glenbow Archives, NA-4135-2.

were among the returnees. Indian Commissioner Edgar Dewdney believed that he had accomplished the relocation of the Assiniboine by October.³

The relocation might have been accomplished, but the treatment of the new residents on these Indian Head reserves was characterized by "neglect, illness, and starvation."⁴ A physician was sent to the reserves in February 1884 to visit the encampments of Piapot, Long Lodge, and The Man Who Took the Coat, and he reported that scurvy was running rampant, observing that this condition "persisted owing to the absence of fresh food and vegetables from their diet."⁵ In his assessment, issuing ammunition for hunting was futile because there were few ducks and prairie chickens in the vicinity.⁶ In 1884, in present-day southeast Saskatchewan near the town of Grenfell, thirty armed warriors from the Sakimay Band, led by Chief Yellow Calf, occupied a federal warehouse in an attempt to secure food. Violence was averted after extensive negotiation by Chief Louis O'Soup. In the Battlefords region, Chiefs petitioned federal officials about the decrease in food rations and the

CHAPTER 7

failure of the government to provide the promised medicine, agricultural tools, and other items.[7]

Famine in the spring and summer of 1884 at the Indian Head Assiniboine reserves was not taken seriously by Assistant Commissioner Hayter Reed. In his correspondence with Prime Minister John A. Macdonald, Reed blamed the Assiniboine for their own misfortune: "No doubt the death rate is large but it must be borne in mind that the first seeds of their complaints were sown during the sojourning of the Indians in the Fort Walsh District, owing to immoral habits, and were it not for this fact the use of [unreadable] would not have such a hurtful effect."[8] These statements are clearly racist and an attempt to disguise deliberate genocidal actions. The comment about "immoral habits" confirms that Reed ignored their cultural rights. He admitted that their death rate was high and then blamed it on their reliance on wild food. He continued this folly: "When the doctor speaks of starvation the same does not mean that the quantities issued were not sufficient but that the Indians were unable to eat the bacon."[9]

In his reports and correspondence, Reed attempted to deflect his responsibility for continuing practices of starvation, claiming that the inability to survive on bacon was in fact the fault of the Assiniboine People. This also reflected the racist mentality of John A. Macdonald, who did not respond indignantly to such foolish excuses. Apparently, Reed did send "a small quantity of meat and potatoes" to the reserves after these reports were sent.[10]

On Christmas Eve 1884, Long Lodge died apparently while south of the border visiting relatives. After a spring and summer of scurvy and malnutrition/starvation, the elderly Chief was no longer able to continue living. It appears that the government's grip finally tightened around the neck of this band. The previous hardships that they endured in the Cypress Hills were spectacular, and the forced movement out of that diverse ecosystem caused many Assiniboine to die of starvation and exposure. Now they had come to a bald prairie setting, and the starvation continued.

But the government was unrelenting. As soon as Dewdney got word of the Chief's death, he recommended an amalgamation of Long Lodge's band with that of The Man Who Took the Coat. Early in March, Agent McDonald was able to convince Long Lodge's band members to accept this proposal, and later in March the department approved of this decision. Dewdney lost no time in communicating with Surveyor Nelson to order a new survey of the reserves at Indian Head to reflect the population of the new amalgamated band. This was done on June 5, 1885. By this time, Piapot had abandoned the reserve previously surveyed for him at Indian Head, preferring a reserve in the Qu'Appelle Valley. This left a single reserve in the Assiniboine Agency.[11] Nelson reported his discussion of the boundaries with The Man Who Took the Coat and Indian Agent McDonald:

> I left Indian Head, accompanied by Colonel McDonald, Indian Agent, to consult with Chief Jack in regard to the boundaries of his reserve. He said since talking with Colonel McDonald in the spring, he had carefully examined the block of land set apart for the Assiniboine Indians, and would like to obtain that part of it which had been abandoned by Piepot [sic], for he found both land and timber good, and preferred it to any farther west. Seeing no objection to this, it was decided between us that the tract which he desired should form part of the reserve for his band and that of the late Chief Long Lodge. The reserve was finally laid out nine miles from east to west by eight from north to south.[12]

CHAPTER 7

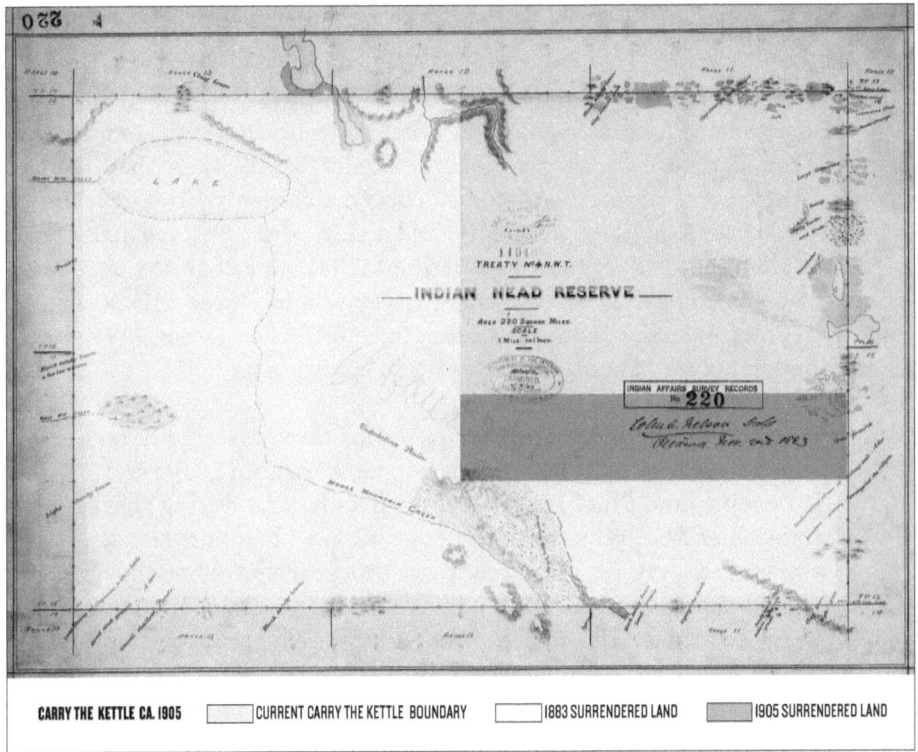

FIGURE 11: Surrendered Lands and Band Amalgamation
Treaty No. 4, NWT Indian Head Reserve. John C. Nelson, DLS, Ottawa, Nov. 2, 1883.
Source: Library and Archives Canada/Department of Indian Affairs and Northern Development fonds/Item 2197. Adapted by Duncan Campbell.

The resulting reserve that would become IR 76 was in area 73.2 square miles, approximately 46,854 acres, and this land was declared to be the Assiniboine reserve on May 17, 1889, by Order in Council 1151-1889.[13] Following the terms of Treaty 4, the amount of land to be set aside per person was 128 acres. The amount in the new survey represented land for 366 individuals. The Annual Report as of December 31, 1884, indicated a total population for the new band of 339 persons, and this consisted of the population of the bands of The Man Who Took the Coat with 251 and Long Lodge with 88.[14] This is in contrast to the estimate of the population of the two bands in 1882 by the farm instructor of over 500 people with almost 75 additional "stragglers."[15] It appears that the population had declined by nearly half (according to these estimates) since the signing of the treaty in the Cypress Hills. This decline was worse than any massacre and comparable to a smallpox epidemic.

It was not, however, a disease but government policy. The formal withdrawal of IR 76 from the operation of the *Dominion Lands Act* was instituted on June 12, 1893, by Order in Council 1694-1893.[16]

Elder Delmar Runs told us in 2015 that these reserve lands—forced on them—had to be shared by many people: "Well, when they got here, they never chose this reserve. This was chosen by the government.... They said there was a lot of elk and the deer. But, see, half of this is Mountain Lodge, and the other half is Take the Coat. It was 200 or 300 some square miles. And this reserve was for three chiefs: the Piapot Chief, Take the Coat, and Mountain Lodge." Elder James O'Watch clarified how Carry The Kettle First Nation got its name:

> When they first got over here, there was three reserves here. There was Carry the Coat and his people, Mountain Lodge and his people, and Chief Piapot and his people. And during that time Chief Man Who Took the Coat was at Mountain Lodge and passed away. So, when the treaty process came along, they amalgamated these people, and they went under Mountain Lodge from Man Who Took the Coat. During that period of time, when they were amalgamated and taking treaty, he passed away, and Carry The Kettle, his brother, was next in line to be Chief. So Carry The Kettle became chief, and our band name stayed that under treaty.

Elder Kevin Haywahe confirmed that in 1906 The Man Who Took the Coat died and that his brother Carry The Kettle assumed the role of Chief.[17]

The role of a Chief was described by Elders:

> They had their Chiefs, but like I said ... the Chiefs can't look after everyone. They kind of had little groups. You know, my grandfather Eashappie, if there is a family that cannot hunt, or can't feed themselves, he will go hunting. Like he's the one that will stand up and gather all the young men, and they will go hunting. He was the head hunting party's leader. So then he'll bring back all the meat, and he'll distribute it and make sure that this family that cannot hunt anymore does have enough food. He does things like that.... That's what she means when she says a leader. Not as a Chief. He doesn't do political decisions, but he does lead the people—his people. (CTK Elder Terri Prettyshield, 2015)

CHAPTER 7

Chief Carry The Kettle and His Wife
Photo provided by Carry The Kettle Nakoda First Nation.

They made me sit alongside of Little Chief and he told me that there were some things that he wanted to tell me. He said that he was a leader of the tribe and always remembered things and did things for his people, and not only him, but there were some other of his friends, meaning the old people at the time, they were the leaders at that time. (Elder Many Coos, September 19, 1929)

You know that massacre that took place out there in the Cypress Hills, that's when there were group bosses. My great-grandfather, he brought his group out here along with his friend. They both had a group like that. You know, they look after them. It's just like, you don't call them Chiefs, but they're leaders. So they brought them out here. . . . Leaders—they called them watchmen. They watched them. They had groups, there's two Assiniboine. Like my great-grandfather and his friend, and I think his name is Little Chief, anyway they both look after two groups of Assiniboine. They belong together, but you know they cut it in half, so it wasn't that many to look after. (Elder Nancy Eashappie, 2015)

FARMING

Reserve life introduced government-run farming to Carry The Kettle People. Elder Victoria Prettyshield noted in 2015 that "they didn't have no, how do you say, tractors, all they had was horses, I guess." Elder Leroy Hassler remembered his grandfather breaking up the land to farm it: "My grandfather was farming a farm right back. He was the one that broke land all back at Vincent. . . . Because they tried to make them farmers at that time. . . . I think there was a community type of farming at that time with the Indian Agent." "At that time," Elder Delmar Runs mentioned, "when they moved here, it was not like Cypress Hills. The queen, the federal crown, promised the Indians everything if they moved here. They will even give them oxes [and] horses to cultivate the land. And at that time they never got any."

DIA crop reports for 1884 and 1885 were mixed, but mostly failure was noted, attributed either to early frost or to drought. Both bands of The Man Who Took the Coat and Long Lodge had experienced many deaths during this period. By 1885, Piapot had given up the Indian Head reserve in exchange for the one in the Qu'Appelle Valley. But W.S. Grant, writing as the acting Indian Agent of the Assiniboine reserve, stated on July 28, 1886, that

> in every respect the Indians here are taking greater interest in their work and becoming more skillful in the use of implements and tools, which is to be appreciated for it is only by good cultivation, ploughing deep and turning over all the soil that good crops need be expected. The area of land now under cultivation has been greatly increased since last year; many Indians who had been somewhat indolent in matters of an agricultural nature, having considered the subject well, at last determined to make a home and farm for themselves.[18]

In the three decades from 1881 to 1911, there was generally increasing prosperity for portions of the reserve population, with intermittent years when degrees of crop failure occurred and when surpluses were eventually sold or bartered under the supervision of respective Indian Agents W.S. Grant (1882-96), Thomas W. Aspdin (1897-1906), and reappointed W.S. Grant (1906-11).

In these years, the agency calculated the worth of accumulated farm implements; houses and outbuildings; other equipment and tools; produce, seed, and even hay; and livestock of all kinds, and it recorded all

CHAPTER 7

Native American Woman Using a Bison Scapula Hoe, c. 1914
Courtesy of State Historical Society of North Dakota, photographer unknown, photo number 00086-0281.

other expenditures. However, there was some confusion about which property was owned directly by the Assiniboine People and which property was under the proprietorship of the agent on behalf of the band. Agency inventories show who was given care of what and which items were returned and retired. The implication was that the agent's oversight of goods, materials, and implements had been part of the treaty. However, many of the implements were purchased by the band literally from the fruits of their labour.

Such record keeping indicated the disposition of the department to foster a work environment that led to the acquisition of property by the band. A different relationship with their environment was promoted by the agent. The commodification of the natural resources of the reserve—such as wood, hay, and other plants, as well as the implements supplied as treaty obligations—became amalgamated with the products flowing from the labour of the Assiniboine People.[19] Everything was treated as something to buy or sell, as a commodity. In addition, it was confusing to the people what was personal property, what was tribal property, and what was under the complete control of the agent. Agency policies of rewarding certain individuals for work and withholding rations from those who did not work, and making everything into a commodity, were foreign to their principle of tribal sharing and traditional culture.

The Department of Indian Affairs was interested in fostering economic prosperity (which it measured in marketable possessions) because it pursued a policy by which affluent bands were made to bear greater proportions of their administrative costs. This included seizing opportunities to create trust funds for bands whenever possible from the proceeds of sales of assets. With such funds, the department allowed more latitude to its agents to authorize more expenses to be paid from the band's resources.[20]

The department was also set on implementing its program of protection, civilization, and assimilation.[21] An example of this discourse, writing to Minister of the Interior Clifford Sifton in 1890, Deputy Superintendent General of Indian Affairs Frank Pedley stated that a basic tenet of the department's policy was "to bring the Indians as near the status of the white man as can be and make them a moral, industrious and self-supporting class."[22] And Indian Agent Grant said that, though "the usual sun dance was held in June, the interest taken in it is quickly dying out and they express themselves to the effect that 'it is their last.'"[23] He was unaware that one of the primary objectives of this Assiniboine religious ceremony, the Medicine Lodge or Sundance, was to bring rain, which would be a sign that the dancers' prayers had been heard.

PEASANT FARMING POLICY

The peasant farming policy was enforced by Assistant Commissioner Hayter Reed despite the complaints expressed by his agents. In an exchange between Grant and Reed dated October 1, 1896, about the department's resistance to mechanization for Indigenous agriculture, Grant protested that "the seasons in this country are too short to harvest any quantity of grain, without much waste, with only old-fashioned, and hand-implements to do the work with."[24] He cited the problems of getting anywhere near the full yield from 240 acres of grain on the reserve. Because of usually hot, windy, and dry weather during harvest, the grain often had to be cut as soon as it was ready to avoid losses. Grant stated that, judging from the amount of grain lost at his agency in the current harvest, it was enough that taken over two years it would pay for a binder at current prices. He went on to say that the loss occurred not only when the grain was too ripe but also from gathering and binding it by hand. Again, using the current harvest as an example, he noted that the prairie straw was often dry and brittle, not prone to being tied without breaking, which also led to considerable loss. Grant therefore emphasized the reactions of the Assiniboine to binding by hand, mentioning the case of Black Mane, who had fifteen acres of very good wheat: "When told he would have to cut and bind it by hand, [he] gave up his oxen, and left his wheat and reserve. I gave his wheat to his brother. I have been told that he is now at Wolf Point, in the States. This will show how hard it is to compel an Indian to harvest his grain by hand."[25]

RESERVE FARMING POLICIES

Within the Saskatchewan treaties, there were written clauses as well as oral promises assuring First Nations the necessary government assistance to establish an alternative "farming" economy following the disappearance of the bison. Government officials, however, were reluctant to distribute what had been promised in the treaties, and the few implements given to First Nations were inadequate at best. Ten families, for example, were to share one Ontario-made plow unsuited to prairie conditions; seed grain in the earliest years arrived damaged and too late for sowing; carts and oxen provided were the cheapest that could be found and altogether unfit for use; and wild Montana cattle were sent to many reserves.

The first Indigenous farmers of the 1870s to early 1880s laboured under many disadvantages, including the permit system, which stated that they could not sell any of their grain or other produce without permission, and after 1885 the pass system, which controlled and confined their every movement off reserve. Still, non-Indigenous settlers had the misconception that reserve farmers were lavishly provided with livestock, equipment, and rations and did not have to worry about the prices at which they sold their products. The solemn promises of assistance made to them in the treaties, in exchange for sharing the land that permitted the settlers to acquire their farms, were regarded as charity.

As a result, the federal government imposed the peasant farming policy whereby Indigenous farmers were to reduce their acreages dramatically and to grow only root crops—no wheat. They were also permitted to use only the most rudimentary implements and to sow their seed by hand, cut their crops with scythes, bind them by hand, and grind their grain with hand mills. Any items that they required were to be manufactured themselves at home. Indigenous farmers were profoundly discouraged by the new rules, and many gave up farming altogether.

Beginning in 1889, reserves were to be divided approximately in two: one half would be surveyed into forty-acre lots on which individual families were to farm; the other half was to be held in common as hay and timber land. Reed believed that an Indigenous farmer was to become self-sufficient but not to compete in the marketplace. This was but another means of restricting how successful Indigenous farmers could be and ultimately contributed to the failure of agriculture on reserves. Although this policy was shelved after 1896, Indigenous farmers gained little ground in the early twentieth century since large tracts of arable land were forcibly "surrendered" to non-Indigenous interests.[26]

Elder James O'Watch noted in 2015 that, as

> the history to our 1905 claim talks about, we had a bunch of horses, and people had cattle, so we needed money to make a community pasture.... They needed twine, fence posts, fences, all those, and when they went to the Indian Agent, rather than exercising their treaty, he told them, "You guys don't have no money, so why don't you sell some land or lease it out?" So they talked about it. They didn't want to sell their land but ended up selling some land in 1905 to purchase a threshing machine, fence posts, wire and nails, and twine, and stuff they needed to make a community pasture with.

COMMON OR INDIVIDUAL OWNERSHIP

Prior to 1905, the vast majority of expenses for threshing and the purchase of all implements were handled by the Indian Agents of the department from the appropriated expenditures and based on approved expenses for each fiscal year, except when surpluses were generated. There was little information about the specific procedures for handling revenues derived from the sales of surpluses. Sales were made from the surpluses of individual Indigenous farmers once seed was set aside and flour milled for the coming year. Presumably, wheat and other grains were cut and placed in stooks in anticipation of threshing. Lacking the means for threshing, the agent arranged to have the crops custom-threshed. The cost of threshing was then broken down pro rata and put against the individual cash accounts. The agent presumably kept track of the amounts of the crops of individual farmers and their value, as well as the value of implements and tools used by these individuals. These cash books and collateral inventories were the records of this range of activity, but unfortunately none of them has survived from the Assiniboine Agency.

Therefore, an examination of the record of life at the Indian Head reserve post-1882 reveals patterns of individual and group ownership. Throughout the annual reports is confusion about property issued to Indigenous individuals and property accumulated by Indigenous individuals on reserve. Individuals gradually came to possess many material goods by developed habit and acquired use, but the transference of property directly to individuals was accomplished only gradually over time. This did not occur when surpluses in departmental property were redistributed to other agencies, which also happened periodically.

INDEPENDENT WAGES AND COTTAGE INDUSTRY
Emphasis on the generation of surpluses overlapped with the increasing demand for men from the reserve to work on neighbouring non-Indigenous farms on a seasonal basis and for women to engage in a range of activities—from tanning hides to knitting socks, mitts, and comforters and selling them—to generate additional income. Reed promoted small-scale cottage industry during his tenure, including raising sheep in a number of western reserves to foster garment production both for reserve consumption and surplus generation convertible into cash.[27]

EXPENDITURES BY THE BAND OR THE GOVERNMENT?
Indian Agent W.S. Grant had to contemplate how the Assiniboine People were to become self-sufficient agriculturalists, horticulturalists, and stock raisers. Moreover, the government—in its role of supplying the treaty-promised implements, stock, and seed—also administered the issue, maintenance, and disposition of these resources for the benefit of the band. The agency administration undertook these services to safeguard the rights of the band as a whole while fostering individualism and initiative among the heads of families. Individualism was encouraged for some practices, whereas group rights were reinforced for others. Agent Grant certainly saw the dilemma of these actions but understood the general purposes of the policy.

OWÓKNAGE / CARRY THE KETTLE NAKODA FIRST NATION

Chief Carry The Kettle, Farm Instructor Hassan, Agent W.S. Grant, Bob Grant, and Band Councillor Ryder. *Photo provided by Carry The Kettle Nakoda First Nation.*

The growing season of 1890 was dry, and the crops taken were light. Grant said that the Indigenous farmers did not complain, and after paying the thresher they stored their seed with him:

> Some had very little left after this, but at the same time it shows that they are doing all they are able to support themselves by farming. These Indians were proud last spring that they did not have to ask the Department for seed of any kind.
>
> The most industrious went out to work last fall for white farmers, pulling flax, etc.; this has been a great help to those who had light crops. The money earned in this way was spent in purchasing blankets, lumber for flooring, and stoves.[28]

Problems with harvesting were attributed to a combination of cold weather and hand-binding of the wheat; however, in an annotation offered by Assistant Commissioner Reed on the original submission by Grant, the difficulties were attributed to the agent's "lack of sympathy with the department's policy regarding keeping labour saving implements as much as possible out of the hands of Indians," suggesting that—if Grant had proceeded with the harvest instead of waiting "to get machinery to cut the grain"—it would have been "finished without loss."[29] However, from the 1889–90 fiscal year to the 1890–91 fiscal year, Grant was able to reduce the rations by 30,000 pounds of solid food, mostly attributed to the increased productivity of the agency's agricultural initiatives.

Inspector T.P. Wadsworth noted that, for the past four months, thirty heads of families augmented their supply of flour by bartering deadfall firewood and day labour for a return of ninety-five sacks. Once their own wheat was threshed, they would have their own flour, and "with outside earnings . . . they were to be kept in meat." The inspector wrote further that

> the above reasoning relates to the farmers, and those who are able to do a day's work, but in this agency there are a number who are unable to work, and have nothing, others have a crop consisting of a few potatoes or turnips, these are the ones who require nourishing food, and i[t] cannot be expected that the farmers and workers . . . will share and share alike with them; for these poor people should be supplied in such quantities, to make them comfortable, that they may have a little daily [food], also a little tea and tobacco.[30]

Wadsworth indicated a few years later that

> the individual earning account does not run into high figures here, as the grain is generally gristed, and therefore is not included in the account; outside of this the total sum earned in the eleven months prior to my inspection was seven hundred and thirty dollars; from sale of firewood, tanning hides, working for settlers, knitting mitts for the Qu'Appelle Industrial School, sale of berries, sale of wheat, prizes gained at industrial fairs. The Indians spent this money purchasing lumber to floor their houses, stoves, food and clothing.
>
> They have been liberally supplied with food by the department, also some clothing. In consequence they have lived in great comfort and happiness.
>
> There is a good market for firewood in the adjacent towns, at the fair price of three dollars a cord, or for long wood, two dollars and fifty cents a load. They can purchase strong baker's flour for one dollar and fifty cents a sack in the same towns.
>
> There is little, if any, market for hay. They can make some money tanning hides, and in a day's work for the neighbouring farmers.[31]

Wadsworth ended by commenting on the keen competition offered by the farmers off the reserve in the farm and garden produce, livestock, and domestic manufactures categories at the Regina and Indian

Head industrial fairs, which often included prizes for all kinds of grain, roots and vegetables, fork handles, ox collars, bread, butter, knitted mitts, socks, gloves, and comforters.

In his first annual report, Indian Agent Thomas W. Aspdin described the natural resources of firewood and hay: "The Indians trade a good deal of wood at the mill at Wolseley for flour." Under the heading "Occupation," he wrote that

> the Indians cut and sell wood (dry) and hay. They have also dug and sold some seneca-root, but the low price of this article has somewhat discouraged them. Some of the young men work for the settlers haying, harvesting and threshing. The women also tan hides for white people. These Indians raise a considerable quantity of wheat and roots. They keep enough wheat for seed and for flour and sell the surplus to buy clothing and other necessaries for their families.[32]

Not satisfied with the condition of houses on the reserve, even though Agent Grant had indicated ongoing attention to infrastructure, Agent Aspdin reported that he "persuaded many of them to build new ones." He encouraged the "more ambitious" to put good floors and shingled roofs as additions by "using the money which they receive from the sale of beef cattle and hay for this purpose." He also promoted "all new fencing around their fields this year," which he reported exceeded twelve miles in length. Improvements were also directed to the agency buildings, and a new fence was constructed around the agency garden to replace the dilapidated one: "The fencing around the agency fields and pasture is very rotten and requires renewing."[33] Aspdin noted the department's purchase of a new well auger to enable the digging of new wells to expand the water supply for both stock and human consumption.[34] Discussing farm implements as property, Aspdin stressed that most were put away in sheds when not in use:

> Some of the Indians own mowers and rakes of their own which they have purchased out of money received for sale of beef and hay. I am getting some more ready to do this, as our haying season is short owing to the harvest coming and it is discouraging for an Indian who wishes to get a lot of hay up to have to wait till five or six others get through with the mower.[35]

In what was undoubtedly a controversial action, Aspdin assessed the stock operations and implemented a series of changes that the reserve residents were expected to accept, but nothing was on the record about his authority to institute these changes, especially whether or not his actions were unilateral, nor was there any direct response or reaction by the stock raisers among the reserve residents. The re-established total dependence on the agency was the result of Aspdin reasserting his control.

He was married to a Lakota Sioux woman, and his daughters were much influenced by their mother both linguistically and culturally. Yet they were educated in residential schools, and Aspdin instilled in them the belief that Indigenous Peoples were compelled to adapt to progress through acculturation. Yet he also viewed Indigenous cultures as sets of knowledge of which he was privileged to have some understanding by virtue of his marriage and experience with the NWMP. However, in his position as Indian Agent, he had become what he thought a catalyst for change in the Assiniboine Agency, and he represented a new regime under a new government and a new minister of the interior.

Aspdin also encouraged the purchase of additional farm implements: "Several of the Indians have purchased new mowers, horse-rakes, bob-sleighs and cooking-stoves, paying for them out of the money they got for beef and wheat that they had raised."[36] Closing his 1899 report, Aspdin was full of self-satisfaction that he was firmly in control: "The past year has been one of contentment and progress among these Indians, and their conduct has been excellent. I beg to thank the department for the new implements and wagons furnished, which have been a great help to us. Daniel Kennedy, an ex-pupil of the Fort Qu'Appelle Industrial School, assists me. I find he performs his various duties in a very satisfactory manner."

CHAPTER 8

Makóče ne Wičákibi

Loss of Lands

During the last days of January 1901, MP James M. Douglas forwarded a letter that he had received from a "Mr. De Tremaudan" of the Montmartre Colony to James A. Smart, the deputy minister of the interior, requesting information about a possible land surrender and particularly seeking the timber resources of the southern end of the reserve.[1] The issue of possible trespassing was investigated, including the allegation that, if the Assiniboine People were not to surrender the lands in question, unnamed settlers were likely to become trespassers.

Secretary J.D. McLean, writing on behalf of the Department of Indian Affairs, asked Indian Agent Thomas W. Aspdin about a proposal that a portion of the reserve "south of Township 16 in Ranges 11 and 12 be detached from the reserve and thrown open to colonization."[2] McLean's formulation of De Tremaudan's inquiry became far more specific:

> It is stated that the land ... is mostly prairie and that no Indians have so far settled thereon, and that hay is spoiled annually for the reason that no one is permitted to cut it unless by payment of 50 cents per ton, which the settlers can ill afford to pay; and that the wood on the east part of the upper part of Lot 15, Range 11, would be of a great help to the settlers for timber and wood, which is more or less spoiled by prairie fires every 2 or three years, also that the Indians never come there for wood.[3]

McLean asked Aspdin to consider whether or not the resources of this land (hay and wood) were "of abundant quantity . . . on the reserve to supply the Indians . . . for all future time," and he wanted to know whether Aspdin thought that such a surrender was advisable and whether the Assiniboine People would be willing to sell "either the timber applied for, or any part of their reserve."[4] McLean closed with the statement that "the department is not at all desirous to urge the Indians to sell either, and it would be well to get quietly the opinions of the chief and the more intelligent members of the band on the subject before replying to this communication."[5] On February 25, Aspdin replied in a four-page handwritten letter that he had met with the Chief and headmen and that "many of the Indians" had listened to "the proposal for their consideration as to selling part of the reserve." He reported that

> the matter was discussed on the whole most intelligently and the unanimous opinion expressed was that not one acre should be sold, and they wished me to convey to the department their resolution in respectful terms and ask for the protection of the government against the white settlers. I assured them that the government was not urging them to sell and if they were unwilling to do so their rights would be rigidly respected. They seemed to be pleased and satisfied at this. The Indians claimed—and I think the point is well taken—that on this point even if all the reserve wood will be made use of. Yet looking at the future, etc. Young men who are growing up and more ambitious than the old men buffalo hunters and that ten times the hay are out for sale or fed to cattle as compared to one ten years ago. There are also twice the number of mowers on the reserve all bought with the Indians money (this of course is excepting purely agency property). This will show that there is a desire to make more use of the natural products of the reserve. Some of the younger Indians are also wanting to buy more mowers.
>
> With regard to the statement of Mr. Tremaudan that there is a part of the reserve where the Indians never go for wood. I think he is meaning a part where there is a quantity of young growing poplar. As I do not allow the Indians to cut this kind of wood this accounts for their not going there.
>
> As to his statement that the settlers have been going for wood on the reserve for many years, I know nothing about it.

CHAPTER 8

I have him in charge there since the summer of 1897 and we keep a look out for trespassers. It is possible some wood may have been clandestinely taken off but not to any great amount I should imagine.

I would draw your attention also to the statement that quantities of hay are not cut but allowed to spoil. Even this will depend upon the kind of year. In each season for instance there is plenty of hay all around, and it sometimes happens that hay may not be cut on the reserve as well as other places.

About the settlers being too poor to pay the fees 50 cents per ton. Last summer for about three days near the 25th of July, I was practically being besieged [corner of page missing] by applicants for permits to cut hay and ready to pay the money for the fees. I had to turn the majority away for fear of trouble with the Indians who had not then begun to cut. The difficulty is not financial but the settlers wish to rush on the reserve and get their haying done before the harvest comes on and the Indians do not like this because some settlers go and cut where they (the Indians) intend to make hay. I tried to regulate the matter by getting the Indians to mark the sloughs, but some settlers are not honourable and in two instances, deliberately went and cut where the Indians had marked.

Regarding the wood being destroyed by fire I may say most of the wood grown on the reserve is small and although fires may occur in the future as in the past, the changes of fire are greatly lessened by increased settlement, graded roads, etc. which will give this young timber a chance to grow. At any rate, it is time enough to think about selling wood after it is [word not legible].

Regarding Mr. Tremaudan's statement about the southern part of the reserve and no Indians living there I may say the Indians follow the ideas of the white people in this respect and where there are nice bluffs of wood they built their houses in preference to going on the bleak prairie. It does not necessarily follow that the land in question is not used as it serves for a haying ground and part is also the summer run for the cattle herd. As the cattle on this reserve are now on a good basis and the young men here taken hold of them and as they are increasing and may in a short time increase to four or five hundred head it will be seen how necessary this part of the reserve is for a summer run, and it would in my opinion be suicidal to the cattle industry to part with any of this land as they will not stop in the [word not legible] in the summer.

There are several other important points which I might state again interfering with the area of the reserve but will merely conclude by saying that I do not think there is any more wood or hay than is or will be wanted for the Indians' own use and I am strongly of opinion that it is not advisable to accede to the request of Mr. Tremaudan with regard to cutting off any part of the reserve.[6]

The sentiments of Aspdin's letter were confirmed in a communication on April 23, 1901, by George L. Chitty, the timber inspector, to the department: "The proposal was laid before the Indians and expressed the unanimous opinion that not one acre should be sold, and they asked the protection of the government against the white settlers."[7] Chitty noted that Aspdin reported on the favourable progress of the Assiniboine on the reserve and asserted that the statements made on behalf of the settlers were incorrect. Referring to Aspdin, Chitty related that "he also states, as his opinion, that there is not any more wood or hay on the reserve than is, or will be, wanted for the Indians, and that it is not advisable to accede to the request of Mr. Tremaudan with regard to cutting off any part of the reserve."[8]

James A. Smart, the deputy superintendent general, in his annual report for 1901, noted in passing the stress caused by drought and crop failures in most parts of the North-West Territories, with the exceptions being File Hills and the Prince Albert and Battlefords districts.[9]

Indian Commissioner David Laird, in his annual report for 1902, made several references to the Assiniboine Agency. He noted that the mixed farming mode of economic subsistence had been so successful that the agency was one of four in Manitoba and the North-West Territories able to supply their own flour and vegetables and meet nearly all of their beef requirements.[10] Laird quoted from Aspdin's September report:

> The Indians made energetic efforts to get the grain cut before the frost came. Their two binders were cutting many times both by day and by night, as there was a good moon to work by; and as one Indian's ponies got tired working in the binder, another Indian would hitch and go on with the work. The same agent also reports that his Indians bought with the proceeds of their industries last year articles to the value of over $1,310,

CHAPTER 8

among which were four new wagons, five binders, one seed-drill, fifteen factory bedsteads, and four cooking stoves.[11]

Laird also noted that the Assiniboine Agency had "not neglected preparing for 225 new acres of broken land [that] had been ploughed at an estimated breaking cost of $3 per acre and that Indians at the Assiniboine Agency and the other singled out by him have added a considerable value to their improvements."[12]

Aspdin, in his annual report for the fiscal year ending June 30, 1904, mentioned that twenty families were engaged in farming and stock raising, and others worked for settlers, and sold firewood, fence pickets, and hay. Women were reported contributing by knitting, tanning hides, and gathering seneca root. However, Aspdin also pointed out various stresses on the resources of the reserve and the limits on his appropriated resources. The houses were shingled and had board floors, and the stables were the best that could be made with available resources since no large logs were available. He described with pride the increase of the reserve cattle herd, and it was important to him that the beef requirements for the band were being met from the herd. In his discussion of implements, Aspdin became explicit about property holding:

> The Indians take good care of their tools and implements, and are constantly adding to their number, as their means permit. The following is a list of the principal implements, etc., purchased by the Indians out of their earnings during the year: two binders, seven mowers, one seeder, two heavy wagons, one democrat-wagon, two thousand five hundred pounds of wire for fencing, one force-pump and one hundred feet of piping, also a numerous lot of useful articles such as axes, shovels, spades, hay forks, hay knives and household furniture, etc.[13]

As the scale of agricultural cropping increased, other issues of capacity had to be addressed, especially threshing. In his general remarks, Aspdin indicated that

> the prospects for a splendid crop are at present very bright indeed, and should no accidents happen, it will be by far the largest ever gathered in the history of the reserve. This combined with the fact that we have now (through the kindness of the department) a threshing outfit of our own, will be a great encouragement for further efforts. In the past the threshing

was very discouraging, as we had to wait 'til everyone else was done.[14]

Deputy Superintendent General Frank Pedley, in his published annual report for the department in 1903, indicated a series of patterns. Aware of the "tide of settlement which seems on the eve of overflowing the prairie provinces," close contact with settlement, in his opinion, brought many Indigenous Peoples "face to face with the necessity for making a radical change in their mode of life."[15] Pedley mentioned that climatic conditions in the North-West Territories had resulted in a very uneven return and for some reserves "disappointment at harvest-time," though the Assiniboine Agency was specifically cited. He declared that the wages earned and various minor industries in which Indigenous Peoples were engaged "contribute very materially to the maintenance of the Indian population," and he pointed to how critical Indigenous wage labour had become in certain regions of the country. Under the subject of lands, Pedley indicated that three western land surrenders had been made and noted the amounts of money resulting from the sales of portions of the reserves.[16]

THE CREATION OF DEBT

Indian Agent Aspdin's annual report for 1904 contained another set of comments in the fixed categories for such reports. "The natural resources were hay, wood, and some seneca-root. The Indians sell quantities of each to the settlers." The number of families engaged in farming and stock raising fell to fifteen from the number reported in the previous year, whereas others "work for wages among the settlers, whilst some engage in selling wood, fence pickets, etc., and also in tanning hides and other sundry work of all kinds." Indigenous-owned implements (including mowers, binders, and seeders), he stressed, were "purchased with their own money."[17]

Although parts of the report were more matter of fact, several segments revealed a tone of frustration and suggested some conflicts between his administrative style and the degrees of compliance by band members to his authority. For example, in his report on the stock-raising operations, besides saying that the cattle were doing very well, Aspdin had to admit some losses the previous winter "owing to the cattle being taken up thin in the fall, caused by the close manner in which they had to be herded in the day time and corralled at

CHAPTER 8

Carry The Kettle Farmers
Photo provided by Carry The Kettle Nakoda First Nation.

night to keep them out of the crops."[18] He reported that it had been a long and severe winter in which a number of neighbouring settlers had much heavier losses to their herds; however, he did not report the precise loss to the reserve herd. Rather, Aspdin reported the situation in these terms:

> The herding is now a thing of the past, as, owing to the department's having kindly loaned the money, a pasture about three miles and a quarter square has been fenced in by the Indians and the cattle roam practically at will on the best of feed, night and day. I may say that the Indians have already made a substantial repayment of the money advanced. It is difficult to get many of the Indians to take hold of stock from the fact that

there is an increasing cash market for hay, which they prefer selling to feeding to stock.[19]

The numerous fencing replacements and expansions described over succeeding years mostly appear to have been paid for from the appropriated funds for the agency, and the new pasture reported in this annual report was promoted as an infrastructural improvement. The precise authority for the loan or credit arrangement was unexplained, and there was no record of how the loan was represented to the band or to the portion of the band involved in stock raising. Neither was the origin of the repayment money from a particular source of cash in the agency accounts explained. Aspdin's specific role in the creation of this debt was also never fully explained other than his statements of gratitude to the department in his annual reports. This arrangement, whatever it was precisely, was allowed even though Aspdin and his superiors within the department were aware that the band did not have trust or capital funds at its disposal.

TRUST FUNDS

There were two circulars dated November 10 and July 26, 1906, and another dated November 14, 1906, though they postdate the surrender in April 1905. The second circular, and the auction in February 1906, were examples of a pragmatic role for the trust funds, the department's use of credit, and interactions between agents or other officers of the Department of Indian Affairs with creditors. Certainly indicative of the department's operations in fiscal matters, a circular was sent by Secretary J.D. McLean to Indian Agent Charles Fisher at Mistawasis Reserve on November 14, 1905, noting that it was necessary for him to send all accounts for expenditures incurred during 1905–06 before July 31, 1906. McLean explained the importance of this practice in these terms:

> The appropriations which are placed at the disposal of the department by parliament are intended only to cover the fiscal year for which they are granted and it is objectionable to pay from the next fiscal year's appropriation, expenditure incurred before the 30th June. It causes grave embarrassment therefore if the regulations are not carried out and you will in future be held personally responsible for any failure to carry out these

instructions to the letter. You should be aware of the outstanding accounts of your agency and should use every effort to collect them, informing merchants and others to whom the government is indebted that it will certainly prejudice the payment of their accounts if they are not presented promptly at the close of the year.[20]

In a second circular, for distribution to agents across Canada, McLean wrote to Indian Commissioner David Laird and asked that, for those bands with surrendered lands and presumably resources from the sale thereof, credit should be available so that, in the estimates for expenses being submitted for the 1907–08 fiscal year, agents should submit only specific expenses as fulfilled treaty obligations. Credit should be considered "sufficient to supply their needs."[21] Therefore, a list of requirements was requested with each estimate so that agents could be authorized upon approval to purchase locally the necessary articles. The department believed that the interest money should be enough to supply the wants of any reserve population, and it was "presumed that in the future that other bands will be similarly independent."[22] Therefore, the cost of maintaining the band was to be borne by the band the moment that it had resources to expend in this manner. Both of these articulations represent the constraints under which Aspdin was expected to operate and reflect the context of credit becoming debt that in turn necessitated the land surrender at Carry The Kettle Reserve.

In the annual report for 1904, Aspdin's discourse on the topic of "Characteristics and Progress" was particularly revealing: "The Indians are steadily progressing towards self-support and no rations are issued to the able bodied. The fact with the exception of a few old and sick, I am glad to report that the band is self-sustaining and the ration house is a thing of the past."[23] Aspdin continued that

> whilst the increase in the quantity of grain raised and also the cattle . . . has been steady, it would have been more so if some of the older Indians had continued farming, but these, finding that they could make what to them is a more congenial living by working for settlers, selling wood, etc., have given up farming. In the past the rations usually given to working Indians from the agency acted as a loadstone to keep them farming in a manner, but as they found the rations cease, they preferred other modes of making a living to tilling the soil. The younger generation will in time no doubt . . . increase the number engaged

in agriculture. The dress and habits of the Indians have undergone a marked change in the last few years, and the blanket, long hair, paint, etc., are gradually giving way to a more civilized attire. The heathen dances are stopped, and although at first their suppression caused some grumbling, I think the Indians have become reconciled to the change. On first settling on reserves the Assiniboines split up; part remaining in Canada and part settling in the United States. A close relationship has existed and their visits to each other have been much against their progress. Endeavours are being made to curtail these in the interest of the Indians themselves.[24]

In the section on "Health and Sanitation," Aspdin noted that "some of the older Indians still prefer their own medicine man, but this class is getting less in numbers and losing its hold on the younger generation."[25] The contest of progress against the traditionalism of older band members remained the focus of his resolve. And finally, under "General Remarks," Aspdin suggested some degree of turmoil and frustration:

The last crop season was a banner one and far exceeding any previous one in quantity. Unfortunately, owing to the prolonged wet weather, hinder[ing] the grain from ripening, it was all frozen. This was most discouraging, as it not only reduced the quantity but the quality as well, some of it being totally unassailable. The band has just taken prizes for work at the Sintaluta and Regina fairs respectively. A larger exhibit at both places could have been made, had time permitted.

In conclusion, I am glad to say that the progress of the Assiniboines toward civilization and self-support is steady and I believe permanent, and in the future the calls upon the department for assistance will be strictly defined to a very few old and sick people [and] the expense very small.[26]

Although Aspdin expressed his unwavering faith in progress as the salvation for the Assiniboine of Carry The Kettle Reserve, there is no direct evidence of the degree to which this was a sentiment held by band members. Unable to control completely all of the decisions made by band members about their economic affairs, especially in terms of some specific or personal interests and choices, Aspdin attempted to manipulate his authority on the reserve by drawing new administrative lines from which band members were not allowed to diverge.

CHAPTER 8

He projected certain achievements by select individuals, represented by the kinds of material goods owned, to be new benchmarks for the band's achievement as a whole. In a season when both of the major sources of surplus (grain and stock) and therefore amounts of cash that individuals could realize were diminished, and the amounts of cash in reserve among individuals or families were presumably reduced or for some wiped out, Aspdin placed the burden on the band for the improvement of a new pasture, which begged an administrative review of some kind. Clearly, this was done without the knowledge of the commissioner or evidence of any direction from headquarters, or at least nothing exists in the surviving record that this set of arrangements had been approved by anyone other than Aspdin asserting his authority.

These two situations, for which remedies necessarily incurred expenses, truly set the stage for a land surrender. But it is not clear that such an action was raised as a solution either partially or wholly for the band to consider. Nothing about an impending auction of the surrendered land was mentioned.

Inspector of Indian Agencies W.M. Graham's first annual report, dated October 8, 1905, stated that Graham had conducted his inspection of the reserve during the last days of March and April 1, and his report was very short. Housing with only a few exceptions met his approval. The cattle herd had come through the winter well, partly because there had been a good supply of hay in the spring; fourteen head were sold to buyers, and several were killed by residents for beef for their own use, leaving 154 head. However, Graham's next remarks were not a tribute to Aspdin or his administration:

> The wheat crop of last year did not amount to much and I am afraid this failure was largely due to poor farming. It is true there was a frost, but this does not account for the failure altogether. The land was poorly farmed and the sowing was late.
>
> Quite a nice lot of new land was broken in the agency this spring, and many of the old fields are being summer-fallowed this summer, and now that the department has placed a practical farming instructor on this reserve, I am looking for a great change in the style of farming.[27]

Graham noted in passing that the Assiniboine People continued to supply wood and hay to the neighbouring towns of Sintaluta and Wolseley, but he also stated that "the Indians own a steam threshing outfit and do their own threshing."[28] Then he returned to his interest

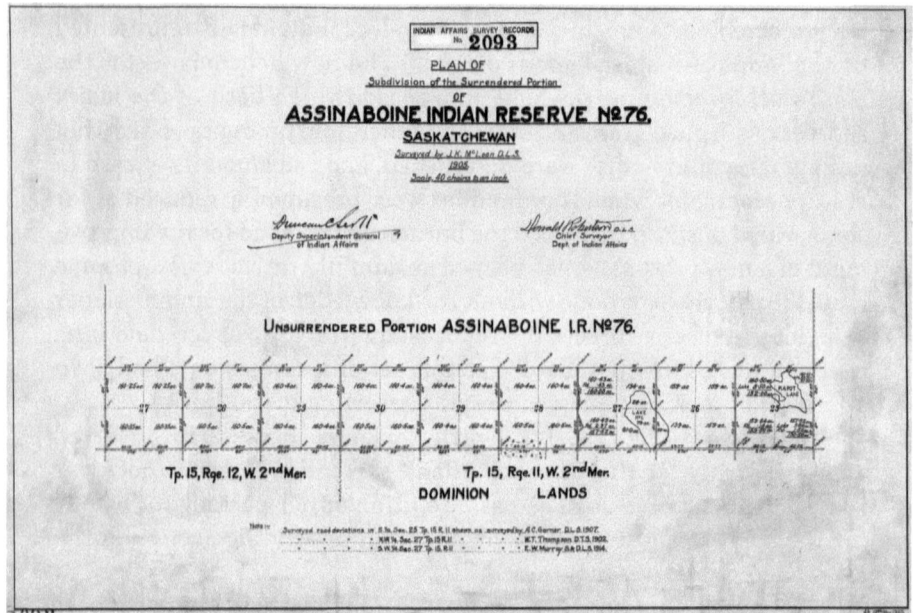

FIGURE 12: 1905 Surrendered Land
Plan of Subdivision of the Surrendered Portion of Assiniboine Indian Reserve No. 76, Saskatchewan. Surveyed by J.K. McLean, D.L.S., 1905; A.C. Garner, DLS, 1907; W.T. Thompson, DTS, 1902; E.W. Murray, S & DLS, 1914.; G.P., May 12, 1925.
Library and Archives Canada/Department of Indian Affairs and Northern Development fonds/Item 2202.

in the farming operations of the agency and stated the basis of the land surrender:

> I may say that I was at the agency early in the summer, and I saw a decided improvement in the farming; in fact, I saw some splendid fields and I am satisfied the Indians will have a large yield this year.
>
> The Indians surrendered nine sections of land from the south of their reserve, and have made a request that part of the proceeds be spent in buying a new engine.
>
> A splendid pasture field was fenced last season and the cattle are now away from the danger of trespassing on the white settlers' crops.[29]

The government-supplied engine, purchased second hand by either Aspdin or someone else in the department (but most probably Aspdin), was linked to why the Assiniboine had to pay the difference on a new engine, but this was never fully explained. Graham indicated only that the Assiniboine had "requested" that a new engine be purchased from the proceeds, or more likely they had complained that the other engine was not working properly. Whether the trade-in originated with Aspdin or Graham, or with certain individuals or the Chief and council, was never explicitly stated, only that it was requested. The expense of this engine (which would become a debt) was not initially described in this manner, nor was the fencing wire for the pasture that Graham praised.[30] Moreover, previous inspection reports had mentioned the need for agency cattle and other stock to be kept out of the gardens on the reserve and from bothering neighbouring white settlers. However, an established need for an agency pasture and how it would be financed were also never stated explicitly in previous records. Moreover, another issue was ways to reduce the person power necessary to herd animals relative to the protection of their own fields and gardens. More than likely fewer individuals were needed to care for the livestock, subsequently freeing them to hire themselves out as wage labourers. The elimination of rations in exchange for work about the agency might also have been a factor in changes in attitude among some band members toward wage labour as a viable source of income. All of these matters were integrally related.

Agent Thomas W. Aspdin died of an emergency medical condition in February in a Vancouver hospital, and his family was paid his salary to February 28, 1906.[31] Inspector W.M. Graham stated that he had looked after the agency in the interim since December, the month that Aspdin had been relieved of his duties because of illness.[32] Therefore, Aspdin was not present for the auction of the surrendered lands, handled by Graham, as he had been authorized.[33] W.S. Grant was reappointed as agent and arrived to take charge of the agency on May 1, 1906.[34]

Grant's first annual report, dated June 30, written after being on the job two months back at the Assiniboine reserve, was almost verbatim the last annual report of Aspdin. The new agent noted in passing that, having only recently returned, he had started in his employment with the department with the Assiniboine People on this reserve twenty-four years previously, and he characterized them as "steadily advancing toward civilization and self-support."[35] In his inspection report, Graham lauded a range of improvements, from farming operations to cattle raising; seventeen head of cattle brought on average thirty-six dollars each. New lands were broken as well. The position of labourer was replaced by that of farmer, and "the result of this change has already been marked on the farming."[36] It was a loss to the Assiniboine to have the foremost wage labour position available on the reserve eliminated. In contrast, other than Graham's enthusiastic remarks, a measured impact was the farmer's guidance along with good weather resulting in increases in crops. In a sense, Grant saw himself as a self-fulfilling prophecy.

Graham's comment on the auction of the surrendered lands was that "the Indians of this reserve surrendered nine sections off the south end of their reserve. This was sold last February, at Sintaluta by public auction. The land was not used in any way, and could well be spared."[37] W.S. Grant, in his last annual report as the agent of the Assiniboine Agency, for 1911, referred to Carry The Kettle Band rather than the Assiniboine Band. Other than concerns about housing to be clean and hygienic in an effort to maintain health, the focus was on economic activities. The marketing of hay and wood (firewood and pickets) was described as "exceptionally" rewarding, and "these products have provided groceries and clothing in exchange."[38] Three-quarters of the men were engaged in farming, and "others derive a livelihood by means of selling wood, hay and pickets; also by tanning hides and working for settlers." Some loss was reported in the cattle and pony herds "owing to the rigorous winter" even though care of the stock improved. Grant commented that "these people are ambitious, energetic, and industrious. They are making progress and rapidly assimilating the ways of white people. This is shown by better houses, better clothing, cleaner surroundings and better household effects. The majority of those farming are making good progress, and are improving in their methods of tilling the soil. They are becoming richer and spend their money more judiciously. They are civil and law-abiding."[39] Mentioning that there were 14,000 acres under cultivation in the inspectorate, Grant noted that more lands were being broken annually as encouraged at Carry The Kettle.

The four administrations of the agency that spanned three decades involved three agents, W.S. Grant (1886–97), Thomas W. Aspdin (1897–1906), followed again by W.S. Grant (1906–11), and finally Thomas E. Donnelly (1912–16). W.M. Graham became increasingly influential after his appointment as inspector of Indian Agencies, Qu'Appelle Inspectorate, in 1905, and he was the department's representative for the land surrender.

In the remainder of this book, we will focus on the traditional land use of the Assiniboine People and Carry The Kettle First Nation as told through historical and Elder interviews, as well as current traditional hunters and gatherers. This discussion will span from when they roamed freely around their Traditional Territory to when they lived on their allotted reserve. We also discuss how they conducted their traditional

CHAPTER 8

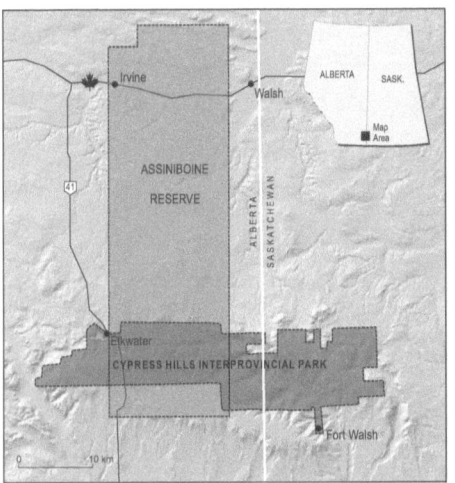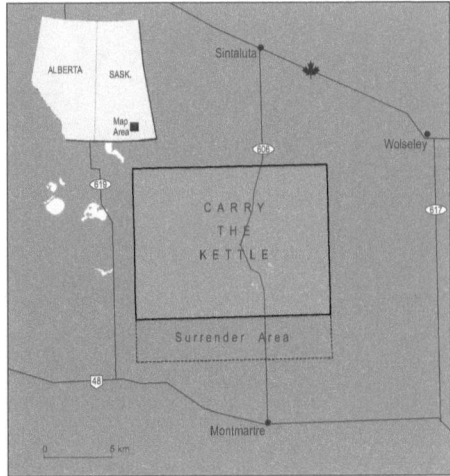

FIGURE 13: Original Cypress Hills Reserve and Current Reserve Details

livelihood on and off reserve now that permits have allowed them to hunt, trap, gather, and fish in the areas that they call home—the land of their Assiniboine ancestors. The restrictions placed on the Assiniboine People were directed not only toward their traditional activities and movements within their boundaries but also toward their spiritual and cultural activities—all in the name of assimilation and the government's attempt at conversion of the Assiniboine to Christianity.

PART 2
Nakón Wičóȟa Iyamé I nagu Wošbebi

Spirituality and Traditional Hunting and Gathering

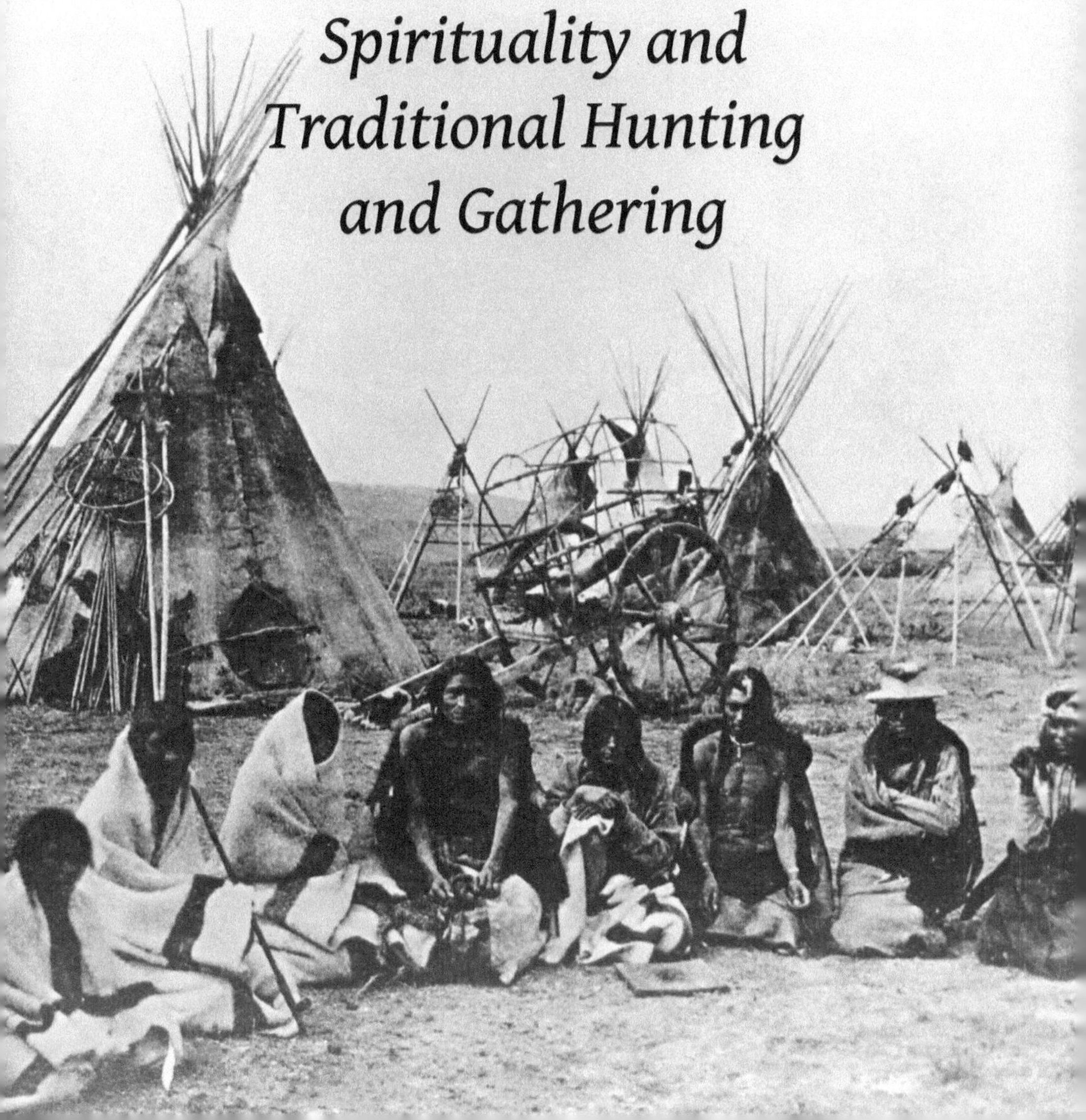

CHAPTER 9

Nakón Wičóȟaŋga, wičói'ábi, wakaŋ makáwida, Owapiya

Spirituality, Language, Sacred Sites, and Burial Grounds

The Cypress Hills area has been a spiritual gathering place and a regular winter camp for the Assiniboine People. It is an area to meet and rejuvenate and to celebrate life and plan for the future. The spirituality of the Assiniboine People is partially experienced through the many ceremonies conducted both in the Cypress Hills and in the Carry The Kettle allotted reserve. Although reserve life and government regulations stifled the culture and spirituality of the Assiniboine People, they maintained their beliefs and ways of life as best they could.

In this chapter, we discuss a few of the traditional ceremonies and celebrations that the Assiniboine People continued to practise even though they were banned by the Canadian government in its attempt to assimilate Indigenous Peoples into white society and Christianity. We also discuss the cultural impact of the government-implemented residential school system and the removal of children from their homes and families, forbidding them to speak their native language or practise their culture.

SPIRITUALITY AND CEREMONIES

Historically, for the Assiniboine People, the Cypress Hills were an area where small wintering hunting parties from all over their Traditional Territory would gather and reunite in larger tribal units to celebrate, plan, and rejuvenate. As Speaks Thunder noted in 1929, "these Assiniboine Indians, they all came together in the month of June, a month before the fourth of July.... The Indians gather in these Sundances and talk about how they are going to live on this earth, live well, live good. They come together and talk about those things, plan ahead."

The Cypress Hills were also the location of one of the most sacred Assiniboine ceremonies, the Sundance. This ceremony is an important spiritual aspect of the Assiniboine culture. "It is a worship," Mrs. Medicine Bear/Iron Cradle clarified in 1929. "They pray to some spirit in heaven away up in the sky.... You people have meetings or gatherings.... It is the same with the Indians." She went on to note that

> the Assiniboines were all one Nation and when they wanted to hold a gathering like that, they tied tobacco in little packages and sent them around to invite them all to gather at a certain spot, like you people do now when you have a gathering some place, you write letters to one another, but the Indians did it this way. Then they all come together and hold their Sundances.... They were generally scattered here and there looking for food, [and] sometimes they would be around White Earth, and also up north and around Woody Mountain and other places.

Held in open areas, the Sundance was a celebration of their survival through the winter and a platform to ask the sun for strength in their bison hunt and bravery in war. It also served as a rite of passage for the younger members of the band. In 2015, CTK Elder Delmar Runs shared the story that his father had passed down to him through generations regarding the creation of this important spiritual ceremony and how it originated in the Cypress Hills:

> Well, on my father's side, ... what he mentioned was ... Cypress Hills, ... that's where that Sundance came from.... It was 400 years before that foreigners came to this country. And the one that found that [Sundance], it was a young boy, I think twelve or eleven years old, in the Cypress Hills. The spirit came for

this boy, spoke to him, and told him how to make a Sundance. So that boy turned around and told his parents . . . that [the] spirit spoke to him. And at that time dad said that there was no war. . . . All tribes, both Canada and the United States, were all at peace. . . . When that boy told his parents that the spirit spoke to him on how to make a Sundance, his father told his wife "We'll do what our little boy told us. We'll go and make a Sundance," and that was the first Sundance that ever was. And when they made that Sundance, across the nation, there was nothing like that. . . . Dad said, after that Sundance, people were there, like wildfire, both Canada and the United States— they started to make the Sundance. . . . That's how it happened, . . . and that's a story my dad told me about Cypress Hills and how the Sundance was created by a little boy . . . in Canada.

CTK Elder Vincent Ryder's grandparents passed on the story of the Seven Sacred Rites given to the Assiniboine People when White Buffalo Calf Woman came to Earth and bestowed the Sacred Pipe to be used for the first rite, Keeping of the Soul. A central part of each sacred rite is smoking the Sacred Pipe, and when it is smoked the holder's voice is sent to the Great Spirit:

Both my grandparents were traditional sacred people. . . . They told me lots of stories about the land. . . . There was a woman that delivered a pipe to the people in the south country, a Buffalo Calf Woman, they always talk about that woman that delivered that pipe to the nation. All over the country of Canada, from west to east, they all knew of the White Buffalo Calf Woman. They teach it . . . that was something sacred. She gave the Seven Sacred Rites that was given to her from the Creator that sent her down with a pipe—the Seven Sacred Rites. The main one is the Pipe Ceremony. She stayed with the Native People . . . and told them about the pipe—all these sacred ceremonies. How to prepare the food, raise the children. She told them about these medicines, . . . what is this medicine good for, how you handle it in a sacred way . . . used to smudge, sweetgrass. . . . They were told to pray because that was put on this land through the Creator.

Ryder explained that one of the Seven Sacred Rights, the most prevalent of ceremonies given to the people, was the Sundance.

CTK Powwow Dancer
Photo provided by Carry The Kettle Nakoda First Nation.

CHAPTER 9

After European contact with Indigenous Peoples, and with the formation of the United States and Canada, governments in both countries created laws banning the practice of cultural beliefs and spiritual ceremonies of those peoples. Indian Agents, based on directives from their superiors, routinely interfered with and disallowed Sundances on reserves from 1882 to the 1940s.[1] Those who continued with their cultural practices were imprisoned or even killed for doing so. As a result, and to preserve Indigenous cultures for future generations, most ceremonies went underground and were practised in secret. According to Elder Nancy Eashappie and Terri Prettyshield in 2015, "Albert, he had a Sundance twice, and two times by Charlie Ryder.... The land is actually out there, ... out past the powwow grounds a bit, ... not too far from there, that's where Albert had his Sundance.... He had one and then a couple years later, and that was the last time, ... around the '40s." Elder Leroy Hassler said that "somehow they let him do it.... I was told it was outlawed, then finally one day Old Man Charlie put one on. And then that's where I first knew about it. Then they had one the next year and next year. Then somebody else had one." Elder Garry Whitecap mentioned that "years ago our grandfather was a Medicine Man, and he used to do a Sundance down there. It's in the old pasture. That was the last Sundance here, for that area ... around the west here, there's some high hills over there, they call that sacred land.... People go up there, and they fast up there, and they pray—Sharp Hills. It's called the Sharp Hills." And, according to Elder Nancy Eashappie, "some of them that could do things like that will have ceremonies. Like Tim Eashappie, I see that he make a raindance, and then they'll have these round dance and powwow.... Things like that they do now and then."

As with medicines, Carry The Kettle Elders are reluctant to discuss the Sundance in any great detail for fear that their traditional ways might be abused, misused, or not passed on in the right ways. In general terms, however, the object of this ceremony is to offer personal sacrifice as a prayer for the benefit of one's family and community. Dances and songs passed down through the generations are celebrated with the use of a traditional drum, sacred fire, ceremonial pipe, fasting, natural medicines, and prayer:

> There's some out here, but again they're on all different neighbouring reserves.... Wherever one has a track record—a history of lodges—then a lot of people go there. Depends on the person—it has to be a gift. It's a gift from God. So it has to be done the right way in order to continue those ways. That's what I was

Gros Ventre Warriors Leaving Camp to Select Sundance Pole, Fort Belknap, Montana, 1896
Courtesy of Glenbow Archives, NA-1419-8.

> told anyway. You need to live a good life, a clean life—a clean mind because you're working close to God, . . . ceremonies that God gave to our people. They tell us that he walked amongst us. He gave them those laws and said you practise these laws, these ways I've shown you. Someday I'm coming back to see. Your children's, children's, children's children [will be] better by carrying those ways. (Elder James O'Watch, 2015)

Elders Victoria, Joyce, and Gladys Prettyshield recalled in 2015 that they used to attend Sundances:

> I remember going to a Sundance a long time ago, and I used to see them all dancing. They used to dance. These guys used to fast for four days—nothing to eat, nothing to drink. They used to stand all around in a circle at the lodge, and they had loincloths, and they didn't have anything else. But the ladies had long dresses, very traditional. The ladies, they had that pride in them. . . . They'd have their dresses tied up with a great big

CHAPTER 9

Raising the Centre Poles at Gros Ventre Sundance, Fort Belknap, Montana, 1896
Courtesy of Glenbow Archives, NA-1419-10.

safety pin here (at the neck), and the dresses were long. They just showed their face. They would wear these babushkas or scarfs (over their heads). . . . They never used to look at anybody except that tree that was up there. . . . That was the central pole, and it was wrapped around with different cloths used for prayer. Those are healing cloths . . . on the reserve, the Sundances.

The Cypress Hills were the location not only for the sacred Sundance and other spiritual celebrations but also for vision quests for the youth and holy men who sought solitude in the hills while fasting. In 2015, Elder Vincent Ryder shared the story passed on to him from his grandfather regarding Elkwater[2]—a very sacred site to the Assiniboine People—where they could look out and see most of their Traditional Territory and fast and pray for their people:

There's a place where Elkwater is. There's a sacred place . . . when they meet . . . they [grandparents] used to talk about this land, this sacred area. . . . When I was a kid, I used to just sit there and listen to them. . . . They talked about a place called Hay-ee-pa—translated it means "Head of the Mountain." That was a sacred land to the Native People. At that time, they used to have ceremonies—their Sundances, Sweat Lodges—down in the valley. It's a beautiful country, and there's a big high hill—that's what they call Head of the Mountain because from there you go west and east, north and south. . . . They used to say you go up to that mountain—Head of the Mountain—you could see the town of Medicine Hat to the north, . . . and from the west you can see the mountaintops, the Rocky Mountains on a nice clear day. . . . And to the southwest you could see Montana, it's called the Sweet Grass Hills in Montana, you could see that place plain as day. . . . And farther south of the Montana border is Helena, Montana. And from that sacred hill, if you look east, there's Cypress Hills, . . . but then you can't see them on account of the hills. There's trees all over those hills.

So that land there, that sacred hill, my grandpa, old Charlie Ryder, used to say they had ceremonies on there, and it wasn't only him that used that mount. There was the Blackfoot to the west, the Blood to the southwest into Montana, they used that land for sacred purposes. And to the south as far as the Montana border—westward—the Crow Nation. The Crows used to come and have their ceremonies there. Other tribes were the Peigan, Sarcee—the Alberta Natives. They knew about that sacred ground. They'd go up on that hill, and there's a sacred ceremony they do—they fast so many days—some say four days. They make a commitment to the Creator, and they go up on that hill, and they perform this fast, and they have visions. Visions of—they call it "cry for a vision." They'd sit up there and pray. Four days, four nights, no food, no water. They fast. They give their bodies, and after that ceremony they have their Sundance for four days again.

When the ban was lifted, more ceremonies were held by Carry The Kettle members, and more celebrations were attended on neighbouring reserves and those farther away with ancestors and relatives. Elder Art Adams's family went to Moose Mountain often for various ceremonial purposes: "They'd go celebrate when they had powwows over there. Go camp over there. I think they went to look for some other medicines they couldn't find over here." Terri Prettyshield noted that,

CHAPTER 9

for a while there, it was kind of need-be almost, back in the '70s, '60s, around there. But now we do have more. Now that the government's more relaxed about it, we do have them a lot more. I know also, I think it's Perry Thomson that holds one every year now as well. So people are starting to get back into that. We have more pipe holders than we've ever had on Carry The Kettle. Even I remember back in the '70s.

Elder Vincent Ryder said that

my grandpa, too, did ceremonies and the pipe. . . . I seen him doing that ceremony, and that's how I learned. . . . In the summertime, they had these things called Sundances. I used to go with them. See, they were spiritual people, and they followed the Native tradition of Sundance and all the ceremonies. . . . From Standing Buffalo to out here—today it's Sakimay. There's a lot of ceremonial, traditional people in there. And they'd come out here and have their Sundances and ceremonial stuff they do. I remember I used to come with them, and there were a lot of other kids I knew who went to residential school, and we'd meet out there. It was a great old time.

Elder James O'Watch confirmed that

out here they had Sundances, and people from across the valley, older people, they used to tell me they'd come over here to Sundances when they were young, with their mom and dad. All the way from Peepeekisis. That's quite a ways. . . . Just north of here, Star Blanket. I know Star Blanket was coming out here when he was a little boy for Sundances. And Mr. Stonechild, . . . he's an Elder now for Peepeekisis, he used to tell us that he used to come out here for Sundances with his mom and dad. . . . And my grandfather George, he did most of the ceremonies.

Finally, Elders Leroy and Myrtle Hassler mentioned that "usually if there's a raindance—mostly raindances at that time—relatives from another reserve would come that's near to travel by wagon. . . . I remember when I was a kid we'd go to Regina in a wagon. Go there and camp out there for a few days."

CTK Elders recalled large powwows put on by the reserve when they were younger. Elder Edna Spencer and Orval Spencer "remember[ed]

CTK Members Watching the Powwow from the Top of the Hill
Photo provided by Carry The Kettle Nakoda First Nation.

the old hall back here, . . . they used to have powwows there. . . . There was an old hall, that's where the gatherings used to be way back then." Elder Tony Ashdohonk recalled that "my mother has pictures of them, 1936 over here, and I have the pictures of that powwow over here. . . . There's no vehicles. . . . The ones that come are sometimes pretty lucky and come in a wagon and team of horses from Moose Mountain, and Goose Lake, and Standing Buffalo. Yeah, Goose Lake, . . . Sakimay. They called it Goose Lake, and they come in a team."

Today Carry The Kettle hosts its own powwow annually, and CTK members attend many other First Nations powwow celebrations. Elder Delmar Runs told us that the band holds many ceremonies on the reserve: "We have a great deal, especially in the wintertime, we have powwows. We have a place over there called the North Hall Powwow. Through the winter, especially at New Year's Eve, we have big powwows there." Many Carry The Kettle members take part in other powwow celebrations held on various reserves. "I go to powwows," Elder Derrick Saulteaux said. "All over, White Bear next weekend, . . . the reserves close around, . . . Kat, Cowessess, Ocean Man. When I was younger, it used to be just this one, because when you're younger you didn't have a vehicle and couldn't get around." Elder Wanda Prettyshield is proud that her children and grandchildren have embraced their Assiniboine culture: "The younger generations, like our own kids and grandkids and great-grandkids now that we have, they're still involved in ceremonies.

CHAPTER 9

And our granddaughter has been a jingle dancer for a long time. She's a mom now, and she still does it. She has a little girl now, and she's teaching her already how to dance. Our boy knows how to beat the drums."

During the group interview conducted in the Cypress Hills in 2015, Elders fondly shared some of the cultural traditions passed on to them through the generations and the importance of keeping these practices alive today. As Elder Freda O'Watch noted,

> everything [is] living. Our ancestors were so close to Mother Nature, they lived in harmony with Mother Nature, so that was giving thanks, appreciation, giving back. Making sure that everything continues to grow and exist for generations in the future to use. Our ancestors are a very spiritual people. They would watch how the animals behave—the muskrats, how high they build their huts. The weather, the constellations, they also lived by. The Milky Way represents that chiwanka—that centre pole that they use in our ceremony, the Sundance. That's the red road of life our ancestors and people should be walking. Keeping it balanced, everything had to have balance. Today we use the word *holistic*, but we all have our four components or quadrants—like we use that in the medicine wheel. All those things, they weren't written down, weren't taught on a chalkboard, just part of living every day. . . . Life values—we still can practise that today—we still can live like our ancestors practised, with humility, respecting, love, caring, sharing.

Carry The Kettle members often return to the Cypress Hills and the United States to practise their sacred ceremonies and celebrate their spirituality with their Assiniboine relatives. "They're from Cypress Hills," Elder James O'Watch said. "I used to go there quite a bit because he'd [his father] practise there, and I still have Assiniboine traditional ways, so we still went down there lots. There was a lot of Sweat Lodges, so we went down there. It was a long way." Elder Art Adams said that Assiniboine went

> to visit other bands . . . with wagon and horses. . . . They used to say it took them too long to get there. Some of them mention it takes a whole week to get there and a whole week to get back. Of course, they weren't in a hurry to get there, to get back. They were just taking their time. . . . They did some berry picking and used to feed themselves on the road.

Carry The Kettle Powwow Dancers, United States, 1958
Photo provided by Carry The Kettle Nakoda First Nation.

Kurt Adams mentioned that "I go all over. I just got back from New York, went with some people to fast over there and did some ceremonies over there. And I go up to Cypress Hills once in a while and fast over there.... In Cypress Hills, there's a lot of places."

Elders Victoria, Joyce, and Gladys Prettyshield commented that

> they go across the border, the States, . . . long ways. Along Old Poplar area.... Before we had a team of horses, and they camped maybe a couple of places, ... it would take them maybe a whole week to go. In those days, they would have the great big hay in the back of their wagons and everything, ... water, food. And they had their camps. And then when they'd get out there relatives would feed them, other people [would] feed them.

Elder Duncan Thomson said that

> I used to go to the States back in the '70s. There was a big powwow celebration in Poplar, Montana, there. Used to go and stay three, four days. And Wolf Point—the next town. Poplar's Sioux, it's a Sioux powwow there. And the next, maybe ten miles down, that's Assiniboine. That's where my auntie, my dad's sister,

lived there and died there. And further down . . . maybe it was Sioux and Assiniboine—the Frasier powwow—that's down that same line. I used to go down to powwows there too and camp three or four days, . . . and Manitoba, Sioux Valley, those are the only powwows I go to.

Other Elders confirmed attendance at powwows:

> Sometimes this white man from Indian Head . . . would come to the reserve, load up everybody who wanted to go to the powwow, so we'd all get into the back of this big truck, and he'd take us. We'd go to White Bear, and he'd take us across to Montana to Poplar, Wolf Point. . . . He'd charge them so much to take them. . . . Some of our relatives came from Montana. (Elder Bernice Saulteaux, 2015)

> All over, wherever the powwow is, they'd go. If it was in the States, they'd go—Montana, Manitoba. . . . It used to be just around here—Fort Kipp. A lot of them used to go to Poplar, Fort Kipp, because there's Assiniboine there too, that's just across the border. But now they go down to Albuquerque, New Mexico. They travel all over Canada and the United States for powwows. (Elder James O'Watch, 2015)

Because Carry The Kettle members have so many relatives from Standing Buffalo, they often attend their ceremonies, celebrations, and powwows. Elder Rena Ryder recalled going to powwows with her family as a child "once in a while. They go in a wagon for a few days. . . . Just the ones that are close around, like Standing Buffalo, around here." And Elder James O'Watch said that "Standing Buffalo was a big powwow here. It was the powwow that belonged to the Sioux and Assiniboine. Crees never had powwow. They only have it now. They learned everything from the Assiniboine and Sioux."

LANGUAGE AND RESIDENTIAL SCHOOLS

The residential school system dates back to the 1870s. The policy behind the government-funded, church-run schools attempted to "kill the Indian in the child." Over 130 residential schools were located across Canada, with the last one closing in 1996. More than 150,000 First

Nations, Métis, and Inuit children were taken from their families and placed in these schools—forbidden to speak their language and practise their culture.[3] The children of Carry The Kettle were no exception.

Elders interviewed in 2015 recounted their experiences of being forcibly removed from their homes and the confusion and trauma that prevailed. Vincent Ryder said that "they took me to school, and just a couple of weeks after that I was seven years old. . . . The RCMP had to come and get me because [my parents] didn't want to let me go." Tony Ashdohonk related that "the priest kept coming and coming, and they handcuffed us and—gone," and Myrtle Hassler noted that

> one day a truck came by, and there was a lady in there, . . . and they picked us up. My dad wasn't home. . . . He was a workaholic—always busy in the fields or chopping wood, and this truck had come. But as kids we didn't know what was going on—we were always supposed to obey adults, right? They load[ed] us up in the truck and took us, and I remember just a long, long trip. . . . They took my brothers because we were holding hands, and they just pulled us apart. And I remember just screaming—my brother just screaming. It was a nightmare.

She also mentioned the fear that her father had of imprisonment if he did not allow his children to be taken away to school:

> He said when he first found out that we were taken from that house, . . . when he got home, my sister said that somebody had taken the kids. . . . It was nighttime, and he ran to the agency, and that's what he was told. We were all taken to boarding school. They didn't ask him or anything, and he didn't know. . . . His hands were tied. "I can't do anything," he said. If [he did] anything, they're going to lock him up in jail, and he'll get no rations.

The children stayed at these schools for ten months of the year, allowed to return home only in the summer. Elder Wanda Prettyshield explained that

> at that time we drove in the back of the truck—the farm truck. . . . I remember when they took us back in August, in the summertime before school, because they would pick up people from here, Fort Qu'Appelle, Broadview, White Bear. . . . We would

CHAPTER 9

Brandon Indian Residential School, Manitoba, c. 1920
Courtesy of Library and Archives Canada, PA-032824.

pick up people as we went. I think they all met in Broadview at that time because they had a bench all around [the] back of the truck, and we had our suitcases underneath, or bags, whatever we were taking, and we had some kind of a tarp, only for the top, . . . but we got the dust anyways.

The Canadian residential school system, as with other government policies discussed in this book, was all about assimilating Indigenous Peoples into white people's ways of living, speaking, and believing—forbidding the children to acknowledge their Indigenous heritage, culture, and language.[4]

Carry The Kettle Elders suffered insurmountable emotional and physical abuse from those in charge of these schools. They recounted how they were starved and in some cases how family members actually died at the hands of these authority figures:

> Oh, we were tortured. Had to take food out to other boys—little boys that were starving. We lost a lot of weight, and they had to give us—there was a group of us that were all underweight—they had to give us around three in the afternoon—cocoa and peanut butter sandwich. . . . They starved so much that they used to sneak to Brandon City Dump and eat what [they] could

find. Burnt oranges or apples or packages of, I don't know what it was, something sweet, I guess. . . . Or even the farms around there, we had to go through their garbage, look around their piles, maybe sometimes they throw stuff away, and we'd eat what they didn't eat up. Bread, oranges, and apples. Stuff like that. Sometimes they get to know you, sometimes they chase you. We used to go to the experimental farm and steal crab apples. It's a long way. (Elders Duncan Thomson and Roswell Saulteaux)

He was older than I was, he was seven, I might have been about three or four, . . . and my sister had seen him. . . . The girls had pulled her over and said "There's your little brother," and she just remembered a maître grabbing and pulling him, and he was crying for mom, and there was blood all over his head, all over his nose, all over his face, his ears. She doesn't know what happened, but the story goes—he went to File Hills—they hear this little boy crying every night. He must have lasted two, three days, and after that, that's it, they didn't hear a little boy crying anymore. And my parents say they didn't tell my parents at all. . . . She [my mother] found out he was buried at the school, and she didn't know about it. (Elder Myrtle Hassler)

She [Elder Rena Ryder] left for residential school when she was five years old (or seven) and didn't get back until she was fourteen. . . . She doesn't speak Nakoda because that's why she's deaf—the nun naître beat her up. But she understands it. . . . That's why she's deaf, because every time they spoke it they would hit her. . . . She's very fluent in Nakoda, but she won't speak it. Like, Grandpa used to speak it to her all the time, and she would understand it, but she won't speak it at all. (Elder Rena Ryder and Stacey Hotomani)

With the children banned from communicating in their native tongue, many lost the ability to speak Assiniboine, understand Assiniboine, or both. This has carried on through the generations of Carry The Kettle People, with residential school survivors unable to pass on their traditional language to their children. "I speak some words, but I don't know the whole language," Lyle Spencer said, and Elder Art Adams mentioned that "I didn't catch on to any of that. I wish I would; I always wanted to speak my own language." Elder Derrick Saulteaux admitted

CHAPTER 9

that "I'm just learning the things now—the language ... Assiniboine," and though the grandparents and parents of Darrell Jack spoke both Assiniboine and Sioux "fluently, they understood it very well because they grew up around it," unfortunately he can speak only "a little bit, not too much. Just words pretty well. I can't speak it, though." Elder James O'Watch noted that "my mom and dad were the last ones who spoke it frequently. After that, there was a lot of mixed marriages, and there was assimilation. They sent us all out to residential school, ... to white schools where they never spoke our language."

Other Elders told similar stories. Victoria Prettyshield said, "you know, I can tell you, I understand [the language] fluently, but when I used to speak it, I would speak like—mixed English. That's because I went to residential school, and I lost it all. But I understand real good." Darlene Whitecap "grew up with it. Words come back to me now and again.... I first went to school in Muscowequan, and I only came home in July and August. So I was losing my language there. But when we were kids, I used to speak it. But words come back to me." And Clayton and Delbert Thomson said that "we were in the States last week, and we stopped at this Wolf Point, Montana, they had this Indian celebration, and this guy was talking Assiniboine, Nakoda words, and it sounded good. I cannot talk that. I could understand what they're saying, but I can't talk it."

Assiniboine (known to its speakers as Nakoda or Nakota) is a Siouan language of the Northern Plains. Assiniboine/Nakoda is one of the five main language divisions within the Dakotan group of the Siouan family. These languages include Dakota (Santee-Sisseton), Dakota (Yankton-Yanktonai), Lakota (Teton), Nakoda (Assiniboine), and Nakoda (Stoney). The Sioux, Assiniboine, and Stoney Peoples are all members of this Siouan language group and form a dialect continuum extending over a vast area of the Northern Plains in the United States and Canada.[5] "I speak the Dakota language," Elder Vincent Ryder said. "And there's the Assiniboine language I didn't know. After I came back here, I was around twenty years old. Talk to other people around here, same language but different dialects."

Elders interviewed for this book proudly discussed the Assiniboine languages that their parents, grandparents, and great-grandparents spoke, which included Nakoda, Dakota, Lakota, Sioux, and in some cases even Cree and Métis. "Well, my mom was Assiniboine," Bernice Saulteaux explained. "She was Nakoda, but my dad, because my mother was Sioux, she spoke Dakota. So we had both languages, Nakoda and Dakota." Delmar Runs had grandparents on his father's side from the

Cypress Hills, and they spoke "the Nakoda language. And the words I learned were Assiniboine, but I don't know where that Assiniboine came in from." Nancy Eashappie's grandparents both spoke Nakoda: "Eashappie . . . means 'cheer' in Assiniboine. . . . They both spoke their language Nakoda. They don't say Nakoda, you know, they say 'Nakod,' they don't sound the a. But that comes from the North Dakota, South Dakota Sioux—they say that, that's how they pronounce that. We just cut it short [to] 'Nakot.'" According to Darlene Whitecap, "he [her grandfather] spoke Nakoda, she [her grandmother] spoke Lakota. You see, my mom spoke Nakoda/Lakota together, on account of her parents, one being Nakoda, the other being Lakota. But they understood one another because it's similar. Just with the *n* in Nakoda, and with Lakota they use the *la*." And Wanda Prettyshield mentioned that "she [her mother] spoke the French-Cree . . . [and her father] Nakoda. . . . They would understand. It was French-Cree that they spoke, but then when you listen to the Cree People from Pasqua and Broadview, in houses around there, it's the same. Because my Auntie Rose was from Broadview, and they all spoke the same language. There wasn't much difference."

Language is a large part of Assiniboine cultural identity and a verbal expression of thought to maintain, convey, and pass on cultural values and ideologies. "Our language has a spirit," Elder Freda O'Watch mentioned in 2015 as part of the Cypress Hills Group Interview. "You know, I could tell a joke to those who understand me—it has an impact. I could turn around and tell that same joke in English, and these guys won't laugh as hard as these guys would laugh because something is missing. That spirit is missing to give it life." Elders interviewed were fearful that the words of their ancestors will be lost forever. Still, many CTK members have retained their ability to speak their native language, and others are diligently learning it in an effort to take back what was stolen from them.

> I talk Assiniboine, . . . and I talk Sioux. I go to Standing Buffalo, and the women talk to me in Sioux right away, and I answered them. And in Manitoba . . . Griswold . . . Sioux Valley. But we went to see this guy over here, he was from South Dakota, he was Oglala Sioux. . . . It would take me a while to understand him, I'll think about it, but by the time I know what he means he's way over there talking about something else. (Elder Tony Ashdohonk)

CHAPTER 9

When I first started out learning my culture, it was 1986, and I started off with the Lakotas. They're part of that group we belonged to, the Seven Council Fires it's called, there's Nakoda, Lakota, Dakota, seven subtribes in there, and we we're part of that. So that started it. I started learning the Lakota language, so that's what I'm sticking with because I feel comfortable with it. And the songs, the Sundance songs, they're all in Lakota that I sing. If I lived here and started my Nakoda, I'd stick with it, but I know more Lakota than Nakoda. (Elder Garry Whitecap)

He [the Creator] gave us the language. When we were in Alberta, this one old man said this young Indian girl died—she went to heaven, and she started talking to him in English, and God said "I don't understand you. I sent you down there, your grandfathers, your grandmothers, I gave them the language. If you don't have that language, it's not your fault, it's your grandparents' fault. You go back there and learn the language [and] then come back here. Otherwise, I don't understand you until then." So it's important that we teach our children the language because someday, when they die and face God, they won't be able to talk to him, because they won't be able to speak our language. . . .

We're working diligently. . . . We got a group of people right now—some of us can understand and speak a bit of it. We try to use as much material and try to meet with as much Nakoda Nations to see if we can come to some kind of agreement and use this one language—the writing and the speaking of it. So we're working very hard to preserve it. And we have it in our schools right now, and we want to expand on that. Right now we have a class through university being done out here. (Elder James O'Watch)

SACRED SITES AND BURIALS

When asked in 2015 about known sacred sites in need of protection, CTK Elders thought of many. Myrtle Hassler said that "I think our whole reserve has to be protected. This is our reserve now, our Traditional Land. But there is some spiritual sites that we need to protect." More specifically, a few mentioned the teepee rings and medicine wheel around Kendal. "There's medicine wheels up on these

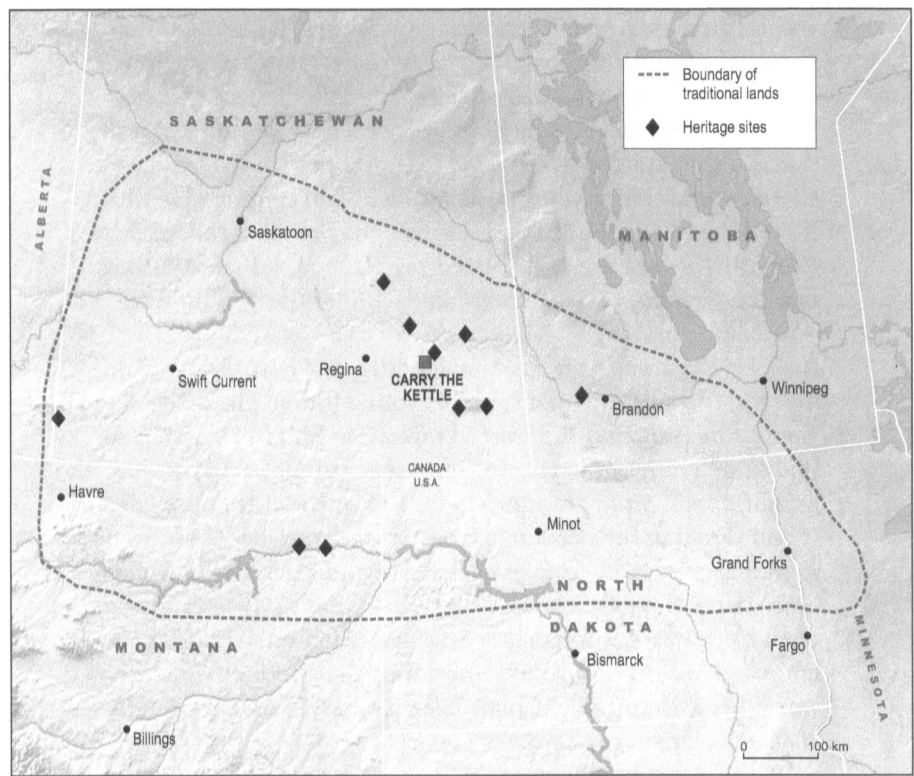

FIGURE 14: Carry The Kettle Heritage Sites (Sacred Sites and Burial Grounds)

hills," Stacey Hotomani noted, "but they're off reserve land. They're in between Kendal and Womack.... There are two hills there." This is not surprising since the Assiniboine People from Wolf Point, Montana, outlined this area as Assiniboine Traditional Territory in interviews conducted in 1929 and stated that only the Assiniboine held their teepees down with stones. As Last indicated back then,

> wherever the Assiniboines roamed, you can see circular rocks, little openings on the south side indicating where the door was. All these rocks are landmarks.... They have roamed in all this territory ... and these marks were made by my fathers and my grandfathers and I consider them as landmarks belonging to the Assiniboines.... Other tribes, those people that do not belong to the Assiniboines, people that heretofore were enemies of the Assiniboine Tribe, never had that custom; they

CHAPTER 9

never used rocks to weight down tepees with. The Assiniboines are the only tribe that ever had that custom.

CTK Elders Duncan Thomson and Roswell Saulteaux indicated in 2015 that

> there's one off reserve here ... in between Kendal and Indian Head. There were lakes around there too, not sure, was it Strawberry Lakes? ... There were big circles, great big circles, and it's nice and flat, and they said there's small circles way big around like this, ... but at that time they stayed in teepees. They stayed in teepees all winter. That's what those big circles were all around. Then there was this big basin, and they said there was water—there used to be water—I don't know if they bathed in that or what. ... I remember just a couple of years ago, north of Strawberry Lake there, four miles west of Indian Head, ... straight south about seven miles, ... stone circles and a buffalo rubbing stone.

Elder James O'Watch also said that

> there's one just east of us here ... about five or six miles. ... We all went back, and there was a bunch of teepee rings back there, just about covered. And, you know, it was a funny thing, we go in there, and it was a cold day. We parked so far [away], and we had to walk, and when we got there, ... the burial grounds there, the warm air came and stayed with us. Our grandfathers walked all about that place ... where the stones were. ... It looked like a turtle. ... There's one exactly the same down in the States someplace. So again giving testimony to at least the fact that we were all Assiniboines from the same territory. Because why would the same rock formation turn up over there?

Moosomin also shows evidence of previous occupation. "There's another place over here," Kurt Ryder said, "the medicine wheel. ... All this area right here from Moosomin. ... There's a lot of tepee rings, and there's a lot of spiritual places inside here. I know someone, the guys from Moosomin, are trying to preserve a lot of this area."

St. Victor is a sacred site at the northern edge of the Wood Mountain Plateau. There you will find the prehistoric carvings in stone of animal tracks, human faces, human footprints, human hands, pictures of

Grizzly bear track, two bison tracks (left and top). Petroglyphs, St. Victor, Saskatchewan.
Courtesy of Tim and Louise Jones, Saskatoon.

a man holding or reaching out to a circle, and a bear paw, along with other designs and shapes of which many are unknown to us today.

The plains grizzly bear is the most prevalent design carved there, depicting the sacred life of this large bear on the plains before the arrival of the fur traders. The friendship between humans and animals is shown by the proximity of the designs of humans and images of hands reaching out to bear paws.[6]

There are also two sites located nearby with shallow pits lined with stones. These sites are on the tops of hills overlooking the valley below. They are known to Indigenous Peoples as "vision pits" and have a clear view of the petroglyph site—strategically placed to view the cardinal directions of north, south, east, and west.[7]

Elder James O'Watch explained in 2015 that there is another sacred site in need of protection around St. Victor:

> That's just southeast of Assiniboia. There's a great big flat rock over there. You climb up, it's way up on kind of a hill, . . . right on top there is a rock with a bunch of writings on it. . . . I was

CHAPTER 9

there two years ago. I sat on the board of the Saskatchewan Native Cultural College, and they took a group of us over there to look at it and see—make our recommendations on what we wanted to see happen.... There's all kinds of writing on there—bear feet.

O'Watch explained that the trail on which his people travelled from Cypress Hills to their current reserve should also be considered sacred, though there was no information about where that trail might be. "They took them back from Cypress Hills ... [to] the reserve land.... They say that's where they moved us here with teams of horses.... So all along there there's burials and all that stuff."

CTK Elders and members expressed that the Cypress Hills region is a major burial site of their ancestors. Stone markers from Nakoda camps dating back hundreds of years can be found there. Delmar Runs noted that "one thing they always said was that our loved ones are buried over at the Cypress Hills. This is our homeland, and we want to go back." Joyce Prettyshield said that "they used to bury their people up in trees. My mom used to say that." And Orval Spencer stated that "I remember them saying ... south over there someone is buried. He died there, and [they] just buried him in the trees that way. Put them up above the ground. I think there was an old powwow grounds there ... just about a mile south of here—two miles south—off the main road here."

Back in 1929, Warren Carl/Brings Back mentioned that

> the original Assiniboines had their burial grounds all over this section of the country ... in the olden days, as far as the Assiniboine territory, within that boundary.... The practice of the Indians in the old days, they didn't usually put them on trestles; the Assiniboines didn't use that method of burial. In those days—and I am pretty sure that all the Assiniboines here will vouch for that—they were buried up in the limbs of trees so that the wolves and coyotes and wild animals cannot reach them.... I don't know that they ever had any marks for them.

In later years, when the community began to build their band office, the fact that their reserve was built on a previous burial ground became evident once again. "When they dig about here ...," Elder Tony Ashdohonk observed in 2015, "it was all bones, lots of bones. And that guy with the Cat, he told me, 'Tony, you know, this is a big graveyard.' ... And skulls—we pushed all the dirt and all these bones, skulls."

Tombs of Assiniboine Indians on Trees, c. 1840–43
Artist, Karl Bodmer; courtesy of Library of Congress, LC-DIG-pga-04424 DLC.

Like some other CTK members, when Lyle Spencer was asked if he knew of any unmarked burial sites or sacred sites, he said yes but was unwilling to share their locations: "I might say no to that because those areas are traditional and protected, and not much people know where they are—traditional burial sites." Still, some of the interviewees shared

CHAPTER 9

Joe Jack Visiting Son Bernard's Grave
Photo provided by Carry The Kettle Nakoda First Nation.

knowledge regarding known burial sites throughout their reserve lands. "Back around Pearl's there," according to Elder Rena Ryder and Stacey Hotomani, "you find a lot of skulls there, a lot of bones. And you know that road—some graves there . . . where the old Chief was buried."

Elder James O'Watch said that

> there was a fire there, twice I guess, that burnt his grave [Piapot]. Right where the band hall is . . . was Piapot land. In fact, the graveyard, when it was first developed, they used to find bones, . . . stuff like that, and a lot of our houses are haunted over there at night. . . . That one house where my son's living—there's a graveyard there. My daughter lived there and used to see—hear things happen.

Other CTK Elders offered similar accounts.

> The hill, it's just right straight across over here. A grave, and they were buried about here [two feet off the ground]. . . . You see the blanket in there, and coyotes had been trying to pull it out. . . . There's another one that I know that's a way over there—a little baby. That's a long time ago. One of those days, one of my relatives put a great big stone right on top of where that body was. That stone is still there. (Tony Ashdohonk)

There's one behind Auntie Kate's old place. Down in the bush there's an old grave from long, long ago. There's a grave back there where south cemetery is, just down the hill on this side. That's where my grandpa used to live. It's in south cemetery, down in the bush there. (Joyce Prettyshield)

There's quite a few of them on the reserve. They found one off the reserve here towards Wolseley. . . . They found one grave in a field out there. What became of it I don't know. But they figure it was some Natives. . . . It wasn't a grave, but they found it in the field. They dug it up, that was it. That's all I heard. There's one in Regina they found there not too long ago, . . . there's four maybe five. . . . There's a residential school there. (Victoria Prettyshield)

In spite of all the efforts to the contrary, CTK People and their traditional activities, spirituality, and culture survived. In the following chapter, we discuss their traditional land use today in areas outside the reserve and how they are trying to protect their Traditional Territories and Indigenous Rights for future generations.

CHAPTER 10

Wanúyabi Wokšubi

Harvesting Big Game

After the move to the southwestern plains of Canada, the Assiniboine People relied on the large herds of bison that formed the basis of their livelihood. As outlined in Chapter 4, the Assiniboine did not recognize the "white man's international boundary line" that divided the northwestern plains of the United States and the southwestern plains of Canada. After the depletion of the bison, the Assiniboine began to depend more on other large game species such as antelope, elk, moose, and deer found throughout their Traditional Territories. In this chapter, we discuss both historical and current locations frequented for large game hunting along with the methods for and uses of these harvests.

HISTORICAL BIG GAME HUNTING

In interviews conducted in 1929, the Assiniboine Tribe of Indians discussed their hunting excursions as well as those of their parents and grandparents. These discussions included the importance of the Cypress Hills, where they travelled, how they harvested, and what their harvests were used for. As Last indicated, "we followed the game everywhere it could be found. If we heard of any herd of buffaloes anywhere, we would break camp and follow it. We were just like wolves; we go wherever there is game." Last also said that "my grandfather told me that at one time there were 700 lodges of the Assiniboine's, but because of the size of the tribe at that time, there was no herd of buffalo sufficient to keep the tribe going. So finally, in order to save themselves, the tribe scattered out into small bands throughout the country."

Red Feather confirmed that "this is a very large tribe of Indians. These Assiniboine's were scattered in different bands throughout this whole territory here, and these different expeditions that I enumerated do not include the entire tribe, just certain bands travelling on these different marches. While we were on these trips the bands would be scattered all over. They didn't go in just one band."

Moreover, Warren Carl/Brings Back commented that "the Assiniboine's did not have any permanent camps, but they were in the habit of moving about as indicated by the fact that, wherever the night overtook them, there they camped; the next day they moved, taking their entire belongings and families. When the winter came they were not camped anywhere—but just located there for a while through the winter. That was the custom of the Assiniboine's."

Nick Alvares explained that there were many bison north of the Missouri River that they hunted well into Canada: "All these hills adjacent to this town (Wolf Point) had all been hunting ground[s]. They chased the buffaloes all over these hills." Likewise, Sam King mentioned that "there were many places I hunted buffalo, on the Little Rocky Mountains, also the Bear Paw Mountains, and the cherry patch regions,[1] out in that country . . . there used to be a lot of buffalo all over." First Eagle explained that the best time to harvest bison was when the weather turned colder: "The buffaloes are in the best condition by the time the leaves turn yellow up to the time of the first snowfall. That is the best period in the year for the buffalo. After that period you can find only a few real good buffaloes, and that is the time when we would go out hunting. We killed only one because we found only occasional animals suitable for meat purposes."

The Cypress Hills provided great shelter for Assiniboine during the winter months as they moved off the open plains to avoid the cold winds. "In the old days when I was a boy," The Man said, "we wintered several times over there (Cypress Hills). Some members of the Assiniboine's that roamed that country would be around Cypress Hills. . . . At that time the Agency was removed up the Milk River,[2] and most of the Assiniboine's went up there" and around White Earth, and "we wintered there most usually."

The game found within the Cypress Hills was plentiful in both summer and winter, and the bison roamed freely on both sides of the border.

CHAPTER 10

In 2015, discussing early bison migration, CTK Elder Delmar Runs believed that many of the bison remained in the Cypress Hills while some of the people migrated farther south during the winter: "Well, really the bison didn't move because the bison could stay in the cold. It was the people who moved. But at that time there was a lot of bison in the States, but I think there were more bison in Canada, and they all survived. And when they'd come back, there were herds of them. And there was plenty of game in Cypress Hills."

Back in 1929, Warren Carl/Brings Back recalled that

> when I was about 15 years old I was a member of a party that camped all winter across the Missouri River here. I was right where the entire Assiniboine Tribe was camped that winter.... There must have been 200 or more lodges at that time ... and as soon as buffaloes were discovered anywhere near we would go on hunting expeditions.... I was in a party that was camped out at Prairie Elk.... The whole tribe was wintered there and pounded some buffalo bones and boiled them for grease. They took everything along with them. They had plenty of dogs and horses. Each family sometimes owned as many as 7 head and sometimes 6, and some families owned as many as 4 head of horses.

The Assiniboine People had many methods of harvesting bison. Sometimes just a few were needed, as Looking indicated in 1929: "I killed two and three at a time when I did kill. If they wanted the hides for the purpose of making tepees, I killed more." At other times, they harvested large quantities using bison jumps or corrals that would attract the animals needed to fulfill their harvesting needs. Blue Horn of the Assiniboine Tribe of Indians described the corrals that his people created near the Yellowstone River across the Missouri River:

> The buffalo corrals were built in a great big pit, a natural kind of reservoir of earth and wooden corrals were built clear up to the mouth and the buffaloes were driven in between these runways, wooden corrals into the pit. The pits were so deep that the buffaloes could not come back because they were just naturally forced into them. When the buffaloes came down into the pit they would trample on some of them and break their legs. At that time the Assiniboine's did not have any horses to chase buffaloes with, the only beast of burden they had at that period

of their life was the dog, and it was in this way—the corralling of the buffaloes—that they could gain their livelihood, by getting the buffaloes. . . .

After the buffaloes are run into this corral, on the north end of the corral there is a stack of poles in the form of corrals. It is built for the leading men instrumental in bringing in the buffaloes. The medicine man sits on top of the corral there, with his legs hanging over into the pit and he is supposed to sing his songs. After he sings these songs, all the while he is singing these songs these buffaloes would all be going in a circle inside the corral. Sometimes while they are doing that the buffaloes will be rubbing against his legs, be licking his feet while he is singing, and while he completes these four songs, the Indians will climb onto the banks all around with their weapons.

One of the rules of the buffalo corrals, according to the rules of the Assiniboine's, is that they were prohibited from using firearms to kill the buffaloes with. It is customary for them to use only bows and arrow, and the way they so construct this bow and arrow, they get a long stick, cut a snag in it, tie it to one end, bend it over, and tie it to the other end. That is the bow. And the way they build their arrows, they get pieces about so long, and they get material, some iron, they get it from frying pan, something like that, flatten it out, and build it into the shape of an arrow point, and put it at the end of this stick. After that is done, they will take feathers and put it at the other end. That is the weapon the Assiniboine's used to kill the buffalo with.

They keep on shooting at these buffaloes until everyone of them is killed within the corral. After the buffaloes are all killed within this corral, the Indians will go down in there and butcher them and haul all the meat out of the corral. They will clean the corral good. Everything that is within the corral is taken out of the corral, and then they will begin to corral another herd. They will continue that four times, four herds of buffalo will be run into the corral, and after that the buffalo corralling is ended.

The bison furnished almost everything needed for the Assiniboine to survive. From the hide, to the meat, to the bones—everything was utilized for their livelihood. "We dried the meat," Sam King said, "made jerk meat, and also prepared buffalo skins for lodges," and The Man

CHAPTER 10

A Buffalo Pound, 1820
Illustrator, George Back; courtesy of Glenbow Archives, Archives and Special Collections, University of Calgary, NA-1344-2.

noted that "it took 12 or 14 buffalo hides to make an Indian Tepee." Red Feather clarified that "the Assiniboines did not live like the Mandans and the Gros Ventres who have permanent villages of their own, but the Assiniboines usually lived in tepees, Indian tepees that are made out of skins. . . . They lived in these skin tepees all the time." Finally, Last mentioned that this "was their living, the killing of buffaloes. . . . They killed buffaloes and they tanned the skins and made tepees out of them. . . . The buffaloes furnished them with a home and wearing apparel. They were game with us for food. The Indian people lived on berries on trees all over the country and game. This is how people grew up in this country."

Prior to 1879, Martin Mitchell explained in 1929, the Assiniboine People lived "mostly on wild meat—deer, antelope, buffalo." They made some of the meat into jerky so that it would keep through the winter, and they tanned the hides. "They tanned them for robes and moccasins. What they could spare they sold for what they needed. . . . They had antelope and deer. They made jackets and shirts, leggings and such things with that." Warren Carl/Brings Back noted "the way the Indians treated their hides, if they are going to tan them they usually fold it together in a small pack, or if they are going to just dry it, they will leave it open; they usually spread it out or nail it down on the ground to dry."

As previously discussed, the demise of the bison was a tragic loss for the Assiniboine People. Last from the Assiniboine Tribe of Indians recalled in 1929 when the "whitemen" began their extermination of the large herds: "Sometimes they would kill a whole herd and leave only a few calves that would be running all over the slaughtered ones." "The whole country was filled with buffaloes," Looking commented. "They started out toward the Little Rockies, and large herds were killed off there." Martin Mitchell elaborated:

> The country was thick with buffalo. I traveled with these Indians quite a bit. . . . In 1881 we crossed the Missouri River here at Wolf Point. . . . There was only a few buffalo. All we found indicated where they took the hides off all over the country. That fall we came across at old Fort Peck Agency and we wintered there. . . . I saw the buffalo hunters coming across the river with buffalo hides loaded just like hay. That is the spring . . . and when the winter came we went there to hunt, we took the sleighs. We found no buffalo, but found the hides piled up. . . . Between 1882 and 1883 these Indians went up the river on a hunt, all the tribe. We got near Glasgow.³ All we found was buffalo hides stacked up like haystacks. . . . That was our last buffalo hunt. When we came back in 1883—that is when the starvation started.

In contrast, "the Indian is not in the habit of killing game for pleasure or the fun of it," Warren Carl/Brings Back noted. "Any time an Indian kills game, such as buffaloes or small game or rabbits, they kill them for the purpose of using the meat for their living."

Bison hunting was but one aspect of the seasonal harvesting cycles that brought the Assiniboine into the Cypress Hills. Many other game animals—small and large—were harvested by these people as essential parts of their traditional diet. Deer, elk, and antelope were important sources of meat as well as smaller birds and animals. "Rabbits are good to eat, and also prairie dogs, sage hens and even deer," Sam King noted in 1929. Crazy Bull recalled that year that "we go out hunting out north. I stated that I had been up on the Belknap Reservation and some of these times we hunted and we roamed over in Cypress Hills and Sweet Grass Hills, and over into Canada. We had a lot of hunting over there."

CHAPTER 10

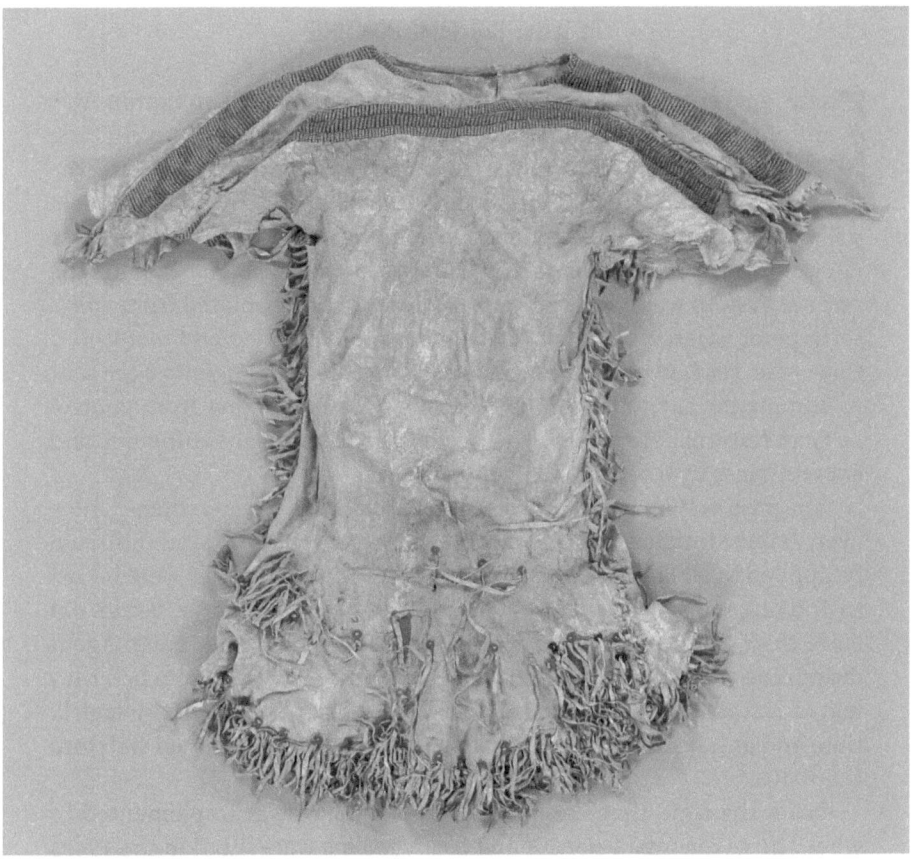

Assiniboine Dress
Courtesy of the Canadian Museum of History, V-C-17.

According to CTK Elder Delmar Runs in 2015, "they survived by rabbits, too, there were so many of them.... There was plenty of game. Plenty of elk, moose, deer, antelopes, buffalo, raccoons. All the wild animals you can name, they were all there in abundance in Cypress Hills.... And there were bears in there, too, cougars. That's how they survived.... Wild turkeys,... pheasants,... ducks, geese."

Traditional life changed dramatically for Carry The Kettle People when they were placed on one little plot of reserve land—not even an area that they considered home. Because of restrictions and permits, they were not allowed to leave the reserve to hunt, trap, fish, or gather. Not even allowed to visit relatives without permission. Because of this, their traditional activities at this time were limited to reserve boundaries.

OWÓKNAGE / CARRY THE KETTLE NAKODA FIRST NATION

RESERVE BIG GAME HUNTING

Early government policy for First Nations in Saskatchewan was administered under the *Indian Act*, with the goal of training First Nations people to become farmers and assimilating them into the greater Canadian society. Through the *Indian Act* and an assimilationist policy based on social Darwinism, attempts were made to dispossess First Nations of their lands and identities: the rationale behind the reserve system was to place them on pieces of land isolated from white settlement where policies could be more easily applied and monitored. Once reserves had been selected and surveyed, Indian Agents were sent to administer them; they had sweeping powers ranging from control of First Nations' movement to control of agricultural equipment and expenditures by a band.

The pass system at first was to be used only for "rebel Indians"; however, Prime Minister John A. Macdonald insisted that the system should be applied to all First Nations. In early 1886, books of passes were issued to Indian Agents, and subsequently First Nations people could not leave their reserves unless they had a pass signed by the Indian Agent describing when they could leave, where they could go, and when they had to return. The pass system, however, was never passed into legislation, and as a result it was never legal, though it was enforced well into the 1940s.[4]

From the time that Carry The Kettle Reserve was implemented to when the government permit and pass systems were lifted in the 1940s, an Indian Agent resided on the reserve, policing the activities of the Assiniboine People. "Down the hills here," Elder Victoria Prettyshield said in 2015, "on this side ... where the school burned down, well just east ... people needed to go to him for permission and would either walk, ride horse, or take the wagon to his home.... They couldn't go out of the reserve because of the Indian Agent. He always had to give the okay." Elder Garry Whitecap mentioned that "they couldn't leave the reserve without the agent's permission. If they did, they'd be thrown in jail.... So they were mostly confined to this reserve.... That was the time when you needed to have permits to go off the reserve, when they implemented the reservations system, implemented the *Indian Act*, to control Indians." And Elder Nancy Eashappie and Terri Prettyshield commented that "we have to stay inside the reserve to hunt and pick. They don't get out.... We're not allowed to hunt off reserve.... The laws state that we can't go off reserve.... You can't hunt out. If you chase a deer on reserve land and it gets out off reserve, well, you don't bother."

CHAPTER 10

When Carry The Kettle People were first moved to the Indian Head reserve, Elders said, there were many animals within the reserve boundaries to harvest and supplement their livelihood. "A lot of deer, but there was just a few elk, not too much," Elder Delmar Runs said. "Maybe the odd moose, but there were a lot of deer. That's what they hunted, . . . that's what they survived on." Clint Haywahe also mentioned "elk, deer (mule deer, whitetail deer), even right down to rabbits. . . . The moose came from the parklands, like Cypress, White Bear and Greenwater. They seldom came through here."

Delmar Runs further noted that

> we had a big reserve at that time. . . . Everything was on the reserve. . . . We lived on deer. The odd time dad would shoot an elk. . . . They come in, because the elk, they travel all the time, . . . [and] they'd come on the reserve. . . . They come in from Moose Mountain Park. . . . Yep, they come by, because I know dad killed some elks when we were little kids. But he never shot a moose. But they said there were some around.

Elder Myrtle Hassler explained that "this reserve was plentiful with everything, from berries to wildlife, we had everything here. But nowadays I hear of people going out to that Moose Mountain there to hunt, maybe up north, and in Cypress Hills. But we didn't do that back then." In fact, Orval Spencer did most of his hunting on the west side of the reserve—"wild deer hunting, rabbits, and stuff"—and Lyle Spencer hunted "elk, deer, moose, . . . there's some on CTK. There's moose and elk out here, with deer." Elder Darlene Whitecap recalled that "they had elk once in a while when they came in," and Darrell Jack said that "I'd rather eat elk than anything else. It's better than beef." Elder Derrick Saulteaux mentioned that "west up here there's lots. Used to be called Greenbush, just southeast of here. There's elk in there now. You go until you get one. Just walk. At that time didn't have a vehicle, and there was no machines around, you did your walking. You dragged them back, carried them, quartered them sometimes—depends how big they were."

Keith Prettyshield and Leroy Walker said that they are providers of wild meat for their families, on "average . . . probably about five elk and maybe two or three moose. We got lots of relatives, lots of family." Clint Haywahe could not say how many animals his grandparents and parents harvested, but they did eat meat every day: "That would be something that's hard to determine because throughout their livelihood they've been hunting year-round just to survive, so I can't put a number on it. . . . They made storage places in the ground, and they'd put it in bags and pack it way down. . . . There's ten of us, five boys, five girls. So you can see why my parents had to continuously hunt."

Carry The Kettle families were very large, with an average of ten or more mouths to feed per household. They survived on wild meat. Because of this, Elders explained, there were no real set seasons to hunt for large game or any set quantity per harvest. Family providers hunted when the meat was required and harvested whatever amount was necessary. Bernice Saulteaux noted that "I have two brothers that were hunters from a young age. They were taken to hunt by our uncles and grandpa and our dad. The importance of hunting was to provide for the family—food, clothing, and shelter, . . . also for moccasins and drums. Everything was used from an animal when they were killed." Elder Art Adams commented that game was hunted "whenever we need[ed] it. We just went out to hunt when we need[ed] it. He never believed in over[hunting]—if you needed one, that's all you shot. If you needed two, then we shot two. . . . Mostly deer and rabbits when we were growing up, . . . just mostly around here, CTK. There were plenty, there were lots."

Darwin Saulteaux clarified when and what he liked to hunt: "Usually, I like hunting the first snowfall, which is now, and before the cows develop young ones inside them. Now is a good time. As well, I prefer myself probably a yearling or a two-year-old calf. To me anyway that's the best meat, nice and tender—fresh. That's what I usually hunt for." Elder Delmar Runs mentioned that his father "would go out and hunt deer [in the fall]. He would kill lots and put them in the shack and just let them hang. He would skin them and just let them hang. And, through the winter, it was deer."

Elder Derrick Saulteaux confirmed that, "just when you needed the meat, then you go out. . . . Summertime we didn't really bother because you get all the flies and the bugs, but when you needed it, yeah. Wintertime we were able to get quite a bit. . . . As long as you're downwind from them, they're easy to get. Don't spook them. You can get pretty close." And Lyle Spencer said that "you can hunt year-round. If you see an animal with a doe—small one—for me I'd rather leave it alone because it has a young one to raise. But you shoot the male. They're good all year round. That's what we live off is wild meat. . . . Sometimes they're hard to find."

Regardless of what was needed when, traditions of "living in harmony with nature," taking only what was necessary, and giving thanks to the Creator for harvests were always abided by. As Lyle Spencer suggested, "it was their way of survival, to honour the culture and the history of our people," and "our native tradition is not to play with life. To honour everything that walks on Earth." He also noted that "our ancestors believed that everything had a spirit, the trees, animals, everything. That's why, when we take something, we give back—even if it's a tree or something, it has a spirit. So we Assiniboine, when we take something, we give something back in honour."

Bernice Saulteaux mentioned that

> we were told by our Elders, parents, grandparents that you don't get greedy, and you don't overkill, because you have to remember that the animal is sacred and that you're using that animal for food. So that is why they said to always share what you got. . . . That was one of the biggest teachings. . . . The other important thing for them was to protect each other when they're hunting because accidents can happen. . . . They had to help each other, protect each other, and watch over each other while they are hunting in the area.

Likewise, Darwin Saulteaux said that

> everything comes into place if you plan your hunt and do your offerings, praying, all that stuff. It all helps. If you're coming here thinking you're going to kill everything and go home, it doesn't work like that. You've got to really prepare yourself, physically and mentally as well. . . . Before we go hunting, we have a prayer, we smudge with the sweetgrass to make sure there's no problems, no hurt, no danger that comes upon us. We offer our tobacco before we start our hunt. We get something, we put tobacco on our hunt to thank the Creator for giving us this animal.

Bernice Saulteaux also indicated that

> the importance for a hunter in our family was to take tobacco and pray that they had a good hunt and they'd be safe. So they offered that tobacco to the Creator. Also, after they killed an animal, they would offer that tobacco to the ground, and that's giving thanks to the Creator for killing that animal, for the food and the shelter, and for the needs that the animal will bring to the family. . . . They also had to cleanse themselves—smudge themselves—before they went into a hunt the next day.

They had to get enough rest because that's a big job for them to go and hunt. So, when they went out, they were asking the Creator to protect them and also to give them the animal to kill. So when they went, they knew that they would be protected.

CTK hunters were also taught how to butcher and prepare their own wild meat: "I make it into sausages sometimes, a lot of people like sausage," Lyle Spencer said. "Other than that I cut it into stewing meat chunks, grind it into hamburger, or chunks of roast." When Elder Wanda Prettyshield lived off reserve for a while as an adult, she still had wild meat: "We used to still get deer out there, . . . a hind quarter or half a deer, and I would cut it up. . . . It would freeze in the wintertime, but in the summertime we would just package it up and put it in the freezer." Bernice Saulteaux noted that

> when they brought back whatever they were able to kill, again they had their certain ways of taking that animal and hanging it up and how they would cut that animal out and take all the insides out. Skin it and all that—the hide—make sure they did a good job because they had to use everything that was in the animal. So they had their ways of how to do that—preparing the animal itself—how to cut it up and what to do.

Drying meat is still a practice performed today. "My uncles used to all hunt," Elder Rena Ryder said. "All deer, no moose or elk . . . on the reserve. . . . They used to dry the deer meat and everything." After Elder Tony Ashdohonk's father passed away, his uncle provided deer meat to his mother for the family, "and they do lots of drying meat. We'd dry meat. . . . We lived good, I guess, we're healthy." Other Elders confirmed traditional hunting and meat-handling practices.

> They got deer, and I don't remember moose too much. I remember elk sometimes, there was the odd one that would go through the reserve. That's the only time they get a moose or elk. And then there was meat. I don't remember my mother ever drying meat, she would can it, but I don't remember her drying meat. . . . I know some families on the reserve would do that. (Wanda Prettyshield)

> I remember grandpa used to dry deer meat on two racks out of poles, you know, and hang that meat on there and light a fire

CHAPTER 10

underneath. There was some kind of smoke they use—some kind of wood they use—that makes a lot of smoke, and they smoke it dry. It was nice, I remember. (Vincent Ryder)

We dried the meat. I remember the old people, my grandma, used to help us in summers. She would help us [to] skin pieces, to help us slice that meat real thin, and they would hang them on, they were twigs, and they'd hang them up high to dry. They'd take those after they would dry . . . and store them. That's for winter. (Myrtle Hassler)

Before reserve boundaries came into effect, the Assiniboine People always hunted for band members unable to provide meat for themselves. Perhaps they had no horses or were widowed, too young, too old, or too sick. It was tradition that all members were fed and provided for—nobody went hungry. This communal practice of sharing is still honoured today by CTK hunters. "After my grandfather lost all his sons, . . . our neighbours helped us with deer," Elder Leroy Hassler recalled. "When he gets a deer, he comes and exchanges with us for potatoes because he's a young guy, and he can go out and hunt." Elder Duncan Thomson said that "everybody used to share if they killed the wild meat. My brother . . . used to kill a lot of deer and pass it around. Just a little bit to eat—help one another." And Elder James O'Watch noted that, "for as long as I know, we always hunted. I hunted when I was young. Whenever we got meat, we passed it around . . . to people who can't hunt."

Other CTK members also commented on the tradition of sharing among the Assiniboine People.

We were always taught to feed your Elders first—give the meat to the people who can't hunt for themselves. Give it away first, and then when everybody has their own meat—their supply for the winter—then we usually carry on and hunt for ourselves and our own families after. (Lyle Spencer)

When I was a younger guy, I used to hunt for everybody. Give rabbits to different families, give my deer to other families and help them out. That's what I would do with my hunting stuff. People would always say "We'll go and get Darrell to go hunt." They'd always ask me for a deer or something, you know, . . . [and I would] just go get it. . . . If they wanted deer, rabbits, or if they wanted ducks, [I would] go out to some sloughs. . . . Whatever they wanted I'd get it for them. That's what I did. (Darrell Jack)

We hunt, if we get two, and somebody wants meat, like deer, elk, or moose, then we go give it to them. . . . Like from now [July] . . . to maybe November or Christmas, we'd get maybe about six or seven. Like you get a phone call, or someone stops you, sees you at the store, they say, "Hey, you got any deer, moose, or elk meat?" Something like that, and we say, "Yep," so we go and get it. (Lyle Spencer)

Everything was used in an animal—the kidneys, liver, heart, even the tongue—and then, when all that was done, they would package all the meat, cut [it] in different sizes, and they would give it to the Elders and to the widows in the community first, and then what's left they would use for themselves. But that meant they would also have to go and make a few trips in order to feed the whole community. (Bernice Saulteaux)

As in pre-treaty days, the hides of big-game animals are considered valuable and traditionally used to make clothing, footwear, jackets, and mittens. "They used them, they tanned the hides," Elder Delmar Runs said, "they made moccasins. Some of them made coats, mitts." Elder Edna Spencer's mother made "moccasins, . . . some shirts, dresses. . . . Some people, they make those mitts." Rena Ryder mentioned that, "yes, my mom used to tan hides. . . . She used to tan them, [make] moccasins. . . . She used to just give them away." And Elder Darlene Whitecap recalled that "I helped my grandmother tan hides . . . to make moccasins, clothes. I remember her making moccasins, she was always beading, making moccasins, and those pants there—I remember my grandfather had one. He had a leather jacket, too, beaded with fringes. They're beautiful."

Other CTK Elders commented on the making of moccasins from tanned hides.

I think all the older people, you know, when we were kids, everywhere you'd go, you'd see people wearing moccasins all the time. We did, too, because I remember running around in moccasins. I don't ever remember shoes until I went to boarding school. And my grandmother was the one that made all

CHAPTER 10

CTK Elders Assist Boy with High-Top Moccasin
Photo provided by Carry The Kettle Nakoda First Nation.

that. I had the wrap-around ones with the flap that would hold them tight. (Myrtle Hassler)

We were wondering why she was making moccasins on the sly. And one time I asked her, "Mom, what are you doing?" "Oh, I'm making moccasins." "For who?" I said. "Oh, for myself," she said, "I'm gonna wear them when I'm done." I didn't see them after, but when she was ready to pass she handed them out. (Victoria, Joyce, and Gladys Prettyshield)

My grandmother used it for beadwork, moccasins, and stuff like that because she used to make my moccasins all the time. When they bought me my first pair of shoes, I was six years old, and I wouldn't even wear them. I threw them away. I used to wear moccasins all the time. (Bernice Saulteaux)

Carry The Kettle Ceremonial Dancers
Photo provided by Carry The Kettle Nakoda First Nation.

CHAPTER 10

> We don't waste. . . . I wore moccasins until I was bigger . . . because my grandmother is a real traditional Indian, and she does all that. She knows how to bead; she knows how to make moccasins. She never wore a made dress. She sews her own dresses. . . . She never wore shoes, she wore moccasins all the time. (Leroy Hassler)

The hide, along with other parts of large game animals, is also used to make ceremonial items. "There's a few that make dancing outfits out here," Elder James O'Watch noted, and Lyle Spencer said that, "yes, the deer hooves or the elk hooves or the moose hooves, like part of the traditional powwow outfits, they use them for belts or armbands." He also told us that the hide of an elk is best for traditional drums: "Oh, yeah, we keep them. My son, he'll tan them and make hand drums or bigger drums." He elaborated that a tanned hide can be used for "jackets, moccasins, that's what it's best for. The hooves, you can make traditional dancing outfits. You can use them for the bells or whatever you want to use them for. Ivory teeth—elk would have teeth right in the back here. There are two they have in the back that are strong—that's why they call them ivory." Elder Art Adams mentioned that "he made hand drums. . . . I know some people would come and pick up the hide, if they knew you had it, they'd ask you to save it. . . . We never tanned the hides. . . . My uncle did once in a while, just to make a hand drum or something." Finally, Elders Delbert and Clayton Thomson indicated that, "with the hides, we stretched them out, and whoever wanted the hides, we give them away. . . . I stopped at the store the other day, and I told them I was going to go hunting here, and this one guy said, if you get an elk, he wants the hide. I said, yeah, you can have the hide. They probably make drums or something like that."

CURRENT BIG GAME HUNTING

With passes, permits, and restrictions lifted, CTK People were finally able to practise their traditional livelihood outside reserve boundaries and expand their hunting, trapping, fishing, and gathering activities throughout the Traditional Territories of their ancestors. Current traditional hunters now harvest big game throughout Alberta, Saskatchewan, and Manitoba.

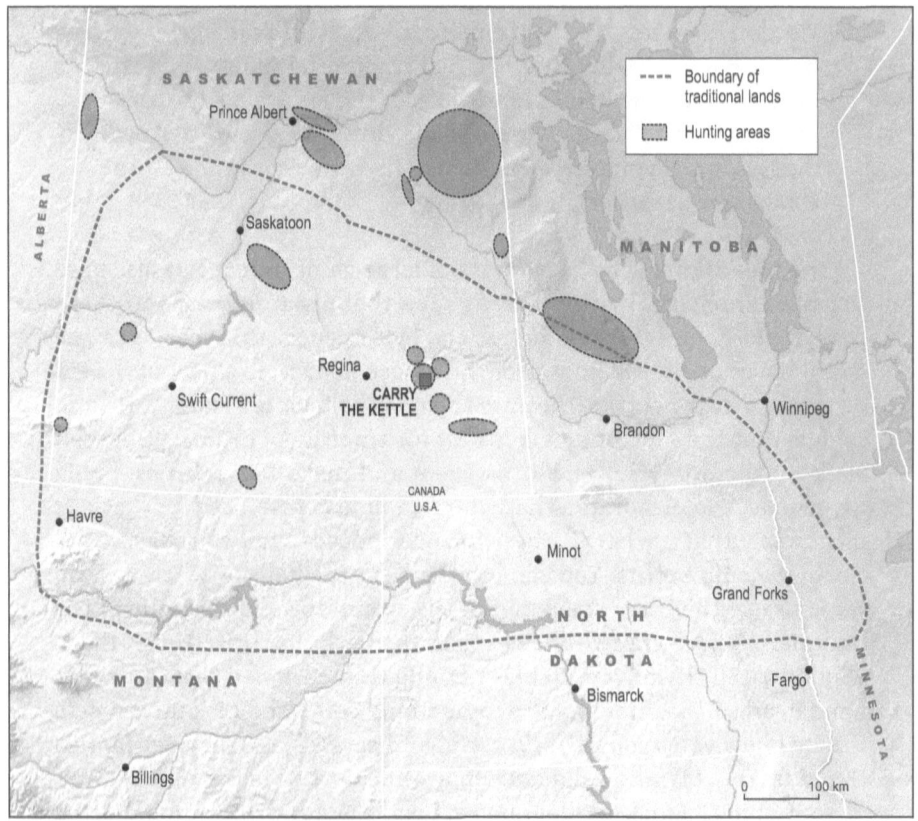

FIGURE 15: Big Game Hunting Areas

THE CYPRESS HILLS AND THE UNITED STATES

CTK members have returned to the Cypress Hills area to hunt, fish, and gather. "Cypress Hills, they have lots of elk out there," Elders Darlene and Garry Whitecap said. "They have moose, bears. . . . They don't hunt the bear, mostly moose, deer, elk." For Clayton and Delbert Thomson, "Cypress Hills, down that way, . . . that's our old stomping grounds. . . . We'd go for two or three days. Camp out." Although Leroy Walker's father died in 1978 when Leroy was only nine years old, he still remembers hunting and fishing with him: "My dad went to Carlyle actually and sometimes [to] the Cypress [Hills]. Only two places he went."

Clint Haywahe noted that,

> well, for years, prior to 1882, our ancestors have frequently done hunting and trapping and fishing and survived off the land there. And that's where we call home yet today. According

CHAPTER 10

to the stories that I've been told from my parents and grandparents, it was just a regular way of life for them out in the Cypress Hills because of the abundance of wild game and the berries and all of the sustenance they can get off of the land. Because that's what they made their living from, was off of the land itself.... Where we are today there's bush but not as great as there is in the Cypress Hills area.

CTK Elders confirmed the traditional land use of the Cypress Hills area:

> There always was talk about wanting to go back over there to hunt, but I don't think my dad did, and I don't think my grandpa did, but my brothers, they went back there. My brothers started to go back there in the '70s—the '60s and the '70s. Every year they'd go over there to hunt, to Cypress Hills. (Bernice Saulteaux)

> When I was working in Moose Jaw there, I used to go to Cypress Hills almost every fall.... There was a few of us that would go, and we would camp over there for a week.... There was moose there, too, but we didn't really bother the moose. Some of us did get moose, but we went for elk or deer. Lots of deer there too.... We'd make sausage out of it and burgers. (Roswell Saulteaux)

> I was listening to some of the Chiefs talking, and a bunch of the boys are going out hunting around Cypress Hills and going someplace else. So everybody's still going there. Doing their wild game hunting wherever they can, and when they can, and pass the meat around to people who can't hunt. (James O'Watch)

Clint Haywahe also noted that "throughout the entire province, and some people go and hunt in the United States, we also have band members that live in the United States, so it's a wide variety of land ... but also into Alberta and Manitoba." And Darwin Saulteaux recalled

> coming here [Cypress Hills] for years, and I was a bush pusher as a young boy. Now I brought my son with me, and I'm going to be teaching him what I was taught. It's going to be a good hunt for us. On the way coming, we saw a bald eagle, and we

just left this morning from Maple Creek, and a golden eagle flew right across from us. So I think we're going to have a good turnout.... It's like an owl. Some people say it brings good luck or bad luck, it just depends. For an eagle, though, it's luck—there's a sign there.

Lyle Spencer explained that there are different areas to harvest large game in the Cypress Hills: "There's different parks. A provincial park and what they call the 'west block'—that's where you hunt.... The only time we hunt outside the park is when it's open season, like for whitetail deer. But you can still hunt if you ask the farmer. But if it says 'no hunting,' 'no trespassing,' you can't hunt—but if you ask you can." He elaborated on the hunting opportunities in the Cypress Hills:

> Our lands that we had out there are for hunting, and a lot of people hunt out there, but it's supposed to be for CTK hunters, but it's a long ways to go up there to hunt.... When they purchased the land, it's hunting territory for CTK, or if you have a friend to go out there with. It's Traditional Lands where you can smoke your pipe on any areas there. They have the feast and ... sweats. But if you want to hunt, you get your animal, one or two, but it's just other hunters go in there, and they don't respect it, they drive all over, it's always better to just walk in.... Other than that, they got the whole provincial park there you can hunt in.

According to Darrell Jack,

> we just went to the park part, that's all where you were allowed to hunt. That's the only place we hunted in there. I never tried anywhere else, just the park, I stayed in the park. There's other places, you go right to the Alberta border here, but you can't hunt into the Alberta side. If you get caught in the Alberta side, you get charged.... So what they do is go around into the other side and chase them back. Don't take a gun, though. Just chase them back.

And Elder James O'Watch mentioned that "we went to three or four provincial parks. There was one in Carlyle, Cypress Hills of course.... It was just so far away.... If you go over there and kill an elk, you almost have to come home right away unless you have a way to keep the meat cold. And you didn't want to go over there just for one, you'd want a few of them."

THE QU'APPELLE VALLEY

The Qu'Appelle Valley, with its proximity to Carry The Kettle Reserve and its lush landscape for animals, fish, and plants, is a frequented harvesting location for the CTK People. Orval Spencer commented that "I never did go off hunting off the reserve.... The only place I would be off the reserve would be in the valley." Elder Delmar Runs hunted throughout this area with his grandparents: "There was a lot of wildlife around the area because there was not much hunters at that time. There was plenty of everything,... a lot of deer. Get a deer and drag it home. In the wintertime, you drag them home and skin them." Elder Vincent Ryder also hunted in the Qu'Appelle Valley with his grandfather and outlined some of the places that they would frequent:

> The valleys, up and down the valleys. There's a valley running from Standing Buffalo north, runs quite a ways back north. I remember there used to be a road there, across from the town [of] Lipton. There was a valley, and that was the reserve line just a ways from that town of Lipton. And we used to go hunting there. And they used to go hunt across the valley south from Standing Buffalo. Today there's a park there.... The valley west, on the south, was the Pasqua Reserve.... We used to hunt as far as Pasqua.

Darrell Jack also noted that "there's a lot of creeks and stuff, walking through running water, rivers to go hunting, which I think was dangerous. That was when we were younger, though. That was in the valley, the Qu'Appelle Valley. We hunted deer in there all the time, around Wolseley in there, back around the valley. A lot of deer in there."

PARKS, CROWN LANDS, AND OTHER WILDLIFE AREAS

It is not just the Cypress Hills and Qu'Appelle Valley regions that CTK People now use for traditional harvesting but also the wildlife areas, Crown lands, and provincial and national parks to which they have access north, south, east, and west of their reserve. "I can remember from long back when I was a kid," Darrell Jack said, "they hunted around here, just out here on the reserve.... When we got to our age, we could go hunting all over the place. We go up to Moose Mountain, ... Carlyle area, Maple Creek, Hudson Bay ... and Greenwater, in there too, ... and Cypress." In their interview, Clayton and Delbert Thomson noted that "I got a little older and started hunting elk in different parks, Greenwater or Carlyle and Cypress Hills." "I hunt all over," said Leroy Walker. "I'm totally different from my parents and grandparents. I hunt from basically Prince Albert all the way over, every place, Saskatoon, Manitoba, ... elk, moose, deer."

Clint Haywahe knows that his parents and grandparents did not hunt and trap just within the perimeters of the reserve:

> Throughout the territory here, in Saskatchewan, right from Cypress Hills to Manitoba, ... my family members have hunted from the park, Cypress Hills, up to Greenwater, and down in White Bear, and then Pipestone Valley. ... We grew up the same way. ... I started hunting when I was about fourteen and hunted throughout the province. ... Me and my brothers would go out. So we've maintained that lifestyle throughout our lives—what we learned from them. That's why I say carry on traditions.

CTK Elders Darlene and Garry Whitecap mentioned that,

> nowadays, people go to Moose Mountain and down [to] Carlyle, way over by Hudson [Bay], ... way up by Yorkton. ... The park, way over there on the border, ... they go all over. ... Greenwater, that's another area. In modern times, they amended the *Indian Act* at certain times, and nowadays—these modern times—you can hunt pretty well anywhere as long as you have a hunting licence. So they travel all over—Alberta, Saskatchewan, Manitoba.

And Elder Delmar Runs confirmed "anywhere. Well, this is the Assiniboine area—that's where all the Nakoda People hunt. And all this was a great place for Assiniboine to hunt. Even in Winnipeg, Manitoba, and close to the Rockies, that's all hunting grounds for Assiniboine there."

Kurt Ryder's father provided for his family by hunting: "We used to go up north hunting long ago. We used to go way up to ... Hudson Bay, ... Yorkton, ... and Porcupine Plain, Greenwater, ... mostly walk for moose. And we'd go to White Bear, ... just in the park." Likewise, Clint Haywahe said that "my dad would go hunt in Hudson Bay with his friends. That's where they used to go hunt. They'd go for a week,

CHAPTER 10

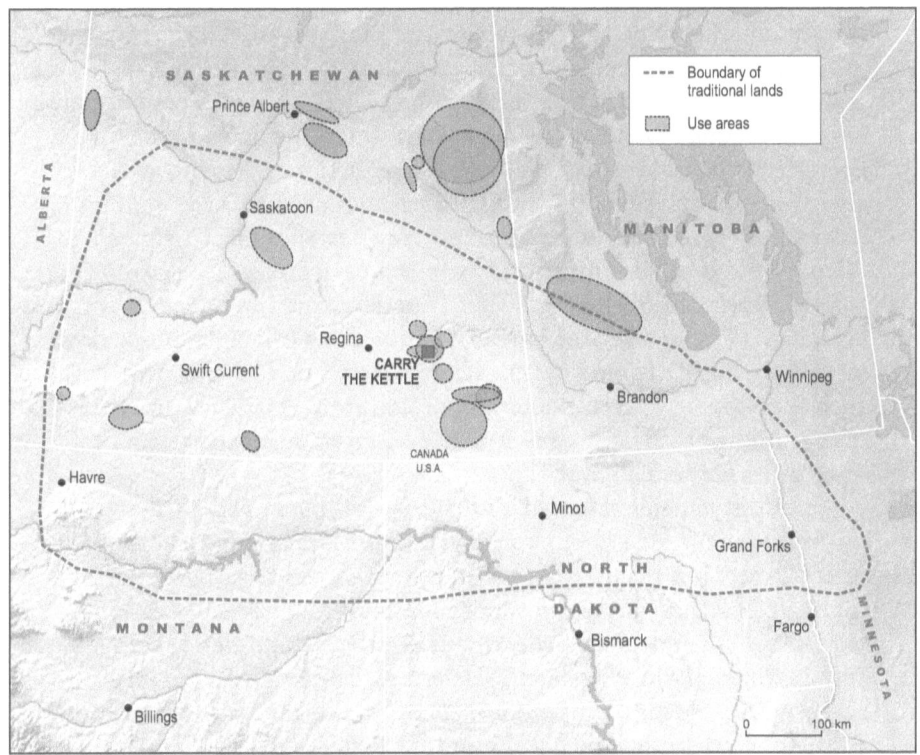

FIGURE 16: Traditional Land Use Areas and Crown Lands (National/Provincial Parks)

week and a half, ... and then ... Greenwater, ... that's where he'd take hunting trips. Down to the park and Cypress was like two-day hunting ... camp out there, ... mainly elk and moose because they were rare around here."

Elder James O'Watch commented that

> the one up north in Kamsack area, it's called Hudson Bay, I think. ... I went one year and north of Kamsack in the forest there. ... Elk, moose were the main targets. Deer we had over here, rabbits. It was the big game that we didn't have over here. And bring it back, cut it up, pass it around, put it into storage. Pass it around, especially to the old people, people with large families.

And Keith Prettyshield noted that "we go to Moose Mountain Provincial Park or Cypress Hills or in the north here, Greenwater. ... Well, actually it's everywhere when hunting season opens up—there's seasons for the 'white guy' hunters. For that season, it opens up the third week in November, and you can hunt anywhere."

The provincial parks surrounding Carry The Kettle Reserve are all hunting grounds for CTK members. Darrell Jack explained that, when harvesting elk, he would travel to "Moose Mountain Provincial [Park] area, then you go up to Riding Mountain National Park, Duck Mountain." Elder Rena Ryder's son Lyle Spencer provides wild meat for her and the family and often hunts in many of the park areas: "He goes to the park in Cypress Hills," Rena said. "Him and Art and them. They go on a big trip.... They go to Greenwater it's called." As Lyle noted, "elk, deer, moose, ... there's some on CTK. There's moose and elk out here, with deer. Otherwise, we go to Moose Mountain Provincial Park or Cypress Hills or in the north here, Greenwater.... Partridge in Moose Mountain, there's lots of them all over."

The Prettyshield sisters—Elders Victoria, Joyce, and Gladys—said that most people did not hunt around Moose Mountain until later years since "it was too far to go." Still, some made the trek. Elder Bernice Saulteaux's father hunted in Moose Mountain: "They went to Moose Mountain, but not often, like whenever they could get there." The grandparents of Elder Art Adams also travelled to Moose Mountain to harvest big game for their families: "They hunted moose and mostly elk and deer. It wasn't around here. Some of the time they would talk about going to the Moose Mountain area whenever they had to, to look for moose and elk. The most thing they had around here was deer."

In later years, with vehicles, Moose Mountain became much more accessible. That's when the Prettyshield brothers began going there more often for elk. "I hunted in Moose Mountain, too, for elk or deer ... just for the day. Close by, it's only an hour's drive," Elder Roswell Saulteaux said in 2015. Elder Garry Whitecap mentioned "the last time I went to Moose Mountain, me and a group of guys.... I plan to go hunting, me and my friends here, this fall." And Leroy Walker indicated "Carlyle, ... Moose Mountain, just that it's close to home, but it's a little tougher hunting grounds.... It's more like quad and bush and things like that.... There's no bear over there."

Both Leroy Walker and Keith Prettyshield hunt in Porcupine Provincial Park, Greenwater Provincial Park, and wildlife areas in between, including Crown lands and farmers' fields when permitted. As Elders Delbert and Clayton Thomson pointed out,

> there's some wildlife parks over here, two of them, we go in there once in a while, ... the CFRAs.... I usually just go for

CHAPTER 10

two [elk], and that should do me for the winter. . . . We went to Greenwater, and we got twelve in one day—one night. And then my brother-in-law came back with a truck and loaded them all out. . . . We passed them all out.

Lyle Spencer said that "Greenwater—that's north of Fort Qu'Appelle—it's a provincial park. . . . Same thing there [as with Cypress Hills], lots of posted land, but if you ask then you may get permission. But sometimes you won't because of the crops and that. We go for elk, deer, and moose there as well. . . . It's wood—flat land." Likewise, Leroy Walker said that he hunted up north, "in this whole area right here, that vicinity. That's where I go. I go up to that park, this park here, and plus I know a lot of farmers in this particular area [Porcupine Provincial Forest, White Fish Provincial Park], Greenwater, and right between. . . . This is all forest in here too. . . . It's all forest in here and wildlife lands."

Keith Prettyshield's family knew many of the farmers in surrounding areas, so it was never difficult to get permission to hunt on their lands, Keith said: "My grandparents, they knew quite a bit of farmers . . . all over—south of the reserve here, east, west. . . . Kendal, Odessa, Gilmore, . . . and down to Preeceville, Ocean Man. . . . Elk, deer . . . they had to hunt. . . . Like all around these little areas, these local areas, we hunt around there." Leroy Walker often gets permission from farmers to help cull animals that are overpopulated in their area: "Sometimes there's guys, our friends, like our non-Native friends, say there's a moose population that's overgrown, and they're bothering the farmers. They'll call us to do some killing for them." Clint Haywahe noted the importance of getting permission to hunt on private land:

> Our daddies tell us that, if you're going to go hunt on farmers' land, go and get permission, so that's what we practised. Because at one time there was a lot of wild game in the area, this was probably I'd say mid-'80s. There was one farmer where deer was getting into his granaries and that, so he contacted us, and we went out. But before we went to his place, we got his permission. . . . Then I went to the RCMP to let them know. So there was people who phoned in . . . and reported it, but nothing happened because the RCMP knew, and the owner gave us permission.

Leroy Walker hunted up

around . . . Yellow Quill. Yellow Quill and Fishing Lake, they have lands around this area, and I got a lot of friends in this area, so we hunt up on their lands. And there's a lot of Crown land that belongs to the government which we're allowed to hunt on and wildlife lands. . . . All the way down to Kelvington, across to Preeceville, up to here—the border—back. . . . That's all forest, bush, wildlife lands, and everything.

Keith Prettyshield noted some other hunting areas: "We have land down around the valley, so we hunt there. We have land by Indian Head, so we hunt there. . . . I used to hunt south of Candiac, right up to south of Glenavon, . . . around Pheasant Rump territory. Never hunted on their reserve lands, but there's lots more land there. Sometimes on the way going down, we'll like zig-zag going up and zig-zag coming back." Leroy Walker sometimes went in other directions:

I go up here by Lloydminster with my buddies. . . . Lots of elk, moose, deer in those areas too. . . . Just south of Lloyd, . . . there's a couple of reserves there. . . . They have a bunch of treaty land entitlements, so we go on their lands. And same with the Prince Albert area, and same with Melfort and that area, and same with Saskatoon area. There's a couple of areas we're allowed to hunt, . . . so we hunt. Like I said, I kind of hunt all over the place. . . . Wherever there's wildlife lands, that's where we hunt.

Historically, CTK People harvested bison as an important part of their plains culture. They travelled continuously, far and wide, to obtain this important source of meat and supplies. Big game has always been a necessity for the Assiniboine People in this region. Although some of the species harvested have changed because of the loss of populations and government interference, the need for these animals for subsistence and cultural continuity is still alive today. In the next chapter, we discuss smaller game hunted by CTK People and the importance of such activities to their traditional way of life.

CHAPTER 11

Iyátaga nagu Hokúwa, Zik'daŋna, Wanúyabi Čusína Wokšubi

Harvesting Smaller Game and Birds, Fishing, and Trapping

Smaller game animals were always a mainstay of the Carry The Kettle diet. They added diversity to big game harvests and were particularly important in times of scarcity. Originally being a Woodlands culture, the Assiniboine adapted well to fishing and snaring smaller game to supplement their diet after the demise of the bison. After being placed on their new reserve lands, fishing was not an option, but harvesting smaller game became more of a necessity to feed their families. In this chapter, we discuss the continuation and adaptation of these seasonal activities after their removal from their Cypress Hills homeland, including species harvested, locations, methods, and uses. We also outline their minimal fishing activities—since their "new" reserve had no lake or river to harvest this essential part of their diet—and discuss the traditional trapping activities undertaken by CTK members long after the fur trade had ended.

SMALLER GAME AND BIRDS

Smaller game animals were a definite mainstay for Carry The Kettle families. The grandparents of Elder James O'Watch "lived off the land . . . on [the] reserve here. There used to be lots of bush here where they hunted and trapped." Referring to small game, Elder Darlene Whitecap said that, "oh, we had prairie chickens, rabbits, grouse, and

Left: CTK Member with an Owl; Right: Adam Spencer Checking Snares, n.d.
Photos provided by Carry The Kettle Nakoda First Nation.

partridge," and Lyle Spencer mentioned "rabbits, gopher[s]. . . . For the birds, I hunt ducks, geese, prairie chickens, and what they call bush grouse." Elder Derrick Saulteaux "used to go hunt rabbits, partridges, deer, . . . skinned them, gutted them, cooked them up. . . . That's all when I was younger." "Yes," Clint Haywahe said, "rabbits, prairie chickens, partridge . . . when we were younger, . . . and today yet my brother and I still go out hunting." "Sometimes," Leroy Walker noted, "maybe geese, grouse, rabbits. . . . It depends if somebody wants muskrat, beavers, anything like that, I shoot them for them."

CTK Elder Delmar Runs mentioned "porcupines, cougars, rabbits. Mainly rabbits were in abundance here [on the reserve]. . . . Porcupine, and sometimes there's skunk, but you need to know how to eat skunk. Partridges, prairie chickens, there were plenty of them, . . . geese and ducks. . . . That's how they survived, by the rabbits, prairie chickens, ducks, geese, they were all here—but their soul and their heart wasn't." His father harvested many rabbits on the reserve: "All we did was snare rabbits. We lived on rabbits."

Elder Wanda Prettyshield recalled her dogs chasing rabbits away from her house as a child, "that's how plentiful they were. You see rabbits everywhere you go. You go for a walk, you see rabbits and prairie chickens, when you're riding. . . . As kids we rode horses, that's what we did, and we talked about the hunting." Similarly, Elder Darlene Whitecap said that "there were plenty of rabbits in the area. . . . They'd go out in the field and hunt them. . . . We lived more in the southwest, . . . [and]

CHAPTER II

they hunted all over." She and Garry Whitecap indicated that "we snared rabbits.... Everybody knew how to snare animals—rabbits—just put a snare in the bush and go back in half an hour [and] you had one.... My neighbour, he was teaching all his nephews. They're small. He's younger than me, only thirty. Keith was teaching his sister's children to snare rabbits behind the house."

According to Darrell Jack, "we checked the sloughs, rabbit snares we checked at the same time as trapping. We had to check our rabbit snares. If you didn't do it in the morning, the magpies got them. You had to be out there early morning, ... [and] when it's getting dark you check them again." There was no shortage of rabbits, Elder Art Adams recalled: "Rabbits, ... there was lots in them days ... everywhere you went. You went inside a house, and all you smelled was rabbits and deer meat.... Wherever you went, they would offer you a cup of tea and a chunk of meat.... Back when I was sixteen, seventeen, ... there was lots of eating rabbits.... There's still lots, but it declined."

Prairie chickens and partridges could be found all around the reserve, and "it was nothing for the boys or my dad to go out and get a prairie chicken.... Prairie chickens were kind of all over the place at that time," Elder Wanda Prettyshield said. "We lived on prairie chicken[s] and ducks," Kurt Ryder recalled, and Lyle Spencer likewise noted the number of "prairie chickens ... anywhere on the reserve ... and the 'bush grouse,' what we call out here, partridge." "Rabbits, partridge[s], prairie chickens," Elder Art Adams noted. "We'd bring them home, and I'd help skin them and all that." Darrell Jack confirmed the abundance of

> prairie chickens, yes, we used to shoot a lot of those too. I'd snare them.... There's some here and there.... Used to just set a tree up made of willow—grey willow or something—stuck them in the ground and put a snare wire there. And so, where they dance on the trails, you would snare them. And otherwise just sit and watch them dance too. It was fun growing up.

Finally, Elders Victoria, Joyce, and Gladys Prettyshield said about prairie chickens that their "dad used to take us to watch them dance—chicken dance.... Out in the prairies you used to see them. You could hear them. They looked so nice. They had their own place to dance. That's when they're mating."

Waterfowl were always harvested annually around the many sloughs throughout the reserve, and "the most common ones to eat is geese and ducks," Lyle Spencer said. Elder Leroy Hassler always had duck as part

Carry The Kettle Child Travelling by Horse
Photo provided by Carry The Kettle Nakoda First Nation.

of his diet: "We have ducks right in our front yard right now. We have beaver in our front yard." "I shoot, like in the spring," Keith Prettyshield added. "I hunt ducks and dog goose but mostly ducks... on the reserve here."

Although it was not permitted, Elder Roswell Saulteaux used to sneak off reserve to hunt ducks: "A long time ago I'd take the shotgun off the reserve, just knock them off, put them in the trunk, and bring them home.... Sometimes where we work we used to come back in the evening shooting ducks. Mostly coming back... on farms off reserve... fifteen, twenty, thirty miles south." Although the birds harvested were used for their meat, other parts of them were used as well: "Yeah, the geese," Lyle Spencer said, "I keep the body feathers for making pillows. Or you can make a fan for dancing." The birds are also important to CTK People for their eggs in the spring, according to Elders Duncan Thomson and Roswell Saulteaux: "I used to get eggs.... Yeah, duck eggs." "We used to collect a bucket of eggs, duck eggs," the Prettyshield sisters said. "Because they had their nests on the water, we'd have to wade in. That was our starving time. I remember getting eggs in the spring." Victoria clarified that, "in our hunting days, our mom and dad would say, 'Go to the slough and find eggs or ducks.' There were young ones then, and they couldn't fly. A whole bunch, we would chase them around. The slough would always go up as far as our waist. We used to collect eggs and catch a few ducks and take them home. We had a hard time, too, getting them home." Elder Wanda Prettyshield commented that "we had duck eggs in the summertime, I remember that. . . . The boys would get those, around the sloughs, wherever the ducks would get their eggs, I guess. I never got any. I was shown once what they looked like, but I never had anything to do with picking them."

Smaller game was also harvested while hunting. Lyle Spencer explained that there are many partridges in the Moose Mountain area and rabbits throughout all the parklands, though he says that they are not always plentiful. "When we're hunting in the provincial parks, . . . for the past four or five years it's been low, but they're starting to come up again. There's too many coyotes that take them, catching them."

TRAPPING

CTK Elders explained that they, their fathers, and their grandfathers trapped quite a bit on the reserve—often as an income activity on its own or done simultaneously during other hunting excursions. "Back then there was a lot of bush and water and sloughs," Elder Bernice Saulteaux remarked, and Keith Prettyshield said that "my grandfather used to trap constantly." "Muskrat for the fur, weasels," Elder Leroy Hassler observed. "Our fathers and grandfathers used to trap, like coyotes and bears, whatever." Roswell Saulteaux explained that "my grandfather, that's what he was trapping, too, muskrats, weasels." Elder Rena Ryder noted that "my dad used to go trapping. Trapped muskrat, beaver, weasel. . . . On the sloughs around over there, he used to walk around all over. It was the morning—come back towards the evening."

Other CTK members also commented on trapping activity on the reserve.

> Starting in December going into January, the coldest parts of the month. . . . Beavers, muskrat, weasel, minks, coyotes, fox—we get those for their fur, in the wintertime, when their fur is nice and thick and shiny. . . . Gophers, get those in the springtime. . . . I mostly trap out here on Carry The Kettle. (Lyle Spencer)

> Trapping, I just barely remember going out with my dad one time chasing mink. That's the only time I remember my dad. In the wintertime, we would chase mink. They just kept running and hiding. We would dig them out and get one. It took us all day just to get the one. . . . We'd shoot it. . . . They were good

money in them days. Even if you just got one, you could feed yourself for a long time. (Elder Art Adams)

I learned how to trap, and I skinned deer and stuff, I learned from my brothers, and weasels, muskrat, and all that. . . . I used to walk a long ways to do that, . . . over all my area in the bush up here. . . . At that time, there used to be quite a lot of muskrats. . . . I trapped a lot of weasels too. I had to trap them before the weasels get to my rabbits and eat them up. (Elder Duncan Thomson)

Long ago when he [his father] was younger, he used to trap for coyotes and stuff like that. A source of income, whatever they could get, . . . coyotes or fox, muskrats. He used to catch a lot of muskrats. Sometimes he had to go a long way to find animals. Even deer, rabbits. Sometimes they go in seasons, and they used to trap a rabbit in one bush and go around and around until it came out, or even deer, . . . on the reserve. (Kurt Ryder)

An adult muskrat weighs from 0.6 of a kilogram to 2 kilograms and is approximately 40–70 centimetres long—half of which is tail. These long tails are covered with scales rather than hair to aid them in swimming. When they walk on land, these tails drag on the ground, making their tracks easily recognized. Muskrat fur is short, thick, and warm, becoming prime at the beginning of December.

In sloughs and marshes, muskrats build houses or "push-ups" up to ninety-one centimetres high, constructed from vegetation and mud. In snowy areas, they keep the openings to their push-ups closed by plugging them with vegetation, which they replace every day.[1]

Darrell Jack recounted his time spent trapping: "I was the lighter guy, so when the ice got thin they'd send me out onto the ice on the muskrat traps. So I'd open up the top and reset the trap for them, take out the muskrats. . . . I felt the water a few times too . . . right back around where we live. Back of the reserve. There were a lot of sloughs then." Elder Delmar Runs also "did a lot of trapping, so did my brothers, . . . muskrat trapping. [There were] a lot of muskrats . . . all around the sloughs and lakes. They had big lakes. . . . Muskrats, they build their houses around the lakes and the big sloughs, and that's where we get them. But I don't think anybody did eat those muskrats—we never did anyway. Weasels, mink, we have all those." Elders Victoria, Joyce, and Gladys Prettyshield noted that

CHAPTER 11

they hunted them.... There was a lot then, because my dad used to follow tracks—that was in the wintertime. And muskrats, they used to make their little houses you could see, and my dad used to set traps, and that's where he caught them, because I went out with him a couple of times—watched him how he did it.... Just down the hill, there was a great big slough, and there were muskrat huts—a few of them anyway.

CTK trappers are skilled in the art of cleaning, skinning, drying, and stretching their furbearing animals. "We did the tanning, and we skinned them and put them in the boiling water.... We did a lot of that," Darrell Jack noted. Elder Tony Ashdohonk said that "my brother here, he skins them. He skins weasels, mink, and coyotes. And he's good at it.... [He] has his stretchers at home, ... his coyote stretchers, his weasel stretchers." Elders remembered often seeing furs drying from the rafters of family mud shacks preparing them for personal use or for sale. Elder Bernice Saulteaux said that "I remember they used to have all these furs hanging on the ceiling to dry so that, when they get enough, they'd take them in—in the spring. They had weasel pelts and muskrat, beaver, and even rabbit." "The men did that with their muskrats and weasels," Elder Myrtle Hassler stated. "They'd clean them and hang them up around the house to dry. And you either made clothing out of them, or they sold them for people on the outside."

The trappers sometimes saved the pelts for their own use. "Mink—that fur—they make mitts with that," Elder Delmar Runs noted. Elder Vincent Ryder claimed that "they used to [make] at one time blankets and stuff from the fur side, especially for babies. Rabbit skin blankets. They tan them somehow to make them soft, just like cloth. They make it nice."

However, the main purpose of trapping furbearing animals was to sell the pelts for income, as mentioned by Elder Gladys Prettyshield: "We used to sell muskrat fur, and beaver, mink, ... out of the slough. Mink was pretty good money at that time." Sometimes they were traded for other essential items, Lyle Spencer said: "We were trapping, beaver and muskrats, coyotes, fox—salvage the furs. Or, if someone wants to trade for whatever, shells, trade for hunting supplies." "Only hides they sell are [furbearing] hides and weasel, those ones," Elder Tony Ashdohonk said. "Mink—dig them out, we'd dig mink out. My brother knows that too. Sometimes you sell them for a dollar an inch, from the nose to the tip of the tail. Coyote is forty bucks straight." And Elder Raymond Prettyshield mentioned

CTK Family with Animal Harvest
Photo provided by Carry The Kettle Nakoda First Nation.

muskrat, mink, and they used to sell the pelts, weasel. They used to collect a lot of pelts and then sell them to Regina. They'd sell them to Heisman's Hide and Fur. Used to go in the train at that time. Used to get on the train in the morning, get to Regina in the afternoon, go to that hide and fur, they sell the pelts there, . . . do a little shopping too. Then they come home. By the time they come back home here, it's about nine o'clock at night. This is the wintertime, it's cold too. It's a good thing they have a stable in Sintaluta where they used to keep the team of horses in there, fed them, hitched them up, and they come home. Used to come back to the reserve here about one o'clock in the morning or something like that. I remember that, I was just a little kid.

Lyle Spencer still traps on the reserve today even though "the fur price in the economy is low, but it's still nice to trap, but you got to get a good amount of fur if you want to take them in. You can't just take one or two."

Furbearing animals were also plentiful throughout the Qu'Appelle Valley, as Elder Vincent Ryder indicated: "Some years we used to trap muskrats . . . on the lake, on the top of the hill. There were big sloughs and lots of muskrats. I guess they come from the lake there. . . . They'd catch the odd mink because my grandfather used to skin the mink with

CHAPTER 11

a drying board. They did that with the muskrat, too, and they'd sell them. They made good money on that mink."

Trapping has played a vital role in the traditional livelihood of Carry The Kettle First Nation both for personal use and for the fur trade. Furbearers were used for their skins and fur, and many of the species were also used for food. Smaller game was always depended on for subsistence, especially in times of food scarcity. Birds, rabbits, and other smaller game have provided food when larger game was not to be found and have been a mainstay in the CTK diet.

FISHING

Unlike the Assiniboine home in the Cypress Hills, Elder Delmar Runs told us in 2015, "there were no fish here [on Carry The Kettle]. . . . They wanted fish, but we couldn't get fish. There were lots across the valley. But we had no transportation in the wintertime to go over there and fish." "I never fished in my life," Elder Tony Ashdohonk said, "because there's no water over here, and for us to go down to the lake over there it's kind of far. . . . But I like fish—I like to eat them." There was a lake near Katepwa Lake that was supposed to be set aside for CTK members to fish, but few knew about it, and those who did found it difficult to get there, as Elders Wanda and Raymond Prettyshield indicated:

> At that time, you had to have permits for everything. So I don't know if anybody ever went off the reserve to go fish there. . . . They had a place along the lake there for CTK to go fish, but to this day I don't know what happened to that. . . . Some of the old people used to talk about that . . . when they didn't have to get permission anymore. Some of them went down to the lake to fish.

Since there was no place to fish on the reserve, Elder Duncan Thomson recalled buying fish from vendors, and Raymond Prettyshield noted that, "in the wintertime, sometimes from Fort Qu'Appelle, someone used to bring fish." Keith Prettyshield and Leroy Walker would "get [their] fish from up north. . . . They do a lot of fishing, and they bring it back and distribute it to [us]. So [we] take what there is." "There is no fish here," Elder Leroy Hassler stated, "you have to go to Fort Qu'Appelle, but somebody would go over there, after we had vehicles, . . . and bring back a load of fish and sell it to us. But that's not really—that's once in

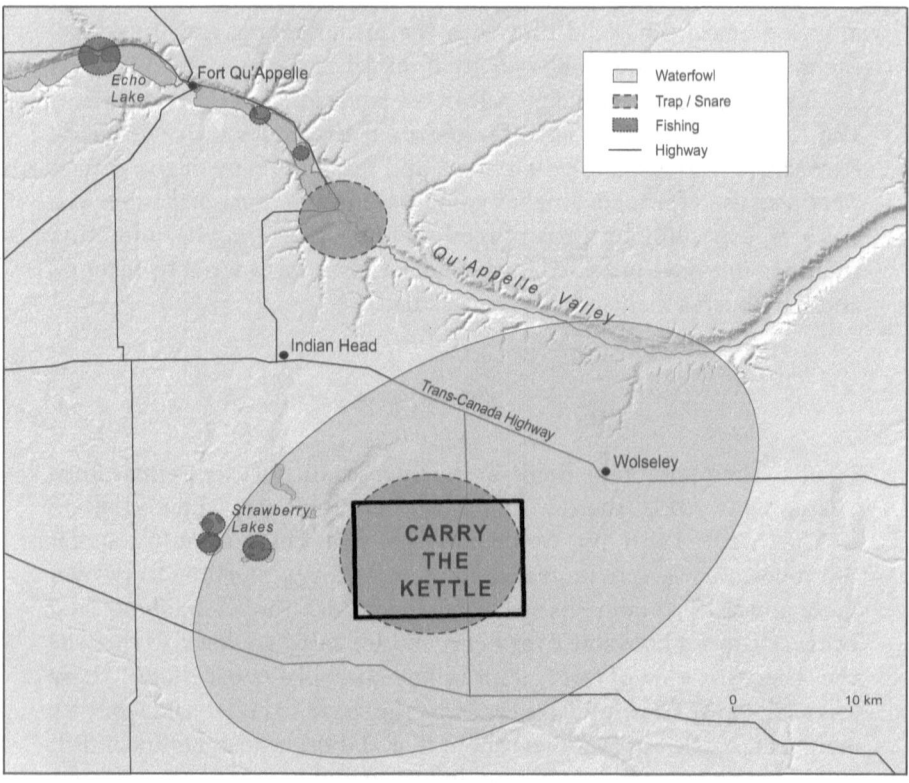

FIGURE 17: Waterfowl, Fish, and Trap/Snare Harvest Areas

a while type of thing." Elder Duncan Thomson also said that "we used to buy them. Standing Buffalo Reserve used to come around here and sell them around the homes—so much a pound. Then there's a guy from Saskatoon. He used to come down here in a truck selling them. Sometimes you'll miss out on them. Every year somebody came out." Finally, Elder Vincent Ryder noted that "my brothers out here, they used to hunt, and sometimes they'd come down to Standing Buffalo, and they'd bring some deer meat, and we'd trade them with fish. Whenever they wanted fish, they'd come down to Grandpa there.... He'd go as far as the next reserve there."

FISHING OFF RESERVE

Elder Delmar Runs explained that his grandfather harvested many fish in the Cypress Hills: "Oh, yeah, ... they catch a lot of fish. You dry the fish, and then you cut them . . ., and then you save them for winter. And then in the wintertime you can eat that fish."

THE QU'APPELLE VALLEY

With water so scarce on Carry The Kettle Reserve, members now travel to the Fort Qu'Appelle region to harvest fish to supplement their traditional diet. "Down in the valley, around Fort Qu'Appelle," Clint Haywahe said. "That's pretty well it. . . . That's one thing growing up, it was hard to get any fish, so it's mainly the big game and that." "Down here by Standing Buffalo, too," Kurt Ryder noted. "In the valley there, yes, my mother used to fish over there, my uncle. We have a lot of relations over there." And according to Elder Delmar Runs, "they said they fished a lot. Nice fishing right there."

Kurt Ryder's father fished "everywhere. We used to go along the spillway. Right near Katepwa. That's the closest place, I guess. . . . Mostly jacks or pickerel." "I fish but not so often," Lyle Spencer said. "Pasqua Lake, Katepwa, . . . it's pretty well all one area. . . . They have jack, rainbow, pickerel, suckers, catfish. What we catch we take." Orval Spencer also noted "Katepwa, around Lebret." Although Elder Art Adams never did much fishing, he ate fish "when it was given to us." He was aware, however, that other CTK members fished in Katepwa Lake:

> They always talked about a fishing area down in Katepwa. . . . I remember going through there, and some guys would tell us that CTK's area for fishing was down there, . . . around Lebret there, down in the valley. Lots of people used to work at that spud farm—we used to work down there, . . . and my mom told me that's where CTK had their fishing—that little waterway there. . . . Some guys still go there today to go fish in the spillway.

Kurt Ryder likewise said that

> we used to [fish there]. My grandfather told me there was a place, they have a place out—it's right by Katepwa as you come off that bridge and you come alongside there, there's a church or something there. . . . It was open, . . . there was a place set aside there for CTK, . . . and I went there one time, and I tried to find it. It was different, it was all grown in.

Elder James O'Watch also said that

> there's some land down there by Katepwa.... This was told to me by my late Uncle Lawrence Thomson. He was a Chief here for many years.... He told me that we had land down by Katepwa there that they set aside for us, so anytime we wanted to fish we could go down there and go fish. Where they talked about, where the Kanokama Beach is, ... there was land over there for us to go fish.... I think there's what, seven bands that own that land there, and we were supposed to be part of that.... I don't know if it was ever recorded, that part of our history.... I don't know what happened, ... they just exploited us on that one.... I used to do that in the spillway, catch some fish and pass it around ... up at Katepwa.... So it's not kind of a rebirth—it's always been happening. We never lost it completely.

Leroy Walker remembered his grandparents fishing "basically just around the Fort Qu'Appelle area, and sometimes they'd go to relatives up north, but where up north I don't know. I couldn't tell you because I was just a young guy."

STANDING BUFFALO

Elder Darlene Whitecap explained that they ate a lot of fish when they went to Fort Qu'Appelle: "Standing Buffalo, we have relatives, we have a grandmother in Standing Buffalo, and our grandfather there was a fisherman.... They used to fish on Echo Lake—Grandfather Paul.... We used to go there and fish and bring home fish." She mentioned that "there used to be plenty of fish in there, not after people started farming. I think after the water was polluted because, you know, the sanatorium, the hospital, is right there near that lake, and I think they flushed all the sewage into that lake. That's why that lake is no good, ... and that lake [Echo Lake] was no good for a long time, ... since probably in the '60s."

Elder Vincent Ryder is worth quoting at length regarding fishing near Standing Buffalo:

> I remember Grandfather, they used to give us nets, but you had to have a permit to use that. The Indian Affairs office there would give us a permit, an Indian permit, to go fish all you

wanted. So that's what we used. . . . The wardens would come—we had to put our name on the board where we had our pick in the ice so they know your name and treaty number. . . . In the spring, when it gets to March, oh, you'd get some big walleyes, whitefish.

There were trails in there to ride around the lake. In wintertime, he used to go and fish in the sleigh. We had a team of horses, and he'd drive on the lake, and they pull our nets. Pull out all the fish and take them home. That's how we made a living. . . . There's a lot of people on the reserve [Standing Buffalo] that still do fishing because they love it, fish with nets, it's a living.

Sometimes outside people would come in and see the fish. "How much?" "Oh, I don't know, ten dollars, twenty-five dollars." "Okay." And other times my grandma used to fillet the fish, and clean them, and take them to the farmers. . . . And my grandparents used to travel in the wintertime in the sleigh and a team of horses and sell their fish. . . . There used to be a settlement north of Standing Buffalo, where Lipton is now, that was the Pacific Railway coming from Winnipeg, just between Standing Buffalo and Lipton, there used to be a little community there. . . . And on the west of the reserve, that was a German settlement. . . . They came in trainloads, . . . lots of settlements, and they liked fish.

PARKS, CROWN LANDS, AND OTHER WILDLIFE AREAS

These areas off reserve also served as fishing holes for CTK harvesters. "My dad used to fish over here too, . . . Round Lake," Kurt Ryder said. "My grandpa married a woman from there, so he used to go there." Elder Darlene Whitecap noted that "lots of them go fishing down over here—they call it the fishing hole—Poplar Point. That's where the guys all go fishing today. . . . My son goes fishing there, but he throws his fish back. . . . We used to eat it." According to Darrell Jack, "we did very little of that, but did most of it down in the valley, up in Kenosee . . . and Greenwater, . . . whitefish." Kurt Ryder mentioned trips farther afield: "We used to go up to Norway House, Manitoba, and my uncle used to go up . . . and bring a lot of fish from over there. Sometimes they brought back one of those great big sturgeon fish, the kind you'd have to cut in half to fit in the deepfreeze."

Elder Darlene Whitecap explained that her family fished "but not on [the] reserve. . . . There is a lake called Strawberry Lake, but maybe they went fishing over there. That was a big lake. It's in the northwest area off the reserve. . . . Probably not today . . . but in that era, probably before 1950." Because there was no fish on the reserve, Elder Delmar Runs remembered, Strawberry Lakes was stocked with fish "once in a while. I don't know how they worked it, but people would bring a lot of fish in here—it was paid by the Indian Affairs—and they would all go out and get their fish. . . . They had to buy it for the reserve. That's the only way we got fish. We had fish once or twice, that's about all I can remember."

Elder Derrick Saulteaux raised his family in Calgary and regularly continued traditional activities while there: "Used to go up Kananaskis area. Kananaskis, the Rockies, . . . big country there. . . . Deer, moose. No elk over there. Mulies mostly." He also harvested fish while living in Alberta, "trout, catfish, jackfish, . . . [in] the Bow River." He also gathered "chokecherries, saskatoons, raspberries. Wherever you can find it. Tsuu Tina, that was a reserve just outside of Calgary on the outskirts." And he attended spiritual ceremonies in "Tsuut'ina, Morley, Siksika."

Traditionally, fish were always an important part of the Assiniboine diet. With no opportunity to fish on Carry The Kettle itself, members still found ways to harvest fish themselves or purchase or trade for fish to include in their traditional diet. In the next chapter, we discuss the foraging activities of CTK members, including their berry and plant harvests, their traditional use, the locations, and the cultural significance of these harvests and activities.

CHAPTER 12

Pežúda Wošpíbi, Wibázoka, Wokšubi

Gathering Medicines, Herbs, Berries, and Wild Vegetables

Gathering has always been an important aspect of Assiniboine culture. Harvesting berries, herbs, and wild vegetables provides a nutritious and essential balance to the Assiniboine traditional diet, but fruits and roots are also used in principal feasts and spiritual ceremonies. Although gathering activities were continuous throughout millennia, after the Assiniboine were confined to reserves, gardens played an important role in balancing Carry The Kettle's traditional diet. In this chapter, we discuss some of the plant-harvesting locations and uses. We also discuss the relevance of medicinal plants to these spiritual people and the need to protect them for future generations.

MEDICINES AND HERBS

Traditionally, the Assiniboine had healers—Medicine Men and Women who knew which herbs to find, where to find them, and how to use them. These "Medicine Elders" are not only traditional healers but also spiritual leaders within the community and embody traditional approaches to healing that are holistic, considering mind, body, and spirit.[1] Elder Darlene Whitecap's grandfather symbolized these attributes: "I know he was a Medicine Man, and he helped people." Elder Nancy Eashappie knew that "some people were using them. Like Charlie

OWÓKNAGE / CARRY THE KETTLE NAKODA FIRST NATION

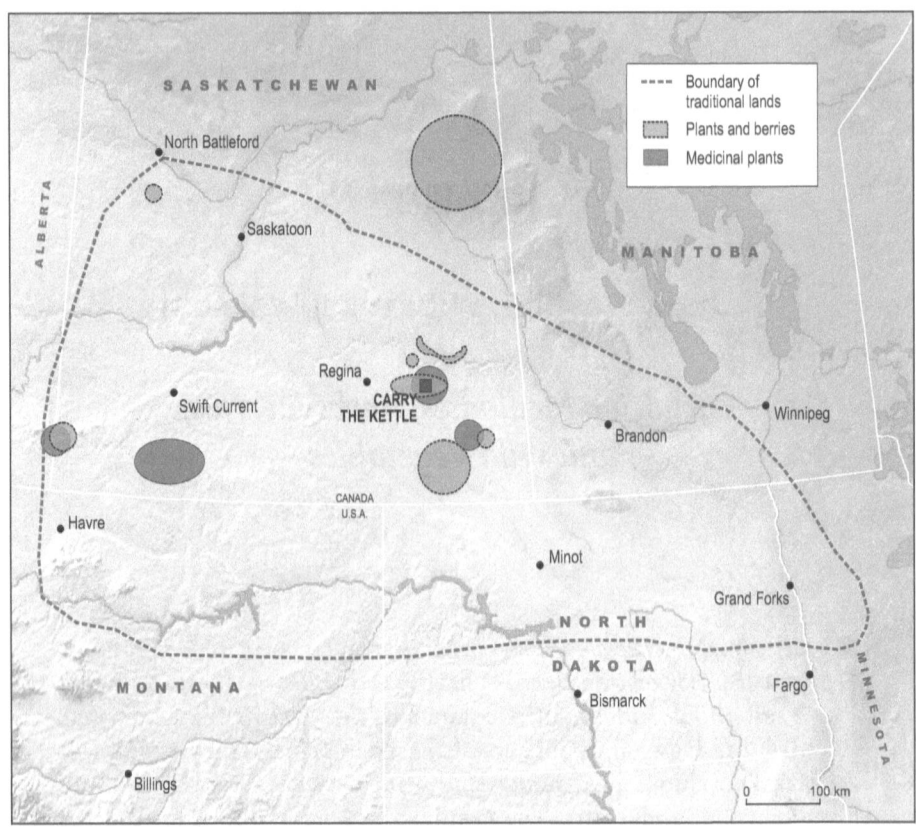

FIGURE 18: Medicines, Plants, and Berry Harvest Areas

Ryder Senior, he was. . . . People will go to him when they're sick, and he cures them with what he has." According to Elder James O'Watch, "every grandparent, the old people, knew the medicine because they used to pass it on, and a lot of them had grandchildren, so all the old women and old men, they all knew medicine—some of them made it. But there was always one or two that . . . were kind of holier, I guess you could say. They're the ones that people would go to because they had a gift of healing." He also noted that "my stepgrandmother, she was blind, and she was a Medicine Woman. In fact, she raised all of us. We never went to see a white doctor too much; she gave us herbs. And they knew where to pick them, in the spring, other ones at certain times of the year. They knew when to harvest anyway. . . . She had a blanket . . . over her shoulder coming back."

Elders Victoria, Joyce, and Gladys Prettyshield said during their interview that

CHAPTER 12

my doctor was my grandma. . . . My great-grandfather is the one that used to sit up in the hill. And my mom said "Your great-grandfather used to sit up on the hill there—fast—four days—he'll get his answer up there, and he'd come down the hill." And he knew what medication—what plants—to get. And he would go out someplace and go and dig out his roots. He'll come home, and he'll make it. And that's how we all got better. Anything that's wrong with us he'll fix us up. . . . My grandmother . . . and Bertha O'Watch used to know all those herbs, used to have them all in those bags. . . . Anyway, we used to go to her place, and if there was anything wrong with us, if we were sick or whatever, my mom used to take us out there, and she used to treat us. But she got them from my grandpa.

There is a certain protocol for collecting medicines, and not everyone knows where they are or what they are used for. To be recognized as the one who performs this function, an individual must be validated in this role by the community. This knowledge is sacred and often passed on through family members and taught by one individual healer. "Right to this day," Clint Haywahe said, "we still have some medicines . . . handed down to my mom and dad—how to go find it, where to go find it. So we still have some today that's been handed down from generation to generation." "Of course," Elder Nancy Eashappie clarified, "you can't just go ahead and use it like that. . . . If you see one out there, you can't take it and use it, because those things are given through Medicine Men. So if you're going to dig one . . . it's got to be given to you to use it."

A number of Elders clarified the process for collecting plants properly.

You have to take tobacco with you to dig up herbs. But it's got to be given to you. I can't go around and start digging around for medication and herbs like that, it's got to be given to me. . . . In order to do that, I have to give that person tobacco in order to give me the okay to go. It's a very spiritual thing. . . . It comes to us, and that's the way it goes. . . . We did a lot of praying back then too. (Victoria, Joyce, and Gladys Prettyshield)

The funny little thing, when you take the plants, you stuff them into the ground so they will grow again. Superstitious. . . . That's what Leroy's grandmother did. . . . You pray for it. . . . You take just what you need and put the rest back. And you pray for that. You give thanks for that. And what you're going to use you keep, and in fact you don't take all of it, you always take a little piece and put it back in the ground. (Leroy and Myrtle Hassler)

When I was younger, my grandmother used to come to our house.... She'd come with her sacks and her little homemade shovels and axes, ... and she used to make me go with her when she went medicine picking. And I'd have to sit there and clean her medicines for her because before she took anything from the ground she prayed. We'd pick it, and she prayed, and she made me clean all these little things, and she'd take what she needed and put it in her bag, and I have to put the rest back in the ground and cover them.... She did a lot of herbs and medicines, ... and when they pick them they'd clean them and hang them up on the ceilings. (Myrtle Hassler)

My grandma, she was raised that way, using herbs and stuff. I always remember when we'd go on the wagon, and she'd look down and holler at Grandpa, "Look, there's the medicine." And we'd stop, and she'd go off the wagon and go dig it. She had a little thing with a handle and a blade on it made of sticks and go digging, ... gather it all and put it in a bag, ... on the prairie roads. At that time, there was just a wagon trail with two deep ruts, and there was medicine there.... And she would use that, and there's people who used to come. I remember the Whitehats would bring their children anytime they were sick—they'd come down, and she'd give them the medicine. (Vincent Ryder)

When I was about eight, nine, ten years old, my Kokum, she was blind, and she had a lot of medicines. We never went to the doctor when we were children. She used to tell me "Come tomorrow and come and help me pick medicines." So I used to go with her, and I used to like going with her because she used to pack a quart sealer of sweet tea with milk and sugar, boiled potatoes, boiled sausages or short ribs, bannock.... She was blind, so she used to feel them. On hot days, we were in the bush picking medicines, on not so hot days we were in the prairie. There were days when we went by a slough. (Freda O'Watch)

Elder Bernice Saulteaux explained that her mother was a midwife who delivered many babies on the reserve: "The grandmother would

CHAPTER 12

Striped Snake Woman, n.d.
Photo provided by Carry The Kettle Nakoda First Nation.

give the mother, back then, this medicine to use because it would help them with the childbearing. And I remember it was a young flower." "We never went to the doctor," Elder Freda O'Watch said. "If we had pneumonia, . . . [my grandmother would] treat us, we had a toothache she fixed us." Likewise, Elder Leroy Hassler commented that

> I lived by that medicine. I fell off a horse one time, . . . and I cut my leg open. . . . So what my grandfather does, he tore his jacket off, . . . tore his shirt off and tear it up, and stuffed some sage in my mouth, and tell me to start chewing. I start chewing. When I got it wet—he's chewing too—and then they plaster me. I got a cut about that long and about that wide. . . . I had to go all the way to Fort Qu'Appelle with my leg wrapped up like that. So every time I cut myself, I treat myself and put it on there. I know how to doctor myself, which is against the law.

Victoria Prettyshield mentioned that her mother

> was telling us long ago that they used to live on plants, medicine, even trees, berries. Anyway, she said she ate too much thorn berries, and she was blocked up, she was just about dying, and my grandpa heard that and said "I'll do something." So he went up on the hill, and he sat up there for four days. Never ate, no water, no nothing. He just sat up there, and he prayed and prayed and prayed. The fourth day he came down. He told my grandma what he was going to do. So he went out, and he dug in the ground. They told him where to go and get this medicine. So that's where he went. He dug it out, he came back and boiled the medicine, and he prayed. Mom was dying already, and my grandpa gave that to her. The next day she was okay. She got up and started walking around. It cleaned her all out, and she wasn't sick after. That's the good thing about berries and medicine, and my grandpa's prayers were really strong up there, getting his prayers answered. I always think of that today, how we can be strong as old people—like our grandfathers and whoever had spiritual ways.

Elders interviewed shared other stories of traditional medicines and their uses but were very hesitant to provide many details regarding what they looked like or exactly where they could be located. Darrell Jack noted that we picked some raspberry roots... just around the house.... [My grandmother would say], "Come on, let's go pick some medicine roots."... We used another kind of root,... a rosebud,... used that too for something else, because I know we put it away.... We picked them in the fall, and she dried them, and they were all over in the house. Like they were for different reasons, like for sicknesses, for flus, and stuff like that.

According to Elder Garry Whitecap,

there's other barks and stuff like that,... the oils, or they scrape, that's medicine. Whatever a human being puts in their body is a medicine.... It keeps you alive. It makes you feel good when you're full and healthy. That's a medicine—these animals. And that includes saskatoons, chokecherries, all that stuff, it's all medicine. All those things have to be protected. But people are trying to claim that—they're all for good health,... water. If you don't have those, you're going to die.

Elders explained that there are many harvesting locations for medicines throughout their Traditional Territories that need to be honoured, protected, and preserved. Bernice Saulteaux mentioned that

they're all over places, in the areas where it's a little bit untouched, there's still some lands that are like that.... I know some of them.... And then, her [her mother] and my other cousin,... I used to drive them around, and we'd go picking here on the reserve. They'd tell me what this was good for and that. So that was good, but it was so late in life, you know, to do that, and a few years later they were gone. My mom passed away in 1995. So that wasn't that many years that she started to come out with it.

Elder James O'Watch mentioned

certain areas where the medicines would grow, where the flowers would grow. There are some that grow after a fire, you got to wait for a fire to go through, and that medicine is used for I think bee stings, any kind of stings. And the bottom root itself, if you're digging, you clean it and make tea. You make enough for a cup and drink it. It's because of the fire..., that's where that plant is. It grows after a fire. Firewater—that's a medicine that was given to me. . . . They picked their medicines at that time of the year, some in spring, some in summer, and some in the fall again.

And, according to Elders Garry and Darlene Whitecap, there were

> medicines all over. . . . Some of them are only known by Medicine Men, traditional people. Lots don't know. Even just out there, there's [a] lot growing, but they don't tell nobody. . . . Rat root, . . . there's lots of that, . . . they know about that. . . . Like sage is a medicine. You know, it's silver and smells nice. They dig it up, and all of a sudden it's growing somewhere else again. You see it all along roads that are newly built and stuff like that. . . . But there's others out there that are sacred that, unless they go out and fast, and Sundance, they won't know about stuff like that. Those need to be protected.

Elder Bernice Saulteaux's mother knew of these medicines and where to locate them. Bernice and her mother often travelled from Carry The Kettle to White Bear Reserve and Mosquito Reserve to pick medicines to trade with those in need: "We would pick medicines here and go over there, and they would trade with my mom and my cousin . . . because some things they have over there we don't have over here. And some things we have here they don't have over there, so we trade." As Elder Freda O'Watch noted,

> at that time she [her grandmother] had mentioned that our ancestors, through stories she heard, there were a lot of medicines here in the Cypress Hills area that didn't grow in the prairies. A lot of good medicine that had a lot of good curing qualities. They had to alternate and learn to use other medicines. They talked—all the Medicine People—and they exchanged. If one didn't have this one, they exchanged. They did that geographically, too, with other people, like our Cree brothers and sisters, the Saulteaux, Dakotas, whatever, because certain medicines grew geographically in different areas. Like, by the mountains, there's also medicines by the mountains that grew. There's a type of fungus that grows in the mountains on the evergreen trees. So they shared these things. So I guess they had, after being forced out of here [the Cypress Hills], our ancestors had

CHAPTER 12

Carry The Kettle Member Attending United Church
Photo provided by Carry The Kettle Nakoda First Nation.

to make new ways of surviving. They had to learn and exchange medicines that were available to where we were put.

Traditional medicine was harshly repressed during the early colonial period as Christianity was introduced and Indigenous spirituality considered "heathen." Many of the oral traditions and teachings essential to the holistic wellness of the Assiniboine People were kept secret out of fear and not passed on to the youth in the usual oral tradition. Elders Garry and Darlene Whitecap explained that

> there was some concern about a lot of the medicines—that a lot of people don't understand them because they're kind of like a sacred thing. But, you see, the way we use them is for good health—so people will get well, be healthy, and live. But a lot of people don't understand that on this reserve and all around. They're kind of leery. This comes from the residential school system. And the churches instill that belief of the devil, ... that fear.... That's really turned the Indians off to their old ways—just saying that they're for evil. They're not, they're for good health.

Elder Bernice Saulteaux said that

> my grandmothers on my mom's side, they were all Medicine Women. And my grandma herself was. But when the churches came in, they discouraged them from picking the medicines anymore. So my parents on my mom's side became Christians— so they gave up all that traditional way of life. But my grandmother, mom's grandmother, her name was Stabbed Many Times, she's the one that was stabbed many times in Cypress Hills. . . . She was a Medicine Woman, and she was teaching my mom the medicines. . . . She [her mom] learned it, but she kept it to herself—she didn't share it. . . . It was only in the mid-1980s when the church apologized to us for the wrong they did. It was only then that she'd start taking us out and showing us the medicines and say "This is good for this and that—that's what my grandma taught me." She remembered.

BERRIES

Elder Myrtle Hassler explained some of the spirituality of picking berries that was passed on to her from her grandmother: "When I went berry picking with her, she told me 'Just pick what you need. Don't get too greedy. . . . Leave the rest because the birds and animals need something to eat in the wintertime.' That always stuck with me." Elder Joyce Prettyshield also mentioned the importance of respect for nature: "We have to respect Mother Earth because she's the one that provides us with everything, our clothes, our food, water that comes out of Mother Earth. The plants, the beautiful different plants. They have all different kinds of tastes. Different berries, different kinds of trees. So we have to have respect for that—for Mother Earth. She comes first."

Carry The Kettle members gather these foods throughout the reserve as their ancestors did before them: "I do all over the reserve. There were saskatoons, chokecherries, raspberry patches, gooseberries. I knew all that area," Elder Duncan Thomson said. Elder Myrtle Hassler recalled how plentiful the berries were when she was a child: "[You could] pick them right out in your backyard. Just around the area, just a few feet away." "We picked them," Elder Delmar Runs mentioned. "They were small, but—pails—we would fill them up." Elder Wanda Prettyshield said that her family picked strawberries in the pasture: "There was a certain area they call the pasture that we used to go through. And there's black

CHAPTER 12

currants too. . . . That was back in the '60s." "Just yesterday I picked about two gallons of saskatoons along the road over there," Elder Garry Whitecap said, and in their interview Elders Victoria, Joyce, and Gladys Prettyshield mentioned "chokecherries. Oh, we picked them all over, they're all over the place. There used to be a lot of trees all over our area there, . . . everywhere you go. . . . I remember . . . hazelnuts, chokecherries, saskatoons, pincherries, raspberries, strawberries, gooseberries. There's something they used to call Hawthornes—they're berries that grow. Hazelnuts in the trees."

Berry picking was recalled by a number of Elders:

> In them days, there was a lot of raspberries, . . . and then we have—a mile south from us around the hills—there are patches of raspberries there. So that's where we get ours. And there are other places, but we just went to the one place, and we had enough for the winter. . . . The saskatoons were just outside of our door behind our house. They were all over. Chokecherries too. We didn't have to go too far for those. (Delmar Runs)

> Berries, I used to eat those. Chokecherries, . . . we used to pick them along the field where my dad worked up the ground. There used to be bushes around there, and we used to pick berries from there. Saskatoons and that. (Edna Spencer)

> All over the place, . . . mostly saskatoons, chokecherries. . . . Just over here, around the powwow grounds, that's one. . . . I think everybody still goes over there today. . . . Other places you could look for strawberries, but you had to go look for them. They just grew in particular spots. The old people knew where they grow. (Art Adams)

> When we'd go for wood, . . . if it was berry picking time, as kids, we had no choice, we had to go along. And my mother would pack, and we'd have sandwiches there. And we'd pick until there was no more there to pick . . . lots. It seemed like a lot because we'd all have our pails, and we'd dump it into a dish pan, and my mother would put a sack on it and tie it up, and we'd bring it home like that. (Wanda Prettyshield)

> Greenbush, lots of berries around here. Saskatoons, chokecherries, pincherries, raspberries, all kinds around. That's what I was gonna

do this afternoon, go picking some chokecherries. They're ripe. Eating some yesterday, they're ready. . . . They're all over, along the pipeline there, west over here. (Derrick Saulteaux)

"Wherever they were in season," Kurt Ryder said, "sometimes we'd have nothing here, so we'd have to drive out for saskatoons or whatever. Just about all over, we had to look for them because sometimes you get a frost, and when you do you have to go a long ways." Likewise, Elder Wanda Prettyshield noted

Carry The Kettle Elders Picking Berries
Photo provided by Carry The Kettle Nakoda First Nation.

that "as kids we had to help pick raspberries, strawberries, saskatoons. There's certain areas that had strawberries; my dad had his certain places where he had to go pick every year. Him and my mother knew where to pick. And they picked pincherries . . . along the house. . . . We'd have to pull the trees down in order to pick the berries." And Elder Tony Ashdohonk said that "they're damn good, pincherries. . . . The other day I see some, a small tree with pincherries on it. I was going to stop and eat some, but I want to wait until they get a little bigger."

CTK members gather berries when in season and then dry or can them to sustain them through the winter. "They'd put all the berries in a big cloth, and it's always way up there, and it's for winter," Elder Myrtle Hassler explained. Elder Delmar Runs mentioned "chokecherries, saskatoons, gooseberries, wild rhubarbs, pincherries, raspberries, strawberries—there were plenty here. Mom always canned all of those and dried them, and we always had fruit through the winter." "She preserves them too, my mother," Elder Nancy Eashappie noted, "or maybe dries them. Saskatoon, chokecherries, gooseberries, hazelnuts, pincherries, and sometimes strawberry." Similarly, Elder Wanda

CHAPTER 12

Prettyshield mentioned that "my mother canned fruit every year. From the time I was little until she passed away, she always canned. . . . My mother made pincherry jam."

According to Elder Tony Ashdohonk, his mother "collect[ed] berries in the fall and put them away. We ate them . . . during the winter too. . . . Eat the same thing all the time, and you live for a long time. . . . [We ate] saskatoons and chokecherries and raspberries. We don't can raspberries; we just eat them right away. And there's gooseberries, but same thing, we eat them right away. Pincherries, we eat them right away too."

Darrell Jack mentioned that

> my grandma always took me picking because I was one of the better pickers. . . . If we went picking, our treat was in the fall, . . . in the winter. . . . We got to eat our raspberries and saskatoons, chokecherries, or whatever. . . . That was the benefit of picking and working. . . . We always had canned raspberries, canned peaches, plums, . . . and the saskatoons, we canned them. Crab apples we canned. And so, when no one was home, my grandma said "Go down into the cellar and get a jar of raspberries or a jar of fruit or something."

Often chokecherries would be crushed and dried to eat on their own later or to be mixed with meat: "I helped her crush some berries," Elder Darlene Whitecap said. "She would put them on a long board and make them into patties to dry. And she'd put them away because she had a cellar that was just full of potatoes and canned stuff." Elders Victoria, Joyce, and Gladys Prettyshield also mentioned that their mother "canned them . . . and dried them. . . . Mom used to can saskatoons. Dried them, made little patties, crushed them with a stone. And their fridge was underground. They used to dig a great big cellar . . . and put them all in there. To keep it cool—for the winter." As Elder Vincent Ryder commented, "Grandma used to go picking with some other ladies. They would get together and all go picking. Chokecherries, saskatoons. They would crush those chokecherries. They find a flat rock and then crush those chokecherries on that. And they dry that. Dry that crushed cherries and mix inside dry deer meat." Finally, Elder Victoria Prettyshield said that "they told me they were digging somewhere, and they found this bag, and they found this—what do you call it?—pemmican. Strawberries, chokecherries, squashed with some meat or something. It was buried in the ground, I guess, and they found that, pemmican, . . . someplace on Carry The Kettle."

WILD VEGETABLES

Wild turnips, onions, and rhubarb were also gathered and used by Carry The Kettle People. "Rhubarb was another one that they grew at home," Elder Wanda Prettyshield noted. "Always rhubarb everywhere, and I got rhubarb back of the house here. So I preserve rhubarb as well." "We used to dig out wild turnips," Elder Gladys Prettyshield said, and "that's what we used to eat, wild turnips." And Darrell Jack mentioned "even wild turnips we used to get, too, but that you had to dig deep, deep into the ground to get those ones. Around where we live, . . . just a couple miles back, down south." Elder James O'Watch recalled that "my sister and them were out picking and said they couldn't find one—wild turnip. I think you have to get those in June or May, so they couldn't find them. But those I like, wild turnips. They grow upside the hill. My uncle took us out one year and went picking them. We ate every one he brought home."

TRADITIONAL LOCATIONS FOR COLLECTING MEDICINES, PLANTS, AND BERRIES

THE CYPRESS HILLS

Known as the "cherry picking place" by Assiniboine ancestors, the Cypress Hills were full of berries, herbs, and medicines harvested annually by the Nakoda People. This region had large concentrations of chokecherries, saskatoons, raspberries, bull berries, gooseberries, and currants. Rosebuds could also be picked, as well as other fruits and wild vegetables such as turnips, onions, and rhubarb, either for immediate use or to dry and store for a later date. "According to them," Elder Delmar Runs said, "when they picked the berries—chokecherries—they dried them for the winter." First Eagle mentioned back in 1929 that "I know we have been over in that section of the country during the summers, gathering berries. . . . White Earth and the Knife River and out north to the Eagle's Nest, and out north to the Canadian border. That is a good place . . . every summer."

THE QU'APPELLE VALLEY

Lyle Spencer gathers berries—"raspberries, saskatoons, chokecherries."—while fishing in the Qu'Appelle Valley Elder Edna Spencer indicated that "we go down the valley, Fort Qu'Appelle around there, because there's hardly any [saskatoons] around here [the reserve]. . . . So we just pick chokecherries around here." Elder Derrick Saulteaux told us that the best berries are in the Qu'Appelle Valley, "like west, when you drive through to the Fort, just like grapes, just hanging." "We used to go to Fort Qu'Appelle, in the valley," Stacey Hotomani said. "But we don't anymore. . . . Our grandpa would take us over there, [but he] passed away six months ago." The grandparents of Elder Delmar Runs did quite a bit of gathering in the Fort Qu'Appelle area: "Berries, a lot of juneberries, . . . plenty of chokecherries and cranberries and saskatoons. Saskatoons wasn't one of the main ones because when they picked saskatoons—today we can them, but in those days they didn't—they dried the saskatoons and they bagged the saskatoons up. And the chokecherries at that time—they crushed them with a stone. And they had enough saskatoons and chokecherries, enough supply for the winter."

PARKS, CROWN LANDS, AND OTHER WILDLIFE AREAS

Lyle Spencer also picks berries around Moose Mountain when he is hunting since "there's berries out there. . . . Well, there's some." The Carlyle area is also an important place for CTK members to gather herbs and medicines. "If you're up in this area," Leroy Walker mentioned, "you got to pick some black root. . . . My old grandparents used to go just the other side of Indian Head, go pick wild turnips and that there." Kurt Ryder said that "we used to go up to the reserve up here, around Broadview [to pick berries]." Strawberry Lake was also a harvesting area for herbs and medicines. "On our side," Keith Prettyshield indicated, "our land used to go out to Odessa . . . and around these Strawberry Lakes, that's my grandfather's area. I used to walk and pick certain kinds of sage, wild turnips, wild onions." He and Leroy Walker also said that

> there's [a] lot of places . . . [where there are] natural herbal medicines and that. . . . There's lots of different areas you go. . . . We used to go over here west of the reserve. . . . And we used to go over—the other side of Carlyle to pick black root and that. It's the only place it grows . . . along the south part. . . . [It is] used for colds and flus and things like that. Just dry it up and drink it. . . . Even up in this area here there's always what you call rat root, and along the valley there's all different places. Certain things only grow certain places.

Although Carry The Kettle People have been maintaining their traditional livelihood as best as possible within their allotted reserve boundaries, increased settlement and development around their reserve have affected wild animal populations and migrations. Large and small game are now less plentiful, as are the fruits and roots on which they have relied.

Once a nomadic people, the Nakoda now tend farm animals and plant gardens. No longer living in teepees, CTK members now build log shacks to live in that require daily care such as hauling water and cutting firewood with which to cook and keep warm. With settlement increasing outside the reserve boundaries, wild animals are becoming scarce, and members need to find ways in which to create income to purchase necessities for their daily lives. Others need to work off reserve in order to provide for their families.

CHAPTER 13

Wičóhaŋga Ičúŋbi: Wašiču Owáŋga Tibi, Maká En Wokšúbi nagu Woyúda

Farms, Gardens, Traditional Diet, and Other Traditional Activities

Before contact, the Nakoda People used corn and fashioned pottery like some of the eastern, more sedentary tribes. It has been suggested that they evolved from a more agricultural society to a more hunter-gatherer society around Lake Winnipeg and traded for corn with those peoples farther east and south. Agriculture was therefore not as foreign to their culture as white people might have thought. In modern times, agriculture was supported by the Nakoda People in the Cypress Hills and then again at the Indian Head reserve, though there were problems introduced by the government over ownership and distribution of the crops. Many Carry The Kettle members planted small gardens and continued to work their small farms to supplement their traditional diet of wild meat and berries. In this chapter, Elders share their stories of family gardens and outline what constituted their traditional diet. Also discussed are the various necessary traditional activities such as hauling water, cutting firewood, and repairing log homes. Also mentioned are various outside income-earning activities that CTK members pursued in order to supplement their traditional economy and livelihood.

Carry The Kettle Members Emmanuel and Katie Farming, n.d.
Photo provided by Carry The Kettle Nakoda First Nation.

FARMS AND GARDENS

Many of the Elders interviewed for this book remembered their grandparents and parents having small farms and farm animals to supplement their food requirements. "When I remember growing up, we had cows, horses, chickens, goats, sheep, geese, everything you can think of," Darrell Jack said. "That was my grandma and grandpa's.... Chicken eggs, oh yeah, that's what we had them for, use them for the eggs." Elders Victoria, Joyce, and Gladys Prettyshield recalled that

> in later years... our Uncle Duncan had a chicken house.... Our grandpa used to have a great big barn—a bunch of eggs, chickens. We used to go there, and he used to give me a little can, I don't know what kind of can it was, go in the bush, and I used to collect eggs. I used to collect lots of eggs.... They had turkey.... Geese, too, he had those.

And Elder Wanda Prettyshield said that

> I think they used to hang the milk down in the well, because we had cows, in the summertime, wintertime too. I remember them putting it somewhere to keep it cool.... And my mother had a cream separator—the cream would come out on one side, and the milk would come out on the other side. And what we

CHAPTER 13

used to do with the milk, she used to put it in a jar, let it go kind of sour, and we used to have to—as kids—sit there and shake it. She put it in sealers.... I don't know, my mother looked after all that stuff. I don't know how she did it. Doing all the washing and cleaning and everything in those days.

Carry The Kettle Family with Their Goats
Photo provided by Carry The Kettle Nakoda First Nation.

Gardens were an important part of reserve life. CTK members ate fresh vegetables during harvest time and preserved large quantities to subsidize their diet in the winter. "People had lots of gardens, beautiful gardens," Elder James O'Watch said. Elder Gladys Prettyshield commented that "Mom used to have a garden. She got those seeds from the Indian Agent, and she used to make this great big garden, and she'd have lots of potatoes and vegetables that we'd eat." Darrell Jack noted that "we'd go out there weeding carrots and peas and stuff." Elder Wanda Prettyshield noted that "my mother and dad always put a garden in every year, and they had potatoes and carrots, and they had a place to put them." Likewise, Elder Edna Spencer said that "my mom and dad used to have a big garden.... Then they used to sell potatoes, and then they'd give vegetables away. We were rich for that anyway."

Other CTK Elders made similar comments.

> Well, that's what we lived on, our own garden. We don't go to town because we don't have the money to go to town.... We had everything here, ... carrots, beets, onions, potatoes, corn, ... just about everything. Onions, carrots, potatoes, and corn were the main things I ate. You see, everybody had gardens at one time. And we had cellars below the house. That's where we kept things. The house kept warm and kept the vegetable[s] warm. (Leroy and Myrtle Hassler)

> I remember, when we were kids, my dad had a little can, and he left maybe chopped-up potatoes in fours, and he told us how to

plant them while he dug up all the holes. He said, "Put one in there, when you're done just cover it up all along the lines." We did the same thing, potatoes, carrots, corn. And then they stuck them in big sacks and put them in the cellar. (Myrtle Hassler)

Potatoes, vegetables, my parents plant all those. They had two big gardens. At one time, they got 100 bags from the one garden—potatoes. Then the farmers would come and ask for the bag, and they give them out free too. (Nancy Eashappie)

We used to put in a garden, a community garden, everybody had to plant.... Around the old agency there, we had a great big garden. Everybody just planted potatoes and vegetables. Corn, carrots, onions, all kinds of vegetables. (Rena Ryder)

TRADITIONAL DIET

The traditional diet of Carry The Kettle members consisted mainly of what they were able to hunt, gather, and grow, "wild meat, wild berries, and gardens if they had a garden," Elders Victoria, Joyce, and Gladys Prettyshield observed. Darrell Jack said "that was usual in them days, just went out and got whatever you needed to eat." Elder Rena Ryder mentioned "rabbit, prairie chickens, ducks, duck eggs, geese. Just everything off the land.... All kinds of berries." Kurt Ryder said that it was "mostly deer and moose. Whatever we could get.... I never really ate too much elk."

According to Elder Darlene Whitecap, "we lived on berries. That was our breakfast, dinner, and supper, because we used to go out and play with the neighbours next door, and we don't go home for meals, and we'd just live on the berries along the road. Chokecherries, saskatoons, gooseberries, currant was in the bush, too, pincherries."

Lyle Spencer had a different diet: "My dad used to trap gophers and muskrat and beaver, and he'd cook it. So we'd eat some of it, but we weren't used to it. My dad even tried some of those groundhogs. He'd skin them up and cook them. He said he carried that on from his dad's time." He said that he even ate "the beaver tail. I never had one before until my father cooked up one. He just cut it in half and put it in tinfoil, wrapped it in tinfoil, and put it in the oven. Left it for about an hour or so, and it just came out fluffy. To me, it was the taste of popcorn." Finally, Lyle noted, "there are moose out there, we hunt moose. That's the top of the

CHAPTER 13

line there is to eat, is moose meat.... The heart, the liver, the kidneys, those are eatable, and we take those.... The nose, we eat the nose."

The Prettyshield sisters had fourteen in their family growing up "in a mud shack—a one-room mud shack.... We all had our own jobs to do," Gladys said. They all survived on berries and wild meat: "I remember, whatever they kill, my mom used to boil them up and can them,"

Elder Tony Ashdohonk mentioned that "we eat bannock,[1] deer meat, rabbits, prairie chickens, partridges.... We eat that all the time—bush rabbits." Elder Roswell Saulteaux also "ate bannock, berries, and rabbit. And I remember eating gophers when we were just little kids. I remember eating porcupine." Elder Vincent Ryder said that "I never used to eat [it], but sometimes they'd eat like muskrat or beaver. They'd eat that."

Kaye Thomson Preparing Her Garden
Photo provided by Carry The Kettle Nakoda First Nation.

Although Carry The Kettle People survived traditionally off the land, Elders recalled the many times that food was scarce. "Well, we had our regular meals. A lot of families didn't have," Delmar Runs indicated, "but we had because we were mostly boys, and we would go out and hunt." Leroy and Myrtle Hassler mentioned "rabbits, deer, gopher, ducks, ... and duck eggs too.... There was always something to eat.... But I wouldn't say there was always lots to eat, because you barely made it." Darlene Whitecap said that "they'd hunt, go berry picking, and eventually, I know, they had a big garden.... We grew up on the land. Wild meat, vegetable garden, ... deer. Whatever they could catch, whatever they could hunt for. I remember when we were small it was kind of scarce, and everybody was having a hard time surviving. So I remember eating porcupine—roasted porcupine."

In addition, Wanda Prettyshield noted, "my mother, in those days, too, they had what you call tripe,[2] and when they had nothing else to eat they would get butcher tripe, and they would wash the tripe. I don't know, my mother had a way of cleaning the tripe, and they would wash it and wash it and wash it." Stacey Hotomani noted that "they make

Donna Prettyshield at Old House
Photo provided by Carry The Kettle Nakoda First Nation.

their own lard. Her and grandpa would get a pig and get all the fat. She still does it, and they would go to farmers to get their tripe from their cows when they would butcher them." And Darlene Whitecap recalled that, "when I was a little girl, it was hard. . . . Five, six, seven, eight years old, we lived off gophers. I remember I was helping my cousin, because we stayed there, and we were drowning gophers—our method of getting them. . . . I remember eating gopher. We were starving then. . . . I think they only brought in bacon, beans, and flour once a year."

This diet was also supplemented with rations provided by the government as promised through treaty. Elder Victoria Prettyshield explained that often these rations were provided minimally and through food stamps by the Indian Agent residing on the reserve: "That's what they gave us, food stamps. You were only allowed so much, and they give a certain day, and they'll bring it to us, or we take it to them, and they'll give us whatever the food stamp qualifies for. Maybe some meat or flour or sugar." Elders Duncan Thomson and Roswell Saulteaux similarly noted that, "at that time, we had rations too. . . . There's a certain day that they give rations down at the agency. And there's a certain time of month or year we go down, and they give you bacon, flour, sugar, stuff like that. Enough that would last you maybe for quite a while. . . . Powdered milk. . . . [Those were] hard times. Elder Tony Ashdohonk mentioned that "my mother got rations from the Indian agency.... They gave her bacon, sugar, flour, ... something like that. I think it's every two weeks you get it. And tea and lard and stuff like that. You get it in little bags." Elder Wanda Prettyshield also recalled relying on rations: "Yes, rations, I remember that.... Tea, lard, and big round biscuits ... every two weeks, I think. And rice, they used to give rice, and later on they'd give flour, hundred pound sacks, ... baking powder, ... sugar, bacon—a big slab of bacon.... That's what we lived on ... combined with wild meat."

Elder Delmar Runs said that the government never really followed through on promises made at the time of treaty, and the minimal rations that it did provide were not enough to help the Assiniboine People live healthy lives as before. "They got some rations, they said it was pork, salted pork. But when they ate the salted pork, many of the people died because they were not used to that. They were used to fresh meat. That was their diet. That's how they lived."

Keith Prettyshield's diet still consists mainly of wild meat "pretty much all the time. I do eat beef, but I try to stay away from processed foods. I eat mostly elk, moose, deer." According to Elders Clayton and Delbert Thomson, "it's better meat than beef . . . or pork, whatever. Some people are diabetic, and they eat that beef with all the chemicals mixed in that beef and everything. I think wild meat is better." Lyle Spencer has always lived on wild meat: "That's what I grew up on, wild meat. . . . They're naturally fed from the roots and the fresh growth from the ground. It's better meat, it's . . . healthier, it's cheaper to get. . . . Back in the day, you used to just walk, or get on a horse and ride, or a team of horses and a sleigh, and go out." Elder Darlene Whitecap mentioned that

> a couple of years ago . . . I ate wild meat for a year and a half, and when I ran out and started to eat the regular hamburger, oh, it tasted so horrible. You taste the chemicals—they make it look so fresh and red—they put that red stuff on it. It tastes really horrible. You have to try it. Live on wild animal for a year, even six months, and you could still taste it. . . . I know liver is really good for your health.

Elder Garry Whitecap also "noticed that taste when Tim shared their moose and elk meat with me for maybe about two months. Then, when I tried bacon, I couldn't stand the taste of bacon. The taste, the smell, I couldn't stand it anymore."

Carry The Kettle Horse-Drawn Sleigh
Photo provided by Carry The Kettle Nakoda First Nation.

Elder Bernice Saulteaux noted that "my grandchildren want wild meat, and I was concerned because sometimes you cook something up, and they don't like it, but they say, 'What kind of meat is this? I like it. It tastes good.' I put some onions in there, and sometimes they don't like onions, too, but you have to chop it up real fine."

OTHER TRADITIONAL ACTIVITIES

Besides harvesting wild foods and tending farms and gardens, there were many other traditional activities, including building and maintaining log homes, cutting firewood, hauling water, and threshing hay for the animals. "You cut the hay for the horse with what you call a scythe," Elder Leroy Hassler said. "[You] get the horses to get it all together, and then you have to put it in a hayrack. You have to make a hayrack. Boy, that's a lot of work." Stacey Hotomani remembered her grandparents farming: "Hay would grow back here.... He'd bale it, rake it, everything. He'd be out there from morning until night.... Put grain in and everything."

In their interview, Elders Leroy and Myrtle Hassler mentioned that

> I have an old picture of my dad's house that was made from logs, plaster, and hay. Because, you know, they made their own

CHAPTER 13

homes at one time. A little mud shack. . . . I remember barefooted—not barefooted—there just was no floor, it was bare. Just a little cabin until I think eventually they put something in it. . . . We made our own houses, . . . put mud on top, mud siding, and they were warm. . . . That was made out of straw. They used to put the straw in a big tub like and clay and water. And as kids we used to have to stomp around in it. They said, "Help us," so we would throw it at the house. Then you take it later on and plaster it all over the logs, the openings. And when it dried, it kept you nice and warm inside. And they did that every spring.

Carry The Kettle Member Doing Laundry
Photo provided by Carry The Kettle Nakoda First Nation..

Elder Tony Ashdohonk said that "we cut wood, gathered wood, especially in the wintertime, because you got to make [a] fire all night almost all the time to keep warm. Sometimes we don't, and if you leave water on the stove it freezes. Next morning you see ice. And our windows are single pane. You know in the morning there's frost about half [an] inch thick on them. Oh, I remember them."

According to Elder Leroy Hassler, "they had warm barns, because what they do is take the manure and use it for kind of like a plastering. They treated their horses really well because they had to rely on their horses. . . . You have to be good to your horse, they're spiritual. . . . They work really hard to put a livelihood."

Elder Tony Ashdohonk related how they got their drinking water:

> We drink slough water. We have to drain it to drink it. Take a team of horses, go to the slough, and with a pail we drain the water into the barrel with lots of bugs in it, that's why we drain

Carry The Kettle Member on Horseback
Photo provided by Carry The Kettle Nakoda First Nation.

it.... But my brother told my mother "That slough over there has no bugs," She said, "Don't get nothing over there, nothing of that, get the one with bugs in it." So we did. She said water with no bugs in it is no good. Even the horse, she said, "Don't let the horse drink that." ... In the wintertime, we melt snow every day. And she had a barrel in there melting snow. She always had a barrel of snow water. That's the way we [drank].

Elder Wanda Prettyshield likewise mentioned that,

> at that time, they had slough water, the Métis. It was clear water, and they used to—my dad would go and get water in a stoneboat and carry these big large iron barrels. I used to think, how did they bathe all of us? ... They used to have big galvanized tubs. I remember sitting in it.... We had two great big barrels. One was for washing clothes—it was soft water, ... slough water—and they used that for washing whatever they had, meat, before they ate it.... And the other was well water, and that's where we got our water for cooking and everything.

And Kurt Ryder mentioned that

> we used to get water a long time ago right along there, just off the reserve, there's a spring there, we'd haul water, barrels of water. Of course, a long time ago in the springtime, we used to just go in the slough with a team of horses and fill up a big barrel and strain the water. That's what we used for washing clothes and everything. They used to drink that water long ago, [but] you wouldn't drink it nowadays.

CHAPTER 13

OUTSIDE INCOME

Living on the reserve, Carry The Kettle members still needed outside income to survive. They chopped firewood and made pickets and fence posts to sell to neighbouring farmers and dug their medicinal seneca and black root for sale in town. Elder James O'Watch recalled that some CTK members also sold berries to help make ends meet: "The other thing was berries, a lot of people done that. They were doing that outside today, picking saskatoons and other berries, clean them, and take them to town and sell them." They also continued their traditional trapping activities within reserve boundaries and sold or traded the pelts, Elder Sarah Eashappie noted: "They did this and a little bit of that. They worked hard. My dad cut hay, wood, trapped, anything he could do.... Hunted... deer, rabbits... all over on the reserve. Southwest, I guess, where there's bush.... Sell wood, people did that at that time."

WOOD, HAY, AND MEDICINE ROOTS

After chopping enough wood to meet the needs of their families, CTK members would chop other loads and take them to town for sale. Elder Wanda Prettyshield's father chopped firewood, gathered hay, and made pickets to make extra income. He sold these items in Womack, Kendal, and Sintaluta, "that's where I remember anyway as a child." Elder Bernice Saulteaux indicated that "they just lived off the land and gained their livelihood like that. That's my grandfather,... and they hauled wood, because the trapping had already gone down. There wasn't as much back in the '60s–'70s, already there was nothing to trap, it was kind of disappearing."

Many of the CTK Elders interviewed spoke about selling wood to earn extra income.

> Each family had a place to take their wood.... Some went to Kendal, some to Womack, some to Indian Head, so you don't really fight over territory that way.... The town people would order it. They would have their own customers. There wasn't really the politeness type of customer, they had good respect ... on both sides. (Leroy and Myrtle Hassler)

> Dad used to cut pickets for their [farmers'] fences, and... he helped them out.... The treated wood—bluestone—he used to sell that.... He'd be gone with the team of horses with a load

Carry The Kettle Men Collecting Wood
Photo provided by Carry The Kettle Nakoda First Nation.

of wood to Kendal, and he'd come home late in the evening and go early in the morning. And then out of that—the money he got—he got the main things, flour, oatmeal, . . . lard. We use a lot of lard. Bacon. We hardly had butter. Tea. (Victoria, Joyce, and Gladys Prettyshield)

He used to cut wood, too, pickets, sell them, both poplar and willow pickets, both of them. . . . They were allowed to cut wood and sell it—pickets—farmers would buy it. There were two sizes of pickets. One was bluestone pickets—the length of a post—and the other was willow pickets. And then [fire]wood, they'd cut wood in the bush, come out and saw it, take it to town, and sell it and buy food. (James O'Watch)

They exchange—they get wood—they get the food. That's how they work. Or they help them at their farm. . . . Because they were using wood, the farmers, so they sell it to them. . . . They give them one big pig that they clean. . . . Or vegetables or whatever. . . . It was all on a barter system. (Nancy Eashappie and Terri Prettyshield)

Besides threshing hay for their own animals, Elders recalled the endless hours that their parents and grandparents spent cultivating and harvesting hay to sell off reserve in order to make ends meet. Myrtle Hassler said that her father "was a really outgoing man, always busy,

CHAPTER 13

always found food for us, always chopped hay, took hay to the farmers around Kendal and Womack. . . . There were three places—Odessa, I think, is one of them—that he mentioned. And if they didn't buy hay or wood from him, he'd trade it for furniture. He'd maybe get a bed, table, chairs, whatever. And that's how we got our furniture." Wanda Prettyshield noted that

> my dad had a mower and rake, and hayrack, a team of horses to pull that. And in my early school years—when we did come home during the summer for our holidays—we used to ride with him on the hayrack, and my dad would lay back like this in the hay [reclining position] and sleep, and we would sit there and watch the horses come home by themselves. That was something. I thought we would go over in a ditch, tip over, but they'd climb up and over.

And James O'Watch mentioned that, in "haying season, sometimes farmers would come in and do a third crop share on hay fields that people used to cut for generations. They would cut that and sell it to them. . . . In fact, the day I was born he [his father] was working in the field. It was about 100 above, and he was working in the field."

Elder Nancy Eashappie explained to us that, when her brother hunted deer, he sold the skins "most of the time, . . . or someone will ask for it. . . . They dry the hide, and they sell them in Regina." The Prettyshield sisters remembered that their mother was often given hides with which to make moccasins to sell in town for extra income: "That's what she did, too, for Fort Qu'Appelle, . . . where they sell all that Indian stuff—Timmy Vans. They'd give her a bunch of leathers to make moccasins, and she'd get paid for it, I think two dollars. Two dollars for only one."

CTK members also sold horses when they could to make extra household income. As Elder James O'Watch said,

> we used to have a two- or three-day roundup in the spring. I used to love it, chasing down wild horses, branding them, cutting the styans. And there used to be horse buyers that used to come out here. Great big trucks. . . . One guy, . . . good friend of the Indians, Harold Pollock, he used to pay the cowboys for chasing horses. He used to bring sandwiches out to them. . . . In the spring, he'd come and pick up all his horses.

They also sewed clothes to make a bit of extra money, as Elders Victoria, Joyce, and Gladys Prettyshield noted:

> My mom was a seamstress. Lots of times . . . we used to have lanterns hanging in the house—coal oil lamps— . . . and Mom would be there sewing, at night. . . . Women would want dresses or something, and Mom would make them to make extra money. . . . She was really good at making western shirts. Oh, it was so nice. Young guys, young men, used to ask Mom to make western shirts for them.

CTK members traditionally harvested seneca root for themselves. "That's medicine," Elder Delmar Runs clarified. "We picked lots of that. We picked bags of it, and we dried them, and we'd leave them for winter until we were sick, and then we take those, and it really works. We're healed on that. . . . Almost good for anything—headaches, stomach, measles." But there was also a market outside the reserve for this root, so extra amounts were dug to sell, as Elder Wanda Prettyshield mentioned:

> I know they used to go hunt seneca roots on the reserve. And I know they would have to go to a certain area, and they had those big sacks, potatoe sacks, they would fill those with seneca roots. They brought them into town and got a lot of money for those. I don't know, maybe five dollars a bag or something. Those days, it was money. It was more than they could make with a load of wood anyway. But it took—you have to know the plant. I remember going with my mom and dad, and they would dig with a little spade. But they had to pick out the top of the plant. They knew what plants to dig out. And the roots were funny, they looked like little carrots, except carrots are orange, these were kind of pale-looking yellow. Not even yellow, they were kind of beigey-brown in colour.

Elder Nancy Eashappie also talked about

> seneca root. We dig a lot of that ourselves too. I know I did. . . . That is everywhere. Like up here we call the Sharp Hills. . . . [My brother] went out there to dig some with my uncle. . . . They don't grow all over, though, it's just some, like sort of a set area. . . . And then they take them to dry them, and then they

CHAPTER 13

George O'Watch and Children
Photo provided by Carry The Kettle Nakoda First Nation.

take them to the city to sell them. We get quite a bit of money for that because, you know, they send them to Winnipeg.

During this time, many restrictions were still in place. As explained in previous chapters, Carry The Kettle members still needed permission from the Indian Agent to leave the reserve and permits to sell any of their products off reserve. "You needed a permit if you sold anything off the reserve," Elder Wanda Prettyshield said. "It would either be hay or pickets, you needed a permit. Or even to leave the reserve you needed a permit." "There was a time when they couldn't go off the reserve," Elder Garry Whitecap noted, "even to sell their crops or produce or anything. Or wood. It was like a concentration camp, we couldn't do anything." Elder Bernice Saulteaux elaborated:

> They did go, but see, back then at that time in the '50s, they had to get a permit to go off the reserve. So I remember even when they went off the reserve to sell wood to a farmer, they had to get a permit. So that was in the mid-'50s, '57/'58, at that time. Because I remember her getting home with my dad—my grandma—and they kind of got stranded there at the farmer's yard because it was pouring rain. And they were afraid—they said that the permit was only for so many hours, so they were afraid that the agent would give them a fine for being

late.... But she said that the farmers—because it was pouring rain—they had them stay for supper. She always told us the story that they asked my dad to pray, so he prayed in the language. He didn't even bless the food, he prayed that they got home safely and the Indian Agent wouldn't give them a fine. I always remember that.

Elders Leroy and Myrtle Hassler

didn't know they were restricted, but I guess they were.... My dad told us about it.... If they wanted to go sell wood, they had to go to the agent and go get a permit. And if they didn't and got caught, they'd go to jail. They were restricted from doing a lot of things.... You had to get a permit to sell a cow. That I know for sure. Even a horse.

"The lifting of the permits, getting rid of that, made a big change," Elder Wanda Prettyshield said. "They were able to get on the train and go to Regina. They had a little more freedom, and you weren't afraid of that gun anymore. My dad used to say that if you left [the] reserve they'd shoot you on sight. I shouldn't say that, but they did apparently in the earlier days. They said that if they caught anybody leaving [the] reserve they would shoot on sight, without a permit."

OFF-RESERVE FARMHANDS
Although continuing to conduct their traditional hunting and gathering activities, as permits and restrictions were lifted, many CTK members began full-time employment as farmhands on neighbouring farms. Elder Nancy Eashappie noted that "my father does work for the German farmers up west Odessa way.... For the farmers that were out off the reserve and for the farm instructor that was here. Both. They do things like fencing, a lot of farming stuff." Clint Haywahe mentioned that "even my mom, seven years old, and she had to go work just to help her parents survive. Then she met my dad, and they made a life together. So she worked alongside him and hunted with him." And Elder James O'Watch "just worked on the farm. Mostly clearing land because a lot of people were clearing land then. Picking stones, picking roots. Some of them had cattle, so they helped with the cattle. And the women went and cooked for them and cleaned house.... Anything they could do they had to do to feed their family.... Everybody worked."

CHAPTER 13

The money brought in from these activities allowed Carry The Kettle families to purchase additional items in town to meet their household needs and supplement their livelihoods. Although their diet still consisted mainly of wild meat and berries, because of restrictions, the decline in animal populations, and time constraints many families began to supplement their traditional diet with store-bought foods. "Stews, soup, meat, bread, bannock of course," Elder James O'Watch commented. "And then after a while, when it got scarce, then we always had to buy meat from the store. That's when dad and them would sell wood and everything." Elder Sarah Eashappie said that, "when I was younger, . . . we survive on this wild meat, wild berries. Get a little bit of meat in town, butter. We not have much. . . . We did all right in a way then. We survived." And Elders Leroy and Myrtle Hassler mentioned "tea, coffee, flour, lard, because we made bannock, . . . all the essentials, . . . salt. . . . That's the main things. . . . You can't just go to town every day, . . . so he goes to Wolseley, and he deals with the people, . . . settlers."

CHAPTER 14

Nakón Wósuye, Makóče at'a Iŋhákta nagu Iknústa

Indigenous Rights and Environmental Concerns

Carry The Kettle interviewees expressed their concerns regarding limited access to their Traditional Territories and their right to harvest traditionally as their ancestors once did. They also offered many comments about the obvious environmental degradation occurring in and around their lands, inflicting illness and disease on their people, as well as the animals and plants on which they have traditionally relied.

TRADITIONAL LANDS AND LIMITED ACCESS

CTK members are concerned that their Indigenous Rights are being increasingly infringed. As Darrell Jack said, "we have rights on our lands, we should have had rights through all of Saskatchewan really, but then we got put into little brown spots on this map, which isn't right, . . . because this is all ours already. . . . The government is taking away our rights, that's about it. It's all government business now. They're taking away all our Treaty Rights and stuff. Slowly, a little bit by little bit." Clint Haywahe likewise said that it is "an everyday thing, even the hunting areas are becoming smaller, because now, too, the governments allow grazing in the parks, so they put up 'No Hunting' signs and stuff. And that runs through the province. So it limits it. . . . Cypress Hills, White Bear–Moose Mountain, Pipestone Valley, even surrounding the reserve here. We have pastures and that, so we also have limited access to that."

Leroy Walker also commented on the changes: "Big changes that they put on First Nations to say that you can't subsistence hunt on certain lands, which is different from how my uncles grew up. They were allowed to go on pretty well any place that wasn't posted and hunt. And now you have to have permission, and now you have to have a licence to hunt, whereas before you didn't have to have a licence." Elder Vincent Ryder confirmed that "they used to go hunt across the valley, south from Standing Buffalo. Today there's a park there. . . . Then, they used to allow us to go hunting anywhere. It was our Treaty Right. But after there was a park there, they shut it down, to keep it as a park I guess. You could sneak in there . . . when the park was there. There were signs 'No Hunting.'" Elder Bernice Saulteaux mentioned decreased access to berry patches: "Oh, there was plenty here—all those years we used to pick berries here. There was lots. Now you can't even get into a patch someplace there's so much fencing. But if you have them around your area, it's good."

Carry The Kettle members have also noticed many changes to access to harvesting lands because of large-scale farming, oil and gas projects, and other industrial development. "It's unreal how much bush they're pushing nowadays for farming," Keith Prettyshield said. "A lot of hunting lands. It seems that the wildlife lands used to be this big [wide open hands], now they're this big [small open hands]. They're shrinking. Some of them got taken away already."

Darrell Jack stated that

> you could go out there and hunt anywhere, and nobody would say anything, now things changed. . . . They have "No Hunting, No Trespassing" [signs] on lands that never had them before. Then, there's a lot of different owners that own the land. . . . The farmers that used to be there, . . . they're gone. . . . So now you have to find different areas to hunt in because different owners and different developments come in. . . . Like the 48 and number 1 [highways]. We hunted all in here, all the way up to this highway here, 8, . . . that's going into Carlyle. . . . We hunted all in here, right from our reserve, right in between these highways. That was just basically like everyday hunting or weekend hunting if you wanted.

CHAPTER 14

Likewise, Clint Haywahe mentioned that

> we've hunted areas where at one time there was none, now mainly there's oil wells and structures and stuff. Even throughout the lands, pipeline[s], oil and gas wells, we've seen that developing over time. So it sort of limited where we could go.... Once roads are built, gas and oil wells are put up, there's also fences put up with "No Trespassing" signs and that. It seems that the wildlife know that, because they jump over the fence so you can't bother them.

Leroy Walker claimed that

> west of the reserve, all the regional prairie, is all going to be dug up for gravel. It's a big area. And . . . down in Carlyle . . . it's a big oil well, and it's just going to keep growing and growing, and like I say it pushes wildlife away.... People are pumping up here like crazy, and there's a lot of lands that are getting bush-pushed and a lot of fields coming up. It's crazy . . . in the past five years how much it grew. But the population grew.... It was isolated, now there's people in those areas.... Watersheds is one of the basic things with small game, ducks and birds and that, it destroys them, ... and some of these animals have cysts and seem sickly and bony.

Clint Haywahe also discussed the importance of preserving certain areas:

> The Cypress Hills area and where the parks are, Greenwater, White Bear, and there's also Crown lands that are set aside for wildlife, and those, it would be good to keep them intact, because there, too, as First Nations people, we're allowed to go hunt on that.... A lot of these lands that we've purchased through the TLE [Treaty Land Entitlement] agreement, they have some of those berries and different medicines, so that's one thing we need to look at as far as protecting all that.

Leroy Walker believes that his people need to know, understand, and practise the Indigenous Rights provided to them through treaty to hunt, fish, and trap before opportunities diminish even further:

I exercise my hunting rights all the time.... I've been in trouble with the law quite a bit of times, and I've always won. So I try to show an example.... Like some of these guys get charged for poaching or ... trespassing out there. I tell these guys that they are allowed to legally hunt on these lands, Crown lands. They don't even know it's Crown lands. So they plead guilty and end up losing their stuff and losing their meat. Whereas I do it all the time and make sure I know our rights.

I've run into DNR [Department of Natural Resources], and they try to charge me, and I say, "Heh, this is Crown land, and I'm allowed to hunt here whenever I can." ... I've been charged, and some of these court cases have lasted three years, but I've walked away still the winner. The only thing that matters to get back is our hunting material—guns and our camping stuff and that there. The meat there it get[s] shipped off, obviously to a good cause, a food bank or something, which is good instead of spoiling.

We're not there for sport, you know, poaching and all that. We're there to feed our families, so I like to prove a point. I'm an advocate to show these guys what should be—stick up for your rights, and other guys should do the same thing instead of being charged . . . and not so easily give up on things which pushes them to losing their hunting rights more and more if the federal government steps in and pushes them off to the side.

ENVIRONMENTAL CHANGES AND ANIMAL AND COMMUNITY HEALTH

COMMUNITY HEALTH

Many concerns were voiced regarding community health issues brought on by large-scale farming, industry, and oil wells surrounding CTK Traditional Lands. "We used to have beautiful gardens out here," Elder James O'Watch said. "I remember people weren't sick in those days. There was hardly any cancer, diabetes, nothing." Leroy Walker mentioned "animals and things, like in certain areas, like Carlyle is really bad for oil wells, and it's scary because there's a lot of H_2S [hydrogen sulfide] gas around, and you don't know if you're safe to hunt in the area. Like it's forests, but it's still scary."

Darwin Saulteaux had similar concerns:

CHAPTER 14

We usually hunt in Moose Mountain, but in Moose Mountain they have a lot of oil and gas production going on in there, and everybody's probably heard of the . . . gases that have been leaking into the air from southern Saskatchewan from Estevan to Weyburn—all that Moose Mountain area. So that air has made humans sick, almost killed people, and it affects the animals and the plants and all the medicines and the berries in that area. So I don't like hunting in Moose Mountain anymore. When I want to hunt, I want to come to Cypress Hills because there's not as much activity here as there is over there, and you don't see a lot of gas and oil inside the park. . . . I guess it would be kind of like a long-term sickness. Just like people get with cancer. It probably wouldn't kill you instantly, but in time it will. And I think eventually, in maybe ten or twenty years from now, a lot of animals will die from that and plants and berries and medicines—everything. It's going to affect everything because it's a poisonous gas. If it can kill people, I'm sure it's going to harm everything else.

Clint Haywahe also discussed health concerns:

With diabetes and cancer, I've noticed a change I'd say within the last twenty-five years. If you take a look at the statistics of sicknesses—how much of our people we've lost due to that—it's higher than anything else. We need to work on finding what's actually causing that. We've had different people make different comments and that, but nobody knows exactly where that stems from. But the pipeline itself, too, there's always that question mark as to is there any leaks? I don't think any company can confirm that they're not health hazards. Because I, too, have also worked with the pipelines, and doing contract work with them I've seen the different things that have happened and what can happen. So we have to be sure and create a more positive lifestyle for our youth, our children that are growing up, because one day they're the ones that are going to be here still dealing with this.

Elder Vincent Ryder noted that at one time

food, water, everything was pure. The people knew how to use medicines. Pure, and the food—the four legged they called them and the winged ones—they lived on that. The winged ones and the four legged, they picked medicine. They always say, the old people, you never see one deer eating from one place. He's always on the move. He starts here, eat something, walk a ways, stop and pick. That's medicine he's looking for—eating. And we eat that meat. That's medicine, all these four-legged animals, wild animals, the moose, elk. They lived on that medicine the Creator put on the ground. You see them eating. The buffalo, you see the buffalo walk, he stops, and he's searching around there, and he goes again. And that's what they lived on, and there was no such thing as hospitals, no disease. Food, water, everything was pure, coming from the Creator. The rain. In the winter, the snow that melts makes big lakes, and the animals lived on that water.

ENVIRONMENTAL CHANGES

The interviewees have seen many environmental changes over the past number of years. Elders Delbert and Clayton Thomson explained that even the weather has changed, become much harsher than in previous years, affecting both the land and wildlife habitat: "There used to be lots of deer at that time, but there's hardly any now. It snowed all winter before, [and] the snow was too deep. We used to climb. We used to find them all along the road here, starving." Elder Nancy Eashappie said that "they did trap weasels too. And sometimes muskrat if there is water. . . . Sometimes there's no water. Like for the last four or five years, it was sort of dry. But now there is, here and there, big waters."

Animal populations have changed and, in most cases, become very scarce. "Some populations have really decreased," Leroy Walker said, "and some gain more over forty years. Just little things like that." "Things are changing," Elder Darlene Whitecap noted. "Things are getting scarce." Likewise, Lyle Spencer said that "there's less whitetail deer because the coyote population picked up, and the deer haven't been coming down," and Elder James O'Watch mentioned that "the animals are very limited, the deer, I haven't seen a deer around." Part of the reason was that "a lot of bush has disappeared," as Leroy Walker indicated. "Like maybe ten years ago you could drive from here to Carlyle, you'd probably see 100 deer, now you're lucky if there's ten deer around. Everything's just pushed away and gone to different areas and bushes."

Other interviewees made similar comments.

CHAPTER 14

How other people survived in the '30s, '40s, those were hard times, but those were how our people survived. Now we don't have them anymore. So we're losing out there. The animals that we used to hunt—we have animals on the reserve that we've never had before—cougars, bears. Twenty, thirty years ago we didn't have elk and moose, now we have an abundance of animals we never had before—wolves. So I don't know what it is, Mother Nature or Mother Earth itself, we have things we've never had before, and we don't have things we had in abundance. (Darwin Saulteaux)

Now there's elk. I spotted two elk about a month ago on the west end of the reserve. And there's moose, because we have a lot of bush, and there's a lot of sloughs, so they're coming onto the reserve, . . . especially in the fall. . . . There are animals about where they never used to be at one time. Maybe because farmers are cutting down all the bush for them . . . to plant their crops, you see that already. You see clumps of trees, all piled up in a big pile. Animals won't stay around that kind of area. (Elder Garry Whitecap)

With those things [development] coming into place, it even cuts down on the supply of game because wild game are used to the wild, and if they see human—even the scent of it—they stay away. So even the wild game is getting scarce today. . . . I've seen that decline over the years. Like at one time, we used to have a lot of deer, a lot of rabbits and that. When we used to go hunting, we used to provide for people in the community as well, and in the last fifteen years a lot of that has gone away. Game is pretty scarce to find now. (Clint Haywahe)

Many changes to plants, trees, and berries have also been noted: "There's lots of different things," Leroy Walker said. "Certain flowers and that, like purple flowers that some of the older people picked, you can't find them anymore. You find them on the reserve, but off the reserve you can't find them anymore. You can't find things like that out there." Clint Haywahe noted that "we have a lot of virgin territory, and it grows throughout the community. . . . In 1982, I had a land technician from the province come out, and I toured the reserve with him, and in his report . . . he mentioned to me there's over fifty species of grass and plants that they don't see anywhere else."

Although Elder Darlene Whitecap still picks berries, she said that they're harder to find now: there were "plenty all over in that era, until they started farming. Look at all the farms around. There were lots of berries around—raspberries." According to Elder Nancy Eashappie and Terri Prettyshield, there were berries "here and there all over the reserve.... But you don't hardly get that now today.... But they do grow." Elders believe that development is the cause of changes to the quantity and quality of berries. "With the lands being worked and farmed, agriculture," Clint Haywahe said, "a lot of bush area has been cleared, so even those are limited to the valleys, the First Nations lands, Crown land, so it's not province-wide anymore." In their interview, Elders Victoria, Joyce, and Gladys Prettyshield mentioned that "there was lots before all these fields came up. Before they started digging around."

In terms of berry quality, Darwin Saulteaux clarified that,

> if the leaves are brown and dried up, then the berries are the same way—dry. They're not worth picking.... When it's being sprayed, you get a coating on your berry, so you know which ones are being sprayed.... I think that the patches of berries, you know where they are, on the reserve, you know it's clean, where it hasn't been bothered. So those are the places you would probably go back to every year to go and pick. So you kind of stay away from the area, maybe close to the edge of the reserve, where there's farmers spraying their fields. Some of that will come over, so you know your own areas.

Lyle Spencer also expressed concern about chemical use:

> Chemicals, they use that for their fields now, and I can't see why they can't just stay to organic growth. It should be like that.... You can tell if a deer or elk or moose is sick or has something on them. You can even tell by the tree. If you got an airplane flying over here, what they call a crop duster, off reserve here, he thinks that nothing is falling off from the sprayer, but it is. Because my hunting lands here, I go all over, and you can see the trees, where there's chemicals on them. Because there's nothing there, no leaves, just dry up and down.

On the issue of bush clearing, Elder Garry Whitecap noted that

CHAPTER 14

we can't really say nothing to the white farmers—that's their property. Them people have the right to do whatever they want with their land, they just plow it down. Like I said, if there's a little bush there where they think they could put another crop in, they'll just bulldoze it all down, make a pile, burn it. Can't say nothing, you know. But us here, First Nations, say Carry The Kettle, we have a right to protect our land here—our territory—and what's growing out there.

Elder Vincent Ryder expressed concern about water quality:

This water we drink today, it's no good. In them days, they could take water out of the slough and cook their food, anything. Out of the slough, that water was just that pure. It came from the sky, the rain, and that was given by the Creator. All this land—everything they could eat—pick medicines, and now today you can't touch that. It's all poisoned, all these chemicals and sprays they use for killing, insecticides or whatever they use for land, growing crops. All that's in the ground, and that's what's polluting all the foods we eat today.

Interviewees believe that the chemicals used on nearby farms are a major contributor to environmental decline, as Elder Darlene Whitecap mentioned: "These farmers spraying their chemicals all over their fields, . . . that's what's affecting the animals." "The fish, you don't see many without little lumps or tumors or sores on them," Keith Prettyshield noted. "The deer are the same way, there's a lot of cysts on the animals. I've seen rabbits that way. Ducks are sometimes full of worms. There's all different kinds of things." And Lyle Spencer said that "the coyote, the fur is what you call 'mangy,' there's too much fleas in it. . . . They're losing fur. They're not all like that, but some are."

Clint Haywahe expanded on the problems of chemical use:

The land itself was considered virgin land. There has been seldom any kind of spraying of crops and that on CTK. I've worked in the land department for twenty-three years, and I've seen where some of the lands were turned to organic because of the pesticides and that . . . put into the ground. And then, adjacent to the reserve, we have farmers right around us that have been constantly spraying their lands with different chemicals. I've experienced myself, where I've seen the wild game—I don't know if they ate too much of the pesticides—have an effect on them where their meat was no good.... Those are the kinds of things that affect our livelihood and our game, because a lot of people are accustomed [to] and prefer wild game other than store-bought processed foods.

Leroy Walker similarly mentioned that

in certain areas there's lots of pesticides and a lot of dead animals at the edge of the fields and that from pesticides—people spraying and that. You'll find lots of that here and there. Like farmers spraying their fields, it kills the birds and all that. And, along the edge of the bush, you'll find dead birds or dead animals, just from the spray. Chickadees, crows, woodpeckers, and things like that. And rabbits—their population—it's hard to find rabbits nowadays.

More dramatically, Clint Haywahe recounted that,

to the west of us here, we went hunting, and I shot this mule deer. I went to cut its throat. It surprised me, no blood come out but foam. So we brought it home and showed our dad, and he said, "You better go and bury it." Not thinking about getting it tested, we just buried it, and my nephews, they had St. Bernards, they were just pups. They [the dogs] found it, dug it up, and within a week they were dead.

Like many of the Elders interviewed, Wanda and Raymond Prettyshield will not eat wild meat anymore because of contamination. Wanda said that "he won't eat it. We did when the kids were growing up.... Even deer meat. He won't eat deer meat or moose meat." Raymond explained that it was "because of all the chemicals. I don't want to eat it. When they started using chemicals on the fields, I said no. Because the wild animals are out in the fields eating the oats and stuff like that. I said no." They also said that "the ducks were full of insects.... Cut up a few ducks, and they were no darn good. So no wild animals.... The Elders still like the taste of wild duck, and I'm sure that some of the ducks are still okay. But the ducks we had that were found somewhere along here, we said, 'No, we'll never eat another duck.'" Wanda also mentioned that "I'd be cautious if I were people nowadays, even hunting deer, make sure that meat is going to be okay to eat. The fish are contaminated too. People are saying in Fort Qu'Appelle, they won't even go down there to fish because of contaminated water.... It's not environmentally safe anymore."

Keith Prettyshield also said that "I don't eat it [fish] because I don't trust it.... That's why the last couple [of] years I haven't touched the Qu'Appelle River, because there's too much sewage going into the whole system. And I mean it, I saw it.... And the mercury levels are really high."

Elder Art Adams said that

> I don't hunt no more.... I used to, like when my uncle was here, I used to do a lot of deer hunting. At that time, the deer meat was real good. As the years went by, you seen all the chemicals that are going through, and you notice the deer are eating them, and you can taste that. All of a sudden the deer meat didn't taste as good as it used to.... So I just stopped. I quit after my uncle passed on ... about twenty years ago.... You hear the stories that the chemicals came in and people stopped eating. I think some of them did quit. It wasn't just me—a lot of us.

Not all of the wild foods that CTK members have access to are contaminated, and Elder Bernice Saulteaux is helping the younger generation understand the importance of incorporating wild meat into their diet again—to promote the good health with which their ancestors were blessed:

> They're trying to go back to the traditional way of life. So I'm on the school board, and we have a new program there that's nutritional. So what we want to do is bring back the traditional foods into the school and teach them to our children to use. Because we have such a high percentage of diabetes, and we don't know if that's related to the foods that we're eating.... It's just a new project that's happening.

Kurt Ryder also mentioned the problem of diabetes: "There's not too many people nowadays that live off the wild meat. That's where you see a lot of people with diabetes and stuff like that, because we're not eating our traditional foods.... I don't have diabetes; I'm the only one in my family that doesn't."

PIPELINE CONCERNS

The TransCanada Energy East Pipeline project proposed to change an existing gas pipeline that runs through CTK lands from gas to oil. This had many Elders and community members concerned about the safety of their people, wildlife, and ecology. "Is it safe?" Elder Derrick Saulteaux asked. "It's time for them to stand up and start to understand what's going on. The youth nowadays, they're pretty smart. Ask questions about the pipeline." As Clint Haywahe noted,

> well, you know, we sit kind of dead centre of everything. Because we have, mainly, not only First Nations but people within the country, we have groups of people that are looking at the safety area mainly and have protested these pipelines because of possible breaks and damages that they can create. So we talk about a safety zone, a buffer zone. . . . That's something that we need to look at today because of the safety of the people in the community. . . . Because we know [the] building of houses and everything within a certain distance of the lines, . . . if one of them were to erupt, you could see damages from half to three-quarter[s] a mile away. And, yes, that's a danger, so we need to continuously work to make sure that the company prevents that.

Elder Wanda Prettyshield expressed concern because "we live close to the pipeline. . . . If there was ever an explosion or anything, we're the first ones that would get hit. . . . So people that live along the pipeline there, never mind the whole reserve, . . . you're always thinking about that—that there's a possibility that something could happen."

Other CTK members expressed their concerns about environmental impacts.

> A lot of people these days wonder about whatever goes up. . . . But the only thing I see is environmental, things that could happen to it because, . . . when they did the seismic up here, we're living on a good water source here, so that's one concern about it. There's an aquafer somewhere around the reserve, down the road here, when they dug it they had to cap it. (Kurt Ryder)

> I can't travel down it no more. It's all ripped up and full of clay and loose black dirt, and roads beat to shit, that high [two feet] from track hoes. So it's pretty rough, it looks ugly too. . . . I don't

CHAPTER 14

like that they're destroying and tearing up all our Traditional Land here. (Keith Prettyshield)

I'd rather have oil than gas. Gas is too dangerous. It contaminates the ground faster and kills a lot of roots. Same thing with oil, but it won't leak out of the pipes as much as gas. Gas could come out of the ground and hurt your trees, hurt the feed for wild animals, they get sick. (Lyle Spencer)

I don't like the idea of pipelines going through. Environmentally, it's a disaster, because we have a big pasture there, and we have dugouts there that the animals drink from, and then we have farmland right along that pipeline, so it could damage the water and land. So I don't like the idea of pipelines going through the reserve, but what are you going to do? They compensate [us], and it pays our bills, but at the same time it's environmentally unsafe. I don't like it at all. (Elder Wanda Prettyshield)

However, because of the economic benefits to the reserve, some interviewees did not mind the idea of a pipeline going through their lands. Art Adams was one: "I don't really mind the pipelines for the economy and the benefit for the band. I welcome that. Because they go through our land, they give us back some revenues that we didn't have before, and we seem to make good use of that. I welcome that opportunity for industry to come through CTK."

Clint Haywahe noted that, "as far as changing it to oil, you're talking about pumping a million barrels a day. When you look at the price of it and then the gas in exchange, . . . our easement agreement should reflect that." He observed that

> our community is faced with many hardships, especially within the infrastructure, because the funding we do get from the federal government is minimal. . . . Maybe we can have our own fire department, emergency response team, a full sportsplex for our children to play in, and a health centre for our elderly people. Not only elderly, we also have young people. Because of the way life has changed, now we deal with illnesses, diabetes, cancer, leukemia, things like that. Sometimes our people need twenty-four-hour care. So in the meantime we need to find a way to build that and have it be self-sustainable. So I believe that by negotiating and dealing with these companies we can

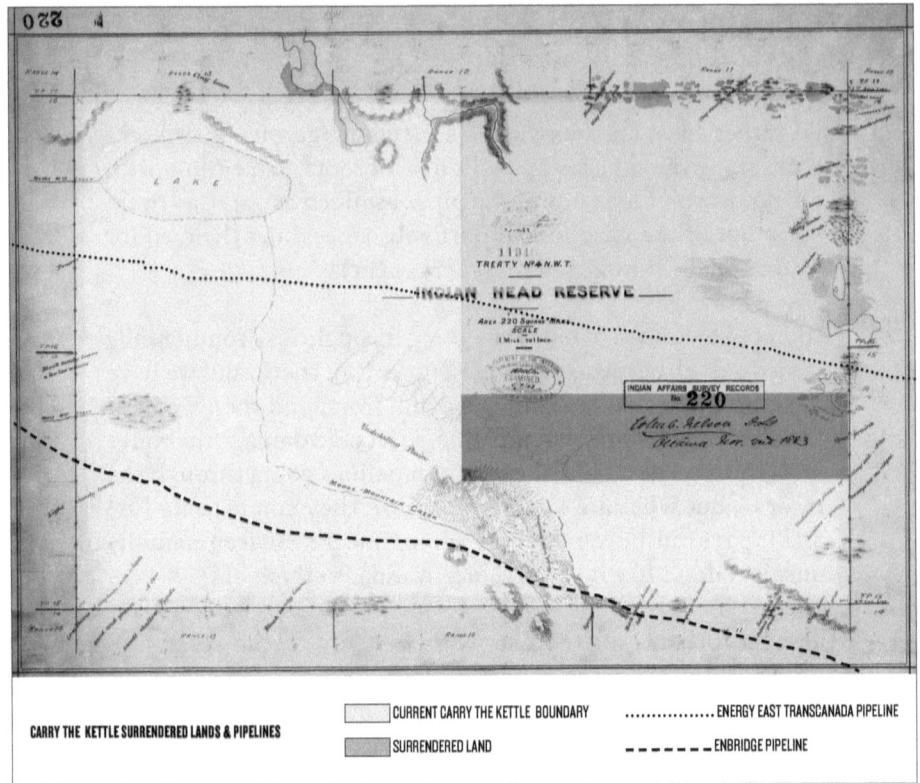

FIGURE 19: Surrendered Lands and Pipelines
Treaty No. 4, NWT Indian Head Reserve. John C. Nelson, DLS, Ottawa, Nov. 2, 1883.
Source: Library and Archives Canada/Department of Indian Affairs and Northern Development fonds/Item 2197. Adapted by Duncan Campbell.

achieve that. It's been a hard life, not only for people from CTK but throughout the country.

Yet, as Haywahe noted, CTK members believe that there should be better consultation regarding this and other projects that might disrupt their lives and Traditional Lands "rather than be dictated to and not given the opportunity to give our concerns." As he elaborated,

> they talk about "duty to consult," ideally "nation to nation." So I'd like to see our leadership at the table when these negotiations and business plans are made, rather than being brought to us after the fact. So I'd like to see where the pipelines, which include TransCanada, Energy East, Enbridge, and any other

CHAPTER 14

company from industry, that come through CTK, that they have a full agreement with the people, made through our leadership, but also approved by the people in general. And that's how I see business should be run yet today. . . . I'd like to see where we are right at the table to negotiate—to deal—to make more solid agreements. . . . It's good when you bring your community of people with you, when you deal with them hand-in-hand, and then you make agreements and work on them together. And sometimes, even though you may fail, you don't fail it alone, you fail it as a group.

ELDERS' ADVICE TO THE YOUTH

The Elders and current users of Traditional Lands interviewed for this book had much advice for the youth in the hope that they will fight to protect their culture, livelihood, environment, and Indigenous Rights for themselves and future generations. "I'd like to see our young people hang on to especially the language, and the powwows and stuff like that," Art Adams said. "That's who we were. We were always proud to be Indian, carry on what our ancestors used to do." Elder Myrtle Hassler also said that "I just want all our traditions, our language and stuff, preserved and passed on so it will never die off. So it will keep constantly going on to the next generation and after. I think it's something that the kids should know. . . . I think it's something unique and should be always kept. Never let it go."

Elder James O'Watch had much advice for the youth:

> Respect your mom and dad, that's first number one of all. Your grandmother, grandfather, brothers, and sisters. Overall, the whole community. Have respect for one another, get along, be kind to each other. . . . You never know what's going to happen. So we're always told be good to each other, have respect, be kind, help, and work, work hard. . . . God gave you two hands to work, two ears to listen, two eyes to look at everything. Analyze everything, study everything. Each day is different, you'll never have one day the same as the next day. So observe the day you were given by the Creator. Look at everything, listen to everything, just listen to the birds, just look at the sky, watch everything, and work. Work hard for your family, for your kids, grandkids. Hard work never did anybody any harm.

He also stated

> be proud of who you are as an Indian. Be proud you have a heritage. Be proud you have a way of life that God gave you. We weren't meant to be poor, but we are, so we have to accept it. Go out there . . . in the white man's world and do what we can to learn their ways and be able to come back and help the old people. . . . That's the advice my dad gave me: "Learn the white man's way and use it as a shield to fight for your people." So I did.

Clint Haywahe mentioned that

> what I think about . . . daily . . . is governing our own lives around community regarding habitat and protection of the lands and putting something in place that would govern ourselves so that it carries on in the future. Because without any structure, even today, with losing our language and all that, it plays a part of that. So we need to maintain our language, our status, and who we are as a nation. If we can accomplish that, then that will carry us a long way.

He also said to

> protect them [our lands], keeping them pretty well as they are to ensure that the supply of the game, medicines, and berries are here to provide for them, . . . as they do for us today. The big picture is, we gotta work with government in order to maintain that. So when you look at the treaties, we need to stand and protect them, but in the meantime we also have to respect them in order for that to happen.

Elders Victoria, Joyce, and Gladys Prettyshield offered this advice: "Listen to the older people. Listen to them, what they got to say, and that way you'll have a good life. . . . That's the only way you're going to keep the reserve, . . . the land, well, just keep it as a reserve. Don't give it away. They should all stick together and try to better themselves here.

Kurt Ryder mentioned "hunt properly, like don't take what you can't eat. . . . When we used to go hunting a long time ago, how I was taught to hunt is we walked and we'd hunt, we went on our horse and we'd hunt.

CHAPTER 14

Nowadays a lot of people go out there and shoot anything and leave it. But the traditional way of hunting is we just hunt what we need to eat, to feed our families." Darrell Jack also mentioned hunting:

> My boys, they know how to hunt already, I've been taking them out since they were just so high.... I would like to keep our land open for our kids to hunt on, wherever they are.... Keep the right to hunt and fish or whatever. It seems a lot harder now to live. Life in them days was easy.... Food was there, and you could live off the land.

Elder Bernice Saulteaux said that,

> when I was going with my mom, and even when they went up to North Battleford, they would say, "This is what my grandma used to cook, we used to eat."... And how to kill, and how to skin, how to clean, and how to cook and all that.... It would be good if they could learn all that because some day everything's not going to last the way it is today. So if they would learn, then they'd have that to survive on.

In other words, she suggested that the youth

> go back to the land again, ... get to know the medicines, the foods, the sacredness of the lands. Because we grew up in that time, aware all this was to be a way of life for me, and then in the '60s, '70s everything started to change. I can see the difference from back then, the way I lived to now the way it is. So the children, they would be much happier, I know, if they would go back to the wild meat and the berries, because there's lots out there—[they] would realize how our people survived. Because there's wild turnip and berries, and there's all different kinds of food that they had and they lived with.

According to Elder Wanda Prettyshield, "I think the language is really important for people to learn.... Traditionally, I'm thinking, ... a lot of generations came over from Cypress Hills and settled on CTK. The language at that time and the language and customs and traditions that went on at that time were true, and today with the generations changing a lot of that stuff ... has changed."

Finally, Elder Garry Whitecap said to "stay away from drugs and alcohol. . . . It causes heartbreak, sorrow, grief, the breakup of families. That's the traditional teachings we tell these young people, otherwise they won't learn the traditional ways."

CONCLUSION

"Our Side of the Story"

It . . . has to do with . . . the Cypress Hills Massacre and our side of the story, that has never been told. So, a lot . . . has been published . . . about the Cypress Hills Massacre and many book[s] done on it, but the people who need to be spoken to have never been spoken to, and [with] all the history that has been written, they've never come to our people and asked us about our history. They've only seen [it] from the archives or from our government relationship, and it wasn't a good relationship. So, from our perspective, what's written is totally different [from] our history. So that's one of the most important things for Carry The Kettle, Cegakin, or Man Who Took the Coat. We need to tell our side of the story. It's been close to 150 years that we haven't told our story, and it needs to be told.
—FORMER CHIEF ELSIE JACK, INDIAN HEAD, SASKATCHEWAN, AUGUST 2021

Carry The Kettle Nakoda People are a proud and strong Indigenous People who have continued close relations with members of their families and tribal communities now located in the United States and in other bands in Canada. They have a long history as a successful, independent society thriving on the prairies and parklands in a larger cohesive group, living on their homelands for hundreds of years before European arrival. As discussed throughout this book, their independent society has a distinct language, spirituality, and culture with knowledge of and wisdom about their surroundings. For millenia, they lived off the bounty of the land and traded with other nations on Turtle Island, their home, and continue to do so.

The arrival of European immigrants was at first a curiosity, but as these immigrants transformed Turtle Island, the lives and livelihoods of the CTK Nakoda People were changed forever. The recent history of the Nakoda People resulting from their treatment by settler society is one of betrayal and neglect. Without conquest, agreement, or valid legal rights, these settlers asserted sovereignty over the Nakoda Peoples, effectively confiscating their lands and livelihoods without compensation nor consideration. As addressed in the early chapters, from initial contact with European traders, the Nakoda People were one of the traders' friendliest and accommodating allies. They acted as guides and go-betweens at the beginning of the fur trade, and later they played the role of peacemakers, not only between robe traders and other Indigenous groups but also between tribes in the northwestern United States. They welcomed the newcomers onto the land and agreed to enter into treaty relations with them as kin. And yet, as a result of their close ties with the early fur trade, they were often the first to be exposed to devastating diseases, and they were manipulated with alcohol. They were able to survive these challenges only to be then confronted by the complete devastation of their livelihood—the near extinction of the bison herds, followed by the confiscation of their Traditional Lands.

Indeed, throughout North American history, European immigrants seized, occupied, and used the Indigenous lands and displaced the First Peoples on them. When Indigenous Peoples fought back, they met with fines, penalties, imprisonment, and even, at times, were hanged or slaughtered. The First Peoples held different concepts of land and property rights that made them vulnerable to European language and legal systems. Realizing this, King George III issued the Proclamation of 1763 in an attempt to protect Indigenous Peoples from the treachery of European settlers. Yet, the protections against the occupation of "Indian Lands" were not followed by the U.S. government after 1776. Even in Canada, under British law, the Proclamation was conveniently manipulated and ignored.

For the Plains Peoples, the most significant betrayal of the Royal Proclamation was Canada's planned and systematic destruction of the bison. The lands and livelihoods of the people were not respected but purposely destroyed. This rampage of greed and death collapsed the livelihood of the entire population of Indigenous Peoples on the Great Plains in both the United States and Canada and in its wake caused the starvation of thousands, creating a refugee crisis. The government's motivation for the extermination of the bison was to remove the Indigenous Peoples from the prairies to allow the immigrant settlement of the west – an act truly immoral, unconscionable, and illegal, and one now deemed genocidal.

CONCLUSION

Elders at the Annual Gathering 2021, Cypress Hills Elkwater Provincial Park, Alberta, Former Assiniboine Reserve 1879.
Photo provided by Carry The Kettle Nakoda First Nation.

Why did both the American government and the Canadian government believe that it was within their right to eliminate the Indigenous Peoples from these territories? In the first half of the nineteenth century, the United States followed a policy of removal and relocation enforced by military actions. President Andrew Jackson violated the Cherokee Treaties and shipped the Cherokee People to Oklahoma in the well-known "Trail of Tears." There were many additional relocations in the United States.

In 1862, in Minnesota, the pattern of expropriation continued. A treaty based on trader participation and failure to pay annuities led to Dakota Sioux strife based on the loss of lands, and many of the Dakota People revolted. This led to the bloody "Dakota War of 1862" and the largest hanging of Indigenous people in U.S. history. Many of the Dakota People were banished from Minnesota and had to flee. Some headed north to Canada, but many headed to an increasingly crowded west where the slaughter of bison had begun. The American military pursued the Dakota and fought a series of battles over the following decades. The American pattern continued whereby Indian Lands were defined, treaties were made, and then immigration overwhelmed Treaty Lands. Then the treaties were ignored or broken. If the conflicts resulted in violence, then Indigenous Peoples were "punished" by revocation of all their rights to land or payment. Then they were imprisoned or relocated.

The American history is important not only because the Nakoda lands stretched into the United States and along the U.S border from Manitoba to Alberta but also because the prairies were one ecosystem and one habitat not only for bison but also for people. The Nakoda followed the bison well into Montana and North Dakota and would travel north to the wooded parklands in Canada. During 1864, the American military committed a genocidal attack on the Southern Cheyenne and Arapaho at Sand Creek, Colorado, killing as many as 200, mostly women and children. In 1868, George Armstrong Custer led the U.S. Cavalry in another genocidal massacre against the Southern Cheyenne at Washita River, Oklahoma, killing 150 people, half of whom were women and children. The Lakota Sioux, Northern Cheyenne, and Arapaho participated in Red Cloud's War from 1866 to 1868 fighting the American military. The brutal treatment of the Dakota and Lakota Sioux and the massacres of the Cheyenne inevitably led to the Battle of the Little Big Horn in 1876, but, before these famous battles, violence had spread too into Canada in 1872 and 1873.

The Sweet Grass Hills Massacre was the cold-blooded murder of four Nakoda men, indiscriminately shot by Tom Hartwick and his crony wolfers, who claimed that the men had stolen their horses. After this incident, American authorities claimed that they would not tolerate such violence, but they did nothing to curb the illegal poisoning of bait, the trade in whiskey, or the continued murder of Indigenous Peoples. The next year—June 1873—the same wolfers committed what was later called the Cypress Hills Massacre, killing many more innocent Nakoda people, the very ancestors of the CTK Nakoda Nation. The wolfers raped survivors in further acts of atrocity against them.

The perpetrators were never punished for their crimes, and the Nakoda became well aware of the treachery of the trade society. In 1874, the Canadian government sent the North West Mounted Police to protect Canadian sovereignty and clean up the whiskey trade. Only three years later, the Nakoda signed Treaty 4 with the Canadian Crown. This was three years after a meeting at Fort Qu'Appelle at which a misunderstood agreement was presented. Despite some advertisements to the contrary, the Canadian government pursued a policy of genocide not too dissimilar to the Americans' methods. The policy was to starve the Indigenous Peoples, thereby forcing them onto reserves selected by government agents. In the case of Carry The Kettle Nakoda First Nation, the government violated the treaty by refusing to let its members stay on their chosen treaty reserve, their normal winter camp, which had been surveyed. Instead, the Canadian officials forcibly relocated

CONCLUSION

Elders Gathering in 2021 for the Annual Memorial of the Cypress Hills Massacre of the Nakoda Tribe in 1873.
Photo provided by Carry The Kettle Nakoda First Nation.

the Nakoda to the bald prairie, where survival of the winter would be extremely difficult if not impossible. This two-year relocation that took place from 1882 to 1883 resulted in significant loss of life and reduced the Nakoda People to a shadow of their former society.

By 1885, after the Riel Resistance and the public hanging of mostly Treaty Indians, the Nakoda were confined to the reserve and subjected to racist and paternalistic rules. They were forced – "encouraged"— to pursue subsistence farming, and their language and culture were discouraged—even prohibited. Given the cultural and genocidal disruptions to their livelihood, their traditional land use was decimated and their farming opportunities limited. The Nakoda would pursue hunting and gathering on their reserve as much as they could, but it was not until much later, after the suffocating regulations were removed, that they restarted their hunting, trapping, gathering, and spiritual practices.

Adding to their dispossession, the Nakoda people were subjected to the Indian residential school system throughout the twentieth century, with countless children being forced from their homes and suffering abuses of all kinds under the guise of an education—but what was truly forced assimilation and genocide. With the recent uncovering of the hundreds of bodies located at the Kamloops Indian Residential School on Tk'emlups te Secwépemc First Nation in Kamloops, BC, in

May of 2021, and the subsequent finding of remains at other schools across the prairies, the Canadian public and the world is finally forced to acknowledge and bear witness to the extent of the horrific events that have taken place throughout the history of the country against First Peoples. The injustices against those same communities continue as First Nations continue to fight for their Treaty Rights and to work through the legal land claims. Movements like Idle No More and the Land Back Movement continue to inspire, educate, and force change in Canada as traditional territories, languages, cultures, and practices are reclaimed, restored, and revitalized across Turtle Island. But there is a long ways to go before reconciliation and decolonization will be achieved. Indeed, in the last interview with Chief Elsie Jack during the final stages of preparing this book, she explained the importance of remembering all of this history, and sharing it with the next generation so that true reconciliation may happen—for there is no reconciliation without first the truth:

> Reconciliation. Where is the honour of the Crown? Reconciliation has to start with her Majesty the Queen and all the Treaty Indians of Canada. Under the Crown's care, you raped the land of the people and then you raped the people themselves. That's acts of genocide. Are we to be idle? If the Canadian government won't honour our Cypress Hills land claim, we will go to the world court and tell them what has been done to our people. We want our rights protected. I will raise my hands somehow, some way, God allowed us to still be here, so we want our rights back, we want our lands protected. We want our Cypress Hills land back.

The many contributors to this book have tried to describe the history of and the challenges faced by the Nakoda People and to record the extent to which they have begun to re-establish their traditional practices. It is clear that the term of the treaty, which gave the Nakoda the right to continue their livelihood, was illegally terminated by the government purportedly to preserve the peace and make way for settler immigration, but really, to protect Canadian sovereignty. Given the broad the violations of the rights of Carry The Kettle First Nation, any settler or any immigrant who has taken up Nakoda Traditional Lands must be deemed complicit with the government in violating the terms of the treaty, which guaranteed the Nakoda their way of life. Now, after 1982, the government is responsible for consulting with the First

CONCLUSION

Elder Karen Ryder at Head of the Mountain at Cypress Hills, 2021.
Photo provided by Carry The Kettle Nakoda First Nation.

Nation with respect to any violation of its rights and any new effects on its Traditional Lands. The racism and the failure to respect the Nakoda People's human rights are not only the failure of the government but also a sickness permeating Canadian society.

And though there have been many recent positive developments—including language revitalization, an increase in traditional hunting and gathering, an exchange and revival of Traditional Knowledge, and a great spiritual reawakening in CTK Nakoda peoples—the peace of the community cannot be achieved and truly reconciled without the rest of the country acknowledging and doing something to mitigate these horrific events and legacies of colonialism. And one way to do so is to tell this story—the story of Carry The Kettle Nakoda First Nation from our perspective, for our children's future:

> I tell our Nakoda children, "You are very fortunate to be here. It's amazing you are still here today, it's amazing that the bloodline of the Nakoda People is still here, because of all the things that happened in our history, how the government tried to wipe us out. It wasn't that long ago either; it was within the last 150 years that the government tried to wipe us out completely." I always say that to our Nakoda children, and to my grandchildren too. And I tell them: "Be proud of who you are because you

Mrs. Rena (Jack) Ryder, Granddaughter of Chief The Man Who Took the Coat (Chief Jack), Signatory to Treaty Adhesion 4.
Photo provided by Carry The Kettle Nakoda First Nation.

are very fortunate with everything that has happened to us in our history. Our history tells us about our own family."

My aunt talked about the blankets, the blankets that were brought from Montana. After days sleeping with the blankets, all got smallpox. How they looked. How they scattered. My grandfather and his brother and his sister separated: one went to Fort Belknap in the United States, one stayed up here to ensure the survival of our nation. She was only a very small child when she went to the residential school in Regina and she never came back. . . . Her body still lies in the Regina residential school.

So, I carry a lot of this history. I let my family know. The move. The starvation and the move. I couldn't imagine my little granddaughter walking from the Cypress Hills to over here [the Carry The Kettle Nakoda Reserve], not once, two times, maybe three times. I can't imagine.

So, a lot of this history, I let my family know. So as to make sure they remember those kind of things we lived through.
—Chief Elsie Jack, Indian Head, August 2021

Notes

INTRODUCTION

1   Dale Russell, *Eighteenth-Century Western Cree and Their Neighbours*, Mercury Series Paper 143 (Ottawa: Canadian Museum of Civilization, 1991), x.

CHAPTER I

1   Douglas R. Parks and Raymond J. DeMallie, "Sioux, Assiniboine, and Stoney Dialects: A Classification," *Anthropological Linguistics* 34, nos. 1–4 (1992): 233–55.
2   James Henri Howard, "The Cultural Position of the Dakota: A Reassessment," in *Essays on the Science of Culture in Honor of Leslie A. White*, ed. Gertrude E. Role and Robert L. Carneiro (New York: Thomas and Crowell, 1960), 249–68.
3   Parks and DeMallie, "Sioux, Assiniboine, and Stoney Dialects."
4   Adapted from the "Assiniboine Creation Story," narrated by Shannon Healy, and notes of Rex Flying, in *Assiniboine Memories: Legends of the Nakota People* (Harlem, MT: Fort Belknap Education Department, Fort Belknap Community Council, 1983), 1–3. The introduction to the stories states that "the stories were collected from Assiniboine Elders on the Fort Belknap Reservation and are their versions as told to them by their grandfathers and grandmothers."
5   Scott Hamilton, Jill Taylor-Hollings, and David Norris, "Human Ecology of the Canadian Prairie Ecozone ca. 1500 BP: Diffusion, Migration and Technology Innovation," in *Human Ecology of the Canadian Prairie*, ed. B.A. Nicholson (Regina: CPRC Press, 2011), 139.
6   The term "tradition" refers to an archaeological concept implying a group of people who used a particular way of life or system of survival. These traditions

NOTES

included the use of particular tools made in particular ways, such as a bow and arrow.

7   This is the period approximately 1,000 years ago.
8   Hamilton, Taylor-Hollings, and Norris, "Human Ecology of the Canadian Prairie Ecozone," 104–06.
9   Hamilton, Taylor-Hollings, and Norris, 138.
10 Hamilton, Taylor-Hollings, and Norris, 138.
11 Hamilton, Taylor-Hollings, and Norris, 138–39.
12 Hamilton, Taylor-Hollings, and Norris, 139.
13 Mound building was evident "throughout much of the eastern plains as far as eastern Saskatchewan (e.g., Moose Bay burial mound), [and it was] coupled with some of the exotic ritual goods associated with Middle Woodland and later Mississippian societies." Ibid. The authors cite Katherine H. Capes, WB Nickerson Survey and Excavations, 1912–15, of the Southern Manitoba Mounds Region, Anthropology Papers, National Museum of Canada (Ottawa: Department of Northern Affairs and Natural Resources, 1963); E.L. Syms, "Cultural Ecology and Ecological Dynamics of the Ceramic Period in Southwestern Manitoba," *Plains Anthropologist* 22, no. 76 (1977): 1–160; and E.L. Syms, "The Devils Lake–Sourisford Burial Complex on the Northeastern Plains," *Plains Anthropologist* 24, no. 86 (1979): 283–308. These associations represent inter-regional influences and an "expanded level of exchange between the eco-regions." This pattern can be "coupled with a transplantation and persistence of broad-spectrum foraging by some groups, and gradually led to the diffusion westward of small-scale village horticultural life after ca. 1000 BP." Hamilton, Taylor-Hollings, and Norris, "Human Ecology of the Canadian Prairie Ecozone," 139. On the Moose Bay burial mound, see Margaret G. Hanna, *The Moose Bay Burial Mound* (Regina: Saskatchewan Department of Tourism and Renewable Resources, 1976).
14 Hamilton, Taylor-Hollings, and Norris, "Human Ecology of the Canadian Prairie Ecozone," 139–40.
15 See Dale Walde, "Sedentism and Pre-Contact Tribal Organization on the Northern Plains: Colonial Impostion or Indigenous Development?" *World Archaeology* 38, no. 2 (2006): 291–310.
16 However, debate continues about potential motivations for changes in pre-dation: (1) whether the primary motivation for mass bison killing was the desire to produce a food surplus; (2) whether surpluses were used for trade in an extra-regional exchange system, as suggested by Brian O.K. Reeves, "Culture Change in the Northern Plains: 1000 B.C.–A.D. 1000," Archaeological Survey of Alberta, Occasional Paper 20, 1983; or (3) whether food was stored for later seasons when deprivation was possible to facilitate seasonal winter aggregation in larger groups, as noted by Walde, "Sedentism and Pre-Contact Tribal Organization."

NOTES

17 See Hamilton, Taylor-Hollings, and Norris, "Human Ecology of the Canadian Prairie Ecozone," who share Walde's perspective in "Sedentism and Pre-Contact Tribal Organization."

18 Hamilton, Taylor-Hollings, and Norris, "Human Ecology of the Canadian Prairie Ecozone," 140, summarizing Walde, "Sedentism and Pre-Contact Tribal Organization," 306.

19 Hamilton, Taylor-Hollings, and Norris, summarizing Walde, "Sedentism and Pre-Contact Tribal Organization," and B.A. Nicholson, "Modelling a Horticultural Focus in South-Central Manitoba During the Late Prehistoric Period—The Vickers Focus," *Mid-Continental Journal of Archaeology* 16, no. 2 (1991): 163–88.

20 The exposition of the Vickers Focus is exploring this connection, as seen in B.A. Nicholson, David Meyer, Gerry Oetelaar, and Scott Hamilton, "Human Ecology of the Canadian Prairie Ecozone ca. 500 BP: Plains Woodland Influences and Horticultural Practice," in *Human Ecology of the Canadian Prairie Ecozone*, ed. B.A. Nicholson (Regina: CPRC Press, 2011), 159–65.

21 Dale Walde, David Meyer, and Wendy Unfreed, "The Late Period on the Canadian and Adjacent Plains," *Revista de arqueologia americana* 9 (1995): 24; also see Guy Gibbon, "Cultures of the Upper Mississippi River Valley and Adjacent Prairies in Iowa and Minnesota," in *Plains Indians, A.D. 500–1500, the Archaeological Past of Historic Groups*, ed. K.H. Schlesier (Norman: University of Oklahoma Press, 1994), 144–45.

22 David Meyer and Scott Hamilton, *Neighbors to the North: Peoples of the Boreal Forest Plains Indians, A.D. 500–1500: The Archeological Past of Historic Groups* (Norman: University of Oklahoma Press, 1994), 115.

23 Brian Reeves, "The Southern Alberta Paleo-Cultural Paleo-Environment Sequence," in *Post Pleistocene Man and His Environment on the Northern Plains*, ed. R.G. Forbis, L.B. Davis, O.A. Christensen, and G. Fedirchuk (Calgary: University of Calgary Archaeological Association and Students Press, 1969), 6–46; Reeves, "Culture Change in the Northern Plains"; based on discussion in Walde, Meyer, and Unfreed, "The Late Period on the Canadian and Adjacent Plains," 25–26.

24 This figure has been adapted from figures in Walde, Meyer, and Unfreed, "The Late Period on the Canadian and Adjacent Plains," 7–9, 11–66; David Meyer and Dale Russell, "The Pegogamaw Crees and Their Ancestors: History and Archaeology in the Saskatchewan Forks Region," Plains Anthropologist 51, no. 199 (2006): 303–24, DOI: 10.1179/pan.2006.027.

25 Walde, Meyer, and Unfreed, "The Late Period on the Canadian and Adjacent Plains," 32.

26 Walde, Meyer, and Unfreed, 32.

27 Based on David Meyer, "The Old Women's Phase on the Saskatchewan Plains: Some Ideas," in *Archaeology in Alberta 1987*, ed. M. Magne, Archeological

NOTES

Survey of Alberta Occasional Papers 32 (Edmonton: Alberta Culture and Multiculturalism, 1988), 60.

28 Walde, Meyer, and Unfreed, "The Late Period on the Canadian and Adjacent Plains," 32–33.
29 Walde, Meyer, and Unfreed, 34–35.
30 Walde, Meyer, and Unfreed, 38–39.
31 The pattern of what constituted a group identity based on archaeological evidence always remains partial, but that does not limit the importance of speculation and efforts to expand the scope of investigation.
32 M.G. Michlovic and F.E. Schneider, "The Shea Site: A Prehistoric Fortified Village on the Northeastern Plains," *Plains Anthropologist* 38, no. 143 (1993): 117–37.
33 Michlovic ad Schneider, "The Shea Site" 117–37.
34 Walde, Meyer, and Unfreed, "The Late Period on the Canadian and Adjacent Plains," 41.
35 Walde, Meyer, and Unfreed, 43.
36 Walde, Meyer, and Unfreed, 43.
37 Walde, Meyer, and Unfreed, 43.
38 Walde, Meyer, and Unfreed, 44.
39 Walde, Meyer, and Unfreed, 44–45.
40 Walde, Meyer, and Unfreed, 45. The One Gun Phase is represented primarily by the Cluny site, and there are many distinctions that differentiated it from the Mortlach Phase (Walde is currently subjecting this to restudy). Cluny is the name given to a site near present-day Calgary that was a fortified village. Although this is far west of Mortlach concentrated village sites roughly in the same time period, the questions of the modern identity of the One Gun Phase are being addressed. Walde suspects that One Gun might be a distinct Nakoda group. He has also found the presence of Cluny ceramics throughout southern Alberta, and he notes the presence of "Mortlach pottery" at several sites in Alberta, including the Junction site near Fort Macleod, the Little Bow sites, and, increasingly, the Old Women's Buffalo Jump.
41 Walde, Meyer, and Unfreed, 45–46.
42 Examples in the historical era include when the Cree accompanying Anthony Henday in 1754 entered Blackfoot country or when the select camping bands of Cree and Assiniboine accompanying Henry Kelsey in 1691 entered the country of the "Naywatamee Poets"; see Henry Kelsey, *The Kelsey Papers*, ed. Arthur G. Doughty and Chester Martin (Ottawa: Public Archives of Canada, 1929).
43 Walde, Meyer, and Unfreed, "The Late Period on the Canadian and Adjacent Plains," 48–49.
44 Walde, Meyer, and Unfreed, 48.
45 B.A. Nicholson, "Ceramic Affiliation and the Case of Incipient Horticulture in Southwestern Manitoba," *Canadian Journal of Archeology* 14 (1990): 15.

NOTES

46 Walde, Meyer, and Unfreed, "The Late Period on the Canadian and Adjacent Plains," 48–49.
47 Walde reasserts this to counter alternative interpretations; see David Meyer and Dale Russell, "The Pegogamaw Crees and Their Ancestors," 309; B.A. Nicholson, David Meyer, Gerry Oetelaar, and Scott Hamilton, "Human Ecology of the Canadian Prairie Ecozone ca. 500 BP: Plains Woodland Influences and Horticultural Practice," in *Human Ecology of the Canadian Prairie Ecozone*, ed. B.A. Nicholson (Regina: CPRC Press, 2011), 153–58. Walde addresses the arguments and evidence of those who disagree about the Mortlach Phase being proto-Assiniboine, and he reasserts his evidence to support his interpretation. Dale Walde, "Ethnicity, the Archeological Record, and Mortlach," *Plains Anthropologist* 55, no. 214 (2010): 151–66.

CHAPTER 2

1 Reuben Gold Thwaites, ed., *The Jesuit Relations and Allied Documents: 1853-1913* (Charleston, NC: Bibliolife Publishing, 1896), reprint 44, 249.
2 Arthur J. Ray, *Indians in the Fur Trade: Their Role as Trappers, Hunters, and Middlemen in the Lands Southwest of Hudson Bay, 1660-1870* (Toronto: University of Toronto Press, 1974), 6.
3 Thwaites, *The Jesuit Relations and Allied Documents*, reprint 44, 249.
4 Ray, *Indians in the Fur Trade*, 6, citing Conrad E. Heidenreich, *Huronia: A History and Geography of the Huron Indians, 1600-1650* (Toronto: McClelland and Stewart, 1973). Modern traditional land use studies have confirmed that the territories of various First Nations did not have strict limits and often changed over time.
5 N.M. Crouse, *Contributions of the Canadian Jesuits to the Geographic Knowledge of New France* (Ithaca, NY: Cornell Publications Printing Company, 1924), 143–44; Ray, *Indians in the Fur Trade*, 6–7, 38.
6 Ray, 11.
7 Ray, 11.
8 Ray, 11, 24; "Memoir on the Present State of Canada and the Measures to Be Adopted for the Safety of the Country," November 12, 1685, in Edmund Bailey O'Callaghan, *Jesuit Relations of Discoveries and Other Occurrences in Canada and the Northern and Western States of the Union, 1632-1672* (Press of the Historical Society of New York, 1983).
9 Ray, *Indians in the Fur Trade*, 11, 24; "Memoir of Duchesneau on Irregular Trade in Canada," in O'Callaghan, *Jesuit Relations*.
10 Ray, *Indians in the Fur Trade*, 11, 24; "M. de Denonville to M. de Seignelay, Ville Marie," August 25, 1687, in O'Callaghan, *Jesuit Relations*.
11 Ray, *Indians in the Fur Trade*, 11.

NOTES

12. Lawrence J. Burpee, ed., *Journal and Letters of Pierre Gaultier de Varennes de La Vérendyre and His Sons* (Toronto: Champlain Society, 1927), 6-7; Richard I. Ruggles, "The Historical Geography and Cartography of the Canadian West, 1670-1795: The Discovery, Exploration, Geographic Description and Cartographic Delineation of Western Canada to 1795" (PhD diss., University of London, 1958); Ray, *Indians in the Fur Trade*, 11, 25.
13. Burpee, *Journal and Letters*, 86.
14. Arthur T. Adams, *Explorations of Pierre Esprit Radisson* (Minneapolis: Ross and Haines, 1961), 227.
15. Burpee, *Journal and Letters*; Ruggles, "The Historical Geography and Cartography of the Canadian West."
16. E.E. Rich, *The Fur Trade and the Northwest to 1857* (Toronto: McClelland and Stewart, 1967), 75.
17. Ray, *Indians in the Fur Trade*, 16, 43n35. "Beauharnois and Hoquart writing from Quebec City said Lake of the Woods and Lake of the Assiniboines were the same lake. [They] cautioned against assuming that the lake was the only one around which the tribe lived. They were said to extend as far as Lake Winnipeg." Lawrence J. Burpee, ed., *Journals of La Vérendrye*, Publications of the Champlain Society 16 (New York: Greenwood Press, 1968), 86-87.
18. See portion of the La France map in Ray, *Indians in the Fur Trade*, 44, Figure 7.
19. Ray, 18.
20. Ray, 44. See *York Factory Journals of 1766-67*, LAC, HBC B 239/d/10, 2.
21. Ray, 19.
22. C. Wissler, Peter H. Buck, Leslie Spier, Ernest Beaglehole, and W.W. Hill, *Population Changes among the Northern Plains Indians*, Yale University Publications in Anthropology (New Haven, CT: Human Relations Area Files Press, 1970).
23. Ray, *Indians in the Fur Trade*, 19, 21.
24. Ray, 19-20. See *York Factory Journals of 1766-67*, LAC, HBC B 239/a/2, 22.
25. Ray, 19.
26. Ray. See also *York Factory Journals of 1766-67*, LAC, B 239/a/1-5.
27. Ray, 21.
28. Wissler et al., *Population Changes among the Northern Plains Indians*.
29. James Daschuk, *Clearing the Plains: Disease, Politics of Starvation, and the Loss of Aboriginal Life* (Regina: University of Regina Press, 2013), 22-24; Henry F. Dobyns, *Their Number Become Thinned: Native American Population Dynamics in Eastern North America*, Native American Historic Demography Series (Knoxville: University of Tennessee Press, 1983), 342.
30. Ray, *Indians in the Fur Trade*, 21.
31. Ray, 21-23.

NOTES

32. Ray, 21. See also Lawrence J. Burpee, "Journal of a Journey Performed by Anthony Henday to Explore the Country Inland, and Rendezvous to Shores of the Hudson's Bay Company's Trade, A.D. 1754–1755," Transactions of the Royal Society of Canada, Series 3, 1, Section 2 (1907): 327, 330, 340.
33. Ray, 22–23.
34. Ray, 23.
35. Walde, Meyer, and Unfreed, "The Late Period on the Canadian and Adjacent Plains," 49–50.
36. Displaced observations propose that it was actually the traders' movement that was recorded, that the Indigenous Peoples were already occupying the "new" lands observed for the first time by explorers/traders.
37. Ray, *Indians in the Fur Trade*, 31. However, before the decline of the bison, they wintered off the prairie sometimes in larger groups. George Arthur, in his PhD dissertation, discusses the large number of bison that wintered in the northern regions of the Canadian parklands and forests. He also cites Northern Plains tribes that prepared pounds for their winter harvests of bison. Arthur suggests that the ranges of the bison were much shorter than previously estimated, making them available to the northern Indigenous Peoples during winter months. He states that the bison might not have been as available or as plentiful after the beginning of the trade bison massacres. This change in the availability of bison was perhaps the most significant effect of the trade on the Nakoda People. George W. Arthur, "An Introduction to the Ecology of Early Historic Communal Bison Hunting among the Northern Plains Indians" (PhD diss., University of Calgary, 1974).
38. Ray, 31–32.
39. Ray, 32.
40. Ray, 35.
41. This contradicts Arthur's estimates of the range of the bison. However, the lack of game was the most compelling reason for movement.
42. Burpee, *Journal and Letters*, 253–54.
43. Dale Walde, "Sedentism and Pre-Contact Tribal Organization on the Northern Plains: Colonial Imposition or Indigenous Development?," *World Archeology* 38, no. 2 (2006): 291–310.
44. Arthur, "An Introduction to the Ecology of Early Historic Communal Bison Hunting."
45. Ray, *Indians in the Fur Trade*, 38–40.
46. Ray, 41–43.
47. Ray, 43–44; see also 50n38. Pink's journal is included in the *York Factory Journals of 1766–67*, LAC, HBC B 239/a/56, 2–21.

NOTES

48   Ray, 43–44; Alexander Henry, *Travels and Adventures in Canada and the Indian Territories, between the Years 1760 and 1776: In Two Parts* (New York: I. Riley, 1809), 267–74.
49   Ray, *Indians in the Fur Trade*, 46.
50   Ray, 46.
51   Ray, 46, 48. Based on the evidence of the Nakoda precontact lands, Ray's explanation would apply to the movements implied to occur even in the 750 BP period and not because of the fur trade effects.
52   George Colpitts, *Pemmican Empire: Food, Trade, and the Last Bison Hunts in the North American Plains, 1780–1882* (New York: Cambridge University Press, 2014), 1–5.
53   Colpitts, 1–5.
54   Daschuk, *Clearing the Plains*, 33–34.
55   Daschuk, 36.
56   Daschuk, 36; Elizabeth Fenn, *Pox Americana: The Great Smallpox Epidemic of 1775–82* (New York: Farrar, Straus and Giroux, 2001).
57   Daschuk, *Clearing the Plains*, 36; see also Fenn, *Pox Americana*.
58   Daschuk, 36–37.
59   Daschuk, 37.
60   Daschuk, 37.
61   Daschuk, 38.
62   Daschuk, 40.
63   Daschuk, 10.
64   Daschuk, 41.
65   Daschuk, 42.
66   Daschuk, 42.
67   Daschuk, 42.
68   Ray, *Indians in the Fur Trade*, 107.
69   See maps in Ray, 87, 95, Figures 30, 31, based on Henry.
70   Ray, 94–96.

CHAPTER 3

1   This compares with the current domestic cattle population of the United States of 89.8 million animals.
2   Arthur J. Ray, *Indians in the Fur Trade: Their Role as Trappers, Hunters, and Middlemen in the Lands Southwest of Hudson Bay, 1660–1870* (Toronto: University of Toronto Press, 1974), 94–136.
3   The first diplomatic relations between the United States and the Assiniboine were a Friendship Treaty agreed with Sub-Agent Peter Wilson, the representative of the United States to the upper Missouri in 1826. Wilson met with a group of Assiniboine trading in the Mandan villages. See Katherine Gideon

NOTES

Colt, *The Letters of Peter Wilson: Soldier, Explorer and Indian Agent West of the Mississippi River* (Baltimore: Wirth Brothers, 1940).

4 William R. Swagerty, "Indian Trade in the Trans-Mississippi West to 1870," in *Handbook of North American Indians: History of Indian-White Relations*, vol. 4, ed. W.E. Washburn (Washington, DC: Smithsonian Institution, 1988), 351–74. One of the issues leading to the War of 1812 was American companies versus companies based in other countries but operating in regions claimed by the United States without permission to do so. The Trade and Intercourse Acts enacted in the 1790s regulated who could enter "Indian Country" and issued licences to control who was engaged in trade. For example, it was forbidden to use alcohol in the trade with Indigenous groups, long a practice of the North West Company and eventually a practice of the Hudson's Bay Company. However, the presence of U.S. authorities in many areas was yet to be realized even though the claim to territory had been made and delineated. See Alan Taylor, *The Civil War of 1812: American Citizens, British Subjects, Irish Rebels, and Indian Allies* (Toronto: Vintage Books, 2010), 6–12.

5 David Wishart, *The Fur Trade of the American West, 1807–1840* (Lincoln: University of Nebraska Press, 1979), 27.

6 Wishart, 13.

7 Wishart, 47.

8 Wishart, 54.

9 Erwin N. Thompson, *Fort Union Trading Post: Fur Trade Empire on the Upper Missouri* (Williston, ND: Fort Union Association, 1994), 9–16.

10 See Ray, *Indians in the Fur Trade*, 95, 97, Figures 30, 31, for the locations of the various Assiniboine bands in summer and winter.

11 Thompson, *Fort Union Trading Post*, 16–17.

12 Thompson, 17.

13 Thompson, 22–23.

14 Thompson, 21.

15 John C. Ewers, *When the Light Shone in Washington: Indian Life on the Upper Missouri* (Norman: University of Oklahoma Press, 1968), 79.

16 Elizabeth Fenn, *Encounters at the Heart of the World: A History of the Mandan People* (New York: Hill and Wang, 2014), 296–97.

17 Quoted in Thompson, *Fort Union Trading Post*, 26–28.

18 Fenn, *Encounters at the Heart of the World*, 299. This would happen again in 1851.

19 Fenn, 300.

20 Fenn, 323.

21 Edwin Thompson Denig, *Five Indian Tribes of the Upper Missouri: Sioux, Arickaras, Assiniboines, Crees, Crows* (Norman: University of Oklahoma Press, 1961), 71.

22 Arthur J. Ray, "Smallpox: The Epidemic of 1837–38," *The Beaver* 306 (1975): 9.

NOTES

23 Arthur J. Ray, "William Todd: Doctor and Trader, for the Hudson's Bay Company, 1816–51," *Prairie Forum* 9 (1984): 13–26.
24 D.R. Miller, J.R. Mcgeshick, D.J. Smith, J. Shanley, and C. Shields, *History of the Assiniboine and Sioux Tribes of the Fort Peck Indian Reservation, 1600–2012* (Helena, MT: Fort Peck Community College; Poplar, MT: Montana Historical Society Press, 2012), 44.
25 Miller et al., 44.
26 Charles Larpenteur, *Forty Years a Fur Trader on the Upper Missouri: The Personal Narrative of Charles Larpenteur, 1833–1872*, ed. Elliot Coues (New York: F.P. Harper, 1898), 134.
27 If we estimate the population of the Nakoda People to be 28,000 in 1833, then it would be reasonable to approximate the consumption of one bison per person per year. The value of just the food from the bison in current consumption prices would be approximately $108 million per year (or a capitalized value of $1 billion). Value would be added for the use of the hide, bones, and other parts of the carcass; moreover, if an estimate of total losses because of the destruction of the bison were made, then there would be a huge adverse impact on their culture and health.
28 David R. Miller, "Introduction," in *The Assiniboine: Forty-Sixth Annual Report of the Bureau of American Ethnology to the Secretary of the Smithsonian Institution 1928–1929*, by Edwin Thompson Denig, ed. J.N.B. Hewitt (reprinted Regina: Canadian Plains Research Center, University of Regina, 2000), xi.
29 Miller, xi.
30 Miller, xi.
31 Miller, xiii.
32 Miller, xiii.
33 Edwin Thompson Denig, *The Assiniboine: Forty-Sixth Annual Report of the Bureau of American Ethnology to the Secretary of the Smithsonian Institution 1928–1929*, ed. J.N.B. Hewitt (reprinted Regina: Canadian Plains Research Center, University of Regina, 2000), 396–97.
34 Walter Hildebrandt and Brian Hubner, *The Cypress Hills: An Island by Itself* (Saskatoon: Purich Publishing, 2007), 120.
35 Denig, *The Assiniboine*, 397.
36 Denig, 397.

CHAPTER 4

1 Hugh A. Dempsey, *Firewater: The Impact of the Whiskey Trade on the Blackfoot Nation* (Markham, ON: Fifth House Publishers, 2002), 17; William Farr, "When We Were First Paid: The Blackfeet Treaty, the Western Tribes, and the Creation of the Common Hunting Ground, 1855," *Great Plains Quarterly* 4, no. 1 (2001): 131–54.

NOTES

2 Erwin N. Thompson, *Fort Union Trading Post: Fur Trade Empire on the Upper Missouri* (Williston, ND: Fort Union Association, 1994), 74.
3 Thompson, 78–79.
4 Thompson, 79.
5 D.R. Miller, J.R. Mcgeshick, D.J. Smith, J. Shanley, and C. Shields, *History of the Assiniboine and Sioux Tribes of the Fort Peck Indian Reservation, 1600–2012* (Helena, MT: Fort Peck Community College; Poplar, MT: Montana Historical Society Press, 2012), 49.
6 Miller et al., 45–50.
7 Thompson, *Fort Union Trading Post*, 81.
8 Thompson, 82–83.
9 Raymond DeMallie, "The Sioux in Dakota and Montana Territories: Cultural and Historical Background of the Ogden B. Read Collection," in *Vestiges of a Proud Nation: The Ogden B. Read Northern Plains Indian Collection*, ed. Glenn E. Markoe (Burlington, VT: Robert Hull Fleming Museum, University of Vermont, 1986), 24–25.
10 Miller et al., *History of the Assiniboine and Sioux Tribes*, 55–57.
11 J.R. Miller, "Owen Glendower, Hotspur, and Canadian Indian Policy," *Ethnohistory* 37, no. 4 (1990): 386–415.
12 Miller et al., *History of the Assiniboine and Sioux Tribes*, 55–56.
13 Miller et al., 57.
14 Miller et al., 58.
15 Miller et al., 58.
16 Miller et al., 59–60.
17 Miller et al., 60.
18 Miller et al., 61–62.
19 Miller et al., 80.
20 Miller et al., 80.
21 Miller et al., 80.
22 Miller et al., 80.
23 Miller et al., 80.
24 These interviews were conducted for *The Assiniboine Indian Tribe, Plaintiff v. The United States, Defendant, Court of Claims of the United States*, No. J-31, 1929. For a list of the interviewees and the dates of their interviews, see "Assiniboine Tribe of Indians Elder and Traditional Land User Interviewees" near the end of the book.
25 The Yellowstone River is a tributary of the Missouri River in the western United States and was an important artery of transportation for Indigenous people. In 1868, the United States granted the territory of the Black Hills and the Powder River country to the Lakota People with the Treaty of Fort Laramie.

NOTES

26   The Powder River is a tributary of the Yellowstone River in southeastern Montana and northeastern Wyoming.

27   The Musselshell River is a tributary of the Missouri River and is located entirely within Montana. The Musselshell region is the location of the last surviving herds of wild American bison.

28   The Little Rocky Mountains, also known as the Little Rockies, are a group of buttes located toward the southern end of the Fort Belknap Agency in north-central Montana.

29   The Cypress Hills are located in southwestern Saskatchewan and southeastern Alberta and have been an important area for various Indigenous groups, including the Assiniboine, Sioux, Atsina, Blackfoot, Crow, Saulteaux, and Cree.

30   Turtle Mountain, or the Turtle Mountains, is located in north-central North Dakota and southwestern Manitoba.

31   The Bears Paw Mountains—also known as the Bear Paw Mountains, Bear's Paw Mountains, Bearpaw Mountains, or Bearpaws—is a mountain range in north-central Montana that extends between the Missouri River and Rocky Boy's Indian Reservation south of Havre, Montana.

32   The Fort Berthold Indian Reservation in western North Dakota is home to the Mandan, Hidatsa, and Arikara Nations.

33   Devils Lake is the largest natural body of water in North Dakota. Devils Lake is an approximate translation of its Lakota name, Ble Waka Sica (blay wah-kahn shee-chah), which means "Lake of the Spirits." This lake naturally flows into the Sheyenne River, a tributary to the Red River, which flows into Canada, eventually exiting into Hudson Bay.

34   The Moose Mountains are located in southeastern Saskatchewan, north of the town of Carlyle.

35   The Sweet Grass Hills are a small group of low mountains near Witlash, Montana. They are a sacred site for Indigenous Peoples on both sides of the forty-ninth parallel, the border between Canada and the United States. The hills were the site of a battle between Indigenous people and wolfers in 1872.

36   Battleford is located across the North Saskatchewan River from North Battleford in Saskatchewan. The town was founded in 1875 as a fur trading post and North West Mounted Police fort.

37   Medicine Hat is in southeast Alberta, located a short distance from the Cypress Hills. The valley was a natural migration path for bison herds, and the Blackfoot, Cree, and Assiniboine Nations used the area for hundreds of years before the arrival of Europeans.

38   Big Lake is located along the Mississippi River in Minnesota.

39   Known for its poplar trees, the village of Wood Mountain, Saskatchewan, was the refuge of Sitting Bull and his Sioux (Lakota) followers after the Battle of the Little Bighorn in 1876.

40	The Souris River or Mouse River (as it is alternatively known in the United States) originates in the Yellow Grass Marsh north of Weyburn, Saskatchewan, and flows southeast into North Dakota before flowing back north, entering Manitoba near Westhope. The river eventually flows into the Assiniboine River near Brandon, Manitoba.
41	Swift Current is a small city in southwestern Saskatchewan. Swift Current Creek, which originates in the Cypress Hills, empties into the South Saskatchewan River and has been a camp for First Nations for centuries.
42	Walter Hildebrandt and Brian Hubner, *The Cypress Hills: An Island by Itself* (Saskatoon: Purich Publishing, 2007), 14.
43	Dempsey, *Firewater*, 67.
44	Dempsey, 67–68.
45	Dempsey, 68–69.
46	Dempsey, 69.
47	Dempsey, 114–16.
48	Dempsey, 116–23.
49	Chief Dan Kennedy, *Recollections of an Assiniboine Chief*, edited by James R. Stevens (Toronto: McClelland and Stewart, 1972), 45.
50	Indian Claims Commission [herafter ICC], *Carry The Kettle First Nation Inquiry Report on Cypress Hills* (Ottawa: Indian Claims Commission, 2000), 15.
51	Dempsey, *Firewater*, 127–34.
52	Miller et al., *History of the Assiniboine and Sioux Tribes*, 109–23; ICC, *Carry The Kettle First Nation Inquiry Report on Cypress Hills*, 12–16.

CHAPTER 5

1	ICC, *Carry The Kettle First Nation Inquiry Report on Cypress Hills* (Ottawa: Indian Claims Commission, 2000), 20. The commission defines Treaty 4 as "encompassing most of the Assiniboine's traditional territories on the Canadian side of the border," which showed a lack of understanding of the importance and extent of Assiniboine Traditional Territories. The Nakoda (Assiniboine) lands take in much of what was Treaty 2 and Treaty 6 as well as most of Treaty 4. It appears that the government method of matching bands and treaty lands was at best ad hoc and based on incomplete information and did not match the homelands of the Indigenous Peoples.
2	ICC, 16–17.
3	ICC, 16–17.
4	James Daschuk, *Clearing the Plains: Disease, Politics of Starvation, and the Loss of Aboriginal Life* (Regina: University of Regina Press, 2013), 99–126.
5	J.M. Walsh, NWMP, to Minister of the Interior, September 12, 1876, in "Report of the Department of the Interior for the Year Ended 30th June 1876," Canada,

NOTES

Sessional Papers [hereafter CSP], 1877, vol. 7, no. 11, Special Appendix D, xxxvii–xxxix.

6   ICC, *Carry The Kettle First Nation Inquiry Report*, 16–17.
7   Inspector J.M. Walsh to E.A. Meredith, Deputy Minister of the Interior, October 28, 1877, "Report of the Department of the Interior for the Year Ended 30th June 1877," in CSP, 1878, vol. 8, no. 10, Special Appendix B, xxxi–xxxiv.
8   Walsh to Meredith, CSP, 1878.
9   Canada, *Treaty No. 4 between Her Majesty the Queen and the Cree and Saulteaux Tribes of Indians at Qu'appelle and Fort Ellice* (Ottawa: Queen's Printer, 1966), 13–14.
10 Walsh to Meredith, CSP, 1878.
11 Walsh to Meredith, CSP, 1878.
12 *Assiniboine Tribe v. The United States, Plaintiff's Request for Findings of Fact, and Brief*, U.S. Court of Claims, Docket J-31, 1929.
13 J.H. McIlree, Diary, NWMP, RCMP Museum and Archives, Regina, SK.
14 John Peter Turner, *The North-West Mounted Police*, 2 vols. (Ottawa: Edmond Cloutier, King's Printer, 1950), 1: 431.
15 L. Vankoughnet, Deputy Superintendent-General of Indian Affairs, to Sir J.A. Macdonald, "Report of the Deputy Superintendent-General of Indian Affairs, 31st December, 1879," in CSP, 1880, vol. 3, no. 4, 12–14.
16 James F. MacLeod, Commissioner, "North-West Mounted Police Force Commissioner's Report, 1879" in CSP, 1880, vol. 3, no. 4, Part III, 3.
17 Sir J.A. Macdonald, Minister of the Interior, to Sir John Douglas Sutherland Campbell, Governor General of Canada, "Report of the Deputy Superintendent-General of Indian Affairs, 31st December, 1879," in CSP, 1880, vol. 3, no. 4, xi–xii.
18 Turner, *The North-West Mounted Police*, 1: 453.
19 Turner, 1: 284–85, 326–32.
20 Brian Hubner, "Horse Stealing and the Borderline: The NWMP and the Control of Indian Movement 1874–1900," *Prairie Forum* 20, no. 2 (1995): 288. See also MacLeod, CSP, 1880.
21 Colonel Acheson Irvine, Journal of This Day, RCMP Museum and Archives, Regina, SK.
22 Irvine; emphasis added.
23 Irvine.
24 Brian Titley, *The Frontier of Edgar Dewdney* (Vancouver: UBC Press, 1999), 66, 67.
25 See W.L. Lincoln, Indian Agent, Fort Belknap, "Reports of Agents in Montana," August 1, 1879, in *Annual report of the Commissioner of Indian Affairs, for the year 1879*, United States, Office of Indian Affairs, Washington, DC: GPO, 1879, 98–100.
26 See Edgar Dewdney, Indian Commissioner, to L. Vankoughnet, Superintendent-General of Indian Affairs, "Report of the Superintendent-General of Indian Affairs, 31st December, 1879," in CSP, 1880, vol. 3, no. 4, 76–103.

NOTES

27 John Tobias, *Interim Report: A Brief History of Little Pine-Lucky Man Bands, 1870–1910*, Cumberland Report, Federation of Saskatchewan Indians, 1985, 8.
28 John G. Kittson, Surgeon, report to James F. MacLeod, Commissioner, January 30, 1880, "North-West Mounted Police Force Commissioner's Report, 1879" in CSP, 1880, vol. 3, no. 4, Part III, Appendix, 27–32.
29 ICC, *Carry The Kettle First Nation Inquiry Report*, 29.
30 ICC, 30.
31 ICC, 30, 31, 33.
32 Edgar Dewdney, CSP, 1880, 76–103.
33 Edgar Dewdney, Diary, 27 August 1879. Dewdney Papers. Glenbow Archives.
34 L. Vankoughnet to Sir J.A. Macdonald, CSP, 1880, 12.
35 John Tobias, "Civilization, Protection, Assimilation: An Outline of Canada's Indian Policy," *Western Canadian Journal of Anthropology* 6, no. 2 (1976): 13–17.
36 Edgar Dewdney, Fort Walsh, to John A. Macdonald, October 3, 1880, Sir John A. Macdonald Papers, LAC, MG26A, vol. 210, reel 1596, 89361–71.
37 Colonel Macleod, Fort Walsh, to his wife, June 3, 1880.
38 A.P. Patrick, report, in CSP, 1881, vol. 8, no. 14, 113–117.
39 *Globe* [Toronto], May 29, 1880.
40 *Globe* [Toronto], June 17, 1880.
41 A. McDonald, Indian Agent, Fort Qu'Appelle, report, September 12, 1880, in *Annual Report of the Department of Indian Affairs for 1880*, 204–205.
42 Edwin Allen, Agent to the Superintendent General of Indian Affairs, report, September 30, 1880, in *Annual Report of the Department of Indian Affairs*, in CSP, 1881, vol. 8, no. 14, 105–07.
43 ICC, *Carry The Kettle First Nation Inquiry Report*, 33–34.
44 ICC, 35–36.
45 Quoted in ICC, 37.
46 ICC, 39.
47 ICC, 40.
48 ICC, 40–41.
49 See ICC, 43–44; no survey plan survives.
50 W.L. Lincoln, U.S. Indian Agent, report to the Commissioner of Indian Affairs, August 11, 1880. In United States, Office of Indian Affairs, *Annual report of the Commissioner of Indian Affairs, for the year 1880*, 114–116.
51 Edgar Dewdney, Indian Commissioner, to Superintendent General of Indian Affairs, November 12, 1880, LAC, RG10, vol. 3726, file 24,729.
52 Edgar Dewdney, Winnipeg, to Superintendent General of Indian Affairs, November 13, 1880, LAC, RG10, vol. 3726, file 24,800.
53 ICC, *Carry The Kettle First Nation Inquiry Report*, 44.
54 ICC, 44–45.
55 ICC, 45–46.

NOTES

56 Quoted in ICC, 47.
57 Edgar Dewdney, Commissioner of Indian Affairs, North West Territories, to Superintendent General of Indian Affairs, November 19, 1880, LAC, RG10, vol. 3726, file 24,800.
58 ICC, *Carry The Kettle First Nation Inquiry Report*, 50.
59 ICC, 50.
60 John A. Macdonald, Superintendent General of Indian Affairs, *Annual Report of the Department of Indian Affairs for the Year Ended 31st December 1882*, in CSP, 1883, vol. 4, no. 5, x–xi.
61 ICC, *Carry The Kettle First Nation Inquiry Report*, 50–51.
62 Dan Kennedy, *Recollections of an Assiniboine Chief*, ed. James R. Stevens (Toronto: McClelland and Stewart, 1972), 66.
63 ICC, *Carry The Kettle First Nation Inquiry Report*, 50–54.
64 Turner, *The North-West Mounted Police*, 1: 498–99, 512–13, 519–20.
65 Turner, 1: 545–46.
66 Edgar Dewdney, Indian Commissioner, report to Superintendent General of Indian Affairs, December 31, 1880, in CSP, 1881, vol. 8, no. 14, 92.
67 Lawrence Vankoughnet, Deputy Superintendent General, memo to Superintendent General, January 30, 1882, LAC, RG10, vol. 3744, file 29,506-2.
68 Hubner, "Horse Stealing and the Borderline," 289.
69 Hubner, 290–93.
70 Colonel Macleod, Fort Walsh, to his wife, May 29, 1880; emphasis added.
71 George Kennedy to Edgar Dewdney, February 1, 1881, LAC, RG10, vol. 3736, file 27,464.
72 Edgar Dewdney to T.P. Wadsworth, February 21, 1881, LAC, RG10, vol. 3726, file 24,763.
73 Edwin Allen to Edgar Dewdney, July 5, 1881, LAC, RG10, vol. 3757, file 31,397.
74 Hildebrandt and Hubner, *The Cypress Hills*, 142.
75 *Globe* [Toronto], June 17, 1881.
76 George Kennedy, Surgeon, report to Edgar Dewdney, July 1, 1881, LAC, RG10, vol. 3760, file 32,057.
77 Dewdney, CSP, 1881, vol. 8, no. 14, 92.
78 Turner, *The North-West Mounted Police*, 1: 527, 529.
79 Tobias, "Civilization, Protection, Assimilation," 13–17.
80 *Globe* [Toronto], May 4, 1881.
81 E.T. Galt, Assistant Commissioner, to Edwin Allen, Indian Agent, May 20, 1881, and E.T. Galt, Assistant Commissioner, to John A. Macdonald, Superintendent General, May 25, 1881, LAC, RG10, vol. 3744, file 29,506-1.
82 E.T. Galt to D.L. McPherson, June 6, 1881, Sir John A. Macdonald Papers, LAC, MG26A, vol. 210.

NOTES

83   Edgar Dewdney to Sir John A. Macdonald, June 19, 1881, Sir John A. Macdonald Papers, LAC, MG26A, vol. 210.
84   Dewdney to Macdonald, June 19, 1881. .
85   D.L. McPherson to Edgar Dewdney, July 15, 1881, Glenbow Archives, NA4035143 M320 Series 16.
86   Colonel Acheson Irvine, Journal of This Day, RCMP Museum and Archives, Regina, SK.
87   Irvine, Journal of This Day.
88   E.T. Galt to T.P. Wadsworth, July 13, 1881.
89   T.P. Wadsworth to John A. Macdonald, July 1, 1881, Sir John A. Macdonald Papers, LAC, MG26A, vol. 210, reel C1596, 89,473–89,476.
90   Daschuk, *Clearing the Plains*, 140. See William Allen, Letter to the Editor, *Globe* [Toronto], September 5, 1881, defending the agent against allegations of theft. See also D.L. McPherson to Sir John A. Macdonald, September 2, 1881, Sir John A. Macdonald Papers, LAC, MG26A, vol. 248. This letter stated that Allen and Baker were invoicing for 800 pounds when the cattle delivered weighed only 400 pounds. The matter made the Toronto Globe in "Supplies to Indians" on March 30, 1882, 10. In the article, a telegram from Allen to Vankoughnet shortly after his July suspension was quoted, in which Allen asked the deputy superintendent general of Indian Affairs directly to reverse the decision, saying that Wadsworth would vouch for him.
91   W.L. Lincoln, U.S. Indian Agent, report to the Commissioner of Indian Affairs, August 20, 1881. In United States, Office of Indian Affairs, *Annual report of the Commissioner of Indian Affairs, for the year 1881*, 117–120.
92   T.P. Wadsworth, Inspector, to L. Vankoughnet, Deputy Superintendent General, August 29, 1881, LAC, RG10, vol. 3744, file 29,506-1.
93   Cecil E. Denny, Indian Agent, to Edgar Dewdney, Indian Commissioner, November 9, 1881, LAC, RG10, vol. 3744, file 29,506-1.
94   ICC, *Carry The Kettle First Nation Inquiry Report*, 54.
95   ICC, 55.
96   Cecil E. Denny, *The Law Marches West*, ed. and arranged W.B. Cameron (Toronto: J.M. Dent and Sons, 1939), 170.
97   ICC, *Carry The Kettle First Nation Inquiry Report*, 64–65.
98   Denny, *The Law Marches West*, 169.
99   Cecil E. Denny to unknown recipient, November 9, 1881, LAC, RG10, vol. 3744, file 29,506-1.
100 Cecil E. Denny, Indian Agent, Fort Walsh, to Indian Commissioner, Winnipeg, November 16, 1881, LAC, RG10, vol. 3744, file 29,506-1.

NOTES

CHAPTER 6

1. Copy of a Report of a Committee of the Privy Council, Approved by His Excellency the Governor General in Council, January 31, 1882.
2. Superintendent Leif N.F. Crozier, *Annual Reports of the Commissioner of the* NWMP, *1882*, in CSP.
3. Cecil E. Denny, Indian Agent, Fort Walsh, to Commissioner, January 17, 1882, LAC, RG10, vol. 3577, file 444.
4. Acting Indian Agent J.H. McIlree, Fort Walsh, to Indian Commissioner Dewdney, February 1, 1882, LAC, RG10, vol. 3744, file 29,506-2.
5. Consent under the circumstances was impossible because the concept of consent requires an independent and uncoerced choice or decision. The government had created a situation in which the Assiniboine had no choice but to agree to move where they would be fed or at least where promises were made that they would be fed.
6. McIlree acted as Indian Agent from January 1882 to August 1882 while still a member of the police, and he was later refused pay from the Department of Indian Affairs on the ground that he was doing his job as a police inspector.
7. Commissioner Dewdney to Superintendent General, February 13, 1882, LAC, RG10, vol. 3577, file Letter from Inspector McIlree to Commissioner Dewdney, February 15, 1882, from Fort Walsh, LAC, RG10, vol. 3744, file 29,506-2.
8. Commissioner Dewdney to Inspector McIlree, Acting Agent, Fort Walsh, February 22, 1882, LAC, RG10, vol. 3577, file 444.
9. NWMP Requisition for Stores No. 247, February 26, 1882, LAC, RG18, Series B1, vol. 1006, file 267a.
10. Commissioner Dewdney to Colonel Irvine, date not clear, LAC, RG10, vol. 3744, file 29,506-2; Edgar Dewdney to Peter Erasmus, March 30, 1882, LAC, RG10, vol. 3744, file 29,506-2.
11. J.H. McIlree, Diary, NWMP, RCMP Museum and Archives, Regina, SK., entries from those dates.
12. Inspector McIlree to Commissioner Dewdney, December 2, 1882, LAC, RG10, vol. 3744, file 29,506-3.
13. Telegram, March 14, 1882, to Captain McIlree, LAC, RG10, vol. 3744, file 29,502-2.
14. Colonel A.G. Irvine to Fred White, Comptroller, May 20, 1882, LAC, RG18, Series B-3, vol. 2186.
15. Indian Agent Alan McDonald to Assistant Commissioner E.T. Galt, July 12, 1882, LAC, RG10, vol. 3744, file 29,506-2.
16. Colonel A.G. Irvine, Fort Walsh, to E. Dewdney, Indian Commissioner, Glenbow Archives, NA 4035143 M320 Series 17.
17. Indian Commissioner Dewdney to Superintendent General of Indian Affairs, April 26, 1882, LAC, RG10, vol. 3744, file 29,506-2.

NOTES

18 ICC, *Carry The Kettle First Nation Inquiry Report on Cypress Hills* (Ottawa: Indian Claims Commission, 2000), 76.
19 Alan McDonald, Indian Agent, to Assistant Commissioner E.T. Galt, June 20, 1882, LAC, RG10, vol. 3744, file 29,506-2.
20 Indian Agent Alan McDonald to Assistant Commissioner E.T. Galt, June 9, 1882, LAC, RG10, vol. 3744, file 29,506-2.
21 See Colonel Irvine's annual report, January 1, 1883, "Part III North-West Mounted Police Force," in CSP, 1883, vol. 10, no. 23, 1–23.
22 Indian Agent Alan McDonald to Assistant Commissioner E.T. Galt, July 12, 1882, LAC, RG10, vol. 3744, file 29,506-2.
23 McDonald to Galt, July 12, 1882.
24 Deputy Superintendent General Lawrence Vankoughnet to Assistant Commissioner E.T. Galt, July 11, 1882, LAC, RG10, vol. 3744, file 29,506-2.
25 Indian Agent McDonald to Assistant Commissioner Galt, July 18, 1882, LAC, RG10, vol. 3744, file 29,506-2; emphasis added.
26 Indian Agent McDonald to Assistant Commissioner Galt, July 29, 1882, LAC, RG10, vol. 3733, file 29,506-2.
27 McDonald to Galt, July 29, 1882.
28 Indian Agent McDonald to Assistant Commissioner Galt, July 31, 1882, LAC, RG10, vol. 3733, file 29,506-2.
29 McDonald to Galt, July 31, 1882.
30 McDonald to Galt, July 18, 1882.
31 Indian Commissioner Dewdney to Superintendent General of Indian Affairs, August 5, 1882, LAC, RG10, vol. 3744, file 29,506-2.
32 ICC, *Carry The Kettle First Nation Inquiry Report*, 80.
33 NWMP Comptroller White to Indian Commissioner Dewdney, October 17, 1882, LAC, RG10, vol. 3744, file 29,506-3. McDonald arrived and paid the annuities for Treaty 4 at Fort Walsh in mid-November 1882. Indian Agent McDonald to Indian Commissioner Dewdney, November 11, 1882, LAC, RG10, vol. 3744, file 29,506-3.
34 Commissioner Dewdney to Colonel Irvine, October 27, 1882, LAC, RG10, vol. 3744, file 29,506-3.
35 Lawrence Vankoughnet, Deputy Superintendent General, to Sir John A. Macdonald, Superintendent General and Prime Minister of Canada, November 2, 1882, LAC, MG26A, Sir John A. Macdonald Papers, vol. 289.
36 Colonel Irvine to Commissioner Dewdney, September 25, 1882, Glenbow Archives, NA 4035143 M320 Series 17.
37 Peter Hourie to Indian Agent McDonald, October 18, 1882, LAC, RG10, vol. 3744, file 29,506-3.
38 ICC, *Carry The Kettle First Nation Inquiry Report*, 87.

NOTES

39 George de Ilges, Lieutenant Colonel, 18th Infantry, Commanding Post, to Major Albert Shurtleff, Commanding Officer at Fort Walsh, May 7, 1882, LAC, RG10, vol. 3745, file 29,506-4, part 1.
40 Colonel Irvine to NWMP Comptroller White, May 18, 1883, LAC, RG10, vol. 3745, file 29,506-4, part 1.
41 Irvine to White, May 18, 1883.
42 Dan Kennedy, *Recollections of an Assiniboine Chief*, ed. James R. Stevens (Toronto: McClelland and Stewart, 1972), 66.
43 Long Lodge, in particular, was loath to accept the site, as noted, and he moved his family and some band members south of the line to Milk River, where he died at the end of 1884. Little Mountain was the headman of the remaining people. J.H. McIlree, Acting Indian Agent, Fort Walsh, to Indian Commissioner Dewdney, December 2, 1882, LAC, RG10, vol. 3700, file 29,506-3.
44 Irvine, in *Settlers and Rebels: Being the Official Reports to Parliament of the Activities of the Royal North-West Mounted Police Force from 1882–1885, by Commissioners of the Royal North-West Mounted Police* (Toronto: Coles Publishing Company, 1973), 3.
45 See *Regina-Leader* news clip, May 10, 1883.
46 Indian Commissioner, report to Superintendent General of Indian Affairs, May 25, 1883, LAC, RG10, vol. 3744, file 29,506-3.
47 Indian Agent McDonald, report to Superintendent General of Indian Affairs, July 6, 1883, in CSP, 1884, vol. 3, no. 4, 69–75.
48 Dr. O.C. Edwards, report to Indian Agent McDonald, May 13, 1883, LAC, RG10, vol. 3745, file 29,506-4.

CHAPTER 7

1 Irvine, in *Settlers and Rebels: Being the Official Reports to Parliament of the Activities of the Royal North-West Mounted Police Force from 1882–1885, by Commissioners of the Royal North-West Mounted Police* (Toronto: Coles Publishing Company, 1973), 3.
2 Indian Agent McDonald, report to Superintendent General of Indian Affairs, August 31, 1883, in CSP, 1884, vol. 3, no. 4, 75–76.
3 Indian Commissioner Dewdney to Superintendent General of Indian Affairs, October 24, 1883, LAC, RG10, vol. 3744, file 29,506-3.
4 ICC, *Carry The Kettle First Nation Inquiry Report on Cypress Hills* (Ottawa: Indian Claims Commission, 2000), 92.
5 D.C. Edwards to Indian Agent McDonald, May 13, 1884, LAC, RG10, vol. 3745, file 29,506-4.
6 There appears to have been no good reason not to issue ammunition to the Assiniboine at this time even if the chance to shoot game was low. It is likely that the fear of armed and starving men was the motivation for refusing to issue ammunition.

NOTES

7 "It Was History in the Making, 1885 Northwest Resistance," *StarPhoenix* [Saskatoon], May 13, 2010.
8 Hayter Reed, Indian Commissioner, to Superintendent General of Indian Affairs, May 20, 1884, LAC, RG10, vol. 3745, file 29,506-4.
9 Reed to Superintendent General of Indian Affairs, May 20, 1884.
10 ICC, *Carry The Kettle First Nation Inquiry Report*, 92.
11 ICC, 93.
12 Surveyor Nelson to Commissioner Dewdney, December 5, 1885, "Annual Report of the Department of Indian Affairs for the Year Ended 31st December 1885," in CSP, 1886, vol. 4, no. 4, 146.
13 Order in Council PC 1151-1889, May 17, 1889, LAC.
14 ICC, *Carry The Kettle First Nation Inquiry Report*, 94.
15 ICC, 55.
16 Order in Council PC 1694-1893, June 12, 1893, LAC, RG2, Series 1.
17 Kevin Haywahe, interview, in *Carry The Kettle First Nation, These Are Our People* (Saskatchewan: Sweet Grass Records, 2010), 19.
18 Acting Indian Agent W.S. Grant, report to Superintendent General of Indian Affairs, July 28, 1886, in CSP, 1887, vol. 5, no. 6, 123-124.
19 Carl Beal, "Money, Markets and Economic Development in Saskatchewan Indian Reserve Communities, 1870 to 1930s" (PhD diss., University of Manitoba, 1995).
20 F. Laurie Barron, "A Summary of Federal Indian Policy in the Canadian West, 1867–1984," *Native Studies Review* 1, no. 1 (1984): 28–39; J.R. Miller, "Owen Glendower, Hotspur, and Canadian Indian Policy," *Ethnohistory* 37, no. 4 (1990): 386–415; John Tobias, "Civilization, Protection, Assimilation: An Outline of Canada's Indian Policy," *Western Canadian Journal of Anthropology* 6, no. 2 (1976): 13–17.
21 Tobias, "Civilization, Protection, Assimilation."
22 Deputy Superintendent General of Indian Affairs Frank Pedley to Minister of the Interior Clifford Sifton, March 24, 1890, LAC, RG10, vol. 3635, file 6567.
23 Indian Agent W.S. Grant, report to Superintendent General of Indian Affairs, July 28, 1886, in CSP, 1887, vol. 5, no. 6, 123.
24 Acting Indian Agent W.S. Grant to Deputy Superintendent General Hayter Reed, October 1, 1896, LAC, RG10, vol. 3964, file 148,285.
25 Grant to Reed, October 1, 1896.
26 Sarah Carter, *Lost Harvests: Aboriginal Reserve Farmers and Government Policy* (Montreal and Kingston: McGill-Queen's University Press, 1990).
27 Assistant Commissioner Hayter Reed to Lieutenant-Governor Amédée-Emmanuel Forget, July 8, 1886, LAC, RG10, vol. 38,877, file 91,839.

NOTES

28 Indian Agent W.S. Grant, report to Superintendent-General of Indian Affairs, August 11, 1890, in CSP, 1891, vol. 15, no. 18, 46.
29 Assistant Commissioner Hayter Reed, October 26, 1891, LAC, RG 10, vol. 3717, file 22,550-4.
30 Inspector T.P. Wadsworth, October 26, 1891, LAC, RG 10, vol. 3717, file 22,550-4.
31 Inspector T.P. Wadsworth, report to Superintendent-General of Indian Affairs, July 1, 1893, in CSP, 1895, vol. 9, no. 14, 220.
32 Indian Agent Thomas W. Aspdin, report to Superintendent-General of Indian Affairs, August 12, 1898, in CSP, 1899, vol. 12, no. 14, 112.
33 Aspdin, CSP, 1899, 112.
34 Aspdin, CSP, 1899, 112.
35 Aspdin, CSP, 1899, 113.
36 Indian Agent Thomas W. Aspdin, report to Superintendent-General of Indian Affairs, September 5, 1899, in CSP, 1900, vol. 11, no. 14, 123.

CHAPTER 8

1 MP James M. Douglas to Deputy Minister of the Interior James A. Smart, January 29, 1901, LAC, RG10, vol. 4001, file 208, 590-1; ICC, *Carry The Kettle First Nation Inquiry Report*, 170.
2 J.D. McLean, Secretary of the Department of Indian Affairs, to Thomas W. Aspdin, Indian Agent, February 12, 1901, LAC, RG10, vol. 4001, file 208, 590-1; ICC, *Carry The Kettle First Nation Inquiry Report*, 175–76.
3 ICC, 175–76.
4 ICC, 175–76.
5 ICC, 175–76.
6 Thomas W. Aspdin, Indian Agent, to McLean, Secretary, February 25, 1901, LAC, RG10, vol. 4001, file 208,590-1; ICC, *Carry The Kettle First Nation Inquiry Report*, 177–80.
7 George L. Chitty, Timber Inspector, to DIA, April 23, 1901, LAC, RG10, vol. 4001, file 208,590-1.
8 Chitty to DIA, April 23, 1901; ICC, *Carry The Kettle First Nation Inquiry Report*, 181.
9 James A. Smart, Deputy Superintendent General, report to Clifford Sifton, Superintendent General of Indian Affairs, December 12, 1901, in CSP, 1902, no. 27, xxi.
10 Indian Commissioner David Laird, to Superintendent General of Indian Affairs, October 15, 1902, in CSP, 1903, no. 27, 186.
11 Laird, 186.
12 Laird, 186.
13 Thomas W. Aspdin, Indian Agent, report to Superintendent General of Indian Affairs, August 15, 1903, in CSP, 1904, no. 27, 134–35.
14 Aspdin, 135.

NOTES

15 Deputy Superintendent General Frank Pedley, report to Clifford Sinton, Superintendent General of Indian Affairs, December 7, 1903, in CSP, 1903, no. 27, xxvi; see also ICC, *Carry The Kettle First Nation Inquiry Report*, 212–27.
16 Pedley, December 7, 1903, xxxi.
17 Indian Agent Aspdin, report to Superintendent General of Indian Affairs, August 15, 1904, in CSP, 1905, no. 27, 125, 126.
18 Aspdin, 126.
19 Aspdin, 126.
20 J.D. McLean, Secretary of the Department of Indian Affairs, to Indian Agent Charles Fisher, November 14, 1905, LAC, RG10, vol. 1621, Carlton Agency Circulars.
21 Secretary J.D. McLean to Indian Commissioner David Laird, July 26, 1906, LAC, RG10, vol. 3086, file 279,222-1.
22 McLean to Laird, July 26, 1906.
23 Aspdin, August 15, 1904, 126.
24 Aspdin, 126–27.
25 Aspdin, 126.
26 Aspdin, 127.
27 Inspector of Indian Agencies W.M. Graham, report to Deputy Superintendent General of Indian Affairs, October 3, 1905, in CSP, 1906, no. 27, 187.
28 Graham, October 3, 1905, 187.
29 Graham, October 3, 1905, 187.
30 Graham, October 3, 1905, 187.
31 AGAR 1905–06, J-24.
32 Inspector of Indian Agencies W.M. Graham, report to Deputy Superintendent General of Indian Affairs, July 14, 1906, in CSP, 1906, no. 27, 158.
33 April 12, 1905, LAC, RG10, vol. 4001, file 208,590-1; ICC, *Carry The Kettle First Nation Inquiry Report*, 239.
34 AGAR 1905–06, J-24.
35 Indian Agent W.S. Grant, report to Superintendent General of Indian Affairs, June 30, 1906, in CSP, 1906, no. 27, 113.
36 Graham, July 14, 1906, 159.
37 Graham, 159.
38 Indian Agent W.S. Grant, report to Superintendent General of Indian Affairs, April 17, 1911, in CSP, 1912, no. 27, 121.
39 Grant, 122.

CHAPTER 9

1 Katherine Pettipas, *Severing the Ties That Bind: Government Repression of Indigenous Religious Ceremonies on the Prairies* (Winnipeg: University of Manitoba Press, 1994).

NOTES

2 Elkwater is located at the western edge of the Cypress Hills in southeastern Alberta and the south edge of Elkwater Lake. The Elkwater townsite is elevated at 1,234 metres, the same altitude as Banff. See Cypress Hills (Alberta) Historical Society, *Cypress Hills Country* (Elkwater, AB: Cypress Hills [Alberta] Historical Society, 1991).

3 Truth and Reconciliation Commission of Canada, *Honouring the Truth, Reconciling the Future, 2015,* https://ehprnh2mwo3.exactdn.com/wp-content/uploads/2021/01/Executive_Summary_English_Web.pdf.

4 Erin Hanson, "The Residential School System," 2009, First Nations and Indigenous Studies, University of British Columbia, https://indigenousfoundations.arts.ubc.ca/the_residential_school_system/.

5 Douglas R. Parks and Raymond J. DeMallie, "Sioux, Assiniboine, and Stoney Dialects: A Classification," *Anthropological Linguistics* 34, nos. 1–4 (1992): 233–55.

6 St. Victor Petroglyphs Provincial Park, 2015.

7 James Keyser and Michael A. Klassen, *Plains Indian Rock Art* (Seattle: University of Washington Press, 2001).

CHAPTER 10

1 The "cherry patch regions" are referred to by this Assiniboine group as Canada.

2 The Milk River (Assiniboine: Asą́bi wakpá, Wakpá juk'ána) is a tributary of the Missouri River in Montana and Alberta. Beginning in the Rocky Mountains, the river drains a sparsely populated, semi-arid watershed, ending just east of Fort Peck, Montana.

3 Glasgow is a city located in Valley County, Montana, just west of Fort Peck. The Nakoda, Lakota, and Dakota Peoples alternately inhabited and claimed the region from the sixteenth century to the late nineteenth century, surviving on the extensive bison and pronghorn antelope herds.

4 Rob Nestor, "Indian Policy and the Early Reserve Period," 2014, http://esask.uregina.ca/entry/indian_policy_and_the_early_reserve_period.html.

CHAPTER 11

1 R. Nowak and J. Paradiso, *Walker's Mammals of the World* (Baltimore: Johns Hopkins University Press, 1983).

CHAPTER 12

1 National Aboriginal Health Organization, *An Overview of Traditional Knowledge and Medicine and Public Health in Canada* (Ottawa: National Aboriginal Health Organization, 2008).

NOTES

CHAPTER 13

1. Bannock, also known as "Indian bread," is a traditional Indigenous quick bread, generally prepared with flour, sugar, water/milk, and leavening agents combined and kneaded (sometimes with dried fruits) and then fried in rendered fat, cooked on a stick over a fire, or baked in an oven. See Michael D. Blackstock, *Bannock Awareness*, 2008, Government of British Columbia, https://www.for.gov.bc.ca/rsi/fnb/FNB.htm.

2. Tripe, from the French meaning "of uncertain origin," is a type of edible offal (organ) from the stomachs of various farm animals. It is usually the first three chambers of a cow's stomach.

Bibliography

Adams, Arthur T. *Explorations of Pierre Esprit Radisson*. Minneapolis: Ross and Haines, 1961.
Arthur, George. "An Introduction to the Ecology of Early Historic Communal Bison Hunting among the Northern Plains Indians." PhD diss., University of Calgary, 1974.
Arthurs, David. "Sandy Lake Ware in Northwestern Ontario: A Distributional Study." *Manitoba Archeological Quarterly* 1, nos. 1-2 (1978): 57-64.
Barron, F. Laurie. "A Summary of Federal Indian Policy in the Canadian West, 1867-1984." *Native Studies Review* 1, no. 1 (1984): 28-39.
Beal, Carl. "Money, Markets and Economic Development in Saskatchewan Indian Reserve Communities, 1870 to 1930s." PhD diss., University of Manitoba, 1995.
Blackstock, Michael D. *Bannock Awareness*. 2008. Government of British Columbia, https://www.for.gov.bc.ca/rsi/fnb/FNB.htm.
Burpee, Lawrence J. "Journal of a Journey Performed by Anthony Henday: To Explore the Country Inland, and Rendezvous to Shores of the Hudson's Bay Company's Trade. A.D. 1754-1755." *Transactions of the Royal Society of Canada*, Series 3, 1, Section 2 (1907): 302-61.
———, ed. *Journal and Letters of Pierre Gaultier de Varennes de La Vérendrye and His Sons*. Toronto: Champlain Society, 1927.
———, ed. *Journals of La Vérendrye*. Publications of the Champlain Society 16. New York: Greenwood Press, 1968.

BIBLIOGRAPHY

Capes, Katherine H. *WB Nickerson Survey and Excavations, 1912–15, of the Southern Manitoba Mounds Region*. Anthropology Papers, National Museum of Canada. Ottawa: Department of Northern Affairs and National Resources, 1963.

Carter, Sarah. *Lost Harvests: Aboriginal Reserve Farmers and Government Policy*. Montreal and Kingston: McGill-Queen's University Press, 1990.

Colpitts, George. *Pemmican Empire: Food, Trade, and the Last Bison Hunts in the North American Plains, 1780–1882*. New York: Cambridge University Press, 2014.

Colt, Katherine Gideon. *The Letters of Peter Wilson: Soldier, Explorer and Indian Agent West of the Mississippi River*. Baltimore: Wirth Brothers, 1940.

Commissioners of the Royal North-West Mounted Police. *Settlers and Rebels: Being the Official Reports to Parliament of the Activities of the Royal North-West Mounted Police Force from 1882–1885*. Introduction by Commissioner W.L. Higgett, RCMP. Toronto: Coles Publishing Company, 1973.

Crouse, N.M. "Contributions of the Canadian Jesuits to the Geographic Knowledge of New France, 1632-1675." PhD diss., Cornell University, 1924.

Cypress Hills (Alberta) Historical Society. *Cypress Hills Country*. Elkwater, AB: Cypress Hills (Alberta) Historical Society, 1991.

Daschuk, James. *Clearing the Plains: Disease, Politics of Starvation, and the Loss of Aboriginal Life*. Regina: University of Regina Press, 2013.

DeMallie, Raymond. "The Sioux in Dakota and Montana Territories: Cultural and Historical Background of the Ogden B. Read Collection." In *Vestiges of a Proud Nation: The Ogden B. Read Northern Plains Indian Collection*, edited by Glenn E. Markoe, 19–69. Burlington, VT: Robert Hull Fleming Museum, University of Vermont, 1986.

Dempsey, Hugh A. *Firewater: The Impact of the Whiskey Trade on the Blackfoot Nation*. Markham, ON: Fifth House, 2002.

———. *Maskepetoon: Leader, Warrior, Peacemaker*. Victoria: Heritage House, 2010.

Denig, Edwin Thompson. *The Assiniboine: Forty-Sixth Annual Report of the Bureau of American Ethnology to the Secretary of the Smithsonian Institution 1928–1929*. Edited by J.N.B. Hewitt. Introduction by David R. Miller. Reprinted, Regina: Canadian Plains Research Center, University of Regina.

———. *Five Indian Tribes of the Upper Missouri: Sioux, Arickaras, Assiniboines, Crees, Crows*. Norman: University of Oklahoma Press, 1961.

Denny, Sir Cecil E. *The Law Marches West*. Edited and arranged by W.B. Cameron. Toronto: J.M. Dent and Sons, 1939.

Dobyns, Henry F. *Their Number Become Thinned: Native American Population Dynamics in Eastern North America*. Native American Historic Demography Series. Knoxville: University of Tennessee Press, 1983.

Ewers, John C. *When the Light Shone in Washington: Indian Life on the Upper Missouri*. Norman: University of Oklahoma Press, 1968.

BIBLIOGRAPHY

Farr, William. "'When We Were First Paid': The Blackfeet Treaty, the Western Tribes, and the Creation of the Common Hunting Ground, 1855." *Great Plains Quarterly* 4, no. 1 (2001): 131–54.

Fenn, Elizabeth. *Encounters at the Heart of the World: A History of the Mandan People.* New York: Hill and Wang, 2014.

———. *Pox Americana: The Great Smallpox Epidemic of 1775–82.* New York: Farrar, Straus and Giroux, 2001.

Gibbon, Guy. "Cultures of the Upper Mississippi River Valley and Adjacent Prairies in Iowa and Minnesota." In *Plains Indians, A.D. 500–1500: The Archaeological Past of Historic Groups*, edited by K.H. Schlesier, 128–48. Norman: University of Oklahoma Press, 1994.

Government of Saskatchewan. *Cypress Hills Interprovincial Park.* Regina: Government of Saskatchewan, 2006.

Hamilton, Scott, Jill Taylor-Hollings, and David Norris. "Human Ecology of the Canadian Prairie Ecozone ca. 1500 BP: Diffusion, Migration and Technology Innovation." In *Human Ecology of the Canadian Prairie*, edited by B.A. Nicholson, 99–152.. Regina: CPRC Press, 2011.

Hanna, Margaret G. *The Moose Bay Burial Mound.* Indians of North America. Regina: Department of Tourism and Renewable Resources, 1976.

Hanson, Erin. "The Residential School System." *Indigenous Foundations.* First Nations and Indigenous Studies. Vancouver: University of British Columbia, 2009. https://indigenousfoundations.arts.ubc.ca/the_residential_school_system/

Healy, Shannon, and Rex Flyway. *Fort Belknap Curriculum Development Project: Assiniboine Memories, Legends of the Nakota People.* Harlem, MT: Fort Belknap Education Department, 1983.

Heidenreich, Conrad E. *Huronia: A History and Geography of the Huron Indians, 1600–1650.* Toronto: McClelland and Stewart, 1973.

Henry, Alexander. *Travels and Adventures in Canada and the Indian Territories, between the Years 1760 and 1776: In Two Parts.* New York: I. Riley, 1809.

Hildebrandt, Walter, and Brian Hubner. *The Cypress Hills: An Island by Itself.* Saskatoon: Purich Publishing, 2007.

Howard, James Henri. "The Cultural Position of the Dakota: A Reassessment." In *Essays on the Science of Culture, in Honor of Leslie A. White*, edited by Gertrude E. Role and Robert L. Carneiro. New York: Thomas and Crowell, 1960.

Hubner, Brian. "Horse Stealing and the Borderline: The NWMP and the Control of Indian Movement 1874–1900." *Prairie Forum* 20, no. 2 (1995): 281–300.

Indian Claims Commission. *Carry The Kettle First Nation Inquiry Report on Cypress Hills.* Ottawa: Indian Claims Commission, 2000.

Kelsey, Henry. *The Kelsey Papers.* Edited by Arthur G. Doughty and Chester Martin. Ottawa: Public Archives of Canada, 1929.

BIBLIOGRAPHY

Kennedy, Chief Dan. *Recollections of an Assiniboine Chief.* Edited by James R. Stevens. Toronto: McClelland and Stewart, 1972.

Keyser, James, and Michael A. Klassen. *Plains Indian Rock Art.* Seattle: University of Washington Press, 2001.

Larpenteur, Charles. *Forty Years a Fur Trader on the Upper Missouri: The Personal Narrative of Charles Larpenteur, 1833-1872.* Edited by Elliot Coues. New York: F.P. Harper, 1898.

Manitoba Natural Resources. *Turtle Mountain Provincial Parks.* 1985. https://www.gov.mb.ca/conservation/parks/pdf/planning/turtle_mountain_management_plan.pdf.

Meyer, David. "The Old Women's Phase on the Saskatchewan Plains: Some Ideas." In *Archaeology in Alberta 1987,* edited by M. Magne, 55-63. Archaeological Survey of Alberta, Occasional Paper 32. Edmonton Archaeological Survey of Alberta, 1987.

Meyer, David, and Dale Russell. "The Pegogamaw Crees and Their Ancestors." *Plains Anthropologist* 51, no. 199 (2006): 303-24.

Meyer, David, and Scott Hamilton. "Neighbors to the North: Peoples of the Boreal Forest." In *Plains Indians, A.D. 500-1500: The Archeological Past of Historic Groups,* Edited by Karl H. Schlesier, 96-127. Norman: University of Oklahoma Press, 1994.

Michlovic, M.G., and F.E. Schneider. "The Shea Site: A Prehistoric Fortified Village on the Northeastern Plains." *Plains Anthropologist* 38, no. 143 (1993): 117-37.

Miller, David R. "Introduction to the 2000 Edition." In *The Assiniboine: Forty-Sixth Annual Report of the Bureau of American Ethnology to the Secretary of the Smithsonian Institution 1928-1929,* by Edwin Thompson Denig, edited by J.N.B. Hewitt, ix-xxi. Reprinted, Regina: Canadian Plains Research Center, University of Regina, 2000.

Miller, D.R., J.R. Mcgeshick, D.J. Smith, J. Shanley, and C. Shields. *History of the Assiniboine and Sioux Tribes of the Fort Peck Indian Reservation, 1600-2012.* Helena, MT: Fort Peck Community College; Poplar, MT: Montana Historical Society Press, 2012.

Miller, J.R. "Owen Glendower, Hotspur, and Canadian Indian Policy." *Ethnohistory* 37, no. 4 (1990): 386-415.

National Aboriginal Health Organization. *An Overview of Traditional Knowledge and Medicine and Public Health in Canada.* Ottawa: National Aboriginal Health Organization, 2008.

National Park Service. *Yellowstone, History and Culture.* 2015. http://www.nps.gov/yell/learn/historyculture/index.htm.

Nestor, Rob. *Indian Policy and the Early Reserve Period.* 2014. http://esask.uregina.ca/entry/indian_policy_and_the_early_reserve_period.html.

Nicholson, B.A. "Ceramic Affiliation and the Case of Incipient Horticulture in Southwestern Manitoba." *Canadian Journal of Archaeology* 14 (1990): 33-59.

———, ed. *Human Ecology of the Canadian Prairie Ecozone*. Canadian Plains Studies 61. Regina: Canadian Plains Research Center, University of Regina, 2011.

Nicholson, B.A., David Meyer, Gerry Oetelaar, and Scott Hamilton. "Human Ecology of the Canadian Prairie Ecozone ca. 500 BP: Plains Woodland Influences and Horticultural Practice." In *Human Ecology of the Canadian Prairie Ecozone*, edited by B.A. Nicholson, Canadian Plains Studies 61, 153–80. Regina: CPRC Press, 2011.

Nowak, R., and J. Paradiso. *Walker's Mammals of the World*. Baltimore: Johns Hopkins University Press, 1983.

O'Callaghan, E.B., ed. *Documents Relative to the Colonial History of the State of New York: Procured in Holland, England and France*. Vol. 9. Paris Documents, 1681–1744. Albany, NY: Weed, Parsons, and Co., 1856.

Parks, Douglas R., and Raymond J. DeMallie. "Sioux, Assiniboine, and Stoney Dialects: A Classification." *Anthropological Linguistics* 34 (1992): 233–55.

Pettipas, Katherine. *Severing the Ties that Bind: Government Repression of Indigenous Religious Ceremonies on the Prairies*. Winnipeg: University of Manitoba Press, 1994.

Prucha, F.P. *Atlas of American Indian Affairs*. Lincoln: University of Nebraska Press, 1990.

Ray, Arthur J. *Indians in the Fur Trade: Their Role as Trappers, Hunters, and Middlemen in the Lands Southwest of Hudson Bay, 1660–1870*. Toronto: University of Toronto Press, 1974.

———. "Smallpox: The Epidemic of 1837–38." *Beaver Magazine* Outfit 306 (1975): 8–13.

———. "William Todd: Doctor and Trader, for the Hudson's Bay Company, 1816–51." *Prairie Forum* 9, no. 1 (1984): 13–26.

Reeves, Brian O.K. "Culture Change in the Northern Plains: 1000 B.C.–A.D. 1000." Archaeological Survey of Alberta, Occasional Paper 20, 1983.

———. "The Southern Alberta Paleo-Cultural Paleo-Environment Sequence." In *Post Pleistocene Man and His Environment on the Northern Plains*, edited by R.G. Forbis, L.B. Davis, O.A. Christensen, and G. Fedirchuk, 6–46. Calgary: University of Calgary Archaeological Association, The Students Press, 1969.

Rich, E.E. *The Fur Trade and the Northwest to 1857*. Toronto: McClelland and Stewart, 1967.

Ruggles, Richard I. "The Historical Geography and Cartography of the Canadian West, 1670–1795: The Discovery, Exploration, Geographic Description and Cartographic Delineation of Western Canada to 1795." PhD diss., University of London, 1958.

Sanders, Davies, and Beebe Jones. In *The Assiniboine Indian Tribe v. Plaintiff's Request for Findings of Fact and Brief*, Court of Claims No. J-31, 1929.

Swagerty, William R. "Indian Trade in the Trans-Mississippi West to 1870." In *Handbook of North American Indians: History of Indian-White Relations*, vol. 4, edited by W.E. Washburn, 351–74. Washington, DC: Smithsonian Institution, 1988.

Syms, E.L. "Cultural Ecology and Ecological Dynamics of the Ceramic Period in Southwestern Manitoba." *Plains Anthropologist* 22, no. 76 (1977): 1–13.

BIBLIOGRAPHY

———. "The Devils Lake–Sourisford Burial Complex on the Northeastern Plains." *Plains Anthropologist* 24, no. 86 (1979): 283–308.
Taylor, Alan. *The Civil War of 1812: American Citizens, British Subjects, Irish Rebels, and Indian Allies.* Toronto: Random House, 2010.
Thompson, Erwin N. *Fort Union Trading Post: Fur Trade Empire on the Upper Missouri.* Williston, ND: Fort Union Association, 1994.
Thwaites, Reuben Gold, ed. *The Jesuit Relations and Allied Documents: 1853–1913.* Charleston, NC: Bibliolife Publishing, 1896.
Titley, Brian. *The Frontier of Edgar Dewdney.* Vancouver: UBC Press, 1999.
Tobias, John. "Civilization, Protection, Assimilation: An Outline of Canada's Indian Policy." *Western Canadian Journal of Anthropology* 6, no. 2 (1976): 13–17.
———. *Interim Report: A Brief History of Little Pine-Lucky Man Bands, 1870–1910.* Cumberland Report, Federation of Saskatchewan Indian Nations, 1985.
Truth and Reconciliation Commission of Canada. *Indian Residential Schools Truth and Reconciliation Commission.* 2015. http://trc.ca/websites/trcinstitution/index.php?p=39.
Turner, John Peter. *The North-West Mounted Police.* 2 vol. Ottawa: Edmond Cloutier, King's Printer, 1950.
United States Geological Survey. *Sweet Grass Hills.* 2015. Geographic Names Information System.
Vickers, Chris. "Aboriginal Backgrounds in Southern Manitoba." Historical and Scientific Society of Manitoba website (Season 1945–46), 1946. http://www.mhs.mb.ca/docs/transactions/3/aboriginalbackgrounds.shtml.
Walde, Dale. "Ethnicity: The Archeaeological Record and Mortlach." *Plains Anthropologist* 55, no. 214 (2010): 155–66.
———. "The Mortlach Phase." PhD diss., University of Calgary, 1994.
———. "Sedentism and Pre-Contact Tribal Organization on the Northern Plains: Colonial Imposition or Indigenous Development?" *World Archeaeology* 38, no. 2 (2006): 291–310.
Walde, Dale, David Meyer, and Wendy Unfreed. "The Late Period on the Canadian and Adjacent Plains." *Revista de arqueologia americana* 9 (1995): 7–66.
Wishart, David. *The Fur Trade of the American West, 1807–1840.* Lincoln: University of Nebraska Press, 1979.
Wissler, C., Peter H. Buck, Leslie Spier, Ernest Beaglehole, and W.W. Hill. *Population Changes among the Northern Plains Indians.* Yale University Publications in Anthropology. New Haven, CT: Human Relations Area Files Press, 1970.

Index

A

Adams, Art (Elder), xvii; on ceremonies, 180, 183–84; on contaminated wild meat from chemicals, 283; on fishing, 235; on hunting and meat processing, 208, 215, 222, 227, 230; on maintaining traditional way of life, 287; on oil and gas pipelines, 285; on picking berries, 249; on traditional language, 188
Adams, Councillor Kurt, xv
agriculture. *See* farming
alcohol (firewater): advice to youth to refrain from, 290; effects on Indigenous Peoples, 52, 62, 64, 292; in fur trade, 39, 42, 51; trade in, 79, 83, 86
Algonquian People, 20, 23; trade contact with Assiniboine, 24
Allen, Edwin, 90, 102, 105, 110–11, 115; rations fraud of, 114
alliances, 108, 112; between Assiniboine and Cree Peoples, 7–8, 20; formed among surviving tribes, 41, 58, 63, 94
Alvares, Nick, xvi, 60, 200
American Fur Company (AFC), 46–47, 50, 54, 56, 58, 68
animal populations: abundance of at Missouri region, 50; affected by development and chemical spraying, 254, 281–82; all parts used, 55, 208, 212; becoming scarce, 254, 271, 278; as sacred, 209. *See also* bison/buffalo herds; furbearing animals
Anishinaabe People, 40
annuity payments, 95–96, 102, 104, 125; paid to Assiniboine bands, 88, 90, 97, 122; promised in treaties, 64, 68, 71, 88, 93, 127, 293
Arikara People, 57, 65
artifacts/archaeological sites: Blackduck site, 13–14, 18; Cluny (One Gun) site, 16, 19; Old Women's Peoples, 13–17, 19; Plains Village/Oneota ceramics, 17; Psinomani site, 13, 16, 20; showing cultural influences, 9, 12, 15, 17. *See also* contact/precontact periods; pottery
Ashdohonk, Felix, xvii
Ashdohonk, Tony (Elder), xvii; on ceremonies and burial sites, 182, 195, 197; on fishing and hunting, 210, 231, 233; on keeping the house warm, 263; on picking berries, 250–51; on rations for flour, sugar, tea,

INDEX

Ashdohonk, Tony (cont.)
    lard, 261; on residential school, 186; on traditional diet, 259; on traditional language, 190
Ashley, William, 47
Aspdin, Thomas W., 144, 167–68; calling for band to improve reserves, 152–53, 165; comments on cattle raising, 160–61; considering surrender of southern end of reserve, 155–56, 158; overseeing credit becoming debt plan, 162–63, 166; resolved to end traditionalism, 164
assimilation, 146, 168–69, 173, 206, 295; and loss of language, 186, 188–89; through residential school system, 187. *See also* Canadian government; genocide; residential school system
Assiniboine Agency/Reserve, 141, 293; asking for protection from white settlers, 156, 158; changes to by Thomas Aspdin, 153; decline in population at, 140; farming and ranching at, 104–5, 122, 149, 157–60; land surrender at, 155–56, 158, 166, 168; progress towards self-sufficiency, 163–64, 167–68; relocation to Indian Head, 121; survey of, 101–3
Assiniboine/CTK Elders, xiii–xv, 7, 81, 213, 250, 293, 295; abuse at residential school, 156, 187; interviews of, 30; knowledge of burial sites, 195, 197; testimony on hunting grounds, 71, 207–9, 229, 231; testimony on seasonal travelling, 34–35, 37; views on protecting sacred sites, 177, 191

The Assiniboine Indian Tribe, Plaintiff v. The United States, Defendant, xvi
Assiniboine Peoples: adherence to 1851 treaty, 67; big game hunting as necessity, 224; consent to leave Cypress Hills, 118; contact with French, 25; Cree-speaking, 128, 131; demoralized and destitute, 95; depopulation of, 41, 58; at Fort Walsh in 1877, 90; horse and warrior culture of, 76; hunting and harvesting cycle, 34–36, 38, 42, 45, 200, 204; migrations of, 23, 31, 34, 37, 41, 45, 60, 63; not invited to Stevens Treaty, 66; processors/users of bison products, 58; relations with Sioux, 25, 29; relocation to Maple Creek, 106; Traditional Knowledge, 31. *See also* Nakoda (Assiniboine) People
Assiniboine Rock Band, 50, 53, 71
Astor, John Jacob, 46, 56
Atsina People. *See* Gros Ventre (Atsina) People
Audubon, John James, 58
Avonlea Peoples, 12

B

barter system, 100, 144, 150, 266
Basquia Cree, 41
Battleford reserve, 110, 117, 119
Battle of the Little Big Horn, 294
Bear Cub, xvi, 73–74
Bear's Head, Chief, 111, 116, 118, 131; band at Battleford, 126, 132
Beauchman, Gabriel, xvi, 73, 76
beaver trapping and trade, 37, 47, 55–56, 226, 228–29, 258–59
Bend the Stick headman, 111
Besant People, 12, 14

INDEX

Big Bear, Chief, 79, 96, 99–100, 107, 109, 120, 127, 129
Bisobbe headman, 111
bison/buffalo herds, 19–20, 99; access to through treaties, 65, 67; competition for, 115; controlled by prairie fires, 88, 92; demise of as great loss, 2, 79, 111, 114, 135, 199, 204; as gift from Great Spirit, 61; on grasslands, 15, 20, 34–35, 37, 39; located south of international boundary, 88, 97, 104, 106, 117, 121, 128; migration cycles of, 35, 45, 108, 201; as primary source of diet, livelihood, 1, 225, 292. *See also* bison/buffalo hunting
bison/buffalo hides, 55, 63–64, 94, 201, 204; made into robes, 39, 47, 50–51, 62, 100, 203; major item of fur trade, 56, 107. *See also* fur trade; hide tanning
bison/buffalo hunting, 11–12, 16, 34, 88, 200, 205, 224, 278; methods for, 29, 36, 38, 53, 201–3
Blackfoot People/Confederacy, 29, 31, 40, 45–46, 79, 95, 99, 117; ceremonies at Cypress Hills, 180; death from smallpox, 56–57; and fur trade, 47, 50, 53; oral tradition, 16; Reservation, 69; searching for bison, 106; territorial expansion by, 39; war parties of, 60
Black Mane, 147
Blood People, 79–80, 95, 99; ceremonies at Cypress Hills, 180; death from smallpox, 56
Blue Cloud, xvi, 73
Blue Horn, xvi, 201
Bobtail Bear, 71
Bodmer, Karl, 55

bow-and-arrow technology, 11, 13, 202
Bozeman Trail, 67–68
Brandon Indian Residential School, 187
British North America Act, 68
Broadview, SK, 186–87, 253, 290
Broken Arm, Chief, 69, 71
buffalo. *See* bison/buffalo herds
burial sites, 11, 129, 195–98
Butler, William, 85

C

Campbell and Sublette Company, 51, 58
Canadian government: banning spiritual ceremonies, 173, 177; cleaning up whiskey trade, 294; and conditions of Indigenous Peoples, 94, 99–100; effects of regulations on Nakoda People, 2; genocidal/racist policies of, xiii, 96, 134–35, 139, 142, 206, 292–95, 297; National Policy and Confederation, 68, 85, 87, 106, 108, 114; needing to consult with First Nations, 296–97; not honouring Cypress Hills land claim, 296; peasant farming policy, 146–48; policy on rations, reservations, 93, 96–97, 100, 104, 113, 134, 139; refusing to let CTK/Nakoda stay on their chosen reserve, 294–95; relocating of Assiniboine, 106, 115; and Sitting Bull, 107; treaty promises not kept, 261
Canadian National Railway (CNR), 107
Canadian Pacific Railway (CPR), 111, 128, 134, 237; derailment during removal of Indigenous People, 132–33
Canoe Paddlers Band, 69, 71

INDEX

Carl, Warren/Brings Back, xvi, 195, 200–201, 203–4
Carlyle: as hunting site, 216, 218–20, 222, 274, 278; oil wells at, 275–76; site for picking herbs, 253
Carry The Kettle, Chief, 142–43, 150, 291
Carry The Kettle Nakoda First Nation, 1, 78, 85, 119, 137, 168, 196; current lands of, 2–3, 31; forced to pursue subsistence farming, 295; having rich history as proud, strong people, xiii–xiv, 291; heritage sites, 192; hunting patterns of, 205, 207–8, 219–20, 224; naming of, 142; as nomadic people, 87, 254; peacemakers with white and Indigenous settlers, 292; residential school survivors, 186, 188; retaining native language, 190; surviving off the land, 259, 291; traditional harvesting areas of, 219, 273; Traditional Knowledge, 63–64, 297; violations to their Treaty Rights, 294, 296
Carry The Kettle Nakoda First Nation youth: advised to refrain from drugs and alcohol, 290; education of as sacred responsibility, xiv; encouraged to maintain heritage and traditional way of life, 182–83, 287–89, 297; not taught about traditional medicines, 247; vision quests for, 179
Carry The Kettle Reserve, 206, 218, 235, 246, 298; ceremonies on, 173; farming at, 161; hunting grounds of, 222; Indian Agent control of band members, 164; land surrender at, 163; Sioux and Cree at, 138; trapping activities of, 229
Cary, William M., 66
Catlin, George, 52–53, 55
cattle raising, 148, 156–58, 160–61, 165, 270; for food, 98, 100, 103, 159; improvements to, 167; for ploughing, 101, 147; sale of, 152
Cegakin, Chief, 291
ceremonies. *See* traditional ceremonies
Cha-ca-chas, Chief, 124
Cheechuk, Chief, 96
Cherokee Treaties, 293
Chic-ne-na-bais band, 115
Chief, role of, 142–43
Chipewyan People, 29, 40
Chitty, George L., 158
Christianity, 169, 173, 247–48
Cocking, Matthew, 37
colonization, 296–97
Columbia Fur Company, 47
contact/precontact periods, 8, 12, 16, 19–20, 23, 26, 35, 177, 255, 292. *See also* artifacts/archaeological sites
Cowen Treaty Commission, 71
Cowessess, Chief, 96–97, 100, 127
Crazy Bear headman, 59, 64
Crazy Bull, xvi, 204
creation story (Assiniboine People), 7–9
credit and debit system: effects on fur trade, 43, 62
Cree People, 3, 25, 28–29, 79–80, 95, 97, 99, 110, 115, 246; as Assiniboine allies, 57; effects of smallpox on, 40, 56; and fur trade, 31, 37, 40–41, 53; home farm for, 100; language of, 190; sacred burial ground of, 130; seasonal migrations, 23, 34, 36; settlements of, 90, 96, 105; Traditional

INDEX

Territory and boundaries of Treaty 4, 28, 30, 32, 87, 135
Crooked Arm headman, 111
Crooked Lake Agency, 115
Crow People, 50, 57, 60, 68, 70, 109, 180
Crozier, Leif N.F., 108, 117
Culbertson, Thaddeus, 59
Custer, George Armstrong, 294
customs and traditions. *See* Indigenous culture
Cuthead Yanktonai People, 70
Cypress Hills Elkwater Provincial Park, 293
Cypress Hills Massacre, xiii, 3, 81–83, 86–87, 134, 143, 291, 294–95
Cypress Hills region, 71, 85, 95, 190, 273; abundant with berries, herbs, medicines, 217, 246, 252; as Assiniboine homeland, 31, 118–19, 132, 136, 195, 225, 233; Assiniboine lodges at, 74, 89, 108, 200–201; as citadel and trading centre, 94; farming and fishing at, 103, 106, 115, 234, 255; forced removal from, xiii, 3, 106, 115, 119–22, 127, 130, 135, 137, 140, 246; hunting game in, 200–201, 204–5, 207, 216–17, 221, 223; hunting grounds, 130, 199, 215, 217–18, 275; reserves at, 97, 100, 169; source of lodgepole pine, 78; as spiritual gathering place and burial site, 88, 173, 179–80, 183, 195; traditional harvesting, 220; winter shelter at, 79, 88, 128, 200

D

Dakota Peoples, 20, 29, 67, 293; languages of, 7; medicines of, 246; territory of, 66, 68

Dakota War (1862), 293
Daschuk, James, 114
deaths: from alcohol, 64; from change in diet, 124–25, 135, 261; of children, 126, 133–34, 295–96; from crop failures, 144; from famine, 139; from smallpox, 2, 56–58, 60–61, 130; from starvation, 93, 96, 126, 128, 133, 135, 140, 292; from warfare, 56, 293; by wolfers, 134, 294
deer hunting, 207–8, 210–11, 219–20, 267, 282–83
Dempsey, Hugh, 79
Denig, Edwin Thompson, 58–59, 61–62
Denny, Cecil E., 114–17
De Noyon, Jacques, 25, 28
Department of Indian Affairs (DIA), 103–4, 109, 115, 118, 155, 238; crop reports of, 144; program of protection, civilization, assimilation, 146; resistance to mechanization of farming, 146, 150; use of credit, 162
Department of Natural Resources (DNR), 276
De Smet, Pierre-Jean, 59
Dewdney, Edgar: amalgamating remaining bands, 140; appointment as Indian commissioner, 95–96; concerned about raids by American bands, 108; encouraging farming, self-sufficiency, 97–98, 103; recognizing food shortages at Cypress Hills, 99, 105; relocating Indigenous bands, 110, 118, 121, 127, 130, 135, 138; uncovering Edwin Allen's fraud, 114; wanting to use Indigenous labourers for railway, 111

INDEX

diseases/illnesses: cancer, diabetes, 276–77, 283, 285; caused by environmental degradation, 273; cholera, 56, 63; consumption, 133; destabilizing effects of, 2, 41, 45, 60, 62–63, 79, 85, 292; diarrhea from change in diet, 124–25; influenza, 63; malnutrition, 39; mountain fever, 96; scarlet fever, 104; scurvy, 138, 140; spread through trade contacts, 2. *See also* smallpox; starvation
Dominion Lands Act, 142
Donnelly, Thomas E., 168
Douglas, James M., 155
Dreidoppel, David, 55
drought: causing crop failures, 144, 158; reducing human and animal populations, 41
Duck, Thomas, xvi
duck hunting/egg gathering, 138, 205, 212, 226–29, 258–59, 275
Duck's Head Necklace band, 110–11, 115
Durfee, Peck, and Company, 69

E

Eagle Brich (Birch) People, 28
Eagle Creek Assiniboine People, 28
Eagle Eyed People (Assiniboine), 29
Eashappie, Nancy (Elder), xvii; on barter system, 266; on ceremonies, 177; on Cypress Hills Massacre, 82, 143; on environmental changes, 278; on gardening, 258; on harvesting and selling seneca root, 268–69; on hunting on reserve, 206; on medicines, 239, 241; on outside farm work, 270; on picking and processing berries, 250, 280; on selling deer skins, 267; on traditional language, 190
Eashappie, Sarah (Elder), xvii; on selling and trading pelts, 265; on traditional diet, 271
Eashappie, Tim, 177
elk hunting, 207, 210, 212, 216–18, 220–22; declining numbers of elk, 279; hides and teeth used, 215; as plentiful, 205, 224; sharing the take, 223
Elkwater, sacred site, 179
Enbridge Inc., 286
English, J.J.: closure of Cypress Hills farms, 110, 115; as farm instructor, 97–98, 101, 104, 110, 121; at Maple Creek farms, 115–16, 132; responsibilities to the Assiniboine, 102–3
environmental contamination/degradation: on and around traditional lands, 273, 278; due to chemical spraying on farms, 281; effects on animal and human health, 276, 278–83
Erasmus, Peter, 118
ethnogenesis, 40
European settlers. *See* immigration; settlers/settler society

F

famine: addressed in Treaty 6, 96; at Indian Head Assiniboine reserves, 139; prevention of, 93–94. *See also* starvation
farm implements, 144–45, 148–49; as inadequate for prairies, 147; purchased by Indigenous Peoples, 152–53, 156, 159–60

INDEX

farming, 95, 97, 103, 110–11, 168, 262; abandonment of, 148; clearing away bush lands for, 274, 280; forced on Indigenous Peoples, 96, 122; improvements to, 166–67; inadequate for survival, 104–5, 107, 165; peasant farming policy and permit system, 146–48, 153; and self-sufficiency, productivity, 96, 148–50; supplementing food requirements, 255–56. *See also* farm implements; Home Farm program

Farr, William, 66

Farwell, Abel, 81

fasting: as part of ceremonies, 177–80, 184, 241, 246

firearms, 29, 114, 202

firewood cutting and selling, 151, 159–60, 168, 254–55, 262, 265

First Eagle, xvi, 200

First Nations children: abuse at residential school, 188; forbidden to speak their languages, 186, 188; taken from their families, 186. *See also* Kamloops Indian Residential School; residential school system

First to Fly headman, 59, 64

Fisher, Charles, 162

fishing activities, 12, 14, 19, 35, 37, 225, 233, 235–38; carried out by Assiniboine, 110; expanded beyond reserve boundaries, 215; as food resource, 34; in Qu'Appelle Valley, 216, 252

Flathead (Eastern Salish) People, 66

foraging. *See* gathering activities

Foremost Man (Nekaneet), 110

forests: economic system of, 38; food cycle in, 32–33; and winter starvation, 34. *See also* parklands; prairies (grasslands)

Fort Belknap Agency, 71–72, 88, 90, 95, 104, 114, 178, 204, 298

Fort Benton, 65, 79, 128

Fort Browning Trading Post, 69

Fort Buford, 67–68, 70, 108

Fort Laramie Treaty (1851), 64, 66–68

Fort Macleod, 95–96

Fort Peck Agency, 55, 71, 88, 204

Fort Pierre, 56, 58, 67

Fort Qu'Appelle, 122, 131, 133, 137, 222, 233, 236, 244; hunting at, 223; Indigenous arrival at, 121, 128; reserves at, 110, 116–17, 186; sale of moccasins at, 267; site of negotiating Treaty 4, 87–88, 96, 135, 294; starvation at, 124; supplies/rations from, 118–19, 127

Fort Qu'Appelle Industrial School, 151, 153

Fort Union, 50–59, 61, 66–68, 73

Fort Walsh, 86, 124; annuities paid at, 88, 92, 97, 118; cattle brought in for food, 98; closing of, 115, 117, 127; crop failures at, 104; destitution, starvation at, 96–97, 100, 102, 109; Indigenous People remaining at, 107, 111, 126, 128; presence of U.S. Indigenous People, 94, 109; reserve/settlement at, 75, 89, 91, 101, 128; survey at, 90, 103, 110

Fort Whoop-Up, 79, 101

Front Man headman, 127

furbearing animals: abundance of at Missouri region, 50; pelts sold for income, 231–32; plentiful in Qu'Appelle Valley, 232; trapping of, 30, 36, 48; use of skins and

INDEX

fur bearing animals (cont.)
fur, 231, 233. *See also* beaver trapping and trade; bison/buffalo herds; hide tanning; mink trapping; trapping activities
fur trade, 1–2, 24, 30, 32, 194, 225, 292; Assiniboine as middlemen, 23, 31, 37, 39, 41–42; competition in during 19th century, 46–47; effects of smallpox epidemic on, 40, 42; in Missouri region, 50–51; negative effects of, 39, 42; trading posts, 28, 41

G

Galt, Elliot T., 103, 107, 109, 111–14, 122, 124–25
gardens, 118, 152, 167, 255, 262, 276; role in traditional diet, 239, 254, 257
gathering activities, 9–11, 238, 270, 295, 297; harvesting herbs and medicines, 239, 241, 245–46, 252–53; picking berries, 239, 248, 252. *See also* hunting activities; medicines; seneca root
genocide: of Indigenous Peoples, 96, 292, 295–96; inflicted through government policies, xiii, 134–35, 139, 207, 293–94. *See also* Canadian government
George III, King, 292
Globe (newspaper), 101, 110
God-Wakan-Tanka (Great Spirit), 8
Graham, W.M., 165, 167–68
Grant, W.S.: appointed agent of Assiniboine reserve, 144; encouraging housing improvement, 152; encouraging self-sufficiency, 149, 167; promoting assimilation,

146, 168; supporting hand threshing of wheat, 147, 150
Great Blackfoot Hunting Ground, 65, 69
Great Sioux War (1865–1868), 68
Greenwater Provincial Park, 207, 220–22, 237, 275
grizzly bear, carvings of, 194
Grizzly Bear's Head, Chief, 121
Gros Ventre (Atsina) People, 29, 37, 66, 129, 203; adaptation to plains livelihood, 3; effects of diseases on, 56–57, 63; enemies of Blackfoot and Sioux, 69–70; friendly relations with Assiniboines, 31; population at Fort Belknap, 71–72; Sundance ceremonies, 178–79; taking treaty, 68
Grunting Calf headman, 111
Gull Lake, bison drive, 10

H

half-breeds, 94, 98, 104, 107–8, 115
Hamilton, Scott, 14, 16
Harkness, James, 66
Hartwick, Thomas, 81, 294
Hassler, Leroy (Elder), xvii; on caring for horses, 263; on ceremonies, 177, 181; on farming and gardening, 144, 257; on firewood cutting and selling, 265; on hay threshing, 262; on homemade moccasins, dress, 215; on house building, 262; on hunting, trapping, fishing, 211, 227, 229, 233, 259; on permit system, 270; on picking herbs and medicines, 242, 244; on store-bought foods, 271
Hassler, Myrtle (Elder), xvii; on ceremonies, 181, 191; on Cypress Hills Massacre, 81; on family

history, 77; on firewood cutting and selling, 265; on gardening, 257–58; on hay threshing and selling, 266–67; on house building, 262; on hunting, trapping, 207, 211, 231, 259; on making moccasins, 212–13; on permit system, 270; on picking and processing berries, 248, 250; on picking herbs and medicines, 242; on residential school, 186, 188; on store-bought foods, 271
hay cutting and threshing, 105, 155, 165, 168, 265, 267; as farm resource, 144–45, 148, 152, 156, 158, 160, 262; permits for, 157, 269; for sale to neighbours, 151, 160, 266
Haywahe, Clint, xvii; on changes to plants and declining animal populations, 279; on clearing bush lands, 280; on effects of chemical spraying, 281–82; on health concerns, 277; on hunting, trapping, and fishing, 207, 216, 220, 223, 226, 235; on Indigenous rights, 273; on maintaining traditional way of life, 288; on medicines, 241; on oil and gas projects, 284–86; on outside farm work, 270; on reduction in hunting lands, 275; on traditional lands, 217
Haywahe, Kevin (Elder), 142
Head of the Mountain, 101, 104, 110, 180
Hearne, Samuel, 37
Heisman's Hide and Fur, 232
Henday, Anthony, 31
Henry, Alexander, 37, 42
Hidatsa People, 13, 28, 46, 51, 57, 65

hide tanning, 149, 151, 160, 168, 203, 212, 231
Holy Lake (Minee-Wakan), 9
Home Farm program, 98, 100–101, 117
horses: eaten for meat, 100–101, 107; equestrianism, 40–41; introduction on northern plains, 31, 39; not surviving winters, 41, 66; owning and selling of, 201, 267; as spiritual beings, 263; stealing of, 108–9, 118, 129; for transportation, 182–83, 195, 226, 228, 232, 261–62; used for farm cultivation, 144
horticulture, village, 11–12, 17, 20
Hotomani, Stacey, xvii; on berry picking, 253; on burial sites, 197; on farming and hay baling, 262; on medicine wheels, 192; on traditional diet, 259; on traditional language, 188
Hourie, Peter, 128
Hubner, Brian, 109
Hudson's Bay Company (HBC), 26, 37, 39, 41–42, 51, 69
Hunkpapa (Sioux) People, 70
hunter-gatherer societies, 9, 255
hunting activities, 114, 142, 199, 207, 225, 270; carried out by Assiniboine, 110, 216, 220; communal practice of sharing, 211–12, 279; importance of, 208; meat-handling practices, 210; permits for, 169; praying before, 209; pursued on and off reserve, 215, 219, 224, 295; revitalization of, 116, 297; traditional hunting grounds, 66–67, 69; as treaty right, 274, 276. *See also* bison/buffalo hunting; deer hunting; elk hunting; moose hunting

INDEX

I

Idle No More movement, 296
I.G. Baker Co., 114, 120
Ik-Tomi, 8-9
immigration: due to warfare, 81; of Europeans, 107, 291-92, 296; of Sioux Peoples, 70, 79. *See also* settlers/settler society; white people
income, supplemental, 168, 255, 271; for cooking and cleaning, 270; sales of wood products, garments, and roots, 231, 265, 267-68. *See also* firewood cutting and selling; moccasins; seneca root; wage labour
Indian Act, 106, 206
Indian Agents: calling for labour for rations, 96; control of First Nations' movements, 206; encouraging farming, 144, 148, 257; Indigenous lack of trust in, 113; and permit system, 269-70
Indian Claims Commission, 82
Indian Head Reserves, 77, 125, 129, 131, 137-38, 207, 223, 286; decline in population at, 140-41; farming at, 133, 255; record of life at in 1882, 149
Indigenous culture, 4, 153, 169, 291; to be preserved and passed down, 177, 182-83, 208, 220, 224, 287, 289, 296; commodification as foreign concept, 146; destroyed by Eurocentric policy, 96; early manifestations, 12, 15; forbidden by government regulations, 173, 180, 295; and oral tradition, 28, 32, 247

Indigenous Peoples: compelled to adapt to progress, 146, 153; contributing to own maintenance through industries, 160; decline in population, 40, 134-35; displaced by European immigrants, 292; expected to submit to white people, 136; forced relocation of, 125, 132, 134; violence and hardship on due to provisions trade, 39. *See also* First Nations children; Indigenous women
Indigenous Rights. *See* Treaty Rights
Indigenous spirituality, 247, 291, 295; celebrated through ceremonies, 173, 183, 238-39; reclaiming of, 198, 297. *See also* sacred sites; traditional ceremonies
Indigenous women, 56, 112; as ceramics-makers, 19; engaged in making products to sell, 149, 152, 159, 267-68, 270; rapes of, 39, 82. *See also* intertribal marriages
international boundary, 51, 62, 65, 72, 81; as foreign concept to Assiniboine, 90, 92; negative effect on traditional practices, 77, 79; as preventing animal hunting, 64, 96, 199
intertribal marriages: to build up populations, 57-58, 63-64, 70
intertribal warfare, 59, 79-81
Inuit children, 186
Iron Arrow Point, Chief, 53
Iron Horn, xvi, 74
Iroquois People, 40
Irvine, Acheson: promoting move to reserves, 115, 120-21, 125, 131, 137; and unsettling conditions at Fort Walsh, 94-95, 112-14, 126-30

INDEX

J

Jack, Bernard, 197
Jack, Chief Elsie, xiii–xiv, 291, 296, 298
Jack, Darrell, xviii; on farms and farm animals, 256; on fishing and hunting, 207, 211–12, 218–19, 222, 227, 237; on gardening, 257–58; on gathering wild vegetables, 252; on Indigenous rights, 273, 289; on medicines, 244–45; on picking berries and fruit, 251; on reduction in hunting lands, 274; on traditional language, 189; on trapping and processing skins, 230–31
Jack, Joe, 197
Jackson, President Andrew, 55, 293
The Jesuit Relations (1658), 23–25
Johnson, President Andrew, 68

K

Kainai First Nation, 101
Kakewistahaw band, 121
Kamloops Indian Residential School: children's remains found at, 295–96
Keeping of the Soul, 175
Kelsey, Henry, 23, 26–28, 35–36
Kennedy, Chief Dan, 82, 130
Kennedy, Daniel, 153
Kennedy, Dr. George, 104, 110–11
Kennedy, Wilma, 133
King, Sam, xvi, 78, 200, 202, 204
King William's War, 30
Kipp, James, 47, 66
Knife River Flint (KRF), 12, 17, 19
Knight, James, 29
Kurz, Rudolph Frederick, 59

L

La France, Joseph, 28–29
Laird, David, 158–59, 163
Lake of the Woods (Lac of the Assiniboins), 25, 28
Lake Winnipeg, 8–9, 26, 28–29
Lakota People, 7, 57, 67, 71, 108
Land Back Movement, 296
Larpenteur, Charles, 58, 68
Last, xvi, 76, 191, 199, 203
La Vérendrye, Pierre Gaultier de Varennes de, 23, 27–28, 34, 36
Lawrence, Emlen N., 66
Lewis and Clark Expedition, 46
Lincoln, W.L., 95
liquor. *See* alcohol (firewater)
Little Black Bear, Chief, 92, 96, 110
Little Black Bear band, 90–91
Little Bull, 70–71
Little Chief, 89–90, 92, 96, 101
Little Child band, 97, 110, 119, 121, 126, 132
Little Mountain headman, 92, 111, 133, 137
Little Pine, Chief, 79, 96, 99–100, 110, 127, 129
Little Soldier, 81
lodgepole pine, 78
Long Hair, Chief, 69
Long Lodge, Chief, 91–92, 111, 118–19, 121–22, 131; death of, 140; grievances of, 124–25
Long Lodge band (Nakoda People), 87, 138, 141; amalgamation with The Man Who Took the Coat band, 140; annuities paid to, 88, 90; census of, 95, 101, 111, 115, 128, 133–34; farming experience of, 144; lodge at Cypress Hills, 89, 91–92, 102, 116, 132; population of in 1883, 137

341

INDEX

Looking, xvi, 78, 201
Louisiana Purchase, 46, 64
Lower Assiniboine People, 69
Lucky Man, Chief, 96, 99–100, 110, 127, 129

M

Macdonald, Sir John A., xiii, 85, 97, 99, 105–6, 112, 139–40, 206. *See also* Canadian government
Macleod, James, 98, 100, 109
Macoun, John, 104
maize (corn), 11, 19, 34, 38, 55, 255, 257–58
The Man, xvi, 72, 77, 200, 202
Mandan People, 51, 203; death from smallpox, 57; lands reserved under Fort Laramie Treaty, 65; villages of, 31, 34–36, 38, 46
The Man Who Took the Coat (Jack), Chief, 90–91, 291, 298; choosing to move to reserve, 97-98, 131; resisting relocation, 106, 118–19, 124–25
The Man Who Took the Coat band (Nakoda People), 87, 138, 141; amalgamation with Long Lodge band, 140; annuities paid to, 92; census of, 95, 101, 111, 115, 126, 128, 133–34, 137; farming experience of, 144; at Indian Head reserve, 142; lodges at Cypress Hills, 116; moving to Fort Qu'Appelle, 119, 121–22, 132
Many Coos, xvi
Maple Creek reserve, 110, 118–19, 122, 218; for Assiniboine, 111; farm at, 115, 121, 131–32
Marest, Pierre-Gabriel, 23
Maximilian, Prince of Weid, 55–56

McDonald, Alan: and amalgamation of remaining bands, 140; and conditions at Fort Qu'Appelle, 124–25, 133; encouraging farming, 122; as Fort Qu'Appelle Indian agent, 102, 110, 118; and movement of Indigenous bands from Cypress Hills, 121, 137; paying of annuities, 127
McIlree, J.H., 92, 117–18, 120, 126, 130
McKenzie, Kenneth, 50, 53, 55
McLean, J.D., 155–56, 162–63
McPherson, D.L., 112
Medicine Bear/Iron Cradle, Mrs., xvi, 75–76, 174
Medicine Lodge ceremony, 146
Medicine Men and Women, 177, 202, 239–41, 248
medicines: affected by environmental degradation, 277; to be protected and maintained, 288–89; harvest, use, sale of, 85, 175, 241, 244, 265, 277; harvesting areas for, 78, 180, 245, 275; knowledge about as sacred, 177, 240–41; promised by government, 139; repressed during early colonization, 247. See also seneca root, 268
medicine wheel, 183, 191–93
Métis People, 186, 264
Meyer, David, 14–17, 19, 26, 31
Middle Missouri village, 17–18
migrations: of Assiniboine and precursors, 9, 38, 60; of bison, 45, 92, 108, 201, 254; trails used for, 86
Milk River Agency, 63, 129, 133, 200; dissolution in 1872, 70–71; inclusion of Assiniboine in, 69

INDEX

mink trapping, 229, 232–33
Missouri River region, 20; as major fur trading centre, 46–47, 64; wintering site of Assiniboine bands, 45
Mitchell, Martin, xvi, 203–4
moccasins, 208, 215; making of, 212–13; selling of, 203, 267. *See also* income, supplemental
moose hunting, 14, 37, 78, 199, 216, 220–22, 258; as plentiful, 205, 223–24, 279, 282; sharing the taking, 207
Moose Mountain, 73, 96, 109, 121, 180, 182; hunting area, 220, 222, 229, 253, 277
Moose Mountain Provincial Park, 222
Mortlach Peoples, 14, 16, 31; phase based on ceramic evidence, 17–19, 23; as Pre-Assiniboine, 13, 17, 19–20, 32
Mother Earth/Mother Nature, 279; living in harmony with, 183, 208; respect for, 248
Mountain, Chief, 79–81
Mountain Crow People, 66
Mountain Lodge band, 142
Mountain Poets Assiniboine People, 28
Muscowequan People, 100, 110
Muskego Cree People, 40
muskrat trapping, 226, 229–33, 258–59, 278

N

Nakoda (Assiniboine) People, 1–2, 134; adjusting to trade outlets in Missouri, 46; attacked by disease, whiskey traders, wolfers, 85; in Cypress Hills, 96, 128; effects of genocidal neglect, 85; language of, 7, 190; oral histories of, 26, 30. *See also* Carry The Kettle Nakoda First Nation; Long Lodge band (Nakoda People); The Man Who Took the Coat band (Nakoda People)
Nation of the Assinipoualak (Warriors of the Rock), 24
Naywatame Poets, 28
Nelson, John, 122, 140
newcomers (Indigenous), 41, 292. *See also* settlers/settler society
Nez Perce People, 95
Nicholson, B.A., 13
Night, xvi, 75
Norman, Frank, 126, 128
Northeastern Plains Village Complex, 17
Northern Plains: displacement and warfare on, 68; hunting/overhunting on, 41, 45; Indigenous territories on, 20; linguistic similarities among tribes, 189; population of, 9, 11–12, 30–31; spread of disease on, 39; starvation of Indigenous Peoples, 88; tribal groups on, 45. *See also* parklands; prairies (grasslands)
North West Company, 41–42, 46
North West Mounted Police (NWMP), 153, 294; base at Fort Walsh, 86, 90–92; and government rations policy, 93, 98, 118, 128; maintaining control at Fort Walsh, 106–9, 117, 125, 129; recognition of Assiniboine reserve, 104; reports on conditions of Assiniboine, 93, 126
North West Territories, 97, 107, 158, 160
Not a Young Man headman, 111

343

INDEX

O

oil and gas projects: consultation with Indigenous groups, 286; economic benefits of, 285; effects on environment, 274, 277, 284; pipelines, xv, 277, 284–86; wells, 275–76

Ojibwa People, 29

O'Soup, Chief Louis, 138

Ottawa People, 25, 40

O'Watch, Bertha, 241

O'Watch, Freda (Elder), xvi; on ceremonies, cultural identity, 183, 190; on maintaining traditional way of life, 287; on medicines, 242, 244, 246

O'Watch, George, 181, 269

O'Watch, James Leon (Elder), xviii; on ceremonies, sacred sites, 178, 181, 183, 185, 193–95, 197, 215; on clearing land for farms, 270; on cutting wood, selling pickets, 266; on declining animal population, 278; on fishing and hunting activities, 211, 217–18, 221, 225, 236; on gardening, 257; on hay threshing to sell to neighbours, 267; on health and disease, 276; on history of CTK/Nakoda First Nation, 78, 142, 148; on horse selling, 267; on maintaining traditional way of life, 287–88; on medicines, 240, 245–46; on picking wild vegetables, 252; on removal from Cypress Hills, 132–33; on selling berries to earn income, 265; on store-bought food, 271; on traditional language, 189, 191

P

parklands, 9, 11, 26, 36; Assiniboine tribes on, 31–32, 34–35, 63, 71; food cycle, hunting on, 32–33, 207, 229; living/thriving on, 291, 294; Mortlach cultural residue on, 19; overlapping economic system of, 37–38; spread of disease on, 40. *See also* prairies (grasslands)

Patrick, Allan Poyntz, 102–3

Pedley, Frank, 146, 160

Peepeekisis People, 121, 181

Peigan People, 57, 79–80, 180

pemmican, 39, 47, 121, 124, 250–51

permits/permit system: to conduct traditional activities, 169; lifting of, 270; to sell goods off reserve, 147, 269; for settlers to cut hay, 157

pesticide/insecticide spraying: effects on traditional lands, 281–82

Piapot, Chief: band at Cypress Hills reserve, 109, 121, 127; burial site of, 197; choosing reserve near Maple Creek, 110, 122, 132; and Indian Head reserve site, 125, 129–30, 137–38, 140, 142; leader of Assiniboine-Cree band, 79, 96, 100, 123, 126, 128, 131; movement to Qu'Appelle Valley reserve, 140, 144; rivalry with Assiniboine, 115

picket cutting, for fences, 159–60, 168, 265–66, 269

Piegan Blackfeet People, 56, 95

Pipe Ceremony, 175

Pipestone Valley, 220, 273

Plains Cree bands, 56, 96

Poor Man (Lean Man), Chief, 90

Poor Man band: annuities paid to, 89–90; hunting for buffalo, 115;

INDEX

at Maple Creek, 111, 116; moving to new reserve, 118, 121, 131–32; population of, 92, 101, 133
Porcupine Provincial Park, 222–23
pottery, 11, 13, 16–18, 20–21, 255
powwow celebrations, 176, 180–82, 184–85, 195, 249; needing to keep alive, 287; outfitting for, 215. *See also* Indigenous spirituality; sacred sites; traditional ceremonies
prairies (grasslands), 15, 19, 291, 296; animals and plants on, 227, 246; and bison hunting, 33–34; economic system of, 38; food cycle on, 32–33; as one ecosystem of Nakoda People, 294
Prettyshield, Gladys (Elder), xvi, xviii; on advising youth to maintain heritage, 288; on ceremonies, sacred sites, 178, 184; on farms and farm animals, 256; on gardening and harvesting wild vegetables, 252, 257–58; on history of Nakoda nation, 136; on hunting practices, 222, 227–28, 230; on loss of bush land, 280; on making clothes and wood products for sale, 213, 266–68; on picking and processing berries, 249, 251; on picking herbs and medicines, 240–41, 244; on traditional diet, 259
Prettyshield, Joyce (Elder), xviii; on advising youth to maintain heritage, 288; on ceremonies, sacred sites, 178, 184, 195, 198; on farms and farm animals, 256; on gardening, 258; on history of Nakoda nation, 136; on hunting practices, 222, 227–28, 230;

on loss of bush land, 280; on making and selling clothing, 213, 267–68; on picking and processing berries, 248–49, 251; on picking herbs and medicines, 240–41; on respect for nature, 248; on selling wood products, 266; on traditional diet, 259
Prettyshield, Keith, xviii; on contaminated wild meat, 283; on effects of chemical spraying, 281; on effects of oil and gas pipelines, 285; on harvesting wild vegetables, 253; on reduction in hunting lands, 274; on traditional diet, 261; on traditional lands, 77; on trapping and hunting practices, 207, 221–24, 227–29
Prettyshield, Raymond (Elder): on contaminated wild meat, 282–83; on fishing, 233; on trapping and selling pelts, 231
Prettyshield, Terri (Elder), xviii; on barter system, 266; on cultural practices, 177, 180; on hunting practices, 206; on role of a Chief, 142; on scarcity of berries, 280
Prettyshield, Victoria (Elder), xvi, xviii; on advising youth to maintain heritage, 288; on ceremonies, sacred sites, 178, 184, 198; on farming, farms, and farm animals, 144, 256; on gardening, 258; on history of Nakoda nation, 136; on hunting practices, 206, 213, 222, 227–28, 230; on loss of bush land, 280; on making and selling clothing, 213, 267–68; on picking and processing berries, 249, 251; on picking herbs and medicines,

INDEX

Prettyshield, Victoria (cont.)
240–41; on rations, food stamps, 260; on selling wood products, 266; on traditional diet, 259; on traditional language, 189

Prettyshield, Wanda (Elder), xviii; on contaminated wild meat, 282–83; on effects from oil and gas pipelines, 284–85; on farms, farm animals, and hay threshing, 256, 267; on fishing and hunting practices, 210, 226–28, 233; on gardening, 257; on gathering wild vegetables, 252; on harvesting and selling seneca root, 268; on hauling water, 264; on maintaining traditional language, 289; on permit system, 269–70; on picking and processing berries, 248–51; on rations for rice, flour, sugar, bacon, 261; on residential school, 186; on selling firewood, hay, pickets, 265; on traditional cultural practices, 182; on traditional diet, 259; on traditional lands, 190

Q

Qu'Appelle River Valley: abundant with berries, fish, 235–36, 252–53; Assiniboine camping locations, 42, 93, 99, 102, 107; buffalo herds in, 19; contamination of the river, 283; furbearing animals as plentiful, 232; harvesting location, 219; reserves on, 111, 121–22, 127, 132, 140, 144. *See also* Cypress Hills region

R

rabbits: as abundant, 229, 258; and communal sharing of meat, 211; as part of diet, 204–5, 207, 226, 233, 259; as scarce or diseased, 279, 281–82; snaring/hunting of, 208, 221, 225, 227, 230, 265

raindances, 177, 181

Rainy Lake (Lac des Cristineau), 20, 25, 28–29

rations: for agreeing to leave Cypress Hills, 119, 121–22; as inadequate, 99, 104, 107, 112, 114, 125–26, 135, 138; increased due to starvation, 116; mismanaged at Fort Walsh, 114, 128; reduced due to farming productivity, 150; as treaty provision, 68, 77, 95–97, 102, 108, 134, 260; used to keep Indigenous People on reserves, 111, 113–14, 122; work for, 98, 101, 103, 111–12, 115, 135, 146, 163

Ray, Arthur, 23–24, 30–32, 34, 37–38

Recollections of an Assiniboine Chief, 82

reconciliation, 296

Red Cloud's War, 294

Red Feather, xvi, 73, 79, 200, 203

Red Snow, 71

Red Stone, Chief, 69–71

Reed, Hayter, 125, 139–40, 146, 149–50

Reeves, Brian O.K., 14

reservations. *See* reserves

reserves: acceptance of, 131; boundaries of, 108, 113, 205, 254; at Cypress Hills, 95, 100, 109; divisions for farming and timber, 148, 155; farming life on, 144; forced on Indigenous Peoples, 61, 64, 68, 142; improvements to housing, 152; individual and group ownership, 145, 149; pass

system on, 106, 147, 206, 215; small-scale cottage industry on, 149; to use interest money for livelihood, 163. *See also* annuity payments; permits/permit system; surveys
reserve settlement (U.S.), 95
residential school system, 181, 188, 298; forced acculturation, loss of language, 153, 173, 185, 187, 189, 247, 295. *See also* assimilation
resources, plant and animal: changes due to environmental degradation, 279; commodification of, 145, 152, 160; depletion causing dislocation of traditional territories, 46, 63, 156, 159; as favourable conditions for migrating bands, 11, 20, 34, 36, 40, 45, 55. *See also* animal populations
Riding Mountain National Park, 222
Riel, Louis/Riel Resistance, 94, 108, 295
River Crow People, 71
Rocky Mountain Trapping System, 47, 58
Royal Canadian Mounted Police (RCMP), 186, 223
Royal Proclamation (1763), 135, 292
Runs, Delmar (Elder), xviii; on animal skin processing, 212, 231; on bison migration, 201; on ceremonies, sacred sites, 174, 182, 195; on farming, fishing, and trapping, 105, 230, 233–35, 238; on history of Nakoda nation, 77, 119, 125; on hunting practices, 205, 207–8, 219–20, 226, 259; on movement to reserve, 142, 144; on picking and processing berries, 248–50, 252–53; on picking and selling medicines, 268; on rations being minimal, 261; on smallpox epidemics, 130; on traditional language, 189
Rupert's Land purchase, 68
Russell, Dale, 2, 31–32
Russell, Lindsay, 103
Ryder, Charles (Elder), 119, 177
Ryder, Charlie, 136, 177, 180, 240
Ryder, Joyce (Rena) (Elder), xix, 298; on ceremonies, sacred sites, 185, 197; on gardening, 258; on hunting and trapping, 210, 212, 222, 229, 258; on residential school, 188; on traditional diet, 258
Ryder, Karen (Elder), 297
Ryder, Kurt, xix; on advising youth to maintain heritage, 288; on diabetes and lack of traditional diet, 283; on effects of oil and gas pipelines, 284; on family origins in Cypress Hills, 77; on fishing, trapping, and hunting practices, 220, 227, 230, 235, 237, 258; on hauling water, 264; on picking berries, 250, 253; on traditional lands, 77, 193
Ryder, Vincent (Elder), xix; on ceremonies, sacred sites, 175, 179, 181; on changing water quality, 281; on effects of environmental degradation on health, 277; on harvesting medicines, 278, 281; on hunting, trapping, fishing, 211, 219, 231–32, 234, 236; on Indigenous right to hunt, 274; on medicines, 242; on picking and processing berries, 251; on residential school, 186; on traditional diet, 259; on traditional language, 189

INDEX

S

Sacred Lodge Pole Tree, 89
Sacred Pipe, 175
sacred rites. *See* traditional ceremonies
sacred sites, 179, 191–95. *See also* burial sites; Indigenous spirituality; traditional ceremonies
Sahaptan People, 65
Sakimay Band, 138, 181–82
Salish People, 65
Sandy Lake Peoples (Assiniboine), 16–18, 20
Santee Peoples, 20
Sarcee People, 180
Saskatchewan Native Cultural College, 195
Saulteaux, Bernice (Elder), xix, 133; on ceremonies, 185; on Cypress Hills Massacre, 83; on hunting, meat processing, 208–10, 212, 217, 222; on living off the land, 265; on medicines and childbearing, 242, 244–46, 248; on moccasin making, 213; on permit system, 269; on right to live off the land, 274; on traditional language, 189; on traditional way of life, 283, 289; on trapping, 229, 231; on wild meat and berry diet, 262, 289
Saulteaux, Darwin, xvi; on change in quality of berries, wild meat, 279–80; on effects of environmental changes on traditional way of life, 276–77; on hunting practices, 208–9, 217
Saulteaux, Derrick (Elder), xix; on ceremonies, 182; on effects of gas and oil pipelines, 284; on hunting practices, 207–8, 226, 238; on picking berries, 250, 253; on traditional language, 188
Saulteaux, Roswell (Ross) (Elder), xix; on burial sites, 193; on hunting practices, 217, 222, 228; on traditional diet, 259; on traditional language, 188; on trapping, 229
Saulteaux People, 95; as Assiniboine allies, 57; at Fort Walsh in 1877, 90; home farm for, 100; and medicines, 246; Traditional Territory in boundary of Treaty 4, 87
Schieffelin, William H., 66
Selkirk People, 17, 20
seneca root, 152, 159–60, 265, 268. *See also* medicines
Setter, John, 98, 110, 115
settlers/settler society, 1, 45, 167; conflict with Dakota Sioux, 66; and development of west, 117; impact on CTK/Nakoda People, xiii, 291–93, 296; interference with hunting grounds, 67; near Assiniboine Agency, 157–58; reserve land for used for timber, 155–56; and trade goods, 19. *See also* white people
Seven Council Fires, 191
Seven Sacred Rites, 175
Shoshoni People, 39
Simmons, Andrew J., 70–71, 81
Sioux Peoples, 23–24, 37, 59, 66, 95, 106, 108; enemies of Assiniboines and Gros Ventres, 70, 104; horse raids by, 66, 68, 81; language of, 7, 189; powwow celebrations of, 184–85; territory of, 29, 45; war parties of, 60
Sisseton People, 70–71
Sitting Bull, Chief, 94, 107

INDEX

smallpox, 2, 66; deaths from, 41, 57–58, 63, 130, 141; effects of, 31, 39–40, 42, 56–58, 60–61, 298; survivors forming new cultural entities, 40–41. *See also* diseases/illnesses
Smart, James A., 155, 158
Smith, Joseph, 36
Sparrow Hawk, 119, 132
Speaks Thunder, xvi, 75, 174
Spencer, Adam, 226
Spencer, Edna (Elder), xix; on ceremonies, 181; on gardening, 257; on making products from tanned hides, 212; on picking berries, 249, 253
Spencer, Lyle, xvi, xix; on declining animal population, 278; on effects of chemicals spraying on farms, 280–81; on effects of oil and gas pipelines, 285; on gathering berries, 252–53; on hunting, meat processing, 207–8, 210–12, 218, 222–23, 226–27; on processing animal skins, feathers, 215, 228; on sacred sites, 196; on traditional diet, 258; on traditional language, 188; on trapping, fishing, 229, 231–32, 235
Spencer, Orval, xix; on ceremonies, 181, 195; on fishing, 235; on hunting practices, 207, 218–19
spirituality. *See* Indigenous spirituality
Stabbed Many Times, 83–84, 248
Standing Buffalo, Chief, 70–71
Standing Buffalo Reserve, 181–82, 190, 219, 234, 274; fishing activities there, 236–37; powwow celebrations of, 185
Star Blanket, Chief, 96, 181
starvation, 96, 98, 116; caused by government inaction, 114, 130, 292, 294; at Cypress Hills, 93, 133, 135, 298; at Fort Qu'Appelle, 124; at Fort Walsh, 94–95, 99, 101, 111–12, 117–18, 126, 128; at Indian Head reserves, 138–40; from loss of buffalo, 79, 93, 204; on Northern Plains, 88, 102; at residential school, 187–88; threat of, 33–34
Stevens, Isaac, 59, 65–66
Stevens Treaty (1855), 65, 69
Stone People (Assiniboine), 28
Stoney People, 7, 31, 189
Strawberry Lakes, 193, 238, 253
Striped Snake Woman, 243
St. Victor (sacred site), 193
Sundances, 178–81, 183, 191, 246; disallowed on reserves, 177; origin of, 175; rite of passage for youth, 174. *See also* Indigenous spirituality; traditional ceremonies
surveys, 111, 119, 122; of international boundary, 64; required by *Indian Act*, 106; of reserve lands, 101–4, 137, 140, 148, 206; stipulated in Treaty 4, 141, 294
Swampy Cree, 41
Sweat Lodges, 180, 183
Sweet Grass Hills Massacre, 81, 134, 294

T

Talks Differently, Chief, xvi, 60, 74
teepees/tipis, 78, 137, 193, 201, 203, 254; rings from, 15, 191, 193
Teton Peoples, 20
Thompson, Kaye (Elder), 82
Thomson, Clayton (Elder), xx; on environmental changes, 278; on hunting practices, 220, 222;

INDEX

Thomson, Clayton (cont.)
on tanning hides, 215; on traditional language, 189; on wild meat diet, 261
Thomson, Delbert (Elder), xx; on environmental changes, 278; on hunting practices, 220, 222; on tanning hides, 215; on traditional language, 189; on wild meat diet, 261
Thomson, Duncan (Elder), xx; on burial sites, 193; on ceremonies, 184; on fishing, 233–34; on hunting practices, 211, 228; on picking berries, 248; on rations for flour, sugar, powdered milk, 260; on residential school, 188; on trapping, 230
Thomson, Lawrence, 236
Thomson, Perry, 181
Thunderchild, Chief, 100
Tk'emlups te Secwépemc First Nation, 295
tobacco, 89, 121, 151, 174, 209, 241
Todd, William, 57
traditional activities. *See* gathering activities; hunting activities; trapping activities
traditional ceremonies, 11, 146, 173, 183; ban on performing, 177, 180; ceremonial items for, 177, 215; dancers for, 183, 214; in need of protection, 191, 193. *See also* Indigenous spirituality
traditional culture. *See* Indigenous culture
traditional diet, 203–4, 225, 233, 238–39, 278; supplemented with rations, 260; supplemented with store-bought foods, 271; of wild meat,

berries, 203, 207–8, 210–11, 217, 255, 258, 271. *See also* wild meat
Traditional Lands. *See* Traditional Territories
traditional languages, 4, 190, 291; to be reclaimed, protected, 288, 296–97; forbidden to speak, 173, 188, 295; kept alive by youth, 191, 287; Siouan language family, 7, 189
traditional livelihoods, 4, 72, 106, 255; affected by development around reserves, 254; disruption to due to treaties, 295; need to protect, reclaim, 287, 296; practiced on and off reserve, 168–69, 215; as purposely destroyed by U.S. and Canadian governments, 134, 292. *See also* gathering activities; hunting activities; trapping activities
Traditional Territories: boundaries of, 24, 27, 30, 40, 46, 74, 87, 273; effects of oil and gas pipelines on, 285–86; extent of, across international border, 72–73, 75–76, 78–79, 106; gain from sale to offset annuities, 163; government duty to consult regarding, 297; and harvesting areas for medicines, 245; and land claims, protection of, xv, 71, 92, 191, 198, 281, 287, 296; land surrender/confiscation of, 165–68, 292; land use areas, xiii–xv, 2–3, 28, 74, 168, 198, 217, 221, 245; large-scale development on, 4, 276; sacred sites, ceremonies on, 174, 179, 191; types of habitat, hunting on, 32, 199. *See also* Cypress Hills region

INDEX

traditional way of life, 183, 224; to be maintained by youth, 283, 290; given up for Christianity, 248
TransCanada Energy East Pipeline, 284, 286
trapping activities, 225, 229, 233, 265, 295; at Cypress Hills, 216; of fur-bearing animals, 30, 36, 48. *See also* beaver trapping and trade; mink trapping; muskrat trapping
treaties: coercion to sign, 134–35; conditions of regarding property, 145; entered into honestly by Nakoda People, 292; government promises not fulfilled, 121, 135, 261, 293, 295; Numbered Treaties, 87; obligations from, 120, 147, 149, 163, 288; and right to hunt, 275–76; spirit and intent of, 98. *See also* Cherokee Treaties; Fort Laramie Treaty; Stevens Treaty; Treaty Rights
Treaty 4, xiii, 102, 131, 286; adhesion to, 88, 90, 92, 298; signing of, 135–36, 294; terms of, 87, 122, 125, 141
Treaty 6: famine and pestilence clause in, 96; increase in rations, 98
Treaty 7, 94
Treaty Land Entitlement (TLE) claim, 1, 275
Treaty Rights, xiv, 107, 273–74, 296; to hunt, fish, trap, 275–76; increasingly infringed upon, 273; as needing protection, 198, 275, 287
tribal reconfiguration (1869), 70

U

Unfreed, Wendy, 15–17, 19, 26, 31
United Church of Canada, 247
United States government/military: banning spiritual ceremonies, 177; genocidal attacks on Indigenous Peoples, 292–94; keeping Indigenous People from international border, 104, 109, 111–12, 118, 128; and northwest settlement, 64; as not protecting Indigenous lands, 292; and Sioux, 67; and Sitting Bull, 107
Upper Assiniboine People, 69–72
Upper Yanktonai People, 57, 70

V

Vankoughnet, Lawrence, 93, 96, 98, 104, 109, 114, 122, 127
vision pits/vision quests, for youth, 179, 194

W

Wadsworth, T.P., 110, 112–15, 150–51
wage labour: contributing to Indigenous economic wellbeing, 149, 152, 160, 167; off-reserve work as farmhands, 149, 152, 168, 270–71
Waggoner, Joseph, 36
Wahpeton People, 71
Walde, Dale, 13, 15–17, 19, 26, 31, 34–35
Walker, Leroy, xx; on changes to plants, 279; on declining animal population, 278; on effects of chemical spraying, 282; on effects of environmental changes, 276; on fishing, 233, 236; on harvesting wild vegetables, 253; on hunting practices, 207, 215, 220, 222–24, 226; on Indigenous rights to hunt, 274; on picking herbs and medicines, 253; on reduction in hunting lands, 275

INDEX

Walsh, J.M., 94, 108; adhesion to Treaty 4, 88, 90; moving Indigenous bands to Fort Qu'Appelle, 110, 118, 121–22; reports on conditions at Fort Walsh, 89, 95, 113

War of 1812, 46, 64

Western Missions and Missionaries, 59

wheat threshing, 148, 159, 165; done by hand, 146–47, 150

Whirlwind, Chief, 69

whiskey. *See* alcohol (firewater)

whiskey traders, 81–82, 85, 100, 106, 134, 294

White, Fred, 120, 126

White Bear Reserve, 246

White Buffalo Calf Woman, 175

Whitecap, Darlene (Elder), xx; on decline animal population, 278; on effects of chemical spraying, 281; on fishing, 236–38; on gardening, 259; on hunting, skin processing, 207, 212, 216, 220, 225–27; on medicines, 239, 246–47; on picking and processing berries, 251, 259, 280; on traditional diet, 258, 260; on traditional language, 189–90; on wild meat diet, 261

Whitecap, Garry (Elder), xx; on advising youth to refrain from drugs and alcohol, 290; on boundaries of Nakoda nation, 61, 78; on ceremonies, 177; on declining animal populations, 279; on hunting activities, 216, 220, 222, 227; on loss of bush land, 280; on medicines and berries, 245–47; on permit system, 269; on picking berries, 249; on reserve life, 206; on traditional language, 191; on wild meat diet, 261

White Earth River post, 47, 200

White Fish Provincial Park, 223

white people, 41, 77, 136, 152, 157, 168, 187, 204, 255. *See also* immigration; settlers/settler society; wolfers

Whoop-Up Trail, 79

Wich-a-wos-taka, 90

Wi-jún-jon—The Light (Pigeon's Egg Head), 53–55

wild meat: butchering and drying of, 210–11, 217; contaminated by pesticides, 282–83; as traditional diet, 203, 207–8, 261–62, 289. *See also* traditional diet

Wissler, Clark, 30

wolfers: attacks on Indigenous People, 81–82, 134, 294. *See also* white people

Wolf Point, 90, 104, 114, 147, 184–85, 189, 192, 200, 204

Wolf Point People, 95

Woodland Assiniboine, 30–31, 35

Wood Mountain, 108, 128, 193

Y

Yanktonai Peoples, 20, 66–67, 71

Yankton Peoples, 20

Yellow Calf, Chief, 138

Yellow Leg headman, 111

York boat, 47, 49

York Factory (HBC), 28–31, 36, 40

Young Dogs, 3, 79

www.ingramcontent.com/pod-product-compliance
Lightning Source LLC
Chambersburg PA
CBHW032025290426
44110CB00012B/668